THIRD EDITION

COMMUNICATION AND SPORT

THIRD EDITION

COMMUNICATION AND SPORT

SURVEYING THE FIELD

ANDREW C. BILLINGS
University of Alabama
MICHAEL L. BUTTERWORTH
Ohio University
PAUL D. TURMAN
South Dakota Board of Regents

SAGE

Los Angeles | London | New Delhi
Singapore | Washington DC | Melbourne

SAGE

FOR INFORMATION:

SAGE Publications, Inc.
2455 Teller Road
Thousand Oaks, California 91320
E-mail: order@sagepub.com

SAGE Publications Ltd.
1 Oliver's Yard
55 City Road
London, EC1Y 1SP
United Kingdom

SAGE Publications India Pvt. Ltd.
B 1/I 1 Mohan Cooperative Industrial Area
Mathura Road, New Delhi 110 044
India

SAGE Publications Asia-Pacific Pte. Ltd.
3 Church Street
#10-04 Samsung Hub
Singapore 049483

Acquisitions Editor: Terri Accomazzo
Editorial Assistant: Erik Helton
Production Editor: Andrew Olson
Copy Editor: Michelle Ponce
Typesetter: Hurix Systems Pvt. Ltd.
Proofreader: Dennis W. Webb
Indexer: Amy Murphy
Cover Designer: Michael Dubowe
Marketing Manager: Jillian Oelsen

Printed in the United States of America

ISBN 978-1-5063-1555-3

Library of Congress Cataloging-in-Publication Data

Names: Billings, Andrew C., author. | Butterworth, Michael L., author. | Turman, Paul D., author.

Title: Communication and sport : surveying the field / Andrew C. Billings, University of Alabama, Michael L. Butterworth, Ohio University, Paul D. Turman, South Dakota Board of Regents.

Description: Third edition. | Los Angeles : SAGE, [2018] | Includes bibliographical references and index.

Identifiers: LCCN 2016044465 | ISBN 9781506315553 (pbk. : alk. paper)

Subjects: LCSH: Mass media and sports.

Classification: LCC GV567.5 .B55 2018 | DDC 070.4/49796—dc23 LC record available at https://lccn.loc.gov/2016044465

This book is printed on acid-free paper.

SUSTAINABLE FORESTRY INITIATIVE
Certified Chain of Custody
Promoting Sustainable Forestry
www.sfiprogram.org
SFI-01268
SFI label applies to text stock

18 19 20 21 10 9 8 7 6 5 4 3 2

BRIEF CONTENTS

DETAILED CONTENTS

PREFACE

Lao Tzu once claimed, "Those who have knowledge don't predict. Those who predict don't have knowledge." We generally agree with this sentiment, yet found ourselves attempting to do both in this third edition of *Communication and Sport: Surveying the Field.* We obviously wish to have knowledge conveyed in the most accessible and accurate degree possible, yet decisions on *which* pieces of knowledge to disseminate involve a series of educated guesses. Particularly with some of our new media information that is enhanced in this book, we attempted to paint a picture that would be useful for several years while acknowledging that communication and sport will have inevitably shifted in noteworthy ways even before the book goes to press. Our interviewee for Chapter 16, Dallas Mavericks owner Mark Cuban, is known for being able to make prognostications about the future—and even he can only write the future story of communication and sport in pencil, not pen. Thus, with the most accurate eye toward the future that we can hope to possess, we are offering this third edition as the closest representation of the issues pertinent to communication and sport, circa 2017.

THE BOOK

Communication and Sport: Surveying the Field is designed to bridge traditional divides between notions of speech communication (a tradition that includes interpersonal, organizational, and rhetorical approaches) and mass communication (a tradition that includes media studies, journalism, and cultural studies) and all of the potential divides and schisms inherently within. The aim was the creation of a book with enough breadth that it would be difficult to have one scholar who could truly claim expertise in all of the terrain. Thus, the combination of the three of us results in a media scholar, a rhetorician, and an applied interpersonal/organizational expert who jointly canvassed what amounts to an amazing scope of work in the field that is now outlined, structured, and synthesized for an undergraduate to grasp the scope and importance of studying communication and sport.

FEATURES OF THE BOOK

The comprehensive focus on communication scholarship is one of the major features of this textbook. In particular, we orient readers to the enactment, production, consumption, and organization of sport. This entails a wide range of communicative processes, including mass communication productions, interpersonal interactions, family and relational development, public speeches, individual expressions of identity through sport performances, collective expressions of community through sport rituals, and much, much more. The chapters within this textbook also feature communication scholarship that directs our attention to the ways that sport produces, maintains, or resists cultural attitudes about race, gender, sexuality, class, and politics.

The broad range of topical material is complemented by a pluralistic approach to communication and sport research. We survey scholarship that can be found in each of the major academic research paradigms: social scientific, humanistic, and critical/cultural. Each of these paradigms values different dimensions of intellectual inquiry. Social scientists, for example, are commonly interested in conducting research that allows scholars to explain how communication has worked in the past in order to offer some prediction of how it may happen in the future. Humanists, by contrast, tend to spotlight more particular instances of communication (rather than universal patterns) so that they may reveal deeper levels of understanding of human experiences. Meanwhile, critical/cultural scholars are committed to identifying relationships of power with the goal of sparking productive social change through academic inquiry. Although most researchers tend to identify with one of these paradigms over the others, they are not mutually exclusive, and, in the best cases, the insights from one approach may complement or supplement another. Communication and sport scholars also approach their research using different methodological tools, including content analysis, statistical modeling, ethnography, interviewing, experiments, survey collection, and textual criticism. Throughout this textbook, we have included examples of each research paradigm and various methods of study. It is our hope, then, that we have truly represented the diversity of scholarship conducted in communication and sport.

Another feature of this textbook is the inclusion in each chapter of a series of inserts, which include interviews, case studies, ethical debates, theoretical connections, and examinations of American niche sports. The interviews feature a range of experts in communication and sport, including renowned television figures such as Bob Costas, leading journalists such as Outsports cofounder Cyd Zeigler, prominent people within the sports industry such as Dale Earnhardt, Jr., and established sports scholars such as Lawrence Wenner. These interviews help to contextualize and extend the ideas that are developed in each chapter. The case studies pick up on a specific dimension from each chapter in order to facilitate discussion about the communicative nature of sport. Ethical debates invite a consideration of various cultural, political, and social consequences of sport, while understanding niche sports hopefully broadens readers' conceptions of the breadth and depth of sport in society. Many of these issues are tied together in our "Theoretically Speaking" sections, and readers can expect all of these inserted features to clarify, extend, and challenge their understanding of communication and sport.

Finally, as those already familiar with sport are well aware, the relationship between communication and sport is one that is rapidly changing. New technologies, changing organizational structures, a pervasive sports media that now includes a multitude of social media formats, and the explosion of fantasy sports are just some of the ways that sport has been dramatically altered in recent years. The final chapters of this textbook, then, offer some insights into these developments and provide some cautious glimpses into the future. Although we cannot peer into that elusive crystal ball, we are certain that communication scholarship will remain an essential lens through which we can view, understand, and modify the universe of sport.

NEW FOR THE THIRD EDITION

The general structure that we moved to for the second edition still holds—16 chapters that run the gamut of communication and sport in a variety of forms from humanistic to interpersonal to mediated. What changes for the third edition is an increasingly contemporary feel, including cutting-edge case studies on issues such as the regulation of fantasy sport and new interviews with people such as Mark Cuban, owner of the Dallas Mavericks, and Cyd Zeigler, the cofounder of the increasingly influential website Outsports. Even more prominently, the entire book is infused with a distinct sense of modern day, including issues such as modern athlete protest movements (such as the one that happened within the University of Missouri football program) and the continued rise of sports media entities ranging from *Bleacher Report* to *The Players' Tribune.* Finally, we must note that relevant citations from recent years are part and parcel of the update, as we strive to make this textbook the most comprehensive and complete option available in the communication and sport marketplace.

ACKNOWLEDGMENTS

With each edition of this textbook, we approach a revision with a combined sense of apprehension (because of the time involved in completing it) and excitement (because so many new works have been published and examples have unfurled within the sports landscape since the previous edition). The goal is to keep the textbook fresh, up-to-date, and at its highest level of utility. This evolution of a project that, at times, could seem unwieldy could not have happened without a great deal of synergy among the three of us, but we also recognize how fortunate we have been throughout this process.

First, we must thank SAGE Publications, particularly Matthew Byrnie, for believing in the first edition of the project and continuing to support our book over the years. It is nice to have a publisher that is willing to be an advocate for the burgeoning field that is the combination of communication and sport.

Second, we wish to thank the following people for their help with developing the textbook with their useful and supportive insights: Marie Hardin (Penn State University), Jacqueline A. Irwin (California State University, Sacramento), Nick Linardopoulos (Rutgers University), Mike Milford (Auburn University), David Sabaini (Indiana State University), Rebecca Robideaux Tiedge (Boise State University), and Joseph G. Velasco (Sul Ross State University).

Third, our institutions/organizations (University of Alabama, Ohio University, and the South Dakota Board of Regents) have allowed us the leeway to pursue this project in the time frame we wished, and for that we are thankful.

Third, we wish to thank all of the faculty and students who embraced the first and second edition of our work, bringing it into classrooms across the country and, indeed, to other nations in an attempt to educate about the role of communication and sport in society. Without your endorsement of the first and second edition of this book, a third edition would not have been conceivable.

Fourth, we thank our graduate students who have assisted us over the course of all three editions with the review of scholarship and other materials for this book. These students include Cory Hillman and Erin Paun from Bowling Green State University and Aisha Avery from the University of Alabama.

Finally, we must also note that we all are approximately in the same life stage, meaning that we have children and understanding wives that accommodate our schedules, which often became demanding near various deadlines. The confluence of events and supporters has resulted in a revised and updated text of which we are proud, and we thank all of the people in our lives who allowed for it to happen.

Andrew C. Billings
Michael L. Butterworth
Paul D. Turman

1

INTRODUCTION TO COMMUNICATION AND SPORT

On July 5, 2015, the United States Women's National Team (USWNT) defeated Japan, 5 to 2, to win the Women's World Cup. The victory marked the third time the United States had won the title, having previously captured the inaugural tournament in 1991 and again in 1999. The game was a fitting send-off for Abby Wambach, perhaps the most accomplished soccer player in U.S. history, and a coming out party for Carli Lloyd, who scored three goals in the championship game. The success of the 2015 team cemented the United States' status as the best women's soccer team in the world and further boosted interest in women's soccer at home.

Players from the United States and Japan line up before the 2015 Women's World Cup final

This brief description is framed primarily in sporting terms: a historically successful team enhanced its international reputation in a dominant performance in the sport's premier event. This is a book about *communication* and sport, though, and we begin with this brief narrative because we believe it introduces a range of topics and questions that we explore at length in the following chapters. Consider the following:

- The FOX **broadcast of the game** (see **Chapter 3**) averaged more than 25 million viewers, the most ever for any soccer game in the United States and an obvious demonstration of the synergy between sport and media (Deitsch, 2015).
- **Social media** (see **Chapter 3**) captured the moment of victory, with prominent celebrities, politicians, and other athletes among the millions who followed the game on Twitter (Mandell, 2015).
- The team's ultimate success came after early criticisms directed at coach Jill Ellis. Among team members, it appeared that Carli Lloyd was especially frustrated (Baxter, 2015). After Lloyd's spectacular performance in the final, it became easier to focus on the team's ability to overcome adversity and develop positive **player-coach relationships** (see **Chapter 11**) and **team cohesion** (see **Chapter 12**).
- Because the game featured the U.S. Women's *National* Team, it inherently captured public interest and reflected sport's capacity to cultivate **community** (see **Chapter 2**) and promote **nationalism** (see **Chapter 8**).
- International sporting events feature prominent **political symbolism** (see **Chapter 8**), with teams often serving as metaphors for nations and fandom as a metaphor for citizenship. This was evident in one minor controversy, when some Twitter users celebrated the U.S. victory by tweeting references to the Pearl Harbor attack of 1941 (Smith, 2015).
- A more substantial controversy, involving questions of **gender and politics** (see **Chapter 6**), occurred leading up to the tournament, based on the Fédération de Internationale de Football Association's (FIFA) plan to play all the games on artificial turf instead of grass (as the men do). As one sportswriter noted, the controversy symbolized "the ongoing inequalities in support for women's and men's soccer programs globally" (Dubois, 2015, para. 3). Because many of the players felt artificial turf increased their risk of injury, the controversy also spotlighted discussions about the health needs of athletes and caused something of a public relations crisis (see **Chapter 13**) for FIFA.
- Other matters of **gender representation** (see **Chapter 6**) were on display. For example, critics lamented that FIFA paid the champions $2 million, a far cry from the $35 million awarded to the 2014 men's champion from Germany (Isidore, 2015). Meanwhile, other critics pointed to continued biases in representations of female athletes, such as Alex Morgan, as objects of sexual desire more than as athletes (Moss, 2015).
- In a break from conventional representations, media also made much of superstar Abby Wambach's postgame celebration, which included a kiss with her wife (Chan, 2015). The moment reflected the rapid changes in American society with respect to same-sex couples and the **performance of identity** (see **Chapter 9**).

- Shortly after the World Cup concluded, EA Sports revealed the cover for its soon-to-be-released *FIFA 16* video game. Having already announced that women's teams would be included in the game for the first time, it revealed that Alex Morgan would share the cover with Lionel Messi (Grez, 2015), another important reference to gender and a reminder of the influence of **sports video games** (see **Chapter 15**).

We could likely add several other items to our list, but we don't wish to belabor the point. As should be clear, a single event such as the USWNT's 2015 victory speaks to a wide range of *communicative* phenomena that reflect the themes that are found throughout this book. Moreover, despite its uniqueness as a spectacular event, the World Cup highlights the degree to which sport plays a prominent role in the daily lives of an overwhelming majority of Americans.

To understand the impact sport has in American life, let us be more specific. Youth sports, for example, are among the most common activities for boys and girls throughout their childhoods. The Women's Sports Foundation reports that 75% of boys and 69% of girls participate in organized team sports (Sabo & Veliz, 2008). While these numbers provide us with some appreciation for the extent to which sports are important, they cannot fully describe the range of sports in which young people participate or the ways children play sports informally. Sports are also significant because they provide models of leadership for young people, environments to develop interpersonal and conflict resolution skills, and stories of inspiration when children use sports to develop their individual skills and character. All of which is to say that *communication* is central to how we play, watch, interpret, and evaluate sports.

Of course, youth sports beget other forms of sport. A quick glance at your college classmates offers an appropriate example. How many of them wear a sweatshirt or hat that features their favorite team? Perhaps your own wardrobe has these articles of clothing? When you wear a collegiate sweatshirt, are you affiliating with an academic or athletic program? Both? Indeed, a positive affiliation with sports is one way that college students construct and communicate identity. Many students even choose where to attend college based on a campus culture organized around sports (Sperber, 2000). And, as the ESPN advertising campaign called "Never Graduate" illustrates, many of us maintain our allegiances to the colleges we attended. Using familiar rivalries such as Michigan-Ohio State or North Carolina-Duke, the ESPN commercials depicted adults who continue to be loyal to their undergraduate institutions. At the heart of the campaign was the idea that our college affiliation—*understood primarily as a sports affiliation*—communicates something essential about our identity. As much as it may be warranted, no university is likely to receive a parade when its business school moves into the top 10 of the *U.S. News & World Report* rankings.

The stakes for understanding communicative practices may be even greater at the professional level. Especially because professional sports are inextricably linked to the media that broadcast, report, and opine about the games, it is next to impossible to escape the influence of professional sports. Consider that leagues such as Major League Baseball and the National Football League routinely set attendance records during the 2000s,

CASE STUDY

SUPER BOWL SYMBOLISM

In order to fully comprehend the extent to which sport intersects with a multitude of participants, media sources, and society, one only needs to look at the activities that surround the Super Bowl each year in the United States. At the conclusion of the 2015 National Football League (NFL) season, a number of relevant story lines emerged from a surprise win by the Denver Broncos over the heavily favored Carolina Panthers. Media attention focused considerable attention on quarterback Peyton Manning who, despite injuries earlier in the season, re-emerged as a starter for the Broncos during the playoffs. At the twilight of his career, Manning faced questions about his eventual retirement if the Broncos were to emerge victorious and erase the memory of an unexpected loss 2 years earlier to the Seattle Seahawks.

After each Super Bowl, sportscasters engage in significant analysis of the final outcome. Key turning points are assessed, coaching decisions are questioned, and a look toward the future begins as commentators begins to speculate about the upcoming NFL draft. Speculation about Manning's retirement fueled sports broadcasts when he declined to comment about his decision during the awards ceremony that evening. Meanwhile, following the game, Panthers quarterback Cam Newton was criticized for his unwillingness to engage the media and discuss the team's defeat. To many, he violated the basic tenants of losing gracefully, as he failed to recognize the performance of the Broncos in defeat.

Not only does the outcome of the event have meaningful implications for the fans of the teams involved, but the local communities are heavily invested in their teams' performances. Whether fortunate enough to attend the Super Bowl in person or to watch remotely, sport fans are afforded an opportunity for a culminating event that is celebrated throughout the country with activities consistent with many national holidays. The day of the event provides activities leading up to the kickoff, opportunities for socialization and engagement during the game, and reflection afterward. When considering implications for consumers and the media outlets that cover the event, the television commercials produced for the game have produced considerable reactions among even nonsport fans tuning into the game who rate the uniqueness and creativity on display by advertising firms from around the country.

In summary, few events can better illustrate how and why sport is able to connect so many interests, ranging from the broadcast itself, to the media coverage that precedes and follows the game, to the advertising industry's investment in the spectacle, to the scores of interactions fans and nonfans experience that make the Super Bowl a cultural touchstone.

1. What are the various factors that bring about the connection sport fans have with the events surrounding the Super Bowl?
2. How has this particular event been able to engage such a large following for fans and nonsport fans alike in the United States?
3. What are the communicative elements that are an integral part of the success of this event?

Members of the Army National Guard show their loyalties to Michigan and Ohio State

the expansion of digital services makes consuming live sporting events more available through satellite providers and Internet feeds, and television networks continue to invest billions of dollars in sports broadcasting contracts. Or, think about the fact that newer "lifestyle" sports such as mixed martial arts have exploded in popularity, fantasy sports have produced an entire industry that is dependent on, but also separate from, sports themselves, community officials often insist that the key to urban development or city pride is to invest in a professional sports franchise and/or arena, and player salaries continue to rise, often driving up the cost of attendance in the process. There are many other ways our lives are affected by professional sports' popularity. What is critical, once again, is that communication practices are essential to the success of sports—from expressions of collective identity found at live events, to the images produced by sports media, to the importance granted to sports in the vitality of a community.

Across all levels of competition, and through the media that cover these events, the very language of sports has become commonplace in American culture. As early as 1959, when Tannenbaum and Noah coined the phrase "sportsugese," there has been an acknowledgement that sports influence how we think and talk. Inspired both by his experience as a sportswriter and the prevalence of sports language in the speeches of President Richard Nixon, Robert Lipsyte (1975) termed this phenomenon "sportspeak." Indeed, as Segrave (2000) has pointed out, sports metaphors are commonly used to communicate ideas and feelings about politics, war, business, and sex. For instance, during the 2008 presidential campaign, both Democrat John Edwards and Republican Mike Huckabee compared themselves to the race horse, Seabiscuit, as both wished to embody similar qualities of determination characterizing the 1930s thoroughbred. During the 1991 Persian Gulf War, General Norman Schwarzkopf famously referred to a military strategy as a "Hail Mary pass," a familiar football reference. Meanwhile, business meetings are routinely punctuated with platitudes such as "this ad campaign is a slam dunk." As for sex, American adolescence is commonly described through the

INTERVIEW

BOB COSTAS, NBC SPORTS AND MLB NETWORK

Q: What is the greatest contribution sport provides to modern society?

A: Sports are still the ultimate shared experience. Sport draws the attention of people from all walks of life in ways that few other things can. People now receive information and entertainment from niche outlets on television, radio, the Internet, and more, but big sports events are still much broader based. For all its flaws and issues, sports at its best can still be a shared experience that bonds individuals, groups, and even nations.

Q: How has the consumption of sport changed since you entered the business?

A: There is just so much more of it, even from the traditional formats. Add all of the ESPN networks, all of the regional Fox Sports networks, and the Internet and the mass of it has grown exponentially. Even if the coverage hadn't changed, the sheer amount available would change sports tremendously. Of course, the coverage has changed—it is more highlight driven because of the presumed shorter attention spans of today's fans. We are barraged with information—which is sometimes good and sometimes overdone. In fairness, much of the event coverage is technically superb and very well crafted, and truly journalistic efforts like HBO's *Real Sports* and ESPN's *Outside the Lines* stand out. On the other hand, in many areas the tone is mindlessly negative—even abusive. The worst of sports talk radio and the sports blogosphere do not just appeal to the least common denominator, they redefine it.

Q: What is the impact of the evolving relationship between athlete, organization, and fan?

A: Athletes are more protected now by layers of agents and advisors. Some may think, "Well, the money is so great, what good does it do me to be all that accommodating to the media? Is it necessary to let the media present my image, or can I control it myself?" Add to that a press corps that is generally more critical and snide, and you can understand why many athletes are more guarded.

Q: How do you see the participation in and consumption of sports changing in the next several decades?

A: In ways we can't fully predict! Over the next decade I'm sure new technologies will leave our present high-definition televisions, mobile phone videos, and Internet links outdated. If you want it and are willing to pay for it, you will have access to just about anything at just about any time. I would also expect at least some American sports to become more global, particularly baseball and basketball. We can't know all the specifics, but it is fair to speculate that the future of sports will be bigger and more elaborate in virtually every way.

quest to "get to first base" or "hit a home run." Sports media professionals, especially announcers, also regularly feature these metaphors and clichés. This is especially the case when announcers are under a great deal of pressure or when the action on the field or court is not following expected patterns (Wanta & Leggert, 1988).

While language use is one indicator of sport's prominent role in American culture, another is the fact that it is among the largest industries in the United States. Financial consultants Price Waterhouse Coopers report that the North American sports market generated $60.5 billion in 2014, up from approximately $50 billion in 2010 ("At the Gate," p. 1). These revenues, coming from ticket sales, media rights, sponsorships, and merchandising, have remained steady or grown even as the worldwide economy has struggled. And, according to the Price Waterhouse Coopers Report, revenues from media rights are expected to surpass gate receipts to become the industry's largest revenue segment by 2019 ("At the Gate," p. 1). Meanwhile, we should point out that sports' ability to generate media interest is almost unparalleled. The two most watched television events in the world are routinely international sporting events—the Olympics and the men's World Cup in soccer (Tomlinson, 2005). With that popularity, television networks eagerly pay astronomical sums for the rights to broadcast sports. In 2010, for example, CBS and Turner Sports paid the National Collegiate Athletic Association (NCAA) $10.8 billion for a 14-year contract to broadcast the NCAA Men's Basketball Tournament (O'Toole, 2010). In 2016, the contract was extended to 2032 for an additional $8.8 billion (Norlander, 2016). For the right to broadcast the Olympic Games from 2014 to 2020, NBC paid the International Olympic Committee nearly $4.4 billion (McCarthy, 2011). All of this demonstrates that the immense popularity generated by sports make them among the most desirable commodities in the media industry.

COMMUNICATION AND SPORT

What should be clear by now is that we are interested in sports primarily as phenomena of *communication*. The academic field of "communication" traditionally covers a range of interests including, but not limited to, intercultural, interpersonal, mediated, organizational, and rhetorical. Other academic publications and textbooks have studied sports through other perspectives. Indeed, the disciplines of anthropology, history, kinesiology, psychology, and sociology have contributed greatly to our understanding of how and why people participate in sports. However, they tend to do so without emphasizing the communicative practices that precede and frame the ways people participate in sport. Kassing et al. (2004) suggest that people enact, produce, consume, and organize sport primarily as a communicative activity. Thus, our focus in this text is to explore how and why sport can be understood and studied specifically from the perspective of communication, a field with a far-ranging set of interests and applications.

This is not to suggest that the field of communication hasn't benefited from other academic disciplines. Sociology, in fact, is likely the academic field that has done the most to promote the serious study of sports. In 1978, the North American Society for the Sociology of Sport was founded, leading to the publication of the *Sociology of Sport Journal* (*SSJ*). Just a few years later, scholar Richard Lapchick founded the Center for the Study of Sport in Society, then housed at Boston's Northeastern University. This led to the publication of the *Journal of Sport & Social Issues*, which alongside *SSJ* publishes the leading scholarship on the sociology of sport. Meanwhile, other academic fields cultivated the study of sport through publications such as the *Journal of Sport Behavior*, the *Journal of Sport Management*, and *Sport in History*.

The field of communication developed its interest in sport around the same time period. In 1975, Michael Real published a study of the Super Bowl, called "Super Bowl: Mythic Spectacle." In that article, Real explained that the televised broadcast of the Super Bowl was arranged to emphasize the mythology of football as a ritualized expression of American identity. That sport could be used to communicate—and thus, affirm and extend—American values became one of the early themes of communication and sport scholarship. Other early studies in mass communication confirmed the importance of sports. Trujillo and Ekdom (1985), for example, analyzed sportswriters' accounts of the 1984 Chicago Cubs to reveal how journalism is a means by which "American cultural values are displayed, affirmed and integrated" (p. 264). Meanwhile, Farrell (1989) recognized that the mediated production of the Olympic Games used international politics to create dramatic narratives that fostered national identity. By the time that Wenner's *Media, Sport, & Society* was published in 1989, it was clear that there was much to be gained through the communicative study of sport. These early studies were significant not only because they demonstrated the significance of sport but also because they blurred the traditional divisions of communication scholarship, therefore making the study of communication and sport a truly interdisciplinary endeavor.

The relationship between communication and sport further developed in the 1990s with studies featuring an increasingly diverse set of topics and scholarly methods. As Trujillo (2003) notes, "[D]uring the 1990s, communication students and scholars became very serious about studying sport" (p. xiii). This attitude stood in contrast to previous decades, during which many academics dismissed the study of sport as being trivial, much like the traditional view in news media that ridiculed the sports page as a "toy department" (Rowe, 2007). By the turn of the century, this seriousness prompted a robust interest in communication and sport that now cuts across virtually every area of inquiry in the discipline. Throughout the 2000s, communication scholars found new avenues for engaging in sport-based research, resulting in numerous conferences and publications, including several special issues of communication journals dedicated exclusively to sport. Such growth leads us to the contemporary moment in which the "field of sport communication now has its own coherent body of knowledge and a community of scholars who are advancing the field" (Abeza, O'Reilly, & Nadeau, 2014, p. 308). This book, therefore, is an effort to synthesize that knowledge and offer a comprehensive survey of the field.

Before we proceed, we should note that this text is not a handbook for practitioners. We know that many of you are interested in careers in "sports communication," perhaps working for the marketing department for a sports franchise or in communications at a university athletic department. We make relevant connections to these professional interests throughout this text. However, primarily we take up how communication and sport can be studied and what they can tell us about one another. The emphasis on *study* over *practice*, therefore, is the logic by which we have chosen to feature the phrase "communication and sport" over "sports communication." With this distinction in mind, but before we offer an overview of the material covered in this book, let us turn our attention to some matters of definition.

Communication

It is virtually impossible to find a definition of *communication* that everyone can agree upon. If you have taken a public speaking course or an introduction to communication theory, you've likely encountered some of the more common definitions of the term. These definitions involve key concepts such as "sender," "message," and "receiver," all of which emerged from telecommunications research in the 1940s (Shannon & Weaver, 1948). Communication scholars have used these simple concepts to develop increasingly sophisticated models of communicative practices. Today, communication is largely understood as a process, wherein meaning is constructed and exchanged through a variety of symbols and media. Thinking of communication as a *process* instead of a *product* allows researchers to examine more than the content of the "message" or the intention of the "sender." Instead, scholarship may examine message construction, interpersonal influence, small-group dynamics, mass media, rhetoric and persuasion, and the performance of identity. Accordingly, in this book we adopt a broad and inclusive approach to communication, recognizing that different definitions and methods allow for greater understanding. Thus, if there is any single definition we would endorse, it is one in the spirit of Alberts, Nakayama, and Martin (2012), who define communication as "a transactional process in which people generate meaning through the exchange of verbal and nonverbal messages in specific contexts, influenced by individual and societal forces and embedded in culture" (p. 20).

Communication is a broad discipline. As we noted earlier, communication scholars study areas such as intercultural, interpersonal, mediated, organizational, and rhetorical phenomena. Each of these labels are insufficient on their own, however, as there are various subfields of interest. An interest in interpersonal communication, for example, might include studies of family relationships, friendships, romantic relationships, or workplace interactions. Mediated communication, meanwhile, encompasses studies of audiences, industries, and productions across an array of forms, including print media, television, and "new media" (which often refers to the Internet, social media, user-generated media, or some combination). Another way to think about communication research is to focus less on the means of communication and more on the contexts. From this view, we might think about topical interests in areas such as environmental communication, health communication, or, yes, communication and sport. It is also important to note that often times these areas and topics of interest interact and overlap, truly reminding us that "communication" is a fluid term.

In addition to the range of topics, communication scholars conduct research from different intellectual traditions, namely social scientific, interpretivist, and critical. *Social scientific* scholars are those who value objective studies of observable communication behaviors. Their research seeks to test, predict, and generalize communication phenomena, typically through quantitative forms of analysis. *Interpretivist* scholars take a more subjective view of communication, using qualitative forms of analysis to explain particular (as opposed to general) examples as a means of gaining a deeper understanding of how and why people communicate as they do. *Critical* (or critical/cultural) scholars prioritize ideologies and power as influences on communication practices. They view both human behavior and scholarship as unavoidably political, using scholarship as a means to facilitate positive social change. Between the three of us as authors, we have expertise across these orientations to communication research. Our approach in this book is therefore inclusive, as we survey broadly the topical and methodological issues addressed by communication scholars of sport.

Sport

If it is important that we have a shared basis for understanding of the term *communication*, then it is equally important to define *sport*. You may have noticed by now that although the word *sports* is used in the opening pages of this book, we have chosen *sport* for the title. Before we explain this distinction, let us first settle on what makes something a sport in the first place. Guttmann's *From Ritual to Record* (1978) is written in the sociological tradition of sport scholarship. Nevertheless, it provides a typology that helps define and delimit the scope of sport. Guttmann wants to distinguish between four levels of activity: play, games, contests, and sports. Play, he suggests, is "nonutilitarian physical or intellectual activity pursued for its own sake" (p. 3). When that play becomes organized, we have "games," and when games have winners and losers, we have "contests." Not all contests are games, however. As Guttmann notes, a war is a contest with winners and losers, but it is most certainly not a game.

Are all contests sports, then? Guttmann doesn't think so. For example, he notes that just because *Sports Illustrated* writes about it, it doesn't mean chess is a sport. Thirty years later, we could amend this to say that just because ESPN televises it, it doesn't mean poker is a sport. What is required, Guttmann (1978) claims, is that sports involve a *physical* component. Therefore, sports are defined as "'playful' physical contests, that is, as nonutilitarian contests which include an important measure of physical as well as intellectual skill" (p. 7). Following this definition, when we talk of specific contests such as basketball or golf, we will likely use the term *sports*. However, and much more frequently, when we refer to the institutional arrangement of leagues, teams, officials, players, fans, and media we will use the term *sport*. In similar terms, we might also think of Bell's (1987) definition, which states, "Sport is a repeatable, regulated, physical contest producing a clear winner" (p. 2).

PERSPECTIVES AND APPROACHES

This book builds on the foundation we have detailed above. We cast a broad net in the effort to survey the field of communication and sport across its methodological, theoretical, and topical diversity. Let us now provide an overview of the chapters to follow.

Sport is a central feature of life in countries around the world. Our focus in this textbook, however, is primarily on the United States and the study of how Americans participate in the community of sport. With that in mind, what does it mean to study the "community of sport?" Bob Krizek (2008), who is interviewed in **Chapter 2**, states that it "is a diverse community with often disparate interests that compel us to employ a wide variety of research practices and theoretical frameworks" (p. 105). Thus, on the one hand, the "community of sport" is about those who study it from perspectives we have described above. However, this community is less about communication scholars and more about those who are invested more directly in the community of sport. Accordingly, in **Chapter 2** we examine how this community is constituted by participants, organizations, media, and fans. For example, think about the discussion that emerged when Major League Baseball (MLB) introduced a rule change in 2014 that sought to minimize the risk of collisions between baserunners and catchers at home plate. The new rule came in response to injuries that occurred from collisions some saw as unnecessary, but the change raised questions about the game's traditions and the toughness of its players. First and foremost, the rule was designed to protect the players (participants), which in turn protected the teams (organizations) from losing a player to the disabled list. Meanwhile, MLB (another organization) promoted the decision as being in the best interest of the game. Broadcasters and sportswriters (media) then debated the virtues of the rule, while observers (fans) watched to see how players would adapt to the change. Collectively, these four constituencies adapted to the new rule and deliberated over whether or not it was good for baseball. Although all four groups represent different interests in the community of sport, those interests overlap, revealing the interdependence of participants, organizations, media, and fans.

Much of the community of sport is influenced by media. Especially when talking about sport at the collegiate and professional levels, it is all but impossible not to think about how the media constructs, delivers, and digests sporting events. Therefore, we provide an overview in **Chapter 3** of the role of media in sport, including traditional forms such as newspapers to "new" media such as Twitter. Twitter, along with other social media sites such as Facebook, Pinterest, and Instagram, are still relatively new platforms. The rapid emergence of these sites has changed communication practices in a variety of contexts, including sports. Sanderson (2011) contends that social media is especially relevant to sport because it breaks down some of the barriers that previously prevented fans from interacting with the sports they follow. As he notes, "Fans are capitalizing on the interactivity offered by social media channels to directly engage athletes and sports organization personnel" (p. xiii). Many of these changes are exciting; others raise concerns. All of them, however, merit our attention if we are to understand how sport affects our lives.

Communication and sport scholarship is also interested in understanding how sport constructs, maintains, or even threatens the communities in which we live. Fans often tell us a great deal about sport's impact on community. Thus, we turn our attention more specifically to Sports Fan Cultures in **Chapter 4**. As an example, consider the fan culture of Major League Soccer's (MLS) Portland Timbers. The team began play in 2011 and has sold out every regular season and playoff game since, with more than 12,000 people on the waitlist for season tickets (Goldberg, 2016). The dedication to the franchise can be explained in part by the fact that Portland is a large metropolitan area with only one other major league franchise (the National Basketball Association's [NBA's] Trail Blazers). But there is also a specific passion for soccer, best symbolized by the popular "Timbers Army" fan club. This group dates back to a previous professional soccer franchise in the city, and this history is rooted in Portland's identity as a progressive, creative city. As the team prepared to join the MLS, the organization launched a "Timbers Army" promotional campaign featuring a diverse array of local fans on billboards throughout the region. The only other content on the billboards was a small Timbers logo. By spotlighting the fans, the campaign channeled local passions and helped establish an immediate connection to the franchise (Dean, 2014). This is only one view of fanship, of course. In **Chapter 4** we examine various forms of fan behavior, including other motivations guiding fans to identify with certain sports or teams as well as the technological changes that have altered the terrain of sport spectatorship and consumption.

Connections to the community of sport are commonly cultivated through mythologies linking fans with their communities or sports in particular ways. As we discuss in **Chapter 5**, myths are stories that are not necessarily true, but their communicative effect is that they feel true. Thus, they provide order and guidance for how people should navigate their worlds. Some myths are local. Grano and Zagacki (2011), for example, demonstrate how civic leaders in New Orleans used the Louisiana Superdome as a site for rehabilitating the city's image after devastation suffered in 2005 because of Hurricane Katrina. The rituals enacted during the ESPN *Monday Night Football* game that reopened the stadium spoke to sport's ability to create a mythic unity, in this case enacting a "spiritual obligation for the community as a whole" (p. 214). Other myths are national. Consider, for instance, the deeply ingrained belief that baseball, as the "national pastime," is somehow representative of America itself. Or, myths may transcend such communities by taking on more cosmological, or religious, significance. Hence, some of the more pervasive sport myths are those equating sports with religion: the "church of baseball" or the idea that the Super Bowl is a "religious festival" (Price, 1992). In each case, myths depend on heroic figures and universal values to impart their lessons. As a result, when we subscribe to a myth's lessons there are substantial consequences to our attitudes, beliefs, and actions.

Communication scholars have revealed that sport is one of the primary sites for the construction, maintenance, and contestation of identity. In a series of chapters, therefore, we turn our attention to the relationships between sport and both individual and collective identities. We begin in **Chapter 6** with a discussion of gender and sport, focusing both on the substantial increase in participation of women in sport since the landmark adoption of Title IX and the problematic representations of female athletes, especially through the media. Overt expressions of sexism are increasingly rare; however, many more subtle iterations of sexism remain. This includes the tendency to provide

Inside the Louisiana Superdome

different coverage to men's sports over women's sports (Billings, 2007), the need to define women first as "feminine" and second as "athletic" (Shugart, 2003), and the all too common emphasis on female appearance over other characteristics.

We clarify as well that "gender" is not a synonym for "women." Although the role of women in sport is a central focus of communication and sport scholarship, we must also attend to sport's role in the construction of masculinity and sexuality. The concept of "hegemonic masculinity," for example, helps explain the dominant features of masculinity for a given culture. These features are often based on power, strength, and control and frequently come at the expense of women or gay men (Trujillo, 1991). Thus, in **Chapter 6** we are careful to acknowledge the multiple identity positions that are implicated by the concept of gender.

If the media have been guilty of sexism with respect to representations of women, then a similar problem arises with respect to race and ethnicity. On the one hand, sport has been the rare institution in American history where racial minorities or non-U.S. natives have been visible, successful, and celebrated. A century ago, when African American Jack Johnson claimed the heavyweight boxing championship, the victory touched off nationwide riots and precipitated cultural anxieties about the diminishment of White cultural authority. Today, American sport is an arena of diverse races, ethnicities, and nationalities. Indeed, often the most beloved stars—Gabby Douglas, LeBron James, Derek Jeter—are racial minorities.

The presence of these athletes, however, does not mean that Americans have transcended racial biases or even reached an understanding of what "race" means. Is

Source: Keith Allison on Flickr. (Originally posted to Flickr as "Derek Jeter") [CC-BY-SA 2.0]

Derek Jeter

race equitable with skin color? Ethnicity? Blood? Questions such as these can threaten the harmony that sport has the potential to cultivate. Meanwhile, despite the apparent level playing field offered by sport, racial minorities are often subjected to questionable portrayals and remain marginal participants in managerial and ownership ranks. Meanwhile, what is communicated by a sport like college football, which consistently fields teams comprised largely of African Americans yet rarely coached by them? Or that in Major League Baseball, where players of Latin American and Asian descent are now commonplace, but the overwhelming majority of owners remain White? These kinds of questions, and many others, characterize our approach to **Chapter 7**.

Moving from the individual identity positions of the previous two chapters, **Chapter 8** evaluates the mutual influence between sport, politics, and nationalism. One of the most deeply held misconceptions about sport is that it is "apolitical," or that it offers *only* an escape from the "real world" concerns of politics. However, if you have ever attended a live sporting event in the United States, you have likely participated in a political ritual that few of us would question. Specifically, most of us take for granted that the performance of the national anthem before a game is simply standard procedure, and few of us would think of it as "political." Yet, consider the uproar that has been caused over the years when someone dares to threaten the sanctity of the ritual. Jose Feliciano, for example, was widely reviled after he delivered what is believed to be the first nontraditional rendering of the anthem at Game 1 of the 1968 World Series. Much more recently, San Francisco 49ers quarterback Colin Kaepernick attracted both praise and criticism for refusing to stand during the national anthem ceremony before the start of games. Kaepernick was motivated by incidents of racial violence that had occurred throughout the country in recent years leading up to the 2016 NFL season. Many others followed his lead (Walker, 2016), sparking substantial discussions about the role of sport in addressing matters of racial justice and the extent to which sport and politics intersect.

Both Feliciano and Kaepernick earned scorn for "politicizing" sport. This charge does not stop elected officials from hoping to exploit sport for their own purposes, however. Presidents routinely throw out pitches at baseball games, invite championship teams to the White House, and appear for interviews during broadcasts in order to foster identification with American citizens. This can generate great favor (President George W. Bush was widely praised when he threw out the first pitch at Game 3 of the 2001 World Series, just weeks after 9/11) or result in embarrassment (such as presidential candidate Mitt Romney's ill-fated attempt to connect with NASCAR fans by talking about his friendships with NASCAR team owners). Less formal uses

Source: By The Official White House Photostream [P071409PS-1207], via Wikimedia Commons

Barack Obama at the Major League Baseball All-Star Game

of sport also have political implications, such as the "rare bipartisan partnership" shared between President Barack Obama and New Jersey Governor Chris Christie in 2013 after they played a game of "Touchdown Fever" during a tour of a New Jersey boardwalk that had been damaged by Hurricane Sandy in 2012 (Shear & Leibovich, 2013). International sport also raises various political issues, from the metaphorical contests of events such as the Olympic Games to heated disagreements about human rights and national ideologies. Recent Olympiads, for example, have spotlighted these concerns, such as the backlash against anti-LGBT laws in Russia that emerged during the Sochi Winter Games in 2014 and the public protests against the Brazilian government's investment in the Rio Summer Games in 2016. In many cases, the mixing of sport and politics sparks controversy about the degree to which they should remain apart from one another.

In the cases of gender, race, and nationality, the construction of identity is often produced, or at least guided, by the media, sports organizations, or politicians. Because *athletes* are also part of this process, we turn our attention in **Chapter 9** to the *performance* of identity in sport. What this means is that participation in sports is often a means for individuals to express who they believe themselves to be or to challenge conventional expectations about identity that they wish to change. The average sports fan, for example, assumes (probably unconsciously) that athletes are *exceptional* physical specimens, and that athletic performance requires a fully able body. Disabled athletes challenge this assumption through their participation in sport. Golfer Casey Martin, for instance, garnered significant attention in 1997 because he had a degenerative leg condition that limited his mobility, and he sued the Professional Golfers Association (PGA) for the right to use a cart on the tour. The PGA insisted that his request undermined the integrity of its rules, but the Supreme Court ruled in Martin's favor. Although his leg condition ultimately prevented him from pursuing a long-term career in professional golf—he is now the head coach of golf at the University of Oregon—the case helped redefine what it means to be an "athlete."

Sexuality can also be understood as a matter of performance. Scholars influenced by the academic field of cultural studies view terms such as *gender* or *sexuality* on a continuum, meaning that there is no such thing as pure masculinity or femininity but rather people *perform* their identities in more or less masculine or feminine ways. Performances can take many forms, from choosing types of clothing, to using specific words, to participating in one sport over another. What is communicated, for example, when a teenage boy opts for figure skating over hockey? As we noted above, one of the common expectations about sport is that it privileges hegemonic masculinity, through which men are expected to be strong, tough, and heterosexual. Thus, the presence of a gay male in sport represents a challenge to the conventions of gender and sexuality. In part, this is why the coming out narratives of Robbie Rogers (MLS), Jason Collins (NBA), and Michael Sam (NFL) were such big news stories in 2013 and 2014. A discussion of the extent to which our performances reinforce or redefine identities, therefore, concludes our focus on negotiating identity in sport.

Sport is often celebrated for its ability to foster relationships, develop teamwork skills, and find creative outlets for resolving conflict. Our attention to these issues begins in **Chapter 10** with a discussion of parent–child relationships in sports. As participation in youth sports continues to climb, its impact on the family takes on growing importance. For many, sports are seen as means to socialize children. Kremer-Sadlik and Kim (2007), for example, revealed that family interactions during sports activities promote the idea that sport communicates and develops important cultural values. Meanwhile, sport also leads to more troubling phenomena, such as parents who identify too strongly with their children's athletic achievements. The emergence of the so-called "helicopter parent" can arguably be traced to parental involvement in sports, as parents have long obsessed over issues such as playing time or the treatment their children receive from their coaches. For some, the stereotypical figure of the overly demanding father as depicted in the film, *The Bad News Bears*, remains a cautionary tale about the line between support and pressure.

If parental pressure is a significant issue, so too is the problem of the few, but high-profile, instances of violence committed by parents. Perhaps the most infamous incident came in 2000, when 44-year-old Thomas Junta beat and killed 40-year-old Michael Costin in a fight prompted by an incident between their sons in a youth hockey game. Sadly, other more recent cases remind us that violence happens in youth sports more than it should. Another hockey father, Thomas Tonda of St. Paul, Minnesota, received a 6-month prison sentence in 2012 for assaulting his son's coach and allegedly threatening to kill him (Pheifer, 2012). In 2010, a Pennsylvania man was charged with assault for punching his own son after the 9-year-old was ejected from a baseball game (Leibowitz, 2010). Such outbursts have led many communities to adopt codes of conduct that require parents to pledge they would maintain good behavior. That parents sometimes become the focus of youth sports invites communication scholars to consider how and why we invest as much in sport as we do.

In some ways, the relationship between players and coaches mirrors the relationship between children and parents. Coaches are often surrogate parental figures, and they are charged with communicating lessons about discipline and hard work, even as they are expected to lead their team to victory. Accordingly, communication scholarship has attended to the ability of coaches to motivate players, including as assessment of different motivation strategies. Although stereotypical portrayals of coaches in television shows and movies—such as the *Bad News Bears* portrayal we referenced earlier—tend to emphasize the role of anger and punishment, Kassing and Infante (1999) discovered that aggressive behaviors commonly lead to unfavorable perceptions of coaches, which leads to weaker performances. In **Chapter 11**, we explore coaching communication strategies, as well as the significance of the coach as a model for organizational leadership.

Coaches can affect the team environment, as well. Communication scholars emphasize the term *small groups* over *teams*, but the terms share many traits. Teams are relatively small units that depend on organization and the distribution of tasks across the group's membership. In this way, team sports are appropriate metaphors for understanding small-group communication processes that are found in organizations of every kind. **Chapter 12** evaluates various issues related to teams, including cohesion, leadership, and organization. Turman (2003), for example, showed that coaches were instrumental in fostering team cohesion. Meanwhile, Hawkins and Tolzin (2002) concluded that baseball teams provide exemplary models of leadership for postmodern organizations.

Small-group communication is typically considered a part of organizational communication studies. In **Chapter 13**, we shift our attention to organizations and the specific set of issues prompted by crises. A crisis can occur at multiple levels—it can be macrolevel, such as the national crisis in the United States precipitated by 9/11, or it can be microlevel, such as the Formula One racing industry's response to a tire controversy. Brown (2004) addressed the first kind of crisis in his study of the role played by sports leagues in the healing process after terrorists attacked the United States. Organizations such as Major League Baseball or the National Football League, Brown suggests, served as positive and unifying forces for Americans shocked by the tragedy. Pfahl and Bates (2008), by contrast, analyzed the various responses from Formula One teams, the Indianapolis Motor Speedway, Michelin, and others, when a dispute over tires threatened to discredit the sport. Their study offers models for communication students and scholars to see how sport provides both positive and negative examples of image repair strategies. One recent volume (Blaney, Lippert, & Smith, 2013) is entirely dedicated to studies of image repair in sport. Similarly, in our chapter we seek to understand crisis communication both for what it does well and for the lessons it invites us to consider.

One challenge in writing a textbook about communication and sport is trying to keep up with changes and new developments. In the final chapters of the book, we address two particular issues that continue to change the landscape of sport: commodification and fantasy sports. We do not suggest that commodification is entirely new to sport. Despite the contrary claims made by nostalgia buffs, sport has been a commercial enterprise just about from the beginning. Nevertheless, changes to the economy in the late 20th and early 21st centuries have produced new relationships between sport and commerce, which have subsequently altered player contracts, how sports are broadcast, who can afford to attend games in person, and what kind of facilities are built to host sporting events. Even as many are comfortable with these developments in professional sports, there growing concerns about the increasingly blurred lines between commercialism and amateur sports. Thus, in **Chapter 14**, we hope to identify the key communication issues that have emerged out of the growing economic reach of sport.

One example of the commercial possibilities of sport can be found in the explosion of fantasy sports. Although many fantasy sports developed in the 1980s, the emergence of the World Wide Web in the 1990s made fantasy sports a widespread phenomenon. With fantasy sports now a multibillion dollar industry, there is little question that it is as much a part of the contemporary landscape as sports themselves. Fantasy sports allow for a new form of fandom and provide an outlet for friends, family, and sometimes complete strangers to communicate and connect with one another. Meanwhile, they also raise questions about addiction or threaten to distract employees who should be working instead of checking their fantasy statistics online. Similar temptations are found with sports video games and gambling. Sports video games are played by millions, some of whom are not even sports fans, and gambling is a multibillion dollar industry. These various forms of games are industries unto themselves, and they have helped to change the way fans consume and interact with sports. For example, not only can fans gamble on a full range of sports thanks to Internet access, they can also make (presumably) informed decisions about their bets thanks to an associated electronic gaming (eGaming) industry, symbolized by publications such as *EGR* (EGaming Review). With these issues in mind, we approach **Chapter 15** with the intention of viewing sports gaming as an integral part of the communication and sport relationship.

Finally, in **Chapter 16** we look to the future of communication and sport scholarship. Especially in light of technological developments that have dramatically changed the way people experience sports, such speculation is no easy task. Speculate we shall, however, with specific attention on sports participants, organizations, media, and fans.

It should be evident that the relationship between communication and sport is one that requires multiple approaches. The chapters in this book are as comprehensive an overview as is available. Yet, we understand that additional topics and questions could be raised. It is our hope that the following chapters provoke you to consider how we might best understand communication and sport. Each chapter incorporates numerous examples and definitions of key terms. We also include five features found throughout the book: an interview with either a communication and sport scholar or a practitioner with experience in sports media; an example that provokes discussion about the role of ethics in communication and sport; a representative case study that demonstrates the central concepts introduced in the chapter; a "theoretically speaking" box that expands on a given academic concept; and an "off the beaten path" insert that spotlights nontraditional sports.

We close this introduction with one final observation about our approach in this book. We are scholars and critics of sport, yes, but we also are fans. We have strong allegiances to our teams, from the Green Bay Packers to the Chicago Cubs to the University of Nebraska Cornhuskers. We played sports as kids, continue to play as adults, and are committed to supporting the athletic activities of our children. And, yes, we even participate in fantasy sports. In short, we are invested in the community of communication and sport in multiple ways. Throughout this book, we hope you will join us.

2

COMMUNITY IN SPORT

No major part of everyday life is left untouched by sport. We join bowling leagues with our coworkers. We play softball with church members against teams representing other denominations. Our schools hold pep sessions to support teams that bear the same school logo and nickname. We attend horseraces by the thousands. In many ways, the topic of this chapter—the community of sport—would be easier to canvass if one were to discuss what does *not* constitute the community of sport. Within American society (and most of the modern world), sport impacts the very manner in which our typical day unfolds. Moreover, it always unfolds within a communicative context. It could involve the interpersonal communication between coach and player, parent and child, or producer and director. It could incorporate the rhetoric of a radio announcer or the bombastic nature of a coach's halftime speech. It could involve intercultural communicative notions of in-groups and out-groups and certainly can be embedded in notions of communication theories that deal with silenced or muted groups or with violations of social expectancies.

Communication informs, persuades, and permeates how we play, how we consume, and how we incorporate notions of sport into our daily lives. The myriad ways in which sport permeates virtually all forms of society make it important to recognize who the various "players" within the mingled communication and sport process are. This chapter outlines the major entities that jointly influence the manner in which sport is communicated in the United States and globally. Trujillo (2003) notes that sport is a "billion-dollar industry and an important purveyor of cultural values" (p. xii). Decades ago, a prevailing attitude rendered was that sport was a microcosm of society; in the modern day, there are many instances in which the inverse also holds true as society is often a microcosm of sport. This chapter is about how these attitudes, ideas, and behaviors are simultaneously influenced by many crucial "players" who collectively constitute the community of sport. More specifically, we explore the (a) **participants;** (b) **organizations;** (c) **media entities;** and (d) **fans** that jointly influence sport and society in increasingly conjoined manners.

PLAYER #1: THE PARTICIPANT

Nearly all of us have played sports—mandatory physical education classes ensure that if nothing else. Games we play range from organized (AAU basketball leagues, school teams, and YMCA clubs) to spontaneous (pick-up basketball games at local parks, throwing a Frisbee with family members in the backyard) games (see Guttmann, 1978). As we grow older, the games become more sophisticated, and the perceived stakes of participation become higher, allowing for a differentiation between play, games, and sports as articulated in Chapter 1 (which is why responses to athletics becoming too intensely serious often involve the rhetoric that "it's just a game"). Relatedly, the decision to continue participation in a given sport is often determined by whether a person is willing to pledge an increased level of commitment. We often hear of the professional player who has forgotten the sheer youthful joy of playing a sport. Thus, to understand our first player, *the participant,* we must begin with childhood play.

INTERVIEW

BOB KRIZEK, COMMUNICATION AND SPORT SCHOLAR, ST. LOUIS UNIVERSITY

Q: What do you feel encompasses the community of sport?

A: The community of sport is a symbolic collective that includes all the people who work in, participate in, are fans of, and /or reporters of sport and sporting events, spanning countries, regions, cities, and schools. It includes everyone who "touches" any aspect of sport, and it is larger than any country or single religion. It connects us to the past and helps us anticipate the future. Nonetheless, it is a symbolic community; it exists because we can imagine and talk about it. The community of sport encompasses all that we as humans find meaningful about our forays into the games we play individually and against one another.

Q: How has this community evolved in recent years?

A: Our awareness of it has become much greater. Economic expansion over the last 4 centuries has provided us with more leisure time, which in turn has allowed the community of sport to develop new ways to experience and define sport. We have introduced "old" sports to new constituencies, as seen in the World Baseball Classic,

(Continued)

INTERVIEW (Continued)

and legitimized "new" sports such as the X-Games and Ultimate Fighting Championship for all constituencies. The evolution of the community of sport blurs traditional city/state sport boundaries as well as challenges traditional meanings of sport.

Q: In what way do media entities influence this community?

A: The media allows us to be socially present in many places in multiple ways. We can watch the Olympic Games in China while listening to our favorite baseball team play a game in the park of a divisional rival. With exposure comes a tremendous amount of power, including notions about what it takes to succeed and what we should value.

Q: Do you see any dangers in the ways in which people interact within this sporting community?

A: The community of sport and all of its mediated representations is pervasive; therefore, this community may be shaping us in ways we do not truly understand. Because the vast majority of people view the activities that the community of sport comprises as ideologically neutral, we rarely consciously reflect upon what occurs in that community. We concern ourselves with wins and losses and not how the community of sport reproduces dominant ideologies that benefit some and disadvantage others.

Q: What is the biggest misconception about sporting communities?

A: It varies based on the lens through which the person answers. Sport communities are not ideologically free zones. Most people perceive sport as being neutral in regard to politics, gender, culture, and sexual orientation. It is not. The best man not only doesn't always win, but sometimes he doesn't even get to play. More often than not, the most talented woman doesn't get recognized for her skills in the same way that her male counterpart does. The community of sport is a privileged place that does not act as a social or political leveller.

Q: To what extent is there a link between community and consumption in sport?

A: In this country, the link is constant and strong. From the sponsors' names on the back of our children's Little League uniforms to the names on our professional sport stadiums, the community of sport encourages us to consume. Even in nonorganized neighborhoods in the community of sport, participants in pick-up ballgames don jerseys, headbands, and protective wear that model exactly how the professional and amateur organizations decorate their athletes. The community of sport has a voracious appetite for consuming fed by a constant flow of marketing campaigns and new products.

Q: How do you see the various "players" within the community of sport changing in the years to come?

A: I would hope that as our critical examination of the community of sport gains momentum, a growing body of knowledge gains traction. More realistically, perhaps, I can see the community of sport becoming even more consumer oriented, maybe not to the extent prophesized in the movie *Rollerball* but certainly more than we currently experience. More positively, more people will actively participate in sport as our life spans increase and as we choose to realign life–work balances.

Source: ©iStockphoto.com/Jacob Ammentorp Lund

Enjoyment and fellowship in the community of sport

Casual Play: Sport as Leisure

By no means is casual play limited to children, but it does represent the formative steps in most people's initiation into the sporting world. Even if children are not indoctrinated into formal types of sports, they naturally create them within the realm of play (such as playing catch with a ball). Four factors influence the degree to which we choose to begin or continue playing sports: personality characteristics (rudimentarily on the continuum of active vs. passive), resources (chances to play and improve via coaching and varied environments), interactions with close contacts (sport-loving parents are more likely to yield sport-loving children), and athletic ability (both inherent and developed in initial experiences). However, variations of these primary four factors occur; for instance, parents who may not overly enjoy sports may nonetheless believe that sport can aid in socializing a child, making the child less likely to participate in delinquent behavior (see Trulson, 1986, for evidence this is true in certain situations). In addition, Chapter 12 focuses on the intergroup dynamics involved in sport that tend to masculinize or feminize the social roles of those who play.

The desire for casual sports play remains for adults, yet the opportunity to participate wanes as life progresses. Whereas children have recess and both informal and structured playdates and parties, these types of occasions rarely naturally occur for the hyperkinetic 21st-century adult. When adults do find occasion for casual play, it is most frequently with their children. Regardless of age, casual sports represent a substantial portion of all athletics and communicate many foundational messages: (a) Sport should be a vital and healthy part of anyone's life, (b) sport is a primary means for functioning socially, and (c) participation in sport is more likely to yield high character and enhanced opportunity for those involved.

Intramurals: Introductions to Organized Sport

The transition from spontaneously played sport to organized activities comes earlier in a person's life now than ever before. Children begin "smart start" programs as young as age 3, and recreation leagues often feature leagues for preschool children. At this stage, the focus of the sporting activities is on understanding rules and basic levels of sportsmanship. Children are often funnelled into these types of structured sporting activities because of the proven correlating benefits between participation in intramural sports and higher grades, lower dropout rates, and greater success in attending and completing college (Lipscomb, 2006). While some experts have been skeptical of these benefits, scholars such as Hartmann and Depro (2006) find positive relationships between activities such as midnight basketball and property crime rates and other forms of deviant behavior. However, research currently has been relegated to finding correlations between intramural activities and positive social benefits; little scholarly attention has been devoted to the communication processes enacted to create this perceived cause-and-effect relationship, making this a ripe area for sport analyses in the future.

Amateur Athletics: Altruism and Idealism

For much of organized sports' history in the United States, being a professional athlete was often equated to being second rate, as the true athletes were the amateurs. They were held in the highest regard largely because they were playing the game because they loved it, not because they needed to in order to make a living. Obviously, the working classes

OFF THE BEATEN PATH

IRONMAN

The event that was imagined in 1977 as a 140.6 mile journey, combining Hawaii's toughest endurance races in swimming, running, and cycling, attracted 15 participants to Waikiki in 1978 for the first-ever Ironman challenge. Ironman's mantra is "Anything is Possible," and its triathletes embrace the essence of the human spirit. The World Championship's home has remained in Hawaii and is now hosted on in the Big Island in Kona and attracts nearly 1,800 athletes from around the world. As a way of showing its appreciation to Hawaii for continuing to host the Ironman World Championship annually, the Ironman Foundation has shown its commitment to the community of Kona through charitable giving. Local non-profit foundations serving members of the community have worked closely with the Foundation to identify the best grant opportunities. The Foundation also recognizes that its triathletes are drawn to the event for various reasons and provides them with the opportunity to race for charities of their choice. This partnership between its foundation, athletes, and the community helps Ironman spread the spirit of *kokua*, Hawaiian for "helping others."

—Aisha Avery

CASE STUDY

BLOOM'S BATTLE

It isn't unusual for sports to blur the lines between professional and amateur athletics. Traditionally the National Collegiate Athletic Association (NCAA) has established rigid policies that attempt to protect student athletes from the high-stakes game of professional sports, yet with each passing year, major athletic conferences push the NCAA to allow a greater portion of college sport revenue to be provided to amateur athletes. In early 2015, members of the AAC, Big 12, Big Ten, SEC, and Pac-12 moved forward with providing the full cost of attendance to athletes involved in the 65 schools affiliated with the five conferences. Traditionally, athletic scholarships at these institutions reflected the cost of room, board, tuition, and textbook costs for student athletes. Scholarships supporting collegiate athletes could not exceed these calculations determined for each institution despite the long held belief that it did not cover the full obligation that students incurred while enrolled. Each sport can require athletes to practice/compete up to 20 hours each week, and when weighed against the demands of school, work makes it difficult to earn additional income that may be necessary for them to cover other expenses associated with college attendance.

Initially approved by the NCAA in August 2014, the vote by the five major conference leaders now allows for institutions to provide stipends (amounts determined by federally established guidelines) of up to $2,000 and $4,000 annually. Shortly afterward, a number of other smaller conferences also followed suit noting that to maintain a competitive advantage in Division I athletes, the need to offer equivalent stipends to at least football and men's basketball players was crucial in the current recruiting environment.

Many believe that successful college athletic programs should allow student athletes to earn a larger portion of the revenue generated from their competitive efforts. For instance, the NCAA currently sells the television rights to its national tournament each year, for which CBS pays more than $6 billion to retain the rights. More than 94% of the money is distributed back to colleges and universities to support all athletic programs. Yet, the athletes responsible for helping to generate this revenue see little of that money beyond the scholarships they receive to attend their institutions.

Should collegiate athletes be eligible for additional stipends from their institution to cover the expenses beyond actual attendance costs?

1. Does it seem appropriate that only athletes from a limited number of sports are eligible for the additional stipends based on their capacity as a revenue generating sport?
2. What potential problems might the shift by the NCAA cause in the future as revenue from collegiate sports continues to increase?

had a much more difficult time staying at the amateur level because of economic realities, so upper classes held to the notions of amateur athletic superiority at least partially because it shut out other classes of people who would be relegated to the professional ranks. For instance, even in the early 1930s, golf's Grand Slam events consisted of the U.S. Open, British Open, U.S. Amateur, and British Amateur Championships, showing just how elevated amateur competition was in comparison to other professional events. Similarly, tennis's "Open Era" did not start until 1968, when professional players were allowed to compete against amateurs.

Things have obviously changed since then, as now even the Olympics allows professionals to compete while other sports, such as tennis, allow players to earn money but place a monetary cap on the amount of prize allotments players can receive while still retaining their amateur status. College athletes do not receive paychecks, yet they receive everything from room and board to tuition waivers to clothing to spending money at college football bowl games in exchange for their participation. Debates remain as to whether such resources constitute adequate compensation for athletes, particularly for prominent athletes in revenue-producing sports. Attempts for larger universities to provide stipends have been rejected in courts (see Solomon, 2015), with antitrust exemptions questioned in the process. Nonetheless, amateurism still is upheld for idealistic and practical reasons, particularly noted within secondary education and university settings. Most athletes participate because they enjoy the competition, yet others do so with their eyes on the ultimate goal of turning professional, with all of the perks that accompany that level of achievement.

Professional Athleticism: Style and Substance

Finally, there are those who participate at the perceived highest level of athletics: the professional athletes. Given how jaded some views have become regarding the notion of pure amateurism in the 21st century, it is no surprise that some have similarly skeptical views about professionalism. Some athletes in high-profile sports can command eight-figure annual salaries, leading fans to feel they cannot relate to the players or that the athletes play not for the love of the game but for a paycheck and the lifestyle that accompanies it.

TABLE 2.1 ■ Top Athlete Salaries (2016)

Sport	Player	Duration	Amount
MLB	Giancarlo Stanton	13 years	$325,000,000
NFL	Andrew Luck	6 years	$139,125,000
NBA	Mike Conley, Jr.	5 years	$153,000,000
NHL	Alexander Ovechkin	13 years	$124,000,000
Auto Racing	Sebastian Vettel	3 years	$240,000,000

Nevertheless, many professional athletes make much smaller amounts of money, often to the point that they need ancillary jobs to support themselves. For example, until 2009, Home Depot provided part-time, flexible-hour jobs to more than 600 future Olympians because, even though the Olympics now involves professional athletes, most could not fulfill their athletic dreams without outside employment. USA Wrestling has implemented their "Achieve the Dream" campaign that awards $1 million to any USA wrestler that earns an Olympic gold medal, encouraging more seasoned athletes to continue in the sport while they are still in their prime.

Despite economic and celebrity-oriented disparities, one commonality that occurs in professional sports is that athletes are playing the game at the highest level. Perhaps this involves someone making thousands of dollars for each pitch he or she throws, but it also involves professional bowlers; the nation's top bowler may make $200,000 a year while most others make far less. Professional seasons are typically longer than amateur seasons, and some notions of athlete welfare are lessened because of the notion that people who earn a living playing a game could (or perhaps even should) endure some hardships in the process. Sports with strong unions are able to ensure some form of equity, but others do not have these bolstered structures in place.

Professionalism involves a ton of talent yet also is about marketability. When a player or sport is marketable, salaries increase along with other sponsorship opportunities. The late BMX biker Dave Mirra made 10 times as much money in outside endorsements and other opportunities as he did from biking competitions. Careers of professional athletes tend to be short, and no two ever appear to be alike because of the deviations in talent, health, marketability, and other outside influences.

PLAYER #2: SPORTS ORGANIZATIONS

Of course, these athletes could not begin to participate at these various levels without governing and organizing bodies to oversee these events. *Sports organizations* serve this vital role by coordinating efforts and providing spaces and events that advance opportunities for sport participation. These groups come in all shapes and sizes, ranging from large conglomerates to events coordinated out of a home of a single person. Some types include *recreation clubs* that often serve as a lifeblood of a local community. Some may have ties to formal, structured sports (think YMCA), yet others regard themselves much more as fitness centers where sports are played in the form of pick-up basketball games and other casual events. These games are then supplemented with a heavy dose of activities that represent physical education in a noncompetitive format, such as aerobics classes and public swimming.

Related and yet quite different are *athletic clubs.* Sometimes, these organizations function in the same "go to the gym and exercise" manner, yet these also may not involve providing a specific, formal physical space in which sports are played. Instead, the focus is on local (and sometimes state and national) organizing as these groups work with city parks and recreation departments and other entities to use spaces for competitive games. A good example of an athletic club is the Amateur Athletic Union (AAU), as the organization is now so well networked in the United States that AAU coaches can wield more influence on athletes than even their high school coaches. Groups such as these provide opportunities for organized play and regional tournaments.

Another type of sports organization involves *state and national federations.* For instance, each state has an organizing federation to handle high school athletics rules and competitions. These groups facilitate play but also aim to fulfill advocacy roles to ensure athlete equity and welfare. For instance, in 2016, the U.S. Women's National Team accused U.S. soccer of wage discrimination because the women's team—the #1 team in the world and reigning World Cup champion—often made less for winning a game than the men's team—ranked #31 in the world—did for losing one. Centralizing national agencies (such as the NCAA) serve similar advocacy functions, intending to offer highly competitive sporting events within the realm of maintaining true amateurism. National groups such as the United States Tennis Association function as federations to promote a certain sport, often by providing youth programs and structures that can aid and help promote sports to those with less access because of their economic or geographic circumstances.

Organizing committees also are integral to the grander sporting events. The biggest sports event of all, the Olympics, has an International Olympic Committee specifically designed to coordinate the Games with a host city. Such a process is so involved for

THEORETICALLY SPEAKING

IDENTIFICATION

Although you might first think of identification in terms of verifying an identity—an ID card, for example—communication scholars who use the term are more likely to think of it as a *process.* In other words, identification refers to the process by which individuals come to see themselves as having things in common. This theoretical approach to identification originates with Kenneth Burke, author of numerous books on literature and rhetoric, including *A Rhetoric of Motives* (1950/1969). In that book, Burke famously declares, "Identification is compensatory to division" (p. 22), meaning that it allows distinct individuals to communicate across their differences to achieve symbolic cooperation. This may happen in one-to-one interactions, but large groups also may form communities through the process of identification. For example, Gill (2012) examines *Gold & Black Illustrated* (*GBI*), a publication that covers sports at Purdue University. Through consistent references to the organizational history, *GBI* cultivates identifications that socialize fans into the Purdue community. As he concludes, "Historical messages reinforce socialization by providing knowledge and recounting experiences that indoctrinate fans into a particular organizational fanhood" (p. 153). Thus, through identification, fans learn how to participate in a given sports community.

the Olympics that host cities are selected 7 years in advance of the competition after several preceding years of a location vetting process by national Olympic Committees. Yes, these organizing committees sometimes are designed to fulfill advocacy roles in a similar manner to federations, yet this is not always the case. College football bowl games have organizing committees that are centralized around a specific event for a specific sport, yet they do not determine rules or sport governance in any way. Instead, these groups work year round to promote a game in which the two competing institutions won't even be known until a month before the game is played. Moreover, NCAA Final Four basketball host cities do not know which schools will be participating until 1 week before the tournament begins.

Finally, there are *team networks*. These types of organizations are not just focused on a specific sport; they are often elaborately designed groups with the intention of promoting a team that plays the sport. All college and professional teams have these types of organizations designed to market and promote a certain team (such as the Cincinnati Reds) or institution with multiple teams playing with the same moniker (such as the Indiana Hoosiers). Branding, media exposure, and the potential for future athletic success are all part and parcel of what these team networks are charged with accomplishing.

PLAYER #3: SPORTS MEDIA ENTITIES

As sports have grown at all levels of society, so too has the plethora of media outlets that now devote substantial time to sport. We will discuss more of the minutiae of traditional, new, social, and user-generated media in Chapter 3. However, it is also important to discuss how media entities impact the community of sport. Aspects of sports media have changed substantially, such as the diminishing opportunities at local sports television networks as a result of increasingly regionalized coverage of sport via regional outlets (Fox Sports Net, New York's YES network, Sports Net L.A.). Even with these changes, parts of *sports media entities* can still be subdivided into visibility jobs and production jobs.

Visibility Jobs

First, *visibility jobs* feature media players with which most people are most familiar: Joe Buck commenting on a football game or Jessica Mendoza opining on the Celtics' off-season moves. These players in the sports media empire are well known and often beloved because fans welcome them into their homes on a regular basis. When Vin Scully was retiring as the voice of the Los Angeles Dodgers in 2016, his 67 years as the voice of the team made millions of fans nostalgic, including one who wrote to *Sports Illustrated* to indicate that he was in diapers when Scully began announcing and that he may be in diapers again when Scully finished his career.

In television, multiple visibility roles exist that are now integral to what is consumed at home. The *anchor* often functions as a host. Anchors are typically highly scripted (via teleprompter) even if the words are primarily written themselves (with the help of editors). An anchor's job is often to focus on the significance and scope of sports games and issues;

Sportscaster Erin Andrews

in other words, anchors relay the "big picture." Yes, they may play a role Bob Costas labels as a "traffic cop" where the goal is to get people from Point A to Point B (say, from pregame announcers to an injury reporter), yet their primary function is to relay a sense of meaning to their audience (see Billings, 2008). What would a win or loss mean within the overall scheme of things? Why should we be interested in today's starting pitching matchup? Anchors frame all of the discussion that will ensue.

At live televised events, commentary still tends to occur within paired broadcasting combinations of a *play-by-play announcer* and a *color analyst*. The play-by-play announcer describes the athletic contest largely in terms of observable facts ("Patrick Kane with a Game 5 hat trick"), while the color analyst interprets the game within a larger context ("LeBron James doing something Michael Jordan never did in the NBA Finals, leading his team in nine statistical categories"). Several decades ago, a study found that 73% of all television commentary was play-by-play (Bryant, Comiskey, & Zillmann, 1977), and this percentage still holds true today, although the strict divisions of who provides which form of commentary are beginning to blur. Even though color commentary represents less than a quarter of all spoken words, color commentators continue to be of extremely high visibility because their dialogue can often be more interesting, memorable, and outside of the box of traditional thinking (consider Dick Vitale's college basketball coverage and his terminology such as a "dipsy-doo dunakaroo" and "diaper dandies").

Television also features another visibility player: the *sideline reporter*. These reporters have been found to be increasingly useful as audience appetite for more "inside" information escalates. More often than not, this role is filled by an attractive female—a topic that will be discussed in greater depth in Chapter 6. Whether it is an interview with the parents of a player, an injury update, or a report on a coach's halftime rant, the sideline reporter offers a form of sports media with an even greater sense of liveness and immediacy.

Beyond television, several of these visibility jobs overlap, while others are functionally quite different. For instance, radio sportscasts usually still have play-by-play and color components, yet they are obviously done without video, resulting in even more play-by-play coverage. However, one visibility job that is starkly different from television is the *radio host*. The formats of shows differ, yet the host is rarely considered to be an anchor as much as a facilitator and/or resident expert. Many local shows are defined by a host taking a series of phone calls from fans and then having discussions and assessments of sports happenings. Others feature a group of people who are usually diverse in roles and backgrounds (studied sports enthusiast, former professional athlete, etc.) who jointly engage in sports talk. A few others, such as FOX Sports 1's Colin Cowherd, perform more of an anchoring function by taking very few calls and instead providing analysis of "big picture" issues. Still, the large majority of radio shows (local and national) are defined by a host who can create a sense of community (such as Jim Rome and his listeners "the clones," who participate in this radio "jungle;" see Nylund, 2007).

Newspapers and magazines also feature two other forms of visibility players: *print reporters* and *feature columnists*. Comparisons can be drawn as reporters often fulfill play-by-play functions and columnists provide the "color" commentary. Still, the benefit of time and hindsight makes these roles quite different. Print reporters often provide event recaps focusing on the chronology of events ("Leading 10–7, the Broncos effectively ended the game with a late touchdown pass"). These reporters also can provide "beat" stories, which involve ongoing commentary on full seasons and events (as these reporters often travel with a team or set of athletes continually). Feature columnists, on the other hand, function as color commentators, yet they often have even more freedom as they can seek out a story that perhaps no one has even thought about.

Production Jobs

Because there is less "glamour" in *production jobs* than in visibility jobs, substantially fewer people (often 10 times fewer) seek out these positions in sports media. Nonetheless, these jobs are critical to any sports media entity. Consider the *photographer* who must capture a single shot worthy of encapsulating a 3-hour game or the *producer* who must determine how the storytelling will unfold between the visual, audio, and graphics components. These jobs are no less important but are instead so plentiful that describing each one takes a substantial amount of time. A typical football game requires a television crew of more than 50 people; only a handful of those are visibility players while the rest are directors, camerapersons, technical directors, and so forth that are jointly responsible for airing the contest. Radio certainly operates with fewer people, yet the ratio of visibility to production people still favors production.

One behind-the-scenes area that is critical in all forms of media is the *editorial department*. Many times people consider these people to be strictly focused on streamlining content, such as a newspaper editor who checks a story for accuracy, length, and appropriate emphases. Yet editorial departments also include writers, researchers, and other information gatherers who can make a visibility player's job much easier. For instance, when watching a profile of an Olympic athlete, an anchor or reporter may provide the voice-over, but often the actual writing and certainly production aspects are choices made by a person (or group of persons) in the editorial department.

There are also public relations departments that contribute to behind-the-scenes matters. Years ago, the *sports information director* was charged with almost all of these aspects; now, there tend to be separate *marketing, promotion,* and *information* departments. Many sports teams have *media relations specialists* who work to merge promotions (such as public appearances) with relevant information (such as media guides prepared by the sports information department) and marketing to yield a product that the media easily understands and can relay to the masses.

Source: ©iStockPhoto.com/visual7

Cameraman at football game

Hybrid Jobs

At this point, one may wonder why the Internet has been omitted from a section on sports media; this is because new media now often feature new roles and media outlets that are not nearly as established or defined. These are best termed *hybrid jobs* because a single person may contribute to the entire process in a singular fashion. For instance, it is now expected that a print journalist will also work in television and on the Internet. Even prominent sports bloggers often write, present, and produce their own content from their homes; these people are not media entities in any formal sense, yet they contribute to the overall sporting landscape. Other more mainstream forms of the Internet overlap with the roles discussed earlier as a feature columnist often has his or her story on the Internet as well, and sports television finds ways to stream a sportscast to essentially make a person's computer into a television. Thus, the principles of sport media hold true, yet the medium changes the way people consume the product in considerably different ways.

PLAYER #4: THE FAN

Motivations for Fandom

Of course, the final "player" of note within the community of sport arguably influences all of the others, as an avid *fan* often is motivated to play more sports as well as consume them, allowing sports organizations and media entities to exist and thrive. Raney (2006) probes the psyche of the typical sports fan, noting motivations in the emotional, cognitive, and behavioral domains. These domains, along with much more detail surrounding the communicative nature of fandom, are discussed in greater detail in Chapter 4. However, an overview of the community of sport is not complete without at least a rudimentary articulation of the role millions of fans play.

First, Raney argues that fans are interested in following sports at all levels because of their inherent emotional appeals. These include the (a) desire to be entertained (often watching athletes playing at the highest level and performing physical feats that they cannot begin to do themselves); (b) "eustress" desires (a form of stress that is actually good for you by providing a sense of fulfilment and achievement); (c) bolstering of self-esteem (for instance, when a person's alma mater wins a national title, he or she may feel pride in selecting and attending that school); and (d) the need to escape from the daily grind of life (one can unwind at the end of a tiring day while consuming a contest that is not a matter of life and death). Collectively, these appeals are very powerful, as sport is used to manage moods (see Zillmann, 1988) in ways that alter the daily existence of millions of people.

Then, there are cognitive motivations for fandom, which Raney divides into the learning and the aesthetic. First, in terms of learning, people glean a great deal of information from following sports at all levels, whether it is about the families involved in a local softball game or the career earned run average of their team's star pitcher. Still, beyond this largely factual level of learning is a higher form of learning, a navigation of a social world. When one watches the Olympics, for instance, a viewer learns about geography (where is Slovenia located?), politics (will political unrest mar the Rio Summer

Fandom even in the rain

Games?), and cultural tastes (is table tennis a major sport in China?). Even beyond that, issues of identity discussed later in Chapters 6 through 9 are negotiated through fan consumption. Second, aesthetic needs are also fulfilled at a cognitive level. Being a fan often involves being transported to a different place and time. These places tend to be majestic (picture a skiing event in the Alps shown in high definition) and epic (consider more than 100,000 people watching a football game in the Rose Bowl). In sum, the fulfilment of cognitive stimulation facilitates many forms of fandom, from the avid to the sporadic fan.

A MATTER OF ETHICS

WE ARE PENN STATE?

In November of 2011, long time Penn State defensive coach Jerry Sandusky was accused of sexually abusing several young boys over the course of many years. The ensuing scandal led to the ouster of Penn State's president (among others), the near erasure of legendary head coach Joe Paterno's image on campus, and, eventually, the conviction of Sandusky on 45 counts of sexual abuse. The revelations that so many children could have been victimized raised numerous questions about the culture of the university's football program and, by extension, the values held by the State College community. For many, both at Penn State and around the country, the university is synonymous with its football program. And it is fair to say that success on the field has yielded positive benefits from the attention, esteem, and money directed toward Penn State. At what point, however, does a community become complicit in creating an illusion that enables the kind of abuse committed by Jerry Sandusky?

This question was addressed by journalist Michael Weinreb. Writing for Grantland.com, Weinreb recalls what it was like in "Growing Up Penn State." His childhood in State College was characterized by safe neighborhoods, good schools, and the common bond forged by the Nittany Lions football team. This bond was most represented by Paterno, of whom Weinreb writes, "He was as much our own conscience as he was a football coach, and we made that pact and imbued him with that sort of power because we believed he would wield it more responsibly than any of us ever could. Maybe that was naïve, but we came of age in a place known as Happy Valley and naïveté was part of the package, and now that word isn't in our dictionaries anymore" (2011, para. 11) Weinreb's lament certainly calls into question the amount of energy, passion, and faith that we invest in sport as a symbol of our communities. Although the specific nature of Sandusky's crimes are unique to Penn State, it is not difficult to imagine other communities across the United States that are similarly dependent on athletics. As you consider this case, do you think Penn State is unique? Why, or why not? How much community investment in a sports team or identity is too much?

Finally, there are behavioral motivations, of which Raney lists five: release, companionship, group affiliation, family, and economics. Many of these five action-oriented reasons are interrelated; for instance, people often find companionship with other like-minded souls when attending a game, but they also do this in family formats, witnessed by countless cases of full families tailgating and sharing tickets together for years on end. Similarly, there is an emotional release that arises from being a fan, and sometimes this is manifest economically in the form of sports bets and other ancillary meanings attached to the outcome of the athletic performance(s).

All in all, there are many reasons for fandom and, relatedly, the overemphasis of some of these same motivations provides proof of unhealthy fandom, another topic that will be explored more fully in Chapter 4.

Modes of Fan Consumption

Hugenberg, Haridakis, and Earnheardt (2008) claim that there are macro levels of sports fandom that include the enactments of identification, motivation, and fan-produced content. Billings (2010) expanded these notions to include four modes of fan consumption (which, admittedly, blend with each other and are not a fully exhaustive list).

The first mode is the *first-person supporter,* who is largely defined not by media consumption but the desire to witness an event firsthand. Season ticket holders for professional and college sporting events certainly fit this criterion but so do those who stop by a youth sporting event to watch a friend's son or daughter play. First-person supporters often consider themselves to be the "true fans" because they are there in the down times as well as the good. Moreover, they often invest significant funds in booster groups and other agencies in exchange for tickets and VIP treatment.

Source: © iStockphoto.com/FranckReporter

An enthusiastic soccer crowd

A direct contrast is found in the second way fans consume sport, the *home-dwelling devotee.* These people also may consume sports in heavy doses but tend to do so using various forms of media (television, radio, etc.) rather than actually attending the game. The motivations for not being a first-person supporter differ, ranging from the economic (lacking the funds to be a season-ticket holder) to the geographic (a Green Bay Packer fan living in the south may find traveling to the game to be quite difficult) to the health oriented (some older fans find the bustle involved in attending games to be overwhelming). Regardless, these people are frequently avid followers, often purchasing television sports packages and better technology to enhance the at-home experience.

Third, there are the *social sports addicts.* These people love sports but only so far as others help them love the games. The rapid rise in sports bars over the past two decades underscores the need for a place where social sports fans can congregate. For most of these people, watching their team win at home is a hollow experience, but watching the same game with friends (even friends they just met that day) in a social place is highly rewarding. Economics become a crucial factor for these people as well, as people often fit into this category when they have surrendered any notion that they could enjoy some of these sporting events live and in person. Often, they congregate where the resources offer them a relative deal financially, ranging from the sports bar offering games that cost hundreds of dollars in satellite packages to visiting a neighbor who happens to get the channel on which the game is being offered. Some people are social sports addicts because they enjoy it; others are because it is the most practical mode of being a modern sports fan.

Finally, Billings outlines a fourth consumption mode: *virtual world aficionados.* We now have fans without televisions, radios, or season tickets who nonetheless are highly involved not only in watching sporting events online but also in actively creating media themselves, whether this means the creation of one's own blog or commenting on various message boards. Some virtual-world aficionados are "lurkers" who prefer to consume and not actively participate, but many others seek to become part of the media themselves, and cyberspace provides considerable opportunity for that.

COMMUNITY OF SPORT IN THE 21ST CENTURY: CHANGING "PLAYER" ROLES

The majority of this chapter has segmented out the four major entities of the modern sporting community, yet one must also recognize that these roles are not completely distinct and are constantly changing. The different players are now intermingled more than ever. Most specifically, the role of the fan in the overarching process now alters the other three players through user-generated and 24-hour sports media. Consider the ownership of the Seattle professional soccer team, the Sounders. All season ticket holders (plus anyone who pays $125 annually) become members of the Alliance. This group makes ownership decisions collectively, including a vote every 4 years on whether to replace the team's general manager. Such decisions are normally left to ownership—the players within the sports organizations discussed previously.

Along with these blurred lines between fans and other aspects of sport comes the enhanced bonding that arises in the process. The concept of BIRGing refers to people who "bask in reflected glory" in team triumphs and good times. Fans in New England may have jointly experienced these feelings when major sports teams (Red Sox, Celtics, and Patriots) all won championships within a few years of each other in the 2000s. There is also the concept of CORFing (cutting off reflected failure), which pertains to the inverse feelings fans feel when their teams lose or underperform. The common refrain that "we" won or "they" lost is underscored by these two concepts. New England baseball fans likely felt this until 2004, when the Red Sox finally ended an 86-year drought in winning the World Series, as did Cleveland until the Cavaliers ended the city's 6-decade-long title drought during the 2016 NBA playoffs. While BIRGing and CORFing have been examined in sport for decades (see Wann & Branscombe, 1990), these fan feelings are exaggerated in recent years, largely because of greater fan investment. It is difficult for fans to put sports in proper perspective when they are increasingly spending thousands of dollars on watching their favorite teams and are constantly consuming messages about sports via sports radio, television, newspapers, magazines, and the Internet. Thus, fans become a part of media and organizations by impacting fan message boards and injecting opinions on radio call-in shows.

The result of all of this interaction between the various players in the community of sport is an enhanced form of identification. There is a feeling of kinship when one spots a person wearing his or her team's logo at the airport or when a community jointly celebrates "its" first championship in decades. Wann (2006) offers three antecedents for sports team identification—psychological, environmental, and team-related—but then notes that there are myriad forms of antecedents to the point that each person's experience of identification is different. Given the increasingly diverse community of sport, this is not at all surprising. Understanding the players within the community is important; yet equally important is the embrace of change and overlap. Members of sports media are undoubtedly still fans; people within sports organizations are more likely to be players of sport as they have dedicated their careers to advancing the importance of participation in athletics. Society is, indeed, a microcosm of sport and, increasingly, that culture is facilitated through media—including a new complex of sports media that eliminate many of the barriers that used to exist between the "players" outlined in this chapter.

Suggested Additional Reading

Bernstein, A., & Blain, N. (Eds.). (2003). *Sport, media, culture: Global and local dimensions.* Portland, OR: Frank Cass.

Carcinelli, S., McGullivray, D., & McPherson, G. (Eds.). (2016). *Digital leisure culture: Critical perspectives*. London, UK: Routledge.

Green, K., & Smith, A. (Eds.). (2016). *Routledge handbook of youth sport*. London, UK: Routledge.

Rein, I., Kotler, P., & Shields, B. (2006). *The elusive fan: Reinventing sports in a crowded marketplace*. New York, NY: McGraw-Hill.

Schultz, B., & Arke, E. T. (2015). *Sports media: Reporting, producing, and planning*. New York, NY: Routledge.

Spinda, J. S. (2012). Perceptual biases and behavioral effects among NFL fans: An investigation of first-person, second-person, and third-person effects. *International Journal of Sport Communication, 5*, 327–347.

Wenner, L. A., & Gantz, W. (1998). Watching sports on television: Audience experience, gender, fanship, and marriage. In L. A. Wenner (Ed.), *MediaSport* (pp. 233–251). London, UK: Routledge.

3

SPORTS MEDIA

Navigating the Landscape

Shifts in the sports media landscape have been seismic since the turn of the century. As of 2016, 34 national sports networks existed, along with an even greater number of regional networks—and yet television was still losing overall media share metrics to the Internet. Sports media has expanded its presence in virtually every manner, while access to media options expand, making advanced sabermetrics a reality while also allowing a junior high softball player to be recruited by a university thousands of miles away. Bleacher Report has 60 million unique visitors per month as of 2016—and did not even exist a decade earlier. Social media allows for breaking news to be disseminated in a manner in which an hour later it is considered "old" and no longer "breaking." Larger conglomerates seek survival in an age of media platform fragmentation. There is no longer one game or competition as an option each night; there are now dozens (see Hutchins & Rowe, 2009). Pulitzer Prize winner Thomas Friedman (2007) argues that the "world is flat," and that is true in sports media as well. The option of streaming a live cricket match from India was not realistic at the turn of the century. It is now.

Although people presume that increased new media traffic results in less traditional media traffic, this amazingly hasn't proven to be the case. Instead, the demand for sports media has proven to be elastic, with the rising tide of sports consumption seemingly lifting all boats. This chapter explores the ever-changing world of sports media using four distinct lenses: (a) traditional, (b) new, (c) social, and (d) user generated. Of course, these areas inherently overlap, yet each brings unique insight into our understanding of how sports media impacts the manner in which we think about and interact with sport. The landscape is constantly changing to the point that

The site of Super Bowl 50

many are overwhelmed by all of the choices available, and the choices are simultaneously exciting and overwhelming. These four delineated areas have different constituencies embracing them, making them both distinct and new.

SPORT AND TRADITIONAL MEDIA

Make no mistake; traditional sports media is still driving the overall media bus. Consider the second half of 2015, in which sports telecasts represented 45 of the top 50 ratings on any channel in the Unites States. Also, the Super Bowl telecast still dwarfs all other ratings. The 2015 telecast of Super Bowl XLIX yielded 114.4 million viewers; in contrast, the television drama *The Walking Dead* regularly places in the top ten programs each week, with a comparatively paltry 13 million viewers.

Also, consider the subscriber fees that each channel charges to a cable or satellite company; ESPN towers over all competition ($6.61 per month) with TNT (home of many live sports including, most notably, the NBA) and the NFL Network following closely behind (Bi, 2015). These channels wield power because, for many viewers, they are "must have" options. Some channels like the Longhorn network survive because they offer must-see live programming just a handful of times per year, making the rest of the low-rated programming slate largely irrelevant, as fans will insist on being able to witness the handful of live games each year, justifying the monthly affiliate fee. Moreover, consider the fees dedicated to the offshoots with the ESPN suite of programming (highlighted in

FIGURE 3.1 ■ ESPN's Programming Suite

Source: The trademarks depicted above are the property of ESPN, Inc. and are displayed only for the purpose of illustrating the various branding of ESPN. Their use in no way indicates any relationship between ESPN, Inc. and SAGE Publications, Inc.

Figure 3.1), and you can get a sense of the portion of any cable or satellite bill devoted to ESPN programming.

First, regarding traditional print media outlets (mainly newspaper and magazines), sports media looks very different than that of even 10 to 15 years ago. There are far fewer "beat" reporters who travel with the team. Decades ago, these reporters could offer vital statistics and game recaps, but now those are handled by major broadcast sports news outlets. Beat reporters could also provide "outside the lines" stories to fans about their favorite players and their personalities, but now those are offered not only by other television outlets but also by the athletes themselves, via Twitter feeds and Facebook pages.

While some prominent newspapers, such as *The Washington Times,* have even eliminated sports sections entirely, others are shortening them by eliminating box scores and other statistical aspects in which the Internet is more immediate, thorough, and

THEORETICALLY SPEAKING

FRAMING

First developed by sociologist Erving Goffman (1974), framing theory has been adopted by numerous communication scholars with an interest in news media. These scholars suggest that news media content creates a "frame" that shapes an audience's interpretation of events, people, and ideas. Much like a picture frame, media frames are incomplete, depicting content only within the frame while ignoring what lies outside of it. Since Goffman's introduction, communication scholars, especially Robert Entman (1993), have used frame analysis to study a wide range of current and political events. Scholars with a specific interest in sport have also turned to frame analysis to better understand the role of sports media in audiences' interpretations. In their study of Olympics coverage, Billings and Eastman (2003) discover patterns that shape viewers' perceptions of individual and national identities. As they note, "What makes these results significant to society is that the potential impact of embedded biases about gender, ethnicity, and nationality goes beyond sports: Ways of thinking that are endemic to sports can frame unconscious thinking about racial and gender groups in nonathletic situations" (p. 582). Frames are not inherently negative; however, communication and sport research does point to possible concerns about what is featured and what is omitted in media content.

accessible. Consequently, sports sections in newspapers have shifted to a greater percentage of coverage devoted to "color" commentary in which columnists dissect, interpret, and ponder future games and moves with proportionally less space devoted to game capsules and statistical recaps. Many newspapers then counter this more streamlined and informed opinion-based print offering with more elaborate online offerings that include statistics and other minutiae about the games and competitions. Local newspapers are usually owned by larger conglomerates, making companies such as Gannett news able to offer the same statistical packages in virtually identical forms to a multitude of sources.

Source: ©iStockphoto.com/Lya_Cattel

Men's magazines with heavy sports components

Regarding magazines, several mainstream magazines remain with *Sports Illustrated* (circulation of 3.0 million in 2013) and *ESPN: The Magazine* (circulation of 2.1 million in 2013) leading the way. However, other prominent magazines have moved into online-only formats, such as stalwart *The Sporting News* moving to a daily digital format in 2011. The mainstream magazines that remain rely on a hybrid model in which articles are tweeted and shared in various sources, with *ESPN: The Magazine* being paired with ESPN's online "Insider" subscription as a way of offering print and digital synergy. Meanwhile, other niche magazines have smaller circulations yet provide a very specific demographic readership that can be optimal for advertisers. For instance, *Golf Digest* (circulation 1.6 million in 2013) clearly is a primary place for people with golf-related products and promotions to advertise, particularly since the readers are more likely to be upscale because of the inherent costs of being a golfer.

Sports newspapers and magazines are more likely than other forms of media to embrace traditional sports (such as baseball or boxing) ahead of newer, emerging sports (such as mixed martial arts or snowboarding). Some of these same traditions are also in place regarding issues of identity with covers and stories disproportionately featuring men athletes. To wit, Weber and Carini (2013) found that women were more likely to be on the cover of *Sports Illustrated* in the 1960s and 1970s than in later years; about half of the women on the covers of *Sports Illustrated* in recent years are not athletes but models for the magazine's swimsuit issue. Still, print sports media is often a place in which key stories can thrive, whether that is the 2004 *San Francisco Chronicle* investigation of the Bay Area Laboratory Co-operative (BALCO) scandal that led to the downfall of many prominent professional athletes or the 2013 *Sports Illustrated* story about the National Basketball Association's (NBA's) Jason Collins becoming the first openly gay active male athlete in an American team sport.

Other forms of traditional sports media are changing as well. Sports radio has traditionally been recognized as the medium most likely to create parasocial relationships with fans, partly because the radio broadcasts of, say, 162 regular season baseball games made names like Vin Scully or Marty Brennaman virtual members of the family. Such broadcasts have existed since the 1920s, yet have changed in many fundamental ways. For instance, radio broadcasts of live sports often were rendered on radio stations that were not purely sports but rather the "home of" a given team. News, music, or other formats were interspersed with these live broadcasts. Now, the sports radio station niche fills every hour of programming not only with live broadcasts but also with a heavy dose of analysis, speculation, and fan feedback. Sports radio stations have become commonplace (the first all-sports format, WFAN, started in 1987) with an emphasis on sports talk more than live-action renderings of games. Satellite radio now offers such renderings but also offers mainstream (such as ESPN or Mad Dog Radio) or specialized (fantasy sport radio or the National Hockey League [NHL] channel) talk and feature-based options for programming.

Meanwhile, televised sports continue to shape the media landscape. While virtually every other genre of programming is being challenged by other cable outlets (TNT, USA, FX), premium channels (HBO, Starz, Showtime), or streaming service (Hulu, Netflix, Amazon), the inventory for premium sports remains relatively constant. For instance, the NFL is more popular than ever, yet there are just 16 regular season games for each NFL team that are available to broadcast, leading to expanded coverage of other aspects of the game, from multiday draft coverage to live reports from the rookie combine. Moreover, the NFL has found multiple ways of selling the same media product, with Yahoo and Twitter becoming recent entrants to streaming live games. While 39% of all television was watched via a time-shifting device (i.e., digital video recorders, etc.) in 2015, just 3% of sports programming was watched in a time-shifted manner, presumably because the liveness of the game makes the need to know the outcome much more immediate than determining what happens within a given plotline of a primetime drama.

Beyond the aforementioned highest of all television ratings within team sports, networks are finding the appetite for televised live offerings to be seemingly insatiable. For instance, college football used to be predominantly a Saturday afternoon phenomena; now, multiple broadcast networks (ABC and FOX) show highly ranked teams in primetime, joining a plethora of cable outlets that offer direct counterprogramming and yet draw reasonable ratings that ultimately yield a profit. Moreover, even some sports are considered a "loss leader" for networks, as being the "home of" a sport or specific team can make a seemingly small channel nonetheless "essential" for fans of a given sport. The 2013 creation of Fox Sports 1 started as an attempt to secure niche markets in sports, such as racing and mixed martial arts, to ensure that virtually any cable or satellite provider would need to purchase it as a part of their packages or fear the wrath of sports fans seeking those sports before then expanding into more mainline offerings such as Major League Baseball and college football. Other channels, such as CBS/Turner-based TruTV used coverage of 2011's National Collegiate Athletic Association's (NCAA's) March Madness as an opportunity for millions of sports fans to find the channel number and then view promotions for its other non-sports-based programming, resulting in record overall ratings in the first quarter of 2011 containing basketball telecasts. These cable channels now often featured sporting events that used to solely reside with broadcast networks (ABC, CBS, NBC, FOX). In 2016, the two most prominent college sporting national championships (football and men's basketball) had their championship games aired by ESPN and TBS, respectively.

SPORT AND NEW MEDIA

The web traffic for many sports websites is truly astounding, particularly in instances where the website is either a niche industry or a relatively new offering. People are likely not surprised that ESPN.com has considerable web traffic (as high as 94.4 million unique monthly users during the football season), yet some could be surprised that almost all of the most-accessed news stories are related to fantasy sports. Main broadcast entities are major players in this corner of the media universe, yet also have ties to Ultimate Fighting Championship and other sports not part of the "big three" major team sports that contribute heavily to web traffic. Moreover, ancillary components of main networks nonetheless receive heavy traffic; NBC Universal, for instance, owns Rotoworld, a popular fantasy sport web service that annually exceeds one billion page views.

The lines between traditional media and new media are now frequently blurred, with mainstream sports journalists and personalities having a presence in a multitude of formats and platforms. A new problem has arisen in which sports organizations have a difficult time determining who constitutes a sports journalist as opposed to a mere fan with a website, an issue that requires substantial discernment when offering media credentials (Holton, 2012). The current standard seems to be to widen the credentialed standards, with the results being record numbers of "media" in attendance; Southeastern Conference (SEC) "Media Days" draws up to 1,500 journalism professionals and recently added a fourth day to accommodate growing interests.

Josh Elliot in the SportsCenter studio

Sports websites have become one-stop shopping for the modern sports fan, with a single site not only offering information on the present game but also offering archives to the past, complex matrices for understanding statistical trends, prediction models for future sports events, and game formats that run the gamut from fantasy football to daily leagues and contests, such as ESPN's *Streak for the Cash.* A particularly noteworthy model comes from Yahoo Sports, a large entity that garners 55 million unique visitors each month. Yahoo opted for an approach that involved free gaming, comprehensive advice, and timely scoring features with a goal of cross-pollination with other parts of the Yahoo digital universe.

Entering the equation as well are blogs, or alternative news sites, such as Deadspin, which breaks news quite frequently (such the 2012 story in which Notre Dame football player Manti Teo was found to have a fictional girlfriend) yet does so often on stories that could be deemed more salacious than newsworthy. The result is a bifurcated system in which print media may not draw the number of readers it did, yet it is more respected than many forms of online media. In the 1970s and 1980s, print media was often jokingly called the "toy department" of news; now, traditional sports media is relatively more respected than its online colleagues (see Whiteside, Yu, & Hardin, 2012), although websites such as ESPN products fivethirtyeight.com and theundefeated.com recently are viewed to bolster the prestige of online platforms.

SPORT AND SOCIAL MEDIA

Social media is a concept that most people think they know and can list examples of platforms that meet the classification, but rarely do they have a specific definition. For our purposes, social media will refer to the digital communities in which creating and sharing content is done within given networks—whether that involves friends (Facebook), followers (Twitter), or hybrids in between. It is also important to know what websites and

TABLE 3.1 ■ Social Media Use (2015)

Social Media Outlet	Percentage	Especially Popular Among
Facebook	72	Adults, ages 18–29; Women, High Income
Pinterest	31	Women; College Educated
Instagram	28	Adults, ages 18–29; Blacks, Latinos; Urban
Twitter	23	Adults, ages 18–49; Blacks, Latinos; Urban
Snapchat	18	Teens and adults 18–29

Note: "Percentage" reflects the percentage of Americans who have ever used the social media site.

applications we are referencing and their relative use. Duggan (2013) studied such usage for Pew Research, with rates reported in Table 3.1.

Several facts can be gleaned from this table and the layers of data uncovered by Pew. First, there is no comparable social media outlet to Facebook. All others are seeking to occupy segments of the market, with Facebook four times higher than any other social media presence. Second, different social media offerings skew wildly demographically: Blacks are almost twice as likely to use Twitter than are Whites; women are 5 times more likely to have used Pinterest.

All of these trends are relevant to sports because of the relative scope and audience each provides. Most scholarly work has been focused on Twitter because of its structure as it is uniquely designed to facilitate breaking news and is considerably more likely to have athletes, teams, and sports organizations using it to relay information to fans (Hutchins & Mikosza, 2010). Such studies have revealed a degree of kinship people feel when they "follow" an athlete, finding that social media fulfills a part of fandom that was otherwise partitioned. When interacting online, people change perceptions of their heroes, showing emotions like empathy (Sanderson, 2008) and kinship (Frederick, Lim, Clavio, Pederson, & Burch, 2014) during the engagement. Athletes seem to generally welcome this form of communication, with Browning and Sanderson (2012) noting that college athletes engage with fans, even when such engagement is negative or overly critical. Social media seems to be a hobby for many professional athletes, as discussing sport-related topics is less likely to occur than interacting with other fans or facilitating a dialogue about other divergent topics that are nonsport related (Hambrick, Simmons, Greenhalgh, & Greenwell, 2010). The opportunity to potentially engage with prominent athletes appears to be a major reason why people choose to follow a given athlete. As Frederick, Lim, Clavio, and Walsh (2012) note, "The 'social world' is heightened because the potential for one-on-one interaction between the media persona (i.e., the athlete) and the media user (i.e., the fan) is a distinct possibility" (p. 496). Moreover, relatively new websites such as The Player's Tribune alter the relationship between athletes and fans; Kevin

INTERVIEW

ANN PEGORARO, DIRECTOR, INSTITUTE FOR SPORT MARKETING, LAURENTIAN UNIVERSITY

Q: What forms of social media seem to be particularly embedded in how we engage in sport?

A: Sport fans were one of the first groups to engage with social media in a substantial way. In fact, they dragged many of the sport organizations with them. As of 2016, Facebook, YouTube, and Twitter are definitely the most established platforms with Instagram and Snapchat as emerging platforms. Facebook seems to be where sport fans go to debate issues around their teams and athletes in more detail and often before or after big games; Twitter is much more a live platform where games are debated live in short bursts of fan reaction; YouTube is the natural home for highlights and short bursts of amazing video. Sport fans engage with teams, leagues, and athletes on all of these channels to satisfy their sport consumption needs.

Q: Are there new social media platforms we should be watching in the coming years?

A: Snapchat has gained a lot of ground in sports recently. I am sure that there will be new emerging platforms that we should always be watching for. Also, platforms continue to evolve to keep the interest of sport fans. This is evident in the 2016 deal for 'live' NFL broadcast through Twitter, undoubtedly a game changer for Twitter and for all platforms as they compete for users.

Q: To what extent can social media sentiment be used (or not used) to gauge general public sentiment?

A: The audience on each social media platform is demographically different and, therefore, any attempt to gauge general public sentiment is problematic. While a larger percentage of the population is on Facebook, Twitter hovers around 12% to 20% of the population for most countries, so any generalizations made are only representative of that small slice of the population. All that being said, these platforms do allow a glimpse of what a section of society thinks or feels about current events, which can be valuable in understanding sport fandom.

Q: What are some of the positive ways you have seen social media used in sport?

A: I have seen some great fan-athlete interactions on social media that would never have been possible before. There is also a lot of "social media for good" out there, perhaps not as much in sport, but it is there. Campaigns where athletes help fans in need by spreading their messages, by shedding light on injustices, and even where athletes have used it to participate in social movements such as #BlackLivesMatter.

Q: Has social media democratized communication and sport?

A: I think that social media has broken some of the stronghold that traditional media has had in sport communication. Individuals can now interact directly with teams and athletes (or whomever runs their accounts) and, in turn, sport teams can essentially bypass media to control their own stories. Essentially, teams can become their own mini media company and control the message that goes out. They can also let fans into areas that they could never access before, providing much sought after exclusive content (e.g., dressing room celebrations) all

(Continued)

Interview (Continued)

through their own channels. We have seen leagues embrace this such as the NBA and its YouTube channel where the league repackages game highlights but also produces exclusive content only available on that platform.

Q: Some athletes and fans have recently moved away from social media platforms, arguing that the negativity and potential for public relations crises outweigh any positive interactions. How can such pitfalls be managed?

A: This is an ongoing issue for most platforms and has been especially acute on Twitter in particular. The downside of the democratization function of social media is that it gives a voice to individuals who perhaps should not have one. The first step is always education and training for athletes who wish to use social media to build their personal brand. And this would include developing a plan for that athlete regarding content as well as dealing with the negativity. The pitfalls are perhaps the worst for female athletes, fans and sports reporters, and until there is enough of a groundswell change in how the "Twittersphere" self-polices trolls, unfortunately it will continue.

Durant's 2016 announcement that he would sign with the Golden State Warriors was released on the site and linked via Twitter, eliminating formal mainstream channels at early stages.

Indeed, social media is something that athletes and fans seem to engage in either in spare time or when witnessing a live sporting event (either in person or via television). With sport media increasingly becoming mobile (Goggin, 2013), fans and athletes find they need to quickly learn the rules of social media engagement or risk the crisis-laden fallout. There is power in websites such as Twitter, some of which can be dangerous to the overall livelihood of the sports media complex. As a result, many prominent college teams such as Clemson and Florida State have banned their players from using Twitter, fearing more negative than positive impact.

Arguing within the context of student-athlete social media use, Browning and Sanderson (2012) claim that "Twitter's rise has been accompanied by what appears, at least anecdotally, to be a hypercritical society in which people seem to feel empowered to send very demeaning or condemning messages to student-athletes" (p. 516). Athletes sometimes find their self-expression on Twitter can lead to controversy and threats, athletes can find themselves suspended for problematic tweets, and these threats extend to media professionals as well; for instance, in 2016, ESPN baseball analyst Curt Schilling was dismissed from his job for a series of incendiary comments culminating in a post that was less than tolerant about transgender Americans.

Nonetheless, social media can have a ripple effect on society as a whole, as evidenced when journalist Guy Adams offered many critical tweets about NBC's taped coverage of the 2012 Olympics and found himself temporarily suspended from Twitter because of the large ramifications and discussions that ensued, particularly with the "hashtag"

CASE STUDY

WATCH WHAT YOU SAY

Prior to the start of the 2010 North Carolina Tar Heels's football season, one of their star defensive players, Marvin Austin, was dismissed from the team for violating NCAA regulations related to receipt of inappropriate benefits. While such cases have become common place in NCAA athletics, the circumstances that led to the dismissal emerged as a result of a suspicious Twitter feed where Austin discussed the outcomes of a lavish shopping spree just following a post about the financial shortcomings of being a college athlete. Media speculation about the post resulted in an NCAA investigation that resulted in sanctions on the Tar Heels football program. Soon after the incident, the athlete handbook at the University of North Carolina was revised to specify that, "Each team must identify at least one coach or administrator who is responsible for having access to and regularly monitoring the content of team members' social networking sites and postings" and that "the athletics department also reserves the right to have other staff members monitor athletes' posts" (Kaiser, 2012, para. 7).

Colleges and universities around the country are faced with a growing need to manage the impact that inappropriate athletes' behavior on social media can have on their public image. As the need has increased, many institutions have begun to monitor their athletes' social media posting by hiring companies or utilizing software that flags what they consider to be inappropriate words or slang expressions. For instance, the University of Louisville flags and has subsequently banned 406 words in their athletes' posts, with a similar number being flagged by the University of Kentucky (Wolverton, 2012). Some of the words include the following:

• Agent	• Alcohol	• Benjamins
• Cheat sheet	• Doobie	• Fight
• Gay	• Payoff	• Rape
• BYOB	• Gozangas	• Porn
• Jeremiah Weed	• GNOC	• Drunk Driving

Institutions that fear inappropriate behavior on behalf of sport agents have also added the names of the 300 most prominent agents to demonstrate to the NCAA that they are taking the appropriate measures to monitor their athletes' behavior.

1. Should an institution have the right to restrict what an athlete posts on social media?
2. Is there a first amendment issue here with the steps that are being taken by a number of these high profile Division I programs?
3. Would these institutions be better served by better educating their athletes about the impact posting on social media websites can have for both them and the institution?

Source: Screenshot from Twitter.com

Twitter Feed for #nbcfail

#nbcfail (Pilkington, 2012). While sports organizations and associations attempt to sort out their policies regarding social media use and ramifications, all seemingly realize that it must be incorporated into the overall media landscape. Most sports personalities have Twitter hashtags included in online graphics; virtually any major sports team has a Facebook page that one can "like" and receive a continual feed of information.

More recently, Instagram has moved into the social media fray; Smith and Sanderson (2015) found that athletes are heavily present in the platform, using the image to carefully cultivate desirable public images. The newest entrants into the social media universe are the currently overwhelmingly female Pinterest and the overwhelmingly youthful Snapchat, for which teams are working to find ways to make a viable outlet for promoting all sorts of aspects of sports culture and fandom. For the former, Conlin, McLemore, and Rush (2014) found that while elements of traditional fandom are rendered on Pinterest, it is especially effective for the selling of merchandise and the overall material lifestyle of a sports fan. Some teams have readily embraced the platform (the Chicago Cubs, for instance, have 1.1 million followers), but other teams are finding ways to use it even with smaller segments of the population. As Laird (2012) writes:

A MATTER OF ETHICS

TUNSIL'S DRAFT NIGHT DRAMA

The National Football League (NFL) draft has become an enormous media spectacle. Each year, ESPN promotes the event—which is not an actually sporting event, of course—for weeks and then airs several days of coverage. Scores of analysts publish scouting reports and draft previews, and social media conversations trade on rampant speculation and the promise of scandal. These various forms of media converged in a particularly striking way in 2016, when University of Mississippi offensive lineman Laremy Tunsil became the biggest story of the draft.

Tunsil was widely regarded as a top 10 pick, perhaps even the number one pick in the draft. Just moments before the event began, however, a video appeared on Tunsil's Twitter feed that showed him smoking marijuana using a gas mask. Later in the evening, his Instagram account published a series of texts that indicated he had accepted money from the athletic department at Mississippi, a clear violation of NCAA rules. Tunsil admitted that both the video and the text messages were authentic; however, he insisted that his accounts had been hacked, and he had not posted the content. Indeed, later reports revealed that Tunsil was perhaps the target of a family member who intentionally sought to sabotage his draft status. To a degree, the effort was successful, as Tunsil fell to the Miami Dolphins with the 13th pick, and several of the commentators on the ESPN broadcast of the draft condemned him for his immaturity and inability to protect his social media accounts, while also raising questions about his future as an NFL player.

Drug use and accepting cash from a university athletic department certainly are rules violations. However, the media dimensions to this story raise additional questions. In particular, what should be the "rules" that govern social media usage in sports? Is it appropriate to share incriminating information on social media, especially if it requires hacking into someone's account? How should mainstream commentators, such as those at ESPN, handle accusations of impropriety that emerge from social media? Ultimately, who is responsible for how best to handle this kind of information?

> The Giants have a section dedicated to their supporters' hearty tailgating culture. The Portland Trail Blazers have boards that collect team-themed wallpapers and photos of pets in Blazers gear. Most teams have boards displaying memorabilia and clothing for sale elsewhere online. Because Pinterest isn't a dialogue-heavy network and allows users to follow either a brand as a whole or just specific boards, teams are able to focus on particular niches of fandom. They're also able to share things that wouldn't be as feasible on Facebook or Twitter. (para. 8–9)

An even newer entrant into the sport media world is Snapchat, which seemingly is growing to mainstream status and has elements that make it appealing for sharing pictures and information related to sports fandom. Billings, Qiao, Conlin, and Nie (2016) found that amongst those that use Snapchat, it is the second most-used platform to render sport-oriented content, trailing only Facebook in this regard.

Recent evidence may suggest some burnout on social media or at least that some usage may be leveling off. Evidence shown from Sporting News Media Group (2013) reveals new trends in social media use in sport, highlighted in Figure 3.2.

Some additional trends were uncovered in the same report, including that

- Facebook was the number 1 option of people who used social media to follow sport,
- football is the most followed social media sport,
- 4% believe second-screen consumption will have the biggest impact on the way sports are consumed in the immediate coming years,
- 29% of all sports fans watch online via a personal computer (PC), and
- 23% of all sports fans consume sports through an Internet-enabled mobile device.

FIGURE 3.2 ■ Percentage of People Using Social Media to Follow Teams, Leagues, and Players Online

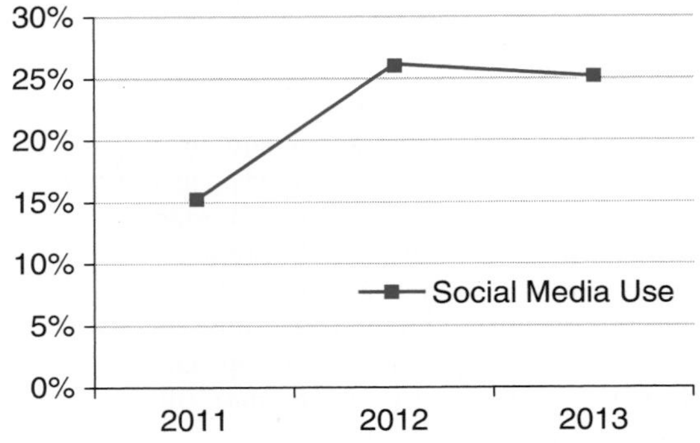

Source: Sporting News Media Group (2013)

Whatever the future of social media holds, it appears the various outlets offer not only new ways of sharing information but also new manners of interaction with fans that previously were considered as attainable only from people with the highest of economic and social class power. As Sanderson (2011) notes, "it's a whole new ballgame" (p. 1).

SPORT AND USER-GENERATED MEDIA

While much of the streaming video and other online traffic is devoted to mainstream sports highlights, the user-generated media industry (predominantly YouTube but including other formats, such as Vimeo and Buzzfeed) also generates large audiences for things that could best be deemed as on the outskirts of sport. For instance, Austrian daredevil Felix Baumgartner's "Red Bull Jump" from outer space was viewed by over 40 million people on YouTube, a noteworthy feat when taking in the comparison that not a single one of President Barack Obama's speeches has generated nearly as many views even over the course of many years of access.

The world of user-generated media is quite vast. YouTube alone has 1 billion unique visitors per month, more than 10% of the entire world population. A total of 6 billion hours of video are viewed on YouTube in a given month. While exact figures are difficult to determine regarding the percentage of views that are dedicated specifically to sports media, both the depth and breadth of videos are impressive. High school use of platforms like The Cube to telecast sporting events or Periscope from Twitter feeds has also grown significantly in a relatively short time period. Moreover, advents such as FloWrestling charge a $150 per year fee for live streaming of youth, high school, college, and Team USA events. Similar to the NCAA expansion, which allows one to watch every match at the NCAA Division I championships through ESPN, FloWrestling has dramatically changed the landscape of

OFF THE BEATEN PATH

MIXED MARTIAL ARTS

The Ultimate Fighting Championship (UFC) considers itself the fastest growing sports organization in the world. It is indeed the premier organization in Mixed Martial Arts (MMA), and its executives, Frank Fertitta, Lorenzo Fertitta, and president Dana White, have revolutionized the sport. Under White's leadership, the organization that was bought in 2001 for $2 million sold for a $4 billion in 2016. In 2011, White announced the first-ever social media incentive program for athletes, setting aside nearly a half million dollars annually to award quarterly bonuses to fighters who have the largest increase in Twitter followers, the largest percentage increase in followers, and send the most creative tweets. The UFC partners with Digital Royalty, a social media brand management company, on this initiative. Digital Royalty provided social media training to over 300 fighters to assist the organization in fully embracing this new communication tool thus increasing fan engagement. The UFC also successfully broke into mainstream media with a 7-year broadcast agreement with FOX Sports Media Group. The result has been rapid growth. The organization has 20.2 million Facebook fans, over 4.45 million Twitter followers, and offers a multiplatform package available to over one billion homes worldwide, in over 149 countries and in 19 different languages.

—Aisha Avery

wrestling with its own documentaries and coverage of the sport that had never been possible a decade ago.

Sports that in the past required one to be physically present now allow much more intimate access to events around the country. Some videos are created and uploaded by media professionals, but the majority are created (or repurposed) by people outside of the sports media complex. Want to see the biggest bloopers of the past month in sports combined and then set to music by The White Stripes? Someone's done it. Want to see people throughout society in Tim Tebow's famous "Tebowing" pose or "Crying Michael Jordan"? So do millions of others, as evidenced by the high number of views. However, there is much more offered online that could best be classified as user-generated sports media. Vimeo has especially avid creators and followers of extreme sports. Meanwhile, outlets like Buzzfeed have matrices to detect viral content from any source, not just establishments inside sports media but anyone with a blog post or video that receives strong upticks in audience interest.

Tim Tebow

Source: The White House from Washington, DC [P111512PS-0111], via Wikimedia Commons

Olympic gymnast McKayla Maroney playfully poses with President Barack Obama at the White House

Some sites straddle the lines between social media and user-generated media. Tumblr is a microblogging site allowing people to attach tags to pictures and other content, with sports being one of the most popular tags on the site. Vine allows people to create 6-second videos to be viewed in a continual loop, perfect for attaching that extreme highlight (good or bad) and then manipulating it for full effect in some form or another. Many of these sites have developed sports components, creating things like Internet memes that, while fun, also convey some form of potentially persuasive message to other sports fans and beyond, with scholars such as Dickerson (2015) arguing for their power in shaping perceptions of issues such as race and gender. For instance, a popular meme in 2012 was of "Smoking Jay Cutler," placing the Chicago Bears quarterback in a variety of other circumstances with the same apathetic look—confirming an image many fans have of him as aloof or undedicated to winning championships. Another popular meme in 2012 was "McKayla's Not Impressed," created from a look American gymnast McKayla Maroney donned after failing to win the gold at the London Olympics in her specialty event, the vault. Maroney's infamous pose was then Photoshopped at other historic events, such as the moon landing or the release of the iPhone 5, providing an opportunity to fuse sporting attitudes into other aspects of culture in the process. More recent memes have functioned as social persuasion, pointedly satirizing issues like the New England Patriots' "Deflategate" or even very serious issues such as Adrian Peterson's child abuse charges.

CONCLUSION

Much of the future of sports media will align with the rest of media evolution, with the key words being "integration" and "convergence." Some new formats have not yet proven to be successful—at least in current form—such as ESPN's 3D programming, which was discontinued in June 2013 because of limited viewer adoption. Yet more formats abound, including 4K ultra high definition, high definition along with the widespread growth of streaming Internet television. The future appears to be ensconced in the merging of media platforms more than the elimination of them, whether that is more radio on the Internet, more social media within a television broadcast, or more print weekly magazines in tablet daily form, sports entities seem poised to take advantage of such convergence, still finding a fan appetite for sports that is insatiable.

Suggested Additional Reading

Billings, A. C., & Hardin, M. (2014). *The Routledge handbook of sport & new media.* London, UK: Routledge.

Boyle, R. (2006). *Sports journalism: Contexts and issues*. London, UK: Routledge.

Hutchins, B., & Rowe, D. (Eds.). (2013). *Digital media sport: Technology, power, and culture in the network society*. London, UK: Routledge.

Lasorsa, D. (2012). Transparency and other journalistic norms on Twitter. *Journalism Studies, 13*(3), 402–417.

Miah, A., García, B., & Zhihui, T. (2008). We are the media: Non-accredited media and citizen journalists at the Olympic Games. In M. E. Price & D. Dayan (Eds.), *Owning the Olympics: Narratives of the New China* (pp. 320–345). Ann Arbor: University of Michigan Press.

Mozisek, K. D. (2015). No girls allowed!: Female reporters as threats to the male domain of sports. *Journal of Sports Media, 10*, 17–29.

Price, J., Farrington, N., & Hall, L. (2012). Tweeting with the enemy? The impacts of new social media on sports journalism and the education of sports journalism students. *Journalism Education, 1*(1), 9–20.

4

SPORT FAN CULTURES

Sport fan cultures are an ever-changing phenomenon, with each sport offering unique opportunities that help define what it means to be a fan in today's global sport environment. Sport viewing and spectatorship continue to be a growing leisure activity, producing more than $60 billion in revenue (e.g., ticket sales, pay-per-view, sport merchandise) each year in the United States alone (Eichelberger, 2013). Within this environment, fans are provided unlimited access to information or *points of contact* and, at times, direct exposure to the sport, teams, and athletes they follow. Through these opportunities, fans are now just as likely to become connected to the sport franchise itself as they are the players or teams that had once served as the center of the fans' allegiance (Oates, 2009).

Sport fan cultures are likely to evolve and develop dependent on the sport type and level at which it is played, and these factors influence the communication that drives how fans enact and consume sports. To highlight this feature of sport fan behavior, we present you with two competing sport contexts to demonstrate the divergent perspectives that can exist across sports. First, the National Association for Stock Car Auto Racing (NASCAR) is a sport that developed during the 1950s and 1960s with humble beginnings and has flourished into a multibillion-dollar-a-year franchise with a fan base of more than 75 million fans. While NASCAR events can generate a considerable television audience, NASCAR is recognized more as the nation's largest spectator sport because of its ability to accommodate as many as 250,000 spectators at major events. In fact, 17 of the top 20 single day sporting events involve NASCAR. Second, at the turn of the 20th century, the National Football League (NFL) developed along similar lines as a sport designed primarily to tap into the commercial success of college football. Despite a number of fledgling leagues, over the past half century, the NFL has emerged as the most dominant sports in the United States, receiving considerable amounts of media coverage. For example, when comparing the most highly ranked television programs in our nation's history, the Super Bowl represents 9 of the top 10 television programs of all time. Prior to 2010, the final episode of *M.A.S.H.* held the record until Super Bowl XLIV between the Indianapolis Colts and New Orleans Saints drew just over 106 million spectators. That record was soon broken, and the current record of 114 million viewers tuned in to watch the New England Patriots and the Seattle Seahawks play in Super Bowl XLIX. For many, the Super Bowl has become an informal national holiday in the United States (Martin & Reeves, 2001). The American Institute of Food Distribution (2004) reports that more products are purchased and consumed during Super Bowl weekend than any other holiday except Thanksgiving. As technology has developed, NFL fans are now given even more opportunities to participate in viewing and responding to league drafts, serving as managers in fantasy football leagues, and even performing simulated play with video games, such as the Madden Football series. In addition to breaking the total viewer record set by *M.A.S.H.* some 3 decades earlier, Super Bowl XLVII set the current record of 231,500 tweets per minute when a power outage caused a blackout in the New Orleans Superdome.

Source: http://www.af.mil/news/story_media.asp?storyID=123010034

Drivers and fans celebrate the start of a NASCAR race

INTERVIEW

LARS ANDERSON, SENIOR WRITER, *SPORTS ILLUSTRATED*

Q: While you write on a plethora of athletes and sports, your two main beats are college football and NASCAR. How would you best describe each of these fan cultures?

A: The typical NASCAR fan attends races for the overall experience of the event: the 3 days of camping and grilling, the socializing with other fans, and finally the race. There is a powerful sense of community among NASCAR fans. In over 10 years on the beat, I've never seen a single fight or argument in the outfields and infields of NASCAR tracks. The intensity level is always much higher among college football fans, who often view their teams as an extension of themselves and, in some extreme cases, of their own self-worth. You don't see people cry at a NASCAR race if their driver doesn't win, but after a big college game, you'll always see fans of the losing team shed tears. I'd argue that college football fans are the most zealous of all American sporting fans.

Q: What aspects of the fandom you witness would best be described as "uniquely American" or, perhaps, unique to a given region of America?

A: Stock car racing is a distinctly American sport (it originated in the South with moonshine runners), and feelings of patriotism surge at high levels at every race. American flags dot the infields, and it's been my experience that nearly one third of the fans have ties to the military. The great American tradition on college football campuses is pregame tailgating. No conference does this with more fervor than the Southeastern Conference (SEC), where tailgating has been turned into an art form. It's not unusual in the SEC to find thousands of fans attending tailgates without tickets to the actual game. To them, the social aspects of the party are more important than what happens on the field.

Q: Sports are purported to be the great economic unifier for all social classes. However, luxury boxes and other modern advents seemingly make the fan experience very different for wealthier fans. How do you see these factors influencing fandom?

A: The sports I cover—NASCAR and college football—are still very accessible to the blue-collar fans. Luxury boxes don't play a big role at NASCAR events, and one of the lures of the sport is that it can be very inexpensive if you choose to camp on the site. Where the middle-class college football fan gets squeezed out is in conference championship games and Bowl Championship Series (BCS) title games. When the average ticket is going for more than $1,000, it simply isn't possible for many to attend. This is why, oddly, national title games can feature some of the quietest crowds of the season; the seats are filled with corporate suits who sit on their hands because they don't have a rooting interest in the game.

Q: What is the relationship between fandom and notions of ritual and tradition?

A: The hardcore fans in both NASCAR and college football are servants to ritual and tradition. NASCAR fans always like to camp in the same spot every year at the races they attend, they spend time with the same people, they cook the same food, and, in many cases, they even wear the same clothes that illustrate who they are rooting for. Tradition is even bigger in college football. I spent time recently with Mike Slive, the SEC commissioner, and he told me the story of seeing a family walking the concourse at an SEC stadium. He then explained how he could envision that moment being repeated in future generations by that family. The DNA of our fandom—and where we tailgate, what we grill, how we celebrate victories, how we mourn losses—gets passed down from fathers and mothers to their children.

With the range of sport cultures in mind, as well as ever-changing fan bases, we set our sights in this chapter on exploring the communicative aspects driving sport fan cultures that exist today. We start by exploring the distinctions between the various types of fans that you are likely to encounter—noting the differences between fans and spectators. As we present these fan types, we expect that you may even begin to recast your own perception of where you might fit on the sport fandom continuum. The change in the way that fans can experience live and mediated coverage of sports has also had a significant impact on the way that sport fan cultures evolve, along with the rituals that are performed in these two contexts. Within this framework, we attempt to explore the range of motives that drive sport fan cultures by examining the rationales behind fan interest in sport, the by-products they receive, and how these vary by sport types. These motives are linked with what many define as sport identification, suggesting that the relationship between sport and identity (self-esteem or personal identity) can affect a large range of variables outside the sport context. Finally, as the NASCAR and NFL examples demonstrate, sport continues to evolve as new technologies provide innovative ways not only of engaging fans with their sports, teams, or athletes but also of affording fans an opportunity to shape the very nature of sport itself. With this broader framework in mind, we begin by exploring the various sport fan types that exist.

Source: Edward Blake - EHB_3384

Duke and Wisconsin players warm up prior to the 2015 NCAA Men's Basketball Tournament

SPORT FAN TYPES

In Chapter 2, we explored how fans serve an important role in the community of sport, noting the differences between modes of fan consumption of sport. Here, we seek to better understand fan types based on the cultures and rituals that emerge, and the difference between fans and spectators is worth establishing at the start of this section. Some use the term sport *spectator* to describe those who simply watch and observe, while the term *fan* (stemming from the term *fanatic*) is more commonly used to depict those who experience a greater sense of devotion to the sport they follow (Trail, Robinson, Dick, & Gillentine, 2003). Fan types often fall somewhere on a continuum between *fair-weather* (those who display rejuvenated waning interest in their sport or franchise only when it is winning) and *die-hard* (those who display heavy loyalty in their sport or franchise regardless of the result). Cottingham (2012) used the term *fair-weather* to contrast with the fans tailgating well into the cold weather months, during his analysis of Pittsburgh Steelers fans, using three forms of evaluation (team performance, weather, and knowledge of the team and game) to find that "fans use the term 'fair-weather fan' to convey a moral hierarchy that idealizes a devoted, 'hardcore' fan as one who is knowledgeable about the game itself, the nuances of playoffs, and rankings, and remains loyal to the team throughout a season of poor performance and inclement weather" (p. 122). You may know a number of people who become excited about college basketball in March each year as the National Collegiate Athletic Association (NCAA) basketball tournament arrives (March Madness). Office betting pools add to the excitement of the games as the tournament unfolds, but many of those who participate in such events are unlikely to follow the sport beyond this time frame (e.g., college recruitment efforts in the off-season, player early entry into the National Basketball Association [NBA]). The initial games for the tournament are so popular that experts estimate that approximately $4 billion in revenue is lost each year due to low productivity in the workplace (Golden, 2016). Others become enamored of their local franchise only after it has won a championship yet quickly lose interest shortly after the team's success fades away. Die-hard fans, on the other hand, are a different story. They look forward to the upcoming season with great anticipation, often transforming into different people as they are overcome by the successes and failures of their teams. For example, Green Bay Packers fans are often described using this particular classification. Their ability to support an NFL franchise in the small Green Bay, Wisconsin, market (population 104,057) serves as a point of pride for these fans as their self-proclaimed identity as "Cheeseheads" further distinguishes them from other sport fans in that community (Giles & Stohl, 2016). Lambeau Field has had a consecutive sell-out streak dating back to 1960, and more than 81,000 fans remain on the waiting list for season tickets. Despite this designation, research by Bryant and Cummins (2010) observed that even die-hard fans have a difficult time maintaining a high level of identification with their team following a loss. They identified "distancing" behaviors in their study of Alabama and Auburn football fans who felt a need to renegotiate their identities in times of hardship.

Sutton, McDonald, Miline, and Cimperman (1997) have classified three types of fans. The first would fall closer to the fair-weather end of the continuum, which they described as the *social fan* (see Figure 4.1). This individual has a limited sense of identification with a particular team, sport, or athlete, seeing sport fandom primarily as a socializing opportunity. The outcome itself is less important than the experience gained from participating. The lived experience of the live event or social gatherings connected with sports is what drives social fans' ongoing interest. The *focused fan* has moderate levels of identification, with some form of invested interest in or affiliation with the team he or she follows: "I'm from Denver, which means that I support the Broncos, Rockies, Nuggets, and Avalanche." Focused fans might have a sense of civic engagement whereby they provide their general support to the city, town, or community sport teams. Finally, the *vested fan* is a die-hard fan with high levels of emotional attachment and identification to the teams he or she supports. Team outcomes are of critical import, and in many cases, self-esteem and identity of vested fans will be connected to contest outcomes. Not being able to work the day after the Chicago Cubs are eliminated from the playoffs might be what you can expect from a vested fan. They have invested time, money, and energy into the support they provide. Advances in technology and the growth of media coverage have had a significant impact on these fan types. More important, such changes have created a distinction for fans who attend the live sporting event. In addition to these three fan types, Courtney and Wann (2010) identified the "dysfunctional fan" as the fans at sporting events who are "overly aggressive with opposing teams, fans and officials" (p. 191). Some sport franchises are more notorious for having a fan base that takes a great amount of pleasure in its notoriety as dysfunctional. The city of Philadelphia went so far as to place a courtroom at Lincoln Financial Field to handle the excessive number of dysfunctional fans on game day. They have even taken pride in folklore associated with pelting Santa Claus with snowballs during a game in the late 1970s.

LIVE VERSUS MEDIATED FANDOM

In Chapter 10, we provide greater detail on the transition that has occurred for sport participants as we have transitioned from a game to a sport culture. A similar transition is also unfolding in contemporary sports, as fandom is no longer defined by our physical presence at the actual sporting event. There are a variety of reasons that fans make a conscious choice to attend the live event. First is the ability to serve as a vicarious participant in the event, because it provides an opportunity to engage in retrospective recall after it is over. Weed (2007) noted that participants at the live event "have some kind of experience of 'otherness' that will set them aside from their peers on their return" (p. 406). You are able to recount not only the specifics about the event but also what occurred in the historic significance of the event itself. Stating that "I was in the crowd when Max Scherzer tied the MLB record with 20 strikeouts in May 2016" garners more attention than the simple recall for those of us who must rely upon the replay of the event. This motivation is the reason that far more people claim to have been present

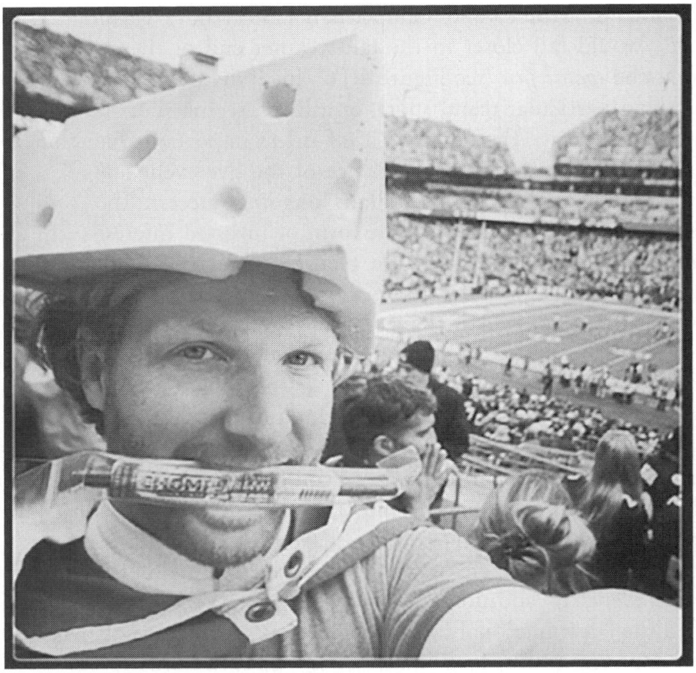

A Green Bay Packer fan sports his cheesehead at Lambeau Field

FIGURE 4.1 ■ Sport Fan Continuum

Sport Interest	Social	Focused	Vested	Emotional Attachment
⟶				

Fan Type	Description	Example
Social	Those individuals whose interest in a sport is driven more by the ability to connect with others. The sport itself is peripheral or secondary to the pleasure obtained from sharing the experience with other fans.	Coworker who takes part in an office pool for the NCAA basketball tournament despite having not followed college basketball the entire regular season.
Focused	Individuals with moderate investment in a particular team, sport, or community who spend considerable time following outcomes.	Dallas native who is vested in seeing the Cowboys and Rangers perform well throughout their respective seasons.
Vested	Sport fans with significant emotional attachment to the success or failure of the teams or sports they support.	Snowboarding enthusiast who attends all national events and makes reservations to attend the Olympics every 4 years to support the sport.

for moments such as the 1980 Olympic hockey "Miracle on Ice" than the arena could possibly have held.

In their investigation of mental imagery for sport spectators, Griggs, Leflay, and Groves (2012) noted the strong contrast between mediated coverage and "being there," whereby a stronger sense of attachment to historic events was more likely to result in highly sensitive personal emotion. Second, fans feel a need to participate in the live event because it serves as not only an opportunity to collect mementos but also, most important, the ability to retell the experience as an intangible outcome of the lived experience. Others have noted the desire for fans to experience the physical connection that comes from being in close proximity to others who are also simultaneously living the event. Being a part of this type of sporting event is one of the enduring features of the lived sport experience. Traditionalists still contend that going to the ballpark is a fundamental feature of the baseball experience, but they have also frowned upon the fact that sport franchises have had to develop a more lucrative experience to stimulate fan interest at these venues. Rushin (2004) noted that Major League Baseball (MLB) attendance, for example, has grown because of the additional amenities that "going to the ballpark" can provide. Wi-Fi access, Ferris wheels, and picnic areas have become common amenities at these venues, causing the sport or competition to become secondary to the social environment that is fostered.

Rituals (sets of actions or behaviors performed to serve a symbolic purpose) have expanded beyond just the context of viewing the event in person. *Sports Illustrated* noted a number of years ago that with advances in media and game coverage, sport fans are able to obtain a better experience by watching the event in alternate locations. For the average American home there are traditionally more television sets than occupants (2.93 sets per home), and Gantz (2012) argued that "the TV viewing experience has become increasingly atomized with parents, children, and roommates able to watch what they want on their own set, when they want to watch it, in their own space, and by themselves" (p. 178–179). Despite this trend, coviewing of sporting events in homes has remained a common feature for how families consume sports. Viewing sporting events together as a family has continued to be an important part of holiday rituals for many Americans, consuming a large portion of family engagement opportunities on the weekend compared to any other in-home activity.

For example, tailgating has become a popular ritual that fans engage in prior to the start of each event, with considerable revenue generated each year by companies that develop a wide range of products that can support this presport experience. Some teams have even begun to view tailgating as a revenue-generating opportunity, by which tailgating and the sporting event itself have been joined in ways that may have never been intended. For instance, it is estimated that more than 30 million spectators tailgate each year, and 30% of those fans are projected never to attend the sporting event itself. When sport franchises seek to build new facilities, providing enough designated space for tailgating has become an important factor of selecting prime retail space in many cities. Weed (2007) observed that in Great Britain, the pub has become a legitimate venue for soccer fans to experience events, noting that more people watch live events in bars or restaurants than those who participate as actual spectators of the event. Three features seem to be influencing this particular trend, including the (a) availability of technology for displaying digital-quality pictures, (b) lack of perceived safety of sport stadiums and negative fan behavior or hooliganism, and (c) increased coverage of all sporting events on television. Regardless of whether a fan takes part in the actual event, a set of rituals often helps to reinforce how fans experience sports.

FAN RITUALS

Rituals produce a permanent change or transformation in an individual or group and represent important rites of passage (Schechner, 2002). Sport is one such situation that is structured around transformational rites of passage for both spectators (e.g., tailgating, cheers) and participants (e.g., pregame warm-up, athlete superstitions). Playful performance is an important part of our everyday life experiences, and sport fans are offered a lasting refuge where playful public performance still exists in the patterns and rituals that define sporting events. Fans often paint their faces and wear common attire or even elaborate costumes as a way to show support or allegiance to their sport teams. A number of scholars have examined the role of ritual for sport spectators (Carbaugh, 1996; Serazio, 2012). Using an ethnographic approach, Carbaugh (1996) assumed the role of participant observer at 40 college basketball games. His analysis uncovered five important rituals consistent at

Spectators watch a soccer game on the large screen at AT&T Stadium

both the professional and college levels: the warm-up, the salutation, the introductions, game talk, and the dissipation. These stages of fan performance were distinguished by the manner of talk (transition from cooperative to competitive as the game started) and the style of talk (low intensity to high intensity) as the contest approached. The purpose of viewing the sporting event live allowed the fan to live vicariously through his or her team and to partake of the highly expressive public discourse.

A source of concern regarding the ritual of sport has been the way sport fans use performance to assist in the perpetuation of racial stereotypes. Miller (1999) contended that the difficulty associated with restricting the use of Native American mascots for professional and college teams resulted from the parallels between stereotypical views and how people assumed the role as "sport fan" for their teams. Dressing in costumes, wearing sentimental team paraphernalia, and performing game rituals and taunting were essential features of their sport experience. Take the University of North Dakota (UND) as a prime example. When the NCAA implemented new requirements for Native American mascots for those programs that hoped to host postseason tournament events, the university sought to replace their Fighting Sioux mascot. Continuous attempts were blocked for more than a decade by alumni lobbying, voting efforts by state tribes to provide support, and even legislation requiring UND to retain the mascot. When designing the Ralph Engelstad Hockey Arena, the benefactor even tied funding for the project to the university retaining the mascot, going as far as embedding images of the mascot in the building facade, granite flooring, and emblems on the leather seating throughout the arena. Finally, in 2015, after an extensive voting process, the institution unveiled the UND Fighting Hawks mascot, eliciting both praise and criticism. As is evident in this example, these important rituals were difficult for some fans to let go, and we explore this at greater length in Chapter 9.

Research has also examined the impact sport venues have on the performance of these sport rituals. During the closing day of the 1991 baseball season, Krizek (1992) assessed the impact the demolition of Comiskey Park (home of the Chicago White Sox) had on fans. Participants reflected on their memories of the park, which formed important rituals of bonding fathers, sons, and families as well as connections with the past. The ritual of going to the ballpark as children had encouraged fans to make pilgrimages from around the country to be a part of the facility's final hours. The park also helped to encompass a number of other important rituals in the lives of these individuals, most notably weddings and bachelor parties, a final slice of life before going off to war, and relationships formed between fans as they cheered for their beloved team. In a number of ways, these rituals have a direct impact on the factors that motivate fan connection and identification with the sport, teams, and athletes they follow, which we discuss in the following section.

MOTIVES OF SPORT SPECTATORS

Research has identified six primary motives that drive fans' connection to the sports they follow. First, fans interested primarily in *aesthetic beauty* are drawn to the sport to see

UND fans watch the former Fighting Sioux hockey team compete at the Ralph Engelstad Arena

it played to its perfection. Having played a sport as a young child and understanding the difficulties associated with performing at the highest level can be a significant motive for some fans. Baseball fanatics are inspired by the perfect double play, a manager's ability to strategize, or the potential for a perfect game. Someone who could never dunk a basketball may be motivated to follow the sport because he or she experiences a greater sense of appreciation for what professional athletes can accomplish.

Second, *achievement* is a motive that is fulfilled when one obtains a sense of accomplishment after a team or athlete wins. This motive can cause a fan to attend every game or contest, as research has shown that highly identified fans have an innate belief that their presence at a sporting event has a direct impact on the competition's outcome (Epting, Riggs, Knowles, & Hanky, 2011). Many sport franchises fuel this belief in their fans. For example, in football, a number of teams emphasize the "12th man," suggesting that the fans can serve as an additional player influencing the game's outcome. Fans and competitors both have a strong understanding of the role the home field advantage has for their ability to win, and one of the significant factors has been the psychological influence that feedback from fans has on an official's desire for fairness (Moskowitz & Wertheim, 2011). Courneya and Carron (1992) observed that home teams have been found to win over 50% of their games when balanced against an even home and away schedule. More recently, Jamieson (2010) conducted a meta-analysis of research on home field advantage and found that the home team will win more than 60% of its events. Furthermore, when exploring factors that impact this winning percentage, Jamieson noted differences based on game and sport type. Home field advantage is more important for intense rivalries, and soccer produced the largest home field advantage effect.

Findings from Wann, Peterson, Cothran, and Dykes (1999) suggest that fans will go to great lengths to support their team's outcome, even indicating a willingness to cause harm to (break a leg, trip) the rival players and coaches. They observed that "because their teams' performance has relevance to their self-concept, they become more willing to assist the team by acting violently. . . . Apparently many sport fans believe that they would go to great (and illegal) lengths to assist their teams" (p. 601). The sense of achievement one experiences after the win (not just for the team but for one's own contribution) can have a direct effect on such behavior. Many fans refer to games that either "we won" or "they lost" as a way of contributing to a win but not hindering a team in a loss.

CASE STUDY

UNANTICIPATED FAN SUPPORT

Since the inception of the Modern Olympics in 1896, the summer Games have comprised a wide range of sports that include throwbacks to the ancient Olympics, such as track and field events, as well as more recent additions, such as basketball, soccer, and baseball. As the modern day Olympics has transformed over the past century, the number of sports has grown to include 35 different types, represented by 30 disciplines and nearly 400 events at its peak. In an attempt to manage the scope and cost of the Olympics for each host city, in recent years, the International Olympic Committee (IOC) limited the number of sports to a maximum of 28 sports and 10,500 athletes.

In its efforts to continue to manage the scope of the Olympics, the IOC established a mechanism for identifying what they refer to as "core sports," which would continue indefinitely in future Olympics. Those sports classified as "non-core" sports would by default be selected for inclusion only on a game-by-game basis. The executive committee for the IOC evaluated the success of the core sports after the London Olympic Games and sought to further reduce the number of core sports down to 25 starting with the 2020 Olympics. At its February 2013 meeting, the IOC voted to drop wrestling to meet this 25 sport standard. A feature of both the ancient and modern Olympic Games, the sport of wrestling has been a common fixture of the summer games. The decision brought about significant outrage from the wrestling community throughout the United States and those countries with a strong history of success in the sport. ESPN devoted a major portion of its programming to the subject during the days preceding the IOC decision. At issue was the executive committee's decision to retain sports like the modern pentathlon and equestrian, both of which have limited appeal beyond those with significant social and economic backgrounds.

As a former high school wrestler, Mike Golic devoted significant time to his daily sports radio broadcast on *Mike & Mike* to denouncing the IOC decision while highlighting the

(Continued)

CASE STUDY (Continued)

benefits for the sport. USA Wrestling members mounted a "Save Olympic Wrestling" campaign in solidarity with wrestling organizations around the world that function to create Fédération Internationale des Luttes Associées (FILA), the international governing body for the sport. Shortly after the IOC decision, the current FILA president resigned, and emphasizing fan interest in making the sport more appealing to the novice spectator, the incoming president implemented, effective immediately, a series of sweeping rule changes that were designed to increase action during the match. The IOC responded shortly afterward that FILA had heard its call to regenerate its fan base and reconsidered its decision to reinstate wrestling as a core sport. During the 2016 Olympic Games in Rio, the IOC also added five sports to the 2020 games to be held in Tokyo including the reinstatement of softball and baseball and introducing surfing, skateboarding, and sport climbing for the first time.

1. What do you perceive to be the viability for a sport that does not provide an opportunity for its athletes to compete either professionally or in the Olympic Games?
2. What does this example of the wrestling community tell you about the role that sport fans, with even a limited fan base, play in shaping the success for the sport they love?
3. Despite how you feel about the sport of wrestling, what are your thoughts about the process developed by the IOC to manage a set of core sports for the Olympic Games? Are they likely to become irrelevant if the IOC doesn't effectively manage spectator interest?

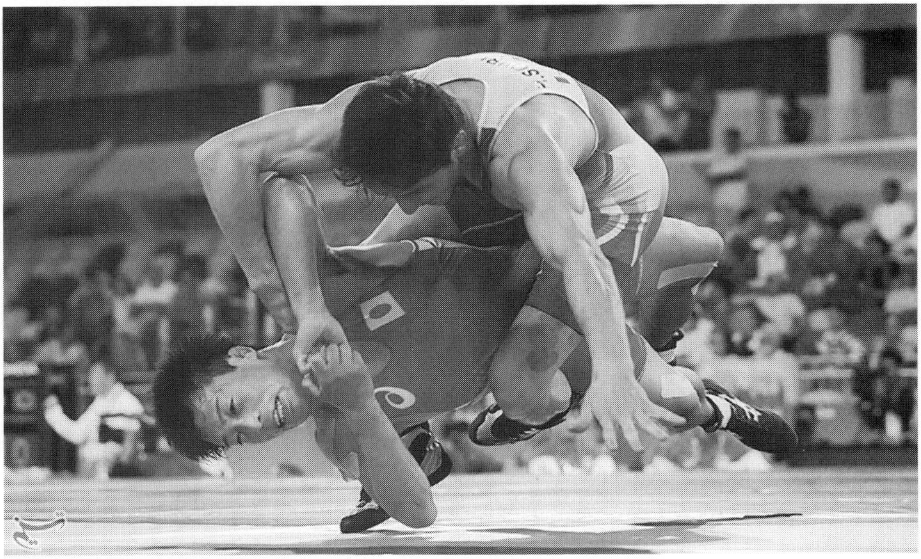

Source: Mohammad Hassansadeh/Tasnimnews

Wrestlers compete at the 2016 summer Olympics in Rio

A MATTER OF ETHICS

A SMART RESPONSE TO A FAN'S TAUNTS?

Many sports teams are famous for having passionate fans. For example, the "12th man" (an "extra" player beyond the 11 on the field) is a central part of the identity of football fans of the Seattle Seahawks and Texas A&M University Aggies. These fan communities are well known for their knowledge of the sport and their loud and active cheers during games. Such commitment often translates to a "home field advantage," giving the fans all the more reason to play a role during the game. For some, that role includes a more antagonistic approach, leading to taunting or heckling of players, coaches, and officials. Chanting "air ball" after a missed three-point shot in basketball or shouting "terrible call" at a baseball umpire with a questionable view of the strike zone may be relatively harmless, but at what point do fans cross the line?

Occasionally, fans end up in physical altercations with athletes and coaches (most infamously in 2004, when some fans fought with players from the Detroit Pistons and Indiana Pacers). In 2014, Oklahoma State University basketball player Marcus Smart fell under the basket during a game played at Texas Tech University. When he got up, he turned toward a fan in the crowd and, after only a few words, shoved him before returning to the court. Smart received a technical foul and, later, was suspended for three games. Without question, his actions were inappropriate, and he received significant criticism (amplified by an already established reputation for immaturity).

As the story unfolded, criticisms of Smart were balanced with greater scrutiny on the fan, Jeff Orr. Orr is a well-known supporter of Texas Tech athletics. As former Texas Tech head coach Pat Knight said, "I was shocked that he was involved. I know he's a crazy fan, a big supporter and a loyal guy, and I know him as a great guy" ("Marcus Smart," 2014, para 27). Other players, meanwhile, recognized Orr and noted his tendency to be vocal. At question in the incident with Smart was exactly *what* Orr said; Smart and other suggested the comments were racially hostile, while Orr insisted he merely called Smart a "piece of crap." In either case, it is fair to ask whether or not purchasing a ticket gives fans license to say whatever they want to the athletes they have paid to see. Do you think there should be limits on what fans can say during a game? How would such limits be enforced? To what extent does behavior like Jeff Orr's reflect on the larger fan culture?

Source: Marcus Smart suspended 3 games. (2014, February 10). *ESPN.com*. Retrieved from http://www.espn.com/mens-college-basketball/story/_/id/10428708/marcus-smart-oklahoma-state-cowboys-suspended-3-games-shoving-fan

Third, fans are also drawn to the *drama* of sports as they experience enjoyment that comes from the thrill of watching the game unfold. Whether a last-second shot, a takedown at the edge of the mat, or a quarterback's ability to march his team down the field in the last 2 minutes, each provides a heightened sense of drama that motivates individuals. You watch because you don't want to miss out on what could be a memorable sporting event or moment.

Fourth, *escape* is a motive for sport fans when they experience a level of relief from the stress in their day-to-day world. This has been one of the most heavily cited motives whereby the sporting context provides an important diversion from the negative aspects of one's daily routines (i.e., work, family, college experience) that can be repressed by temporary immersion in sporting events (Wann, Allen, & Rochelle, 2004). Sport offers a distraction for fans as they frequently get distracted by something that has less impact on their day-to-day existence. Others suggest it simultaneously serves as an important source of release from overstimulation (Wann et al., 1999).

Fifth, fans can also be motivated by *knowledge,* as they gain insight into how the sport is played by viewing it. Watching a television analyst break down the technique involved in a successful double play can assist young athletes as well as youth coaches who are attempting to instill the same technique into their kids. Additionally, people wish to be experts on a given subject, motivated by the desire to be the "smartest person in the room." For instance, Ruihley and Hardin (2011) coined the term *Schwabism* for those people who wish to be like Howie Schwab on ESPN's former show *Stump the Schwab* as they tested their sport knowledge against one of the foremost sources of sport trivia.

Finally, sport fans are motivated by the *social connection* that sport can provide. The desire to interact with others who have similar affiliations with sport can help manage friendships and relationships (Wann, Royalty, & Rochelle, 2002). For example, females are more likely to be motivated by increased family time that comes from sport spectating. Each of these motives is influential in determining the level of identification that fans experience.

SPORT IDENTIFICATION AND FANDOM

Many fans are likely to make connections with athletes and teams they support, and a body of research has used sport identification (the psychological connection fans experience to their team, sport, or athletes) to describe the extent to which fans are connected to sport. Highly identified fans are more likely to experience stronger postgame affect (both positive and negative, depending on the team's performance), and studies have also observed positive correlations between team identification and collective self-esteem, psychological well-being, optimism for the team's future performance (Wann et al., 2002), and academic success but negative correlations with loneliness and alienation (Branscombe & Wann, 1991). For example, college and university graduates who attend their institutions' sporting events have been found to have higher grades, retention, and graduation rates (Wann & Robinson, 2002). Positive impressions of an institution's sport program increase the likelihood that a college student will persist or be retained at the campus and have also been found to serve as a critical factor in the decision for freshmen to return to their institutions a second year. Love and Walker (2012) even observed unique patterns in phonetic shifts when asking fans of American football compared to English soccer to describe their teams, resulting in a unique language community based on their identification with their teams.

The sense of identification fans experience can also help define a city and the circumstances that fans have collectively faced. The New Orleans Saints and the aftermath resulting from Hurricane Katrina serve as a prime example, as the organization had been perennial losers in the NFL, having lost more than 60% of their games since their inception in 1966. However, despite the hardships New Orleans faced following the aftermath of Katrina in 2005, the team's win in Super Bowl XLIV was considered by many to be a temporary respite of sorts for the city and its fans (Burns, 2014).

TABLE 4.1 ■ Typology of Fan Motives for Sport Spectatorship

Fan Motive	Definition	Example
Aesthetic Beauty	Drawn to the sport because one appreciates the way it is played or performed	Enjoying the sport of motocross because of the unique skill necessary to perform the range of jumps or tricks required to win judge approval
Achievement	Internal sense of accomplishment that comes from the success of the team one is supporting	Sense of joy experienced by a New Orleans Saints fan after the individual's team finally won the Super Bowl in 2010 just 4 years after Hurricane Katrina almost destroyed the fan's city
Drama	Thrill obtained from a heated rivalry or key matchup between marquee athletes or teams	Watching the final round of Wimbledon as Roger Federer and Rafael Nadal compete for a Grand Slam win
Escape	Following a team to experience a sense of departure from the day-to-day world around us	Americans watching the 1980 Olympic hockey team win the gold to help forget about difficult economic times
Knowledge	Monitoring how the sport is performed to increase one's understanding for how it should be played	A parent watching the slow-motion coverage of an ice dancing routine in the hopes of further refining the technique employed by her daughter during future competitions
Social Connection	Ability to interact with friends, family members, or colleagues with sport serving as a background or rationale for supporting the relationship	Mother and daughter taking a trip to watch the NCAA women's field hockey championship as a way to bond

Individual players have been shown to have a similar impact on the identification that fans have with their teams. Consider the emotional turmoil that a highly identified fan experiences when his or her favorite team relocates or a star athlete demands to be traded. Fans' feelings about LeBron James are a prime example of the tension fans are likely to experience. James began his NBA career with the Cleveland Cavaliers, fortunate to remain in his home state of Ohio after an illustrious career at St. Mary High School. After seven seasons in Cleveland, where he was a two-time Most Valuable Player (MVP) and six-time all-star, James was confronted with a significant free-agency decision to remain in his home state or pursue free agency in an attempt to secure an NBA championship. After being courted by five other teams, James took part in a 75-minute live special aired on ESPN named "The Decision" where he announced his choice to sign with the Miami Heat along with two other free agent all-stars (Dwyane Wade and Chris Bosh). The television special was heavily criticized along with James's betrayal of the Cavaliers, drawing comparisons to Art Modell's relocation of the Cleveland Browns decades earlier. Cleveland fans struggled to support their former player as he went on to win two NBA titles with the Miami Heat, yet were highly supportive of his decision to return to Cleveland after the 2014 season. This support was extended significantly in 2016 when James brought the Cavaliers back from a 3–1 deficit to earn Cleveland's first professional team title in more than five decades. Sport identification appears to have the ability to overcome serious obstacles that may be confronting a sport. For example, the rise in doping has emerged in sports such as baseball, cross-country skiing, and cycling, yet research has found that fans with a high

OFF THE BEATEN PATH

RUGBY

Most associated with sports fans abroad, rugby is growing in popularity among sports fans in America. Rugby is played at all levels, including youth, collegiate, and national by both males and females. The sport has been active in America for 38 years and is slowly transitioning up the sport fan continuum. USA Rugby, the national governing body, dreams of inspiring Americans to fall in love with the sport. Rugby continues to be a niche sport in America, and its fan base is estimated at only 1% of Americans. However, rugby participation has increased by 350% since 2004 and receives more mainstream media attention. In 2011, Universal Sports and NBC Sports provided multiplatform live coverage of the IRB Rugby World Cup in New Zealand for the first time in the United States, in order to accommodate the country's growing interest. NBC and Universal retain the rights to broadcast the 2015 tournament, and this increased exposure can help fans in the United States become more emotionally connected to the sport.

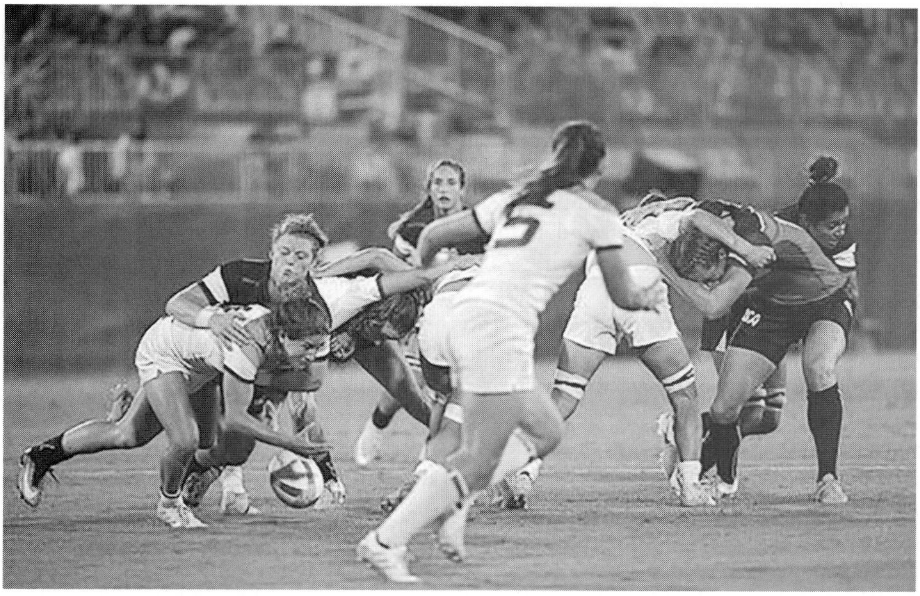

Members of the USA Women's Rugby team compete in the 2016 Rio Olympic Games

level of identification with the sport "expressed more liberal attitudes toward doping than others" (Solberg, Hansfad, & Thoring, 2010, p. 197). Despite the fallout from Lance Armstrong's confirmation of using performance enhancing drugs to achieve his record setting Tour de France wins, cycling fans still maintain a strong affiliation with the sport.

Similar experiences are likely to occur when a sport franchise decides to relocate, leaving fans behind to question their loyalty to their respective teams. For example, the Hartford Whalers moved from Hartford, Connecticut, during the 1997 to 1998 season to become the Carolina Hurricanes. Fans of the franchise described their loss using terms like *death* and *divorce*. This was consistent with work done by Krizek (1992) during his assessment of White Sox fans during the final days before closing the old Comiskey Park in Chicago. Many of the former Whaler fans noted that they no longer support a particular NHL hockey team, with many indicating that the move forced them to lose interest and faith in all professional sports (Hyatt, 2007). A number of prominent sport teams with strong affiliations with their cities have made the decision to relocate in the NFL (Baltimore Colts, Houston Oilers), in Major League Baseball (Brooklyn Dodgers, Milwaukee Braves), and in the NBA (New Orleans Jazz, Vancouver Grizzlies). Overall, identification has the potential to evoke a variety of emotional responses, which can be further enhanced as advancing technologies provide fans with new opportunities for interacting with athletes and their teams.

IMPACT OF NEW TECHNOLOGIES ON SPORT FANDOM

Fans' increased use of new forms of media have certainly impacted the sense of connection that they can have with their favorite teams as these tools allow fans greater control over the sporting experience. Haridakis (2010) noted that "Sports fans are utilizing the on-demand nature of the Internet to immerse themselves in their association with their favorite teams and to connect and identify with other geographically dispersed fans" (p. 258). By allowing authors a vehicle for providing commentary on sports of all kinds, Internet blogs have become an increasingly common way for sports fans to further identify with their sports. As the relevance of microblogging and Twitter continues to grow, numerous news outlets have devoted segments in their daily newscasts to reporters who track and comment on popular websites. This practice has aided in establishing the blog as a potentially credible source of information, although much of the discussion that flows from these sources represents simple assertions, opinions, and conjecture having limited journalistic quality. In the past, news coverage was reported almost exclusively by seasoned journalists who served as the voice of record. Some have used the coined term *reclinerporting* to describe the quality of the growing number of blogs that allow commentary with little to no direct contact with the individuals involved and that is written for an audience with a desire for bias toward their favorite teams or athletes. Sports at all levels have expanded into this growing media outlet. For instance, many professional sports teams have gone as far as allowing fans the opportunity to set up fan profiles on their websites, write blogs, and interact with other fans (Elliot, 2007). Blogs have become an increasingly relevant feature of the sports landscape, so much so that a number of outlets, including the *Sporting News,* have devoted sections of their publications to tracking the most memorable quotes from numerous sport blogs. There is little doubt among seasoned reporters and legitimate news outlets that fan websites are increasingly making and breaking news in a way that is transforming the relationship between fans, athletes, coaches, and organizations (Byers, 2013).

The socially constructed website Wikipedia is an additional source for fans interested in creating a cultural product that represents their favorite players, sport, or franchise. The collective work of the fans generates a potentially problematic profile through consensus that allows for a dialogue and historical creation that has never before been possible. Ferriter (2009) noted that "the relationship between user, structure, and content on Wikipedia set the stage for unique interactive space for those 'in-the-know' about sports" (p. 129). This imagined community has become an interesting space where fans and those who are not in the know about a particular sport can come to celebrate the varied accomplishments of their favorite athletes and teams. Just as *The Baseball Encyclopedia* provides baseball fans with a historical account of Major League Baseball, the Wikipedia site provides a more interpretive formulation of sport history and a uniquely different type of historical account for both the average reader and those who seek to contribute to the narrative.

Last, a growing number of social media outlets continue to provide fans with additional opportunities for interacting with teams and athletes. A number of athletes (Cristiano Ronaldo, LeBron James, Chad Ochocinco) have high-profile Twitter accounts that expose fans to the ongoing activities in their daily lives. Instagram and Facebook pages also afford athletes the opportunity to connect more individually with fans and offer their own interpretations of events that in the past would have been filtered by media outlets. News organizations have also now begun to monitor these sites to assist them in providing commentary on breaking news events. In Chapter 16, we spend time foreshadowing how these outlets will continue to change the communicative function of sport fan cultures. Brown and Billings's (2013) analysis of the University of Miami fans use of Twitter for communication image repair strategies after alleged NCAA violations depicts the usefulness of this tool for fans to construct their own interpretation of the allegations. They observed that the allegations produced a high level of anxiety for Miami fans whose own perceived self-worth was being affiliated with the charges. As a result, they felt a need to respond using this medium and to deploy a variety of reputation repair strategies to shape public opinion.

CONCLUSION

Sport will continue to evoke a range of fan types with varying motives for following the sports, teams, and athletes they have become attached to. As sport continues to define and redefine itself, we are likely to experience ongoing changes to the way that fans can experience sport while also bringing about modifications to those sports that have traditionally held deep-seated fan cultures. In this chapter, we have demonstrated that rituals serve an important function in the sport fan experience, and as fans' identification with sports increases, they find themselves experiencing a host of positive (and potentially negative) outcomes. Just as technology continues to shape how we can experience the spectacle of sport, innovative approaches for sharing the sport experience are likely to draw even more fans in directions that we may never have felt possible. For example, participation in fantasy football leagues (see extended discussion in Chapter 1) has become an important ritual for many sport fans who are just as concerned with individual athlete performance as they are with the outcome of their favorite team. This has shaped television broadcasting of individual athlete highlights and spectator viewing habits as well as generated considerable revenue for sport franchises. What happens when "going to the ball game" becomes meaningless because fans no longer cheer for one respective team and are more concerned about the performance of individual players spread out across 10 or 12 teams throughout the league? The underlying features of devotion still exist in this situation, but the evolving nature of sport and competition puts sport spectatorship at a crossroads for how sport fandom is experienced.

Suggested Additional Reading

Aden, R. C. (1994). Back to the garden: Therapeutic place metaphor in *Field of Dreams*. *Southern Communication Journal, 59*, 307–317.

Butterworth, M. L. (2005). Ritual in the "church of baseball": Suppressing the discourse of democracy after 9/11. *Communication and Critical/Cultural Studies, 2*, 107–129.

Meân, L. J., & Kassing, J. W. (2008). Fan identifies at youth sporting events. A critical discourse analysis. *International Journal of Sport Communication, 1*, 42–66.

Earnheardt, A. C., Haridakis, P. M., & Hugenberg, B. S. (Eds.). (2012). *Sports fans, identity, and socialization: Exploring the fandemonium.* Lanham, MD: Lexington Books.

Hugenberg, L. W., Haridhis, P. M., & Earnheardt, A. C. (2008). *Sport mania: Essays on fandom and the media in the 21st century*. Jefferson, NC: McFarland.

5

SPORT AND MYTHOLOGY

In June 2016, two overlapping stories demonstrated sport's unique capacity to capture a public's attention. During the National Basketball Association's (NBA) championship series, the Cleveland Cavaliers rallied from a three games to one deficit against the defending champion Golden State Warriors to win their first title. The Cavaliers became the first team ever to overcome a 3–1 finals deficit and, more compellingly, they were led to the championship by LeBron James, whose infamous departure and celebrated return to his hometown team only amplified the symbolism of King James as a "savior" for a city long associated with painful sports failures. Later in the month, the Coastal Carolina Chanticleers unexpectedly

LeBron James shoots during a 2016 NBA Finals game

won the men's College World Series, defeating traditional powers such as Florida and Arizona on the way to the first national championship in the university's history. Numerous media outlets defined their victory with the familiar reference to a sports underdog as "Cinderella."

Such underdog narratives are commonly narrated as a Cinderella story. When an unheralded or overmatched athlete or team faces a familiar champion, sports media and fans often refer to the event as a "David versus Goliath" match-up. When individuals of modest backgrounds achieve greatness, we invoke the rags-to-riches idealism of the "American Dream." Triumphs over adversity—such as the long-awaited opportunity for LeBron James and the Cavaliers to purge Cleveland of its sports suffering—offer "redemption," historic accomplishments are considered "heroic," and tests of strength and endurance are performed by "warriors" and "gladiators." Such terminology is so familiar in the world of sports that we have likely forgotten the origins of such references. They are elements of stories, of course, but not merely stories. Rather, they operate as *myths*, providing a compelling lens through which we can view, as well as communicate about the importance of, athletic achievements and events.

For many of you, the word *mythology* may prompt thoughts about ancient Greek and Roman myths. For example, you may know that the phrase "Achilles' heel" derives from the story of Achilles, whose mother inoculated him from an enemy's attack by dipping him in the river Styx. Because she held him by the heel, however, he was left vulnerable in that lone spot, which subsequently led to his death when he was struck by an arrow. Or, you may be familiar with the phrase "Midas touch," a reference to King Midas, whose touch turned everything to gold. Although contemporary myths sometimes reference these ancient stories, or incorporate elements of them, they also draw from historical and cultural conditions of a given time. Thus, mythology is as much about the present as it is about the past.

Rhetorical scholar Walter Fisher (1984) contends that human beings essentially communicate through stories, and that the most persuasive stories we tell "are mythic in form" (p. 16). Sports provide especially persuasive people and places for communicating mythology. In this chapter, we explore several of the ways that sports are influenced by myth and how sports affirm myths found in the broader culture. We begin with some important definitions of terms, including *myth*, *ritual*, and *hero*. Then, we provide examples and discussion of these terms in order to reveal the persuasive power of sports mythology.

DEFINING TERMS

We begin this section with an example most of you probably know something about: the national pastime. This label commonly used to refer to baseball is really shorthand for various expressions of mythology. For example, baseball is said to have been invented in

National Baseball Hall of Fame and Museum entrance

Cooperstown, New York, an idyllic rural village embodying the virtues of small-town America. Yet this story is an invention, crafted by Albert Spalding, one of baseball's most influential figures in its earliest decades. As the United States became a more mature nation in the late 19th and early 20th centuries, there were those who wanted to prove America's superiority over the "Old World" of Europe. Thus, Spalding commissioned a report designed to find evidence showing baseball was uniquely American. The resulting Mills Commission report, issued in 1907, provided "evidence" that Abner Doubleday invented the game in Cooperstown in 1839. This story has been completely discredited, yet it remains central to baseball's mythology. Indeed, Cooperstown serves as the home to the National Baseball Hall of Fame and Museum, which legitimizes the location as the "birthplace" of baseball.

The Hall of Fame's location is about more than baseball's mythic origins. It also serves as repository of baseball's memories, and it celebrates the heroes that have contributed the most to the game. In addition, the myth is enacted by the millions of visitors who make the journey to Cooperstown to renew their connection to the "national pastime." As Newman (2001) demonstrates, the trip to this small New York village can be understood as a "pilgrimage." The idea of the pilgrimage, of course, evokes a parallel to religion and, indeed, many have noted that Cooperstown functions for baseball fans as the Vatican would for Christians or Mecca would for Muslims (Rader, 2002). The ritual of traveling to the Hall of Fame, therefore, dramatizes the overlap between religion and mythology. In sum, Cooperstown symbolizes the *myth* of American exceptionalism, sanctifies the *heroes* of the national pastime, encourages fans to visit the Hall of Fame in *ritual* fashion, all through enactments that are similar to organized *religion*.

Communication scholars examine these features of baseball's history and ask, "Why and how did this mythology develop?," "What does this mythology communicate about us as a people?," and "What needs are served by constructing this myth?" Certainly Americans invest a great deal in the game they call the national pastime. In other words, baseball is more than a sport; it is a cultural institution that claims to be an exemplar of American character. From this standpoint, mythology becomes an essential means for communicating and reinforcing the very identity that binds Americans together. What is interesting about myth, then, is not whether or not it is "true" but to what extent it *feels* true (perhaps, to borrow Stephen Colbert's famous term, myths have "truthiness").

The most basic definition of a myth is that it is a "story," which is precisely what its root term, *mythos*, translates to in English (Doty, 1986, p. 3). Yet, as our opening example suggests, myths are about particular kinds of stories. More specifically, they are stories designed to explain the world, or as Hart (1990) puts it, to describe "exceptional

THEORETICALLY SPEAKING

THE NARRATIVE PARADIGM

Operating from the assumption that scholarship largely viewed communication as inherently "argumentative," rhetorical scholar Walter Fisher (1984) developed an alternative perspective that he terms the "narrative paradigm." Fisher begins by observing that human beings are essentially story-telling creatures. For Fisher, stories—narratives—refer to "symbolic actions—words and/or deeds—that have sequence and meaning for those who live, create, or interpret them. The narrative perspective, therefore, has relevance to real as well as fictive worlds, to stories of living and to stories of the imagination" (p. 2). From this view, both factual and mythical stories have communicative impact. Given this, communication and sport scholars who are interested in myths are building from the narrative paradigm's foundation. For example, Von Burg and Johnson (2009) examine the media and public reactions to allegations of steroid use by Major League Baseball players in the mid-2000s. They contend that much of the anxiety provoked by this controversy is attributable to the public's discomfort with a disruption of the "national pastime" as a mythological symbol of American identity. As they write, "Therefore, when such athletic accomplishments are called into question and the accounts of success become fragmented, the faith in the symbolic value of these athletes and the narratives of fairness and American exceptionalism are shaken" (pp. 352–353). In this way, narratives can be understood as mythic stories that connect large groups of people across time and space.

- Fisher, W. R. (1984). Narration as human communication paradigm: The case of public moral argument. *Communication Monographs, 51*, 1–22.
- Von Burg, R., & Johnson, P. E. (2009). Yearning for a past that never was: Baseball, steroids, and the anxiety of the American dream. *Critical Studies in Media Communication, 26*, 351–371.

people doing exceptional things that serve as a moral guide to proper action" (p. 305). In addition, media and sports scholar Michael Real (1989) notes that, "myths arise as community stories that celebrate collective heroes, origins, and identity through expressive rituals" (p. 66). Thus, an especially important element of mythology is that the stories are *shared,* and they provide a foundation for a community's identity. This is why baseball's mythic origins continue to resonate long after the Doubleday story itself has been discredited.

Real's definition also includes other important terms for this chapter. *Ritual* can be understood as the means by which myths are enacted or performed. Accepting communion during a Christian religious service or casting a ballot on Election Day are ritualistic performances that reaffirm the importance of larger purposes—that is, Christian faith or democratic governance. Meanwhile, *heroes* provide dramatic exemplars by which others may come to understand the "proper action" to which Hart refers. Along with the significance of religious symbolism, these terms provide the foundation for our subsequent discussion of sports and mythology.

SPORTS MYTH

Myths may be either particular or universal. The popular American story about George Washington cutting down his father's cherry tree is an example of a particular myth. It is used, typically with young children, to instill values about truth and honesty. This particular myth might stand on its own, or it might be used as an exemplar of a larger mythology—for instance, as a story that speaks to the United States' commitment to liberty and justice. Sports myths also function this way. Thus, the celebrated victory of the men's Olympic hockey team over the Soviet Union in 1980 might be a particular expression of the triumph of the underdog, while the universal purpose of the myth communicates the moral superiority of American democracy over Soviet communism.

We begin this section with a discussion of myths that are particular to the world of sports. Sports leagues and organizations are acutely aware of their histories, and they often draw upon the past to create mythological narratives that help guide the present. Consider, for example, the stories defining the modern National Football League (NFL). During the first half of the 20th century, collegiate football was very popular, but the professional game still mostly existed at the margins. When the Baltimore Colts defeated the New York Giants on live television to win the 1958 NFL Championship, however, the game began a rapid ascent to become the most popular sport in the United States. More than 50 years later, that contest, which ended in overtime, is commonly referred to as the "Greatest Game Ever Played." It is doubtful that the game is truly the *best* professional football game in history, but that is not important. Rather, its *greatness* lies in the *mythological* character of the game as the genesis of the modern NFL. The persuasiveness of this myth is evident in a range of books equating football with the essence of American identity, from *America's Game* (MacCambridge, 2004) to *How Football Explains America* (Paolantonio, 2008).

INTERVIEW

DICK MAXWELL, FORMER SENIOR DIRECTOR OF BROADCASTING, NATIONAL FOOTBALL LEAGUE

Q: In 1975, scholar Michael Real published an article, "Super Bowl: Mythic Spectacle," that is commonly cited as the first essay in our field to take sports seriously. Given your experience with Super Bowl broadcasts, what does the phrase "mythic spectacle" mean to you?

A: Football is structured to build to a climax. Because of the physical nature of the game, there is a limiting factor in the number of competitions you can stage and still retain a viable product. Consequently, there is one game a week; only 16 contests during the regular season, and a winner-take-all post-season single elimination tournament. This naturally builds to a finale. Super Bowl Sunday is an unofficial American holiday. Media adds to the hype with 2 weeks of worldwide media coverage. Put it all together, and the NFL Championship Game certainly qualifies as a "mythic spectacle."

Q: To what extent does a televised sporting event match the "reality" of the event on the field/court?

A: I always thought the NFL was smart to have multiple rights holders as a positive off-shoot is the competition among the networks themselves to provide extraordinary coverage of the event. When I started my 36-year career in the NFL, I would never have envisioned cameras allowed to be over the playing field, microphones on players and coaches during the games, or microphones in shoulder pads of offensive linemen to pick up the sound of player contact. As far as other sports? I doubt any TV event totally replicates realty.

Q: How important are mythic narratives—"Cinderella stories," "David versus Goliath," and so on—to sporting event broadcasts?

A: Every producer and his or her broadcast team head into a sporting event with a storyline or two or three. Mythic narratives are the natural ones to follow. They are time-tested to hold an audience. When "David" is beating "Goliath" (or at least beating the spread), viewers stay tuned. When a journeyman pitcher throws a no-hitter, people stay tuned until the necessary final out. Sport is entertainment. And the best entertainment is when we, as viewers, don't have to work real hard to be involved in the game's storyline.

Q: Why do you believe professional football has become, as it is now often called, "America's Game"?

A: Football is America's Game and has been since the 1960s, or at least the 1970s. There are strong fundamentals involved. The NFL is played in the fall and winter months when TV viewership is the highest. The calendar shadows major advertising periods—back to school, Thanksgiving, and Christmas. The game of football has stoppages convenient for commercial breaks. As far as the NFL expressing a particular American mythology, I'd point to the basic tenets of the League's structure. The NFL is set up to sustain "competitive balance" year in and year out—just like in America, your team always has a chance to be successful.

Q: Thinking about the history of sports in the United States, what events or moments do you think of as "mythic"? Why?

A: There aren't many. Perhaps Jesse Owens at the Berlin Olympics or Jackie Robinson breaking the color barrier in baseball. Having been directly involved in 32 consecutive Super Bowls, I'm not sure I'd qualify any of them as truly "mythic." However, there are two games that standout in my mind as "mythic-like," and each of them occurred in the Louisiana Super Dome, ironically. The first was the Super Bowl after the 9/11 terrorist attack. There was a patriotic theme for the entire day's event, and the entire country was one America that day and evening. The other was the first game back in the Louisiana Superdome following Hurricane Katrina. The hometown Saints powered over the Atlanta Falcons on pure emotion and the town's energy of "being back."

There are many accomplishments or moments within sports that have achieved mythical status: Babe Ruth's alleged "called shot" during the 1932 World Series, when he supposedly pointed to a spot in the Wrigley Field outfield then delivered a home run to that exact location; Muhammad Ali's "phantom punch" that dropped Sonny Liston in a heavyweight rematch in 1965; Willis Reed's miraculous recovery from a leg injury and re-entry into a playoff game for the New York Knicks in 1970; the 1980 U.S. Olympic Men's Hockey team and the "Miracle on Ice" (which is often mistakenly assumed to have been the gold medal game); Kerri Strug's final vault to solidify the women's gymnastics gold medal for the United States at the 1996 Summer Olympics; Brandi Chastain's shirt-removal celebration after kicking a penalty shot that secured the women's 1999 World Cup soccer title for the American team; Tiger Woods's one-legged victory at the 2008 U.S. Open; and American Pharoah in 2015 becoming the first horse racing Triple Crown winner since Affirmed in 1978. Surely you can identify several other moments. What each of these has in common is

American Pharoah completes the Triple Crown at the 2015 Belmont Stakes

that they feature either transcendent athletes or championship moments that persist in our collective sports memories. In this way, sports mythology is a way of preserving the best of our past as we try our best to move forward in the future.

These types of myths often serve a positive function for sports organizations, media, and fans. Yet there is also the possibility that mythology obscures some of the problems found in sports. For example, the National Hockey League (NHL) has long balanced the need for control and order with the excitement generated by the violence of fighting between players. As the familiar cliché says, "I went to a fight and a hockey game broke out." In part, this violence is encouraged and perpetuated by a mythology equating strength and toughness with hand-to-hand combat. Unfortunately, even as the game's violence may attract some fans, it has the potential to detract many others from following what can be an exciting sport. In his study of hockey in Canada, Grant (1998) concludes that "the mythic power of sport is being used to the detriment of sport itself" (p. 58). The aforementioned myth about the NFL's "Greatest Game Ever Played" risks obscuring some of the league's persistent problems. As Grano (2014) contends, the mythologizing of the game moves beyond celebrating the popularity of the NFL. Indeed, by idealizing the historical context in which the game was played, it also "seems to promise a return to simpler times" that deflects our attention away from labor struggles or the physical consequences of a violent sport like football (p. 17). That conflict is perhaps most evident by recent controversies about head injuries and concussions, given all the more attention through the book and documentary *League of Denial* (Fainaru-Wada & Fainaru, 2013) and the dramatized Hollywood film, *Concussion* (2015).

Although many myths are confined to the world of sports, many other sporting myths are communicated in the service of broader mythologies. For example, O'Rourke (2003)

Hockey fight during an NHL game

analyzed the public's response to the announcement that the Cleveland Browns would be leaving the city for Baltimore. In his study, O'Rourke demonstrates the extent to which fan identification with the team was grounded in their mythic identity with their city. As he notes, "Cleveland is a diverse, multicultural urban community that accepted waves of immigrants as labor for heavy industry" (p. 72). As the Browns found success in the 1940s and 1950s, they became associated with this diverse, "blue-collar" ethic. When economic changes in the 1960s and 1970s adversely affected cities like Cleveland—much like similar "Rust Belt" communities such as Pittsburgh and Detroit—local sports teams, especially the Browns, were viewed as both symbols of past glory and of hope for the future. Thus, when Browns owner Art Modell announced in 1995 that he would relocate the team, local fans reacted as if they were losing a family member. O'Rourke explains that the fans' collective response contributed to the NFL's eventual decision to award an expansion franchise to Cleveland for 1999, a move that also preserved their beloved nickname, "Browns."

Even as the above example demonstrates how mythology can positively bind a community around a collective identity, we should also be cautious about myths that threaten communities. Among the most common narratives in sports is the myth of the "American Dream," in which an athlete of humble origins works hard and achieves greatness on the field or in the arena. Throughout sports in the United States there are athletes who fit this description. Yet the downside to this myth is that it equates success with individual effort and potentially ignores economic, political, and social factors that could prevent someone from achieving success. An excellent example of this concern is found in the critically acclaimed documentary film, *Hoop Dreams* (1994). The movie chronicles the lives of two African American boys in Chicago who aspire to be professional basketball players. Over the course of 3 hours, viewers witness the growth of Arthur Agee and William Gates as they move from eighth grade to high school graduation. Although there are many important themes in the film, many observers commented on the hope that basketball provided these two young men and the idea that sports can provide a pathway out of poverty. However, as Cole and King (2003) argue, the film also, perhaps inadvertently, perpetuates stereotypes about urban life in the United States. In particular, *Hoop Dreams* relies on the "already known," meaning that audiences are able to identify with Agee and Gates because they believe they already understand what it means to be African American in the city. Unfortunately, then, the film allows viewers to think positively about the main characters without having to confront the social and economic inequities that serve as the backdrop to the narrative.

Hollywood cinema tends to reproduce this dynamic, showing sport as a means to overcome cultural and social divisions. Films such as *Remember the Titans* (2000), *Glory Road* (2006), and *Invictus* (2009), all based on real events, dramatize sport's capacity to foster racial harmony. None of them are *wrong* exactly, but each movie simplifies the complexities of real life. Documentary features can also present overly simplified narratives. For example, over the course of four decades, Bud Greenspan produced 13 official films to document the Olympic Games. Roessner (2014) argues that Greenspan's films featured "Victorian and modern universal narratives of heroic triumph to construct a dominant promotional brand of Olympism" (p. 340). This orientation was in keeping with Olympic ideals about athletic virtue and the peaceful competition among nations. However, as Roessner points out, the films also work ideologically by making "the argument that everyone can succeed by adhering to a decidedly Western set of cultural values, such as individualism, competitive performance, and national loyalty. This, of course, is unrealistic, even in the setting of elite sport, where success is often driven by corporate sponsorships that provide access to state-of-the-art training facilities and other necessary resources" (p. 348). Each of these examples demonstrates that myth can perform both a positive and negative function. Because sport is often viewed as an "escape" or "diversion" from real social or political problems, we may be less prepared to think about the mythologies that are bolstered by sports narratives. To be sure, some sport myth making is either good fun or provides important links to histories and traditions. Nevertheless, it is important to keep in mind the various levels at which myth functions.

SPORT AND RITUAL

As we discussed in Chapter 4, ritual is an essential element in the enactment of sports mythology. Writing about the culture associated with the University of Nebraska's football team, Deegan and Stein (1989) write, "Extraordinary events—formal rituals—provide the community with an alternate social world to that found in everyday life. Part of the power of these events lies in their ability to evoke symbols and myths relating to the community" (p. 79). That power is evident in Aden's (2008) book, *Huskerville*, which reveals multiple ritual practices that allow Nebraska fans, even those who have moved far from home, to preserve their sense of community. For these fans "Huskerville" becomes a place that is created not necessarily through physical contact but through symbolic expressions such as wearing team colors or attending team parties, as well as maintaining a commitment to core "rural" values such as working hard and being good neighbors.

Herbie Husker

Sports rituals are also commonly performed through media. Olsen's (2003) analysis of the National Basketball Association (NBA) draft, for example, illustrates the ritualistic emphasis that sports media place on creating "characters" out of players and exploiting dramatic moments. He explains that various elements of the NBA draft occur regularly throughout the years: Players wait nervously in the green room, they come dressed "in costume" and immediately wear their new team's hat once their name is called, they transition then to the live interview, and so on. As Olsen notes, "Each element of the coverage reinforces the dominant notion of a ritual transformation" (p. 192), meaning that the draft broadcast becomes a sports rite of passage that is shared between media, teams, players, families, and fans.

As is the case with myth more broadly, then, sports rituals can serve communities by providing communicative means of joining people together. Consider, for example, how commonplace songs and chants are among sports crowds. Baseball's 7th-inning stretch would feel incomplete without "Take Me Out to the Ball Game," no self-respecting Ohio State University fan would hear someone shout out "O-H!" without yelling back, "I-O!," and soccer matches buzz with a near-constant soundtrack of "Olé, olé, olé," and other songs. In other words, ritual allows us to feel a sense of ***belonging***. As Serazio (2013) concludes in his study about fandom and the Philadelphia Phillies, "as primary social ties through neighborhood, work, and religion increasingly wither, identification with a sports team can satisfy the need for quasi-intimate relationships" (p. 306).

Participation in ritual is not always comforting, however. As Rothenbuhler (1998) suggests, "Almost always, rituals are accompanied by a certain social compulsion. The costs that result from choosing not to participate may be such that we do not experience certain rituals as voluntary" (p. 10). This is the point Butterworth (2005) makes in his study of baseball ceremonies that took place after the terrorist attacks of September 11, 2001. As he explains, through repeated performances of "God Bless America" and inclusions of nationalistic imagery, baseball tributes "moved from healing ritual to a potential exercise in ideology that could preserve a privileged interpretation of national identity" (p. 114). Moreover, because of the heightened anxiety felt in the United States after 9/11, any resistance to this ritual was likely to be considered subversive or unpatriotic (see Chapter 8 for more on these ideas).

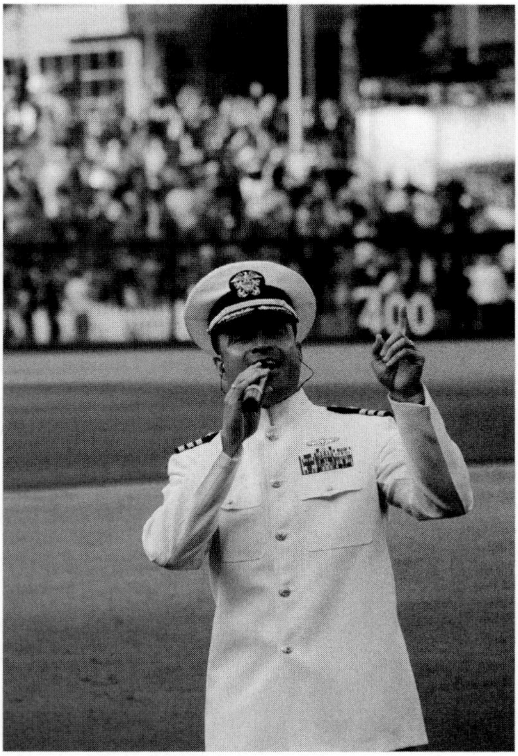

Source: By U.S. Navy photo by Chief Mass Communication Specialist Terry L. Feeney, via Wikimedia Commons

A Naval officer performs the national anthem at San Diego's Petco Park

Communal rituals may also emphasize unity in ways that diminish the significance of differences and inequities. When Hurricane Katrina struck the Gulf Coast in 2005, the city of New Orleans struggled to recover economically and socially. As Grano and Zagacki (2011) argue, the New Orleans Saints became a vehicle for performing rituals designed to rehabilitate the community. Yet, even though the reopening of the Louisiana Superdome was spectacular, an overemphasis on spiritual healing through football "may lead to a visual forgetting or erasure of the very subjects the rituals seek to memorialize, effectively re-marking those subjects as invisible in the name of national healing" (Grano & Zagacki, 2011, p. 202). In other words, the restored Superdome creates the illusion that those who most suffered after the storm—poor African Americans—had now been healed by virtue of the communal

CASE STUDY

MYTHOS SURROUNDING THE MIRACLE ON ICE

ABC commentator Al Michaels described the closing seconds of a hockey game that still resonates in the collective memory of many Americans more than 35 years ago in Lake Placid. "Eleven seconds, you've got 10 seconds, the countdown going on right now! Morrow, up to Silk. Five seconds left in the game. Do you believe in miracles? . . . YES!" These closing statements are connected to what has become known as the Miracle on Ice, where a highly underrated USA team defeated the Russian team on its way to Olympic gold during the 1980 Winter Olympics. The David versus Goliath match-up pitted a group of young amateur players led by now-legendary coach Herb Brooks against a team of Russian veterans (many of whom had been competing together for more than a decade). This game has been solidified as a sporting event that served as a turning point for many Americans who were struggling through a turbulent decade in the 1970s. However, the general mythos that has been generated around the game itself has caused many to forget a number of relevant facts surrounding the team and the gold medal that resulted from the victory.

Although it is accurate that Herb Brooks was able to pull together a group of amateur hockey players to defeat a more "professional" team, the collective talent on the 1980 team was generally stronger than any previous team representing the United States. For instance, of the 20 players on the team, 13 went on to play in the National Hockey League with eight playing 500 or more games in their careers. In fact, Ken Morrow eventually went on to start his career with the New York Islanders and became the first hockey player to win the Olympic gold and the Stanley Cup in the same year. Additionally, many people forget that the team did not win the gold medal after the victory over the Russians. Two days later, the team needed to come from behind against Finland to win. Years after the Miracle on Ice, the structure of the medal round was modified to the single-elimination model that is employed today. Yet in 1980, a round robin was used, whereby it was still mathematically possible for the USA team to be eliminated from medal contention had it lost to Finland 2 days later. In the locker room before the third and final period, it is reported that Brooks reminded his players that they would "take it to their graves" if they didn't find a way to come from behind to win. Had the team lost, the social significance of the victory over Russia would have ultimately been lost as well, and the team's presence in the mythos of American sport history would have been eliminated despite the fact that the outcome for the event they are most remembered for would have remained the same.

1. What other facts about this particular event tend to get lost in the retelling of the Miracle on Ice?
2. How does the selective recall of sporting events lead many of us to establish our own recollection of the events that transpired?
3. How have the media been influential in depicting the general mythos that has surrounded the 1980 Olympic Hockey team since its win in Lake Placid?

rituals taking place because of football, an argument that remains far from true more than a decade later.

SPORTS HEROES

Star athletes are among the most recognized and beloved people in American culture. Their athletic feats produce joy and admiration, they evoke pride among members of the communities in which they play, and they are among the most persuasive spokespeople for commercial products and services. In addition to performing their *jobs* as athletes, they clearly are *entertainers* as well, and consequently, they frequently appear as talk-show guests, at red-carpet openings, and as grist for the tabloid rumor mill. All of which raises an important question for communication and sport scholars: Can athletes be considered *heroes*, or are they simply *celebrities*? Drucker (1994) is one who argues that sports figures are not heroic. Rather, they are media creations, "products of the celebrification of the pro athlete rather than the creation of a hero" (p. 83). Drucker seems to suggest here that celebrities are *manufactured* for the purposes of spectacle, whereas heroes earn public admiration by being *authentic*.

In light of such a critique, it is worth rethinking what it means to call someone a "hero." Traditionally, the hero is a transcendent individual who faces tests and trials of strength and character. Through such challenges, the hero is transformed, "leaving one condition and finding the source of life to bring forth . . . a richer or mature condition" (Campbell & Moyers, 1988, p. 124). This archetypal image of the hero is designed to provide lessons for others in a culture, using the hero as a model for action and behavior. As Drucker and Cathcart (1994) note, "Heroes transcend ordinary human qualities embodying the divine, the ideal, the quest, the courageous, the virtuous, the superior. All cultures have heroes, but the hero and heroic varies from culture to culture and from time to time" (pp. 1–2). From this view, although Drucker may be correct that sports figures are not heroes in the traditional sense, she and Cathcart acknowledge that in our current time, contemporary figures such as sports stars may meet a redefined standard of heroism. Thus, Wenner (2013) maintains that "in our quest for meaning, we hope for more, and the media feed the notion that extraordinary athletic competence is often undergirded by character and fortitude" (p. 8).

Michael Vick

The ideal sports hero is one who not only achieves greatness on the field but also is an admirable person off of it. Failure to serve as a role model often earns an athlete public scorn or indifference. Consider the case of Michael Vick, whose conviction in 2007 on charges that he organized illegal dog

A MATTER OF ETHICS

BEING THE "WARRIOR"

Sports stars provide us with modern heroes. They are adventurers who seek glory and conquest, warriors who confront their own physical (and mental) limits in the quest for greatness. Ancient Greece had Achilles; modern Americans have had Babe Ruth, Muhammad Ali, and Tom Brady. To the extent that sports heroes provide us with joy and inspiration, and serve as models for achievement, this mythology can be a positive force in our culture. Yet, what happens when we push the myth too far?

There are "warriors" found in a range of American sports, but this is especially the case in football. Football demands so much toughness that players routinely comment on the physical and, sometimes, mental anguish that they endure for the rest of their lives. Recent years have seen an increased attention on brain trauma, especially chronic traumatic encephalopathy (CTE) that results from repeated blows to the head common in football. The effects of CTE can include dementia and depression, and the suicides of notable players have been linked to this condition. The most notable of these cases has been Junior Seau, who played 20 seasons at linebacker in the NFL and was among the most dominant defensive players of his era. He was particularly known for his physical style, which made him extremely popular with both fans and the media. After Seau retired from the NFL in 2010, he suffered from depression. In 2012, he shot and killed himself. Research on his brain conducted by the National Institutes of Health revealed evidence of CTE.

NFL players are all too aware that playing professional comes at a physical cost. But are we, as fans, expecting too much of them? Has the myth of the warrior clouded our judgment about how best to achieve a balance between excitement on the field and the players' well-being off it? Do you think that Seau's aggressive style of play contributed to his struggles after retirement? Is it time to reconsider how football is played?

fighting transformed one of the NFL's most popular players into one its most despised. In the years since he served his prison term, Vick has made considerable efforts to rehabilitate his image and has once again enjoyed some success as a starting quarterback. Nevertheless, he now occupies a more ambiguous space, in part because of public cynicism about the degree to which athletic heroes are merely inventions. In the case of Vick, "Whether rising star, fallen hero, or redemptive soul, his 'story' is just that, a mediated fiction served up for public consumption" (Giardina & Magnusen, 2013, p. 176).

The Vick case reminds us that Americans are notorious for their fickle relationships to heroic figures. Nothing is more predictable, it seems, than the cycle of identifying, celebrating, destroying, and then rehabilitating a hero. To work through this rise and fall narrative, let us review the case of baseball slugger Mark McGwire. McGwire, who began his career with Oakland in 1987, was always a prodigious home run hitter. By the 1998 season, he was regularly the subject of speculation about breaking the single season home run record, held by Roger Maris, who hit 61 home runs in 1961. Playing then for the St. Louis Cardinals, McGwire embarked on the heroic journey toward the record, joined unexpectedly by a then relatively unknown outfielder for the Chicago Cubs, Sammy Sosa. By the end of the season, McGwire reached 70 home runs (and Sosa had 66) to shatter the record. The "home run race" of 1998 was one of the most compelling sports stories of recent decades, with some sportswriters claiming that the goodwill generated by the pursuit had "saved" baseball after the work stoppage that led to the cancellation of the 1994 World Series. *Time* magazine even went so far as to call McGwire its "Hero of the Year" (Okrent, 1998).

Although it was largely a "feel-good" story, anointing McGwire as a hero was not without problems. For one, the sports media elevated him to such heights that his eventual fall—from revelations that he had used steroids—was almost inevitable. Indeed, when McGwire was called before Congress in 2005 to testify about the presence of performance-enhancing drugs in baseball, his refusal to "discuss the past" meant the "end of Mark McGwire as an American icon" (quoted in Butterworth, 2007). In other words, although his achievements on the field were remarkable, McGwire nevertheless remained human, a simple fact lost in the exaggerated reports of his heroic greatness. Much like Vick, then, it wasn't a question of *if* McGwire would make a mistake, but *when*. In addition, the coverage also frequently featured McGwire as a "Ruthian" figure, hailing the legacy of Babe Ruth. Meanwhile, they relegated Sosa to the role of a "sidekick," often using his Latin American heritage as a point of comic relief. As a result, the portrayal of the two players, unintentionally though it may have been, privileged a White, American hero and diminished the status of a non-White, Latin American figure (Butterworth, 2007).

Not all mediated sports heroes are White, of course. However, superstar athletes of color such as Derek Jeter and Jerry Rice are often careful not to disrupt the dominant expectations of the hero's behavior. Indeed, even as their silence on controversial political issues has been criticized by some in the media and by academics, apolitical athletes have profited by crafting public personae that are consistent with heroic ideals. When non-White athletes do express viewpoints that are not considered "mainstream"—Richard Sherman or the Williams sisters, for example—they are criticized either for "playing the race card" or failing to appreciate their substantial privilege. Thus, as Vande Berg (1998) notes, there is space alongside the sports hero for the "antihero," a figure who often disrupts or challenges commonly accepted beliefs and practices that may be oppressive. Minority athletes, women, or gay and lesbian athletes all have the potential to embody the antihero persona. Vande Berg specifically uses examples such as Billie Jean King and Dennis Rodman, athletes who, in different ways, destabilized common interpretations of gender (for more on gender, see Chapter 6). As Grano (2009) illustrates in his analysis of Muhammad Ali, the irony is that antihero athletes are typically reviled in their own time and are "granted heroic status only retrospectively" (p. 192). Indeed, contemporary sports fans may not realize just how despised a figure Ali was—first for converting to Islam and changing his name from Cassius Clay and second for opposing the Vietnam War and refusing to be drafted in the United States Army (we discuss this in more detail at the

OFF THE BEATEN PATH

ARCHERY

In April 2012, the World Archery Federation named America the best nation in archery since 2008 based on athletes' performances in international competitions. Three months later, the first American medal won in the London Olympics was a men's team silver in archery. Arguably, the archers that helped America achieve these accomplishments will not be remembered as sporting heroes. However, archery is growing in popularity and MSNBC and NBC Sports Network reported that archery was the top watched Olympic sport on cable.

Recent movies, such as *Avatar, The Avengers, The Hunger Games*, and *Brave*, have also helped draw more attention to the sport. Although the movies use it for different purposes, the actors performing archery are all portrayed as heroes. In March 2012 when *The Hunger Games* premiered, USA Archery's website attracted over 30,000 unique visitors, a 59% increase from March 2011. This shows how heroic usage of archery in movies increases excitement for the sport.

beginning of Chapter 8). Instead of remembering Ali's role in resistance to war and racial oppression, people today tend to associate him with his battle against Parkinson's disease and the inspiration he provided by lighting the torch at the 1996 Summer Olympics in Atlanta.

Thinking of contemporary sports figures as heroes is complicated; they are human beings like anyone else and are thus bound to make mistakes (we explore responses to mistakes in Chapter 13). Although they often provide suitable role models, there are also numerous examples of athletes whose behaviors are indefensible. For example, Minnesota Vikings running back Adrian Peterson and golfer Tiger Woods have each been implicated in scandals involving allegations of child abuse (Peterson) and chronic marital infidelity (Woods). Nevertheless, in a media-saturated world where sports continue to grow in popularity, there is little doubt that Americans will continue to grant their sports superstars heroic status. And, as cases such as Kobe Bryant—who admitted having an extramarital affair in 2003 after he was alleged to have raped a resort employee—illustrate, the community of sport is often eager to welcome back athletes who rehabilitate their images. Indeed, Peterson appears to have been welcomed back to his sport with significant enthusiasm. All of which reminds us, "One of the few places where heroes can still be found is sports" (Vande Berg, 1998, p. 152).

Not all fallen heroes are able to reclaim their vaunted status, however. In the case of Woods, the scandal has largely become a footnote, but it lingers as part of the explanation for why he no longer dominates the sport as he once did. Thus, Billings (2013, p. 61) concludes that he remains a "nuanced, multifaceted, and flawed public persona." Other heroic figures, such as football coach Joe Paterno at Penn State University, are now so thoroughly embedded in scandal or tragedy that their images have suffered irreparable damage. Paterno is forever linked to assistant coach Jerry Sandusky, who was revealed in 2011 to have been sexually abusing young children for decades. Even the most adamant defenders of Paterno have struggled to preserve his image, as new information continues to suggest that the former coach knew more about Sandusky's behaviors than he claimed (Perez, 2016). Paterno's death in the aftermath of the scandal was tragic in its own right, and his decades of good work for the university make his legacy complicated. Nevertheless, his downfall provides a cautionary tale for those tempted to elevate any individual coach or athlete to such unreasonable heroic heights (Rinehart, 2012).

SPORT AS RELIGION

Because sports fans devote so much passion, loyalty, and faith to their favorite players and teams it is common to hear sports equated with religion. In particular, as Hoffman (1992) identifies, "The aspect of sport that so invites a comparison with religion is the intense excitement and the spirit of community it generates" (p. 7). It is the emphasis on community found in both sport and religion that suggests we should consider this relationship as a version of mythology. Remember, we are not evaluating myth based on its "truth" value but on its ability to communicate explanations about the role of human beings in the world and to guide appropriate actions. In this respect, religion certainly functions mythologically, as it is principally concerned with molding the beliefs and behaviors of its adherents.

This orientation to religion focuses less on denominations or organized churches and more on the logic that guides religious practice. Rothenbuhler (1989) takes this approach in his study of the values and symbols that are communicated by the Olympic Games. As he explains, the Olympics can be understood as a kind of religious experience because they bring individuals into community with one another in ritualistic fashion. Moreover, this mass ritual is designed to promote core values, such as pride in one's country (patriotism) and respect for other cultures (internationalism). For American audiences, the Games reaffirm particular ideals about the role of sports in society, including "sportsmanship, friendship between even those who compete, pride in victory, artistry in performance, and the willingness to make personal sacrifices, to submit to training, and to build skills" (p. 152). These values, so often at risk in contemporary commercial sport, are preserved by the religious logic at work during television broadcasts of the Olympics. Far from being restricted to the Olympic Games, Kurtz (2016) suggests that sport inherently expresses a kind of religious faith because it hails ideals of "moral character and virtuous athletic performance" (p. 32). All of which is to say that sporting events, such as an Olympic broadcast, can serve as a means to reaffirm one's *faith* in sport itself.

If religious meaning can be found in sports spectatorship, it can also be found in the personal journeys that are inspired by sport. For instance, earlier in this chapter we referenced the idea of the "pilgrimage," a journey that is designed to have spiritual significance. This theme is evident in Aden's (1999) discussion of the film *Field of Dreams* and the tourist location of the same name in Dyersville, Iowa. Rooted in the mythology of rural innocence and purity, the story of *Field of Dreams* is one of personal redemption and familial reconciliation. For the millions who visit the ballpark in Iowa, this mythology is bound to the ideals of the nation that have historically been assigned to baseball. Thus, as Aden summarizes, "The fields—both real and reel—are strongly infused with the romantic spiritual elements of community" (p. 222).

Equating sport and religion in metaphorical terms has become so commonplace that we react with little surprise when we hear someone suggest that a given sport is "like a religion" in a particular country or region. Lewis (2013) explores this phenomenon in his study of college football in the American South. In particular, he notes that four key metaphors—"cathedral," "worship," "glory," and "sacred"—characterize the experience of a majority of southern college football fans. This is not accidental he claims, but rather it is an outgrowth of the South's cultural attachment to the Christian Church. Most interestingly, Lewis notes, "Church identification may be a Southern cultural expectation, but collegiate football identification is far more communal and powerful. Currently, the local church and the local stadium seem to be peacefully coexisting, but the football stadium may be winning out with more converts these days" (p. 212).

Although these religious parallels might help us understand sports' broad appeal, some worry that overstating the case diminishes religion and inflates the importance of sports. Religion may be a powerful metaphor for sports, but the outcome of a game fails to match the gravity of religion's larger purpose. Whether one subscribes to a given religious doctrine or not, it is fair to conclude that religion is about the *transcendental*—that is, about things beyond the grasp of human experience. Sports, meanwhile, are bound to our earthly experience, which is probably as good a reason as any to maintain a distinction between religion and sports.

There might also be reason to be cautious about the influence of religion on sports. Especially during the late 20th and early 21st centuries, religious organizations have gained more and more influence among athletes and teams. Athletes in Action, Baseball Chapel, the Fellowship of Christian Athletes, and Upward Bound Sports are just a handful of the groups that view sports as a means for extending the reach of Christianity in American culture. In the 1990s, a group started by a former college football coach gained significant notoriety for trying to merge the purposes of sport and religion. The Promise Keepers not only sought to link religion and sports—their meetings took place in sports arenas, after all—but also to compensate for sociopolitical developments in American culture. As Beal (1997) explains, the movement was largely a response to a perceived "feminization" or "sissification" of American men. Thus, sport was "used to demonstrate the qualities of masculinity linked with superior leadership" (p. 279).

By weaving political commitments into the relationship between religion and sports, the Promise Keepers earned as much criticism as they did praise. Yet they represent only one iteration of what has become a familiar phenomenon. Baseball fans may now attend promotional events called "Faith Nights," some of which have been sponsored by controversial groups such as Focus on the Family or the Creation Museum. Butterworth (2011) critiques this comingling of sport, religion, and politics not so much because of the presence of Christianity but because the sponsorship of "Faith Nights" excludes other religious and political views "at the expense of a healthier democratic pluralism" (p. 326). Meanwhile, NASCAR driver Bobby Labonte had his car sponsored by *The Passion of the Christ* when that film was released in 2004. University of Florida quarterback and Heisman Trophy winner Tim Tebow has been the subject of countless cover stories commending him as heroic more for his missionary work than for his completion percentage (Butterworth, 2013). These are but a handful of the religious expressions that are now commonplace. All of which extend the range of ritual and mythology that routinely characterize contemporary sports.

CONCLUSION

In this chapter, we have explored the connections between mythology and sports. Between mythic stories, ritual performances, celebration of heroes, and use of religious metaphors, it should be clear that sports depend on mythology for much of their communicative power. In many cases, this heightens the drama of sports and offers a means for spectators to participate in a larger community. In other cases, sports mythology reproduces troubling practices or restricts the ability of some to participate in such a community. But in all cases, it makes connections between past and present, individuals and groups, and fans and players, all of which makes mythology an essential element in our understanding of communication and sport.

Suggested Readings

Berg, K., & Harthcock, A. (2013). "Brett Favre is a god": Sports fans' perpetuation of mythology on newspaper websites. In A. C. Earnheardt, P. M. Haridakis, & B. S. Hugenberg (Eds.), *Sports fans, identity, and socialization: Exploring the fandemonium* (pp. 137–150). Lanham, MD: Lexington Books.

Grano, D. A. (2007). Ritual disorder and the contractual morality of sport: A case study in race, class, and agreement. *Rhetoric & Public Affairs, 10*, 445–474.

Higgs, R. J., & Braswell, M. C. (2004). *An unholy alliance: The sacred and modern sports.* Macon, GA: Mercer University Press.

Milford, M. (2015). Kenneth Burke's punitive priests and the redeeming prophets: The NCAA, the college sports media, and the University of Miami Scandal. *Communication Studies, 66*, 45–62.

Perks, L. G. (2012). Sox and stripes: Baseball's ironic American dreams. *Communication Quarterly, 60*, 445–464.

Roessner, L. A. (2009). Hero crafting in *Sporting Life*, an early baseball journal. *American Journalism, 26*, 39–65.

Scheurer, T. E. (2005). Musical mythopoesis and heroism in film scores of recent sports movies. *Journal of Popular Film & Television, 32*, 157–166.

Trujillo, N. (1991). Hegemonic masculinity on the mound: Media representations of Nolan Ryan and American sports culture. *Critical Studies in Mass Communication, 8*, 290–308.

Trujillo, N., & Ekdom, L.R. (1985). Sportswriting and American cultural values: The 1984 Chicago Cubs. *Critical Studies in Mass Communication, 2*, 262–281.

6

GENDER IN SPORT

Sport is buried in gender stereotypes, with disparaging phrases such as throwing a ball "like a girl" or the need for a team to "man up" still percolating within modern conversation. The gender barriers present within sport started as obstacles of opportunity (not allowing women to play and, if so, mocking them for participation) yet now are barriers of lack of respect, resources, coverage, and equity. Progress has been made, yet many barriers remain. For instance, the rise of women's participation in sport has caused the creation of more women-only leagues and less coeducational sports opportunities for gendered unity. In a similar law of unintended consequences, the rise of women's sports media offerings has come at a time of increased sports media channels as a whole, making women's sports (and really all American men's sports that are not football, baseball, or basketball) less likely to be on mainstream sports channels (such as ESPN) and more likely to be on harder-to-find sports channels (such as NBC Sports Network). Discussions of women in sport are different than those about gender issues in sport; the former is about the struggle for participation, opportunity, and equal treatment for one identity group, while the latter is about the power-laden *interaction* between this identity group and those who currently have the access and opportunities: men. Sometimes, notions of sex roles and gender identity become intermingled, with sex roles being based on biological differences between men and women and gender roles being largely socially constructed. Thus, sex becomes more binary (either an XX or XY chromosome makeup ends the discussion), whereas notions of gender become far more malleable (indeed, notions of gender change depending on aspects of background, culture, and life experience being exerted upon the binary chromosomal makeup). Put simply, we explore gender issues (since communication is structured through words and other social interactions) through what sport often creates as sex divisions (associations that allow either only men or women to play exclusively). This chapter explores both feminist and interactive gender issues by (a) surveying the history of women's sport, (b) discussing gender roles under the broader theoretical construct of hegemonic masculinity, (c) assessing the amount of current coverage and exposure afforded to men's and women's sport, (d) addressing gendered language differences in sports media, (e) outlining current opportunities and struggles for women in modern sporting society, and (f) offering gender in sport as a possible agent for social change within an increasingly global society.

A HISTORY OF WOMEN'S SPORTS PARTICIPATION

The history of women's participation in sport is not as long as the history of their desire for inclusion. In fact, records show that even in the 1700s, women were arguing in print that they should be included in athletics (Sandoz & Winans, 1999).

Hargreaves (1994) delineates three distinct time frames for women in sport. She claims the first ranges from the inception of modern sports in 1896 until 1928—an era of overwhelming exclusion and dismissal of any combination of women and sport.

The second spans from 1928 to 1952—a period when primarily "feminine-appropriate" sports received relatively meager forms of societal attention. Hardin and Greer (2009) articulate the sports that are considered feminine (such as gymnastics and swimming) and also those that society more often regards as not appropriate for women (such as basketball and boxing). Opportunities happened in the sports in which ladies could still behave as they were expected to for the time period. For instance, golf became a mainstream women's sport during Hargreaves's second time span. Hauser (1999) claims that "golf was said to be the 'gentlemen's game,' but it was also the perfect sport for a gentle woman" (p. 81). Women's professional golf (and the Ladies Professional Golf Association, or LPGA) was founded during this time period, as players such as Babe Didrikson Zaharias were respected for their abilities. Sports such as tennis became mainstream for women; Wimbledon hosted its first women's tournament in 1884, just 7 years after the gentlemen's championships began, yet the women's championships became much less a perceived sideshow during this time period. Other sporting opportunities arose as men went to fight in World War II. The rise and fall of the All-American Girls Professional Baseball League is chronicled with a fair dose of historical accuracy in the 1992 film *A League of Their Own*. Opportunities for women in a wider range of sports were still quite limited, however. Of all the athletes participating in the 1948 London Olympics, just 90 women competed (as opposed to nearly 5,000 today). Hargreaves argues that

Carli Lloyd (center, in white) at the 2015 Women's World Cup

because of increased recognition for women's sporting accomplishments, the standards of skill and international competition accelerated substantially.

The third era provided by Hargreaves ranges from 1952 to the present day, representing decades in which women's sports have been able to conquer traditional power structures while challenging long-held stereotypes about women's athleticism. While this third era is certainly progressive in relation to the previous two, women often find their access to facilities, trainers, coaches, and media exposure still lacking when compared to their male counterparts. Nonetheless, the 1970s brought two tipping points that aided a surge in women's athletics that still escalates today.

Tipping Point #1: Title IX

The most significant change for women's sports in the United States occurred in the early 1970s, when Title IX of the Education Amendments of 1972 made gender equity into law, stating, "No person in the United States shall, on the basis of sex, be excluded from participation in, be denied the benefits of, or be subjected to discrimination under any education program or activity receiving Federal financial assistance." Title IX is now largely regarded as an athletic law, but note that sport was not specifically mentioned in the wording of Title IX. Rather, athletics was previously considered the largest violator of this principle, making gender equity in sports the most immediately observable change in American gender policies.

Compliance with Title IX has long been a hotly debated issue (see Suggs, 2006), with the three-prong approach of 1979 still being used today (see Hardin, Whiteside, & Ash,

INTERVIEW

DR. CHERYL COOKY, ASSOCIATE PROFESSOR, PURDUE UNIVERSITY

Q: Female participation in sport is at an all-time high; roughly equal numbers of females and males report an interest in playing at a high school level. Yet, your research shows that media coverage of female athletes does not reflect this change. Why is media coverage not following this growth in female athletic participation?

A: Researchers have speculated as to why such unevenness exists. Some of the coverage of women's sports has migrated to niche media outlets such as espnW.com and blogs such as those featured on Women Talk Sports. While this is good for fans of women's sports, it lets the "mainstream" sports outlets like ESPN's *SportsCenter* off the hook from engaging in sustained coverage of women's sports. Since most viewers will learn about sports through mainstream outlets, this prevents the growth of women's sports beyond the "hard core" women sports fan. Others have suggested that sports media is male-dominated, and unless more women are involved in the production-side of sports journalism, we will continue to see the trends in the lack of media coverage of women's sports. The assumption here is that women journalists and broadcasters will want and be empowered to cover women's sports. While it is a worthwhile endeavor to increase the numbers of women in sports journalism (Richard Lapchick's annual report on gender, race, and sports editors attests to this need), in our research we have called for the hiring of sports broadcasters and camera crews that are willing and able to invest in covering women's sports regardless of their gender and who are willing and able to cover women's sports in a way that mirrors the coverage of men's sports (e.g., high production values, exciting and colorful commentary). Of course, some journalists and sports broadcasters will argue that the trends in coverage exist because the media are simply giving viewers what they want (i.e., supply and demand). Our research demonstrates that the media creates demand and builds audiences for men's sports while ignoring women's.

Q: Society has moved toward gender fluidity (Facebook has 50 different gender designations). Yet sport is still defined in the binary: male/female. Is this problematic?

A: Yes. Instead of recognizing sports performance as a continuum rather than a binary, as Mary Jo Kane argued in the mid-1990s, where some women outperform some men, sex segregation (the mechanism by which the binary is enacted) in sports is both legally enforced (via Title IX) and culturally accepted. Moreover, the sex/gender binary as it is reproduced in sports contexts is hierarchical such that notions of male physical superiority and female physical inferiority are reproduced. An illustrative example of this is in the sex testing/gender verification/regulations on female hyperandrogenism that falsely constructs a sex/gender binary, in spite of the realities of sex as a continuum. Many athletes come under "suspicion" in part because of their gender appearance. Athletes who subscribe to Western standards of beauty and femininity are less likely to have their sex/gender called into question and thus are less likely

(Continued)

INTERVIEW (Continued)

to be subject to sex testing/gender verification. Of course, governing bodies like the International Olympic Committee and the National Collegiate Athletics Association have policies that allow for the participation of trans-athletes, yet these policies require invasive medical surgeries and procedures (and not all trans individuals wish to fully transition from one sex to the other or are able to afford these expensive surgeries).

Q: To what extent is sport still an entity of exclusion for females?

A: Over the past 40-plus years in the United States—and elsewhere—we have seen impressive growth in opportunities for girls and women to participate in sports. We have also seen a shift toward cultural acceptance and even celebration of female athleticism. Despite these gains, girls and women continue to experience exclusion. Women are also underrepresented in leadership positions on sports teams (as coaches) and in sports organizations (as managers, owners, etc.) and in sports media (as writers, commentators, broadcasters, editors). Lack of media coverage, sex testing in sports, the everyday exclusionary cultures of sports bars and sports stadiums wherein women fans continue to be sexualized, objectified, and are victims of sexual harassment and assault are other examples of the exclusion.

Q: Opportunities for women in sport-related fields are still far more limited than for men. What can be done to allow more women into the industry?

A: We have to change the cultural association of sports with masculinity. If sports continue to be "a man's world," women will continue to struggle to not only get hired in the industry but to thrive. Women who assimilate to the masculinist cultures of sports organizations may experience less resistance to their presence within those organizations and may even be embraced, promoted, and celebrated. For women who do not assimilate or who wish to challenge the masculinist cultures of sports, they are either marginalized or excluded. However, it should be noted that the underrepresentation of women occurs in other facets of our society and so addressing the lack of women in the sports industry cannot happen outside of the societal forces that contribute to the underrepresentation of women in other industries and sectors, such as the lack of women directors and producers in Hollywood, the lack of women in C-suite positions in corporations, and so on.

2014). More specifically, college and high school athletic programs are considered to be in compliance if any one of the following three prongs is satisfied:

1. Athletic opportunities are provided that are proportionate to the student enrollment.
2. Athletic opportunities are continually expanded for the underrepresented sex.
3. Athletic interests of the underrepresented sex are fully satisfied.

Most college athletic programs strive for compliance under the first prong but use the other two prongs as a means for demonstrating they are continually striving to provide more opportunities for women's athletics. In 2010, the use of student surveys to register compliance based on student interest was eliminated (Thomas, 2010).

Compliance is becoming increasingly difficult as the percentages of men and women enrolled in college have changed dramatically. At Title IX's inception, men and women attended colleges and universities in roughly equal numbers; by 2005, for every 100 male students, there were 135 female students (National Bureau of Economic Research, 2016). These demographic shifts cause athletic departments to do one of two things to achieve proportionality compliance: They must either add more women's sports or end existing men's sports. The fact that Division I football programs are permitted 85 scholarships exacerbates the problems confronting lower profile men's sports. Men's sports such as wrestling and gymnastics have experienced diminished resources and, in many cases, elimination from athletic programs to balance the scales, causing even greater criticism of the ramification of Title IX within these sporting communities. Moreover, the University of Oregon dropped its wrestling program shortly after investing over $3 million for a new football locker room, illustrating how such decisions are not only the result of Title IX but also seemingly the result of an ever-expanding budget argued to be necessary to compete at the highest level.

Regardless of where one stands on proper implementation of Title IX, the impact on women's athletics has been eye popping. Consider the participation rates for five sports 25 years after Title IX was established (see Table 6.1).

TABLE 6.1 ■ Women's High School Sports Participation Rates (1972, 2007)

Sport	1972 Participants	2007 Participants	% Change
Soccer	700	337,632	+ 48,133%
Lacrosse	450	54,771	+ 12,071%
Cross Country	1,719	183,376	+ 10,568%
Golf	1,118	66,283	+ 5,829%
Bowling	370	20,931	+ 5,557%

Source: Angel, A., Bella, T., Brady, S., & Brauner, D. (2009, March 23). Lady killers. *ESPN: The Magazine*, p. 34.

Tipping Point #2: The Battle of the Sexes

Nothing can match the impact of Title IX, but another landmark event of the 1970s still can be regarded as a tipping point for women's opportunities in sport: the 1973 tennis exhibition between former men's number 1 player Bobby Riggs and women's superstar Billie Jean King. The 55-year-old Riggs claimed he could still beat the best women's tennis had to offer; he had already defeated Margaret Court, 6–2, 6–1, which only further motivated King to rise to this challenge. Most knew beforehand that this match would be part of the history of women's rights in society regardless of the outcome. However, when King won in straight sets, the event took on even greater meaning. While gender equality was resisted in false urban legends that Riggs got only one serve while King got two and that Riggs bet large sums of money against himself to fix the match, the outcome galvanized women athletes seeking a place within the sporting landscape

Memorabilia from Billie Jean King's match against Bobby Riggs

and also, for millions of people, signaled that more equal treatment of women at home and at the workplace would surely follow. Given that the event was nationally televised with great promotional fanfare, the impact of the event was that women's athletics was much more widely considered to at least deserve a place at the sporting table. Whereas Title IX was government-mandated inclusion of women in athletics, the Battle of the Sexes was a direct challenge to men's near-exclusive hold on sport.

Moments of Recent Decades

Women's athletics had many highs and lows in the subsequent years, yet the overarching mindset shifted from one of fighting for a space to play to one where women athletes are perceived as commonplace, embodied in the feeling noted by Meân and Kassing (2008, p. 126): "I would just like to be known as an athlete." Still, overarching structures appear constantly in flux. The Women's Professional Basketball League lasted a mere three seasons, folding in 1981. The LPGA continues to struggle for sponsors and media exposure. The first generation of women to benefit from Title IX clearly forged new ground; NBC's Bob Costas refers to the 1996 Atlanta Summer Olympics as the Title IX Games because so many of the American women who took center stage were born close to the advent of the legislation. Progress can be measured in many ways, such as the high rating garnered for the 2015 Women's World Cup soccer final, the fact that all Grand Slam tennis tournaments now pay men's and women's champions equal sums of money, and Annika Sorenstam's valiant effort to make the cut in an all-male Professional Golf Association (PGA) event, missing by four shots at the 2003 Colonial tournament. Still, some moments have been bizarre (the highest rating ever for women-oriented sport

CASE STUDY

U.S. SOCCER'S GLASS CEILING

Few would argue that the USA Women's Soccer Team has had significantly more success on the international stage compared to their male counterparts. The women's team has been one of the most successful competitors in international soccer, having won three Women's World Cup titles and four Olympic Gold Medals. Since the Women's World Cup was implemented in 1991, each of the U.S. Women's teams have medaled and held onto the #1 ranking from early 2008 until 2014. In comparison, the U.S. Men's team has medaled in World Cup competition only once (dating back to 1930) and, until recently, has struggled even to qualify for international competition.

However, despite these accomplishments, the formula for funding the U.S. men's and women's team has a clear imbalance. For example, when the U.S. Men's team earns a win against a significant opponent each player receives a bonus of $17,625, compared to only $1,350 for members of the women's team. To make the issue even more egregious, members of the men's team earn a $5,000 stipend for each loss compared to no such benefit afforded to the women's team following a loss or tie. In an attempt to address this issue, the U.S. Women's National Soccer team filed a complaint in early 2016 with the Equal Employment Opportunity Commission claiming wage discrimination for being paid nearly four times less than their clearly less successful male counterparts. Such a structure may be conceivable in an environment where the male equivalent serves as the primary revenue generator for the sport. However, that is not the case for U.S. Soccer. The women's team consistently achieves higher ticket sales as well as television ratings than the men's team, resulting in a formula that is outdated considering the revenue generated by the women's team on an annual basis.

1. U.S. Women's soccer is certainly unique in its ability to generate considerably higher revenues than their male counterparts, but what factors do you feel drive the national organization's formula for distributing revenue to players?
2. Outside a decision not to compete on the U.S. Women's team, what other options might the players have for working to address this perceived inequity?
3. How are the historical issues associated with women's athletics discussed earlier in this chapter influential in producing this type of outcome for the U.S. Women's team?

remains the 1994 Olympic skating of Nancy Kerrigan and Tonya Harding, at least partly inflated by the earlier physical assault on Kerrigan by people close to Harding), while other advancements seem to have been begrudgingly accepted, such as when Augusta National Golf Club admitted two women members in 2012—former U.S. Secretary of State Condoleezza Rice and South Carolina businesswoman Darla Moore—but only after years of protests. The history of women in sports has been one of steady progress, with setbacks outnumbered by advances as women continually seek out new ways to join the community of sport. Nevertheless, women continue to break boundaries in sport, establishing noteworthy firsts, such as Ronda Rousey's becoming the first woman Ultimate Fighting Championship (mixed martial arts) Bantamweight Champion in 2012, Mo'Ne Davis pitching a shutout in the 2014 Little League World Series, and Becky Hammon (San Antonio Spurs) and Kathryn Smith (Buffalo Bills) becoming the first full-time women assistant coaches in their professional sports leagues in 2014 and 2016, respectively.

HEGEMONIC MASCULINITY IN SPORT

Foundational theorists, such as Gramsci (1971), have used the concept of hegemony to explain how power becomes entrenched in established beliefs regarding power and myth. As Connell (1987) says, "In Western countries . . . images of ideal masculinity are constructed and promoted most systematically through competitive sport" (pp. 84–85). Given that hegemony is not only about power but also about winning, it is not surprising that scholars have used hegemonic masculinity to explain how male athletes maintain dominance in sport that ranges from access to economics to participation rates to media coverage. More specifically, Trujillo (1991) claimed that hegemonic masculinity "refers to the social ascendancy of a particular version or model of masculinity that, operating on the terrain of 'common sense' and conventional morality, defines 'what it means to be a man'" (p. 291). Using pitcher Nolan Ryan as exemplar, Trujillo articulated five features: (1) physical force and control, (2) occupational achievement, (3) patriarchy, (4) romantic frontiersman or modern outdoorsman, and (5) heterosexuality; these features jointly

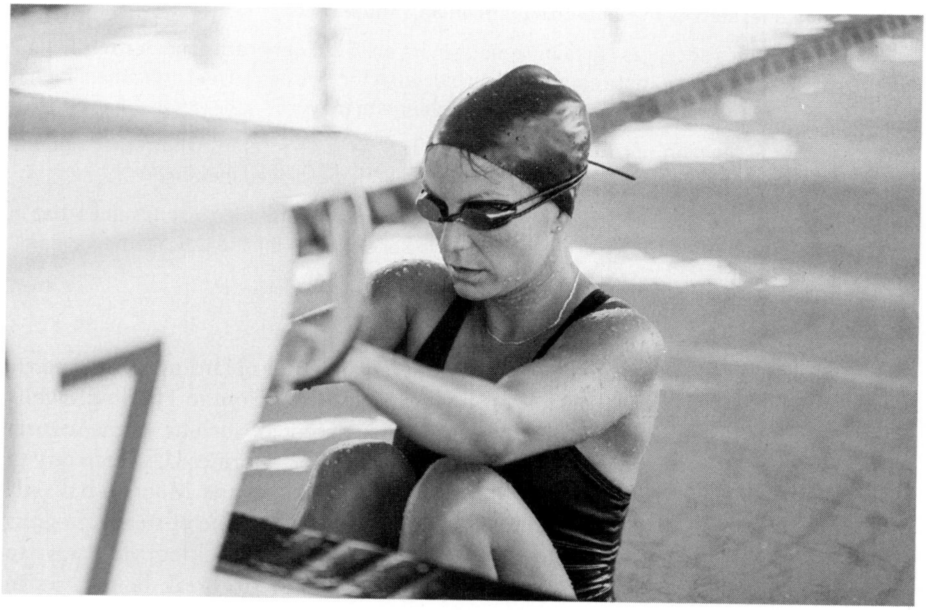

Source: © iStockphoto.com/Microgen

Swimmer prepares for backstroke

reinforce masculine ideals at the expense of other forms of masculinity, homosexual men, and women.

Sport often is defined as who is bigger, faster, and stronger, and yes, males have proven in world records that they are objectively bigger, faster, and stronger because of biological circumstance. Nonetheless, one cannot discount the endless cycle of certain sports (boxing, basketball) that are considered masculine that then results in media coverage that is predominantly masculine, which then embeds discourses to society that reinforce notions that sports are not for all but for males (see Hardin & Greer, 2009). Applying hegemonic masculinity also can explain how male athletes sometimes are typified in more objective manners (again, the bigger, faster, stronger) than the more nuanced and repeatable athletic skills (finesse, touch, control; see Kane, LaVoi, & Fink, 2013). For instance, mediated basketball coverage on programs such as ESPN's *SportsCenter* is more likely to show powerful men performing slam dunks than talented men executing a spot-on assist for a timely layup. Nevertheless, the increased popularity of women athletes in power-oriented sports (such as Ronda Rousey and Holly Holm in UFC) could indicate an increased public willingness to seek out women in a wider array of sports.

THEORETICALLY SPEAKING

FEMINIST STANDPOINT THEORY

Standpoint theory dates back at least to early 19th century theories developed by German philosophers, including Georg Hegel and Karl Marx. These theorists were interested in different perspectives about the world between members of the dominant social class and those who were on the margins. Variations of standpoint theory, including Nancy Hartsock's (1983) feminist standpoint theory, have subsequently theorized the experience of different oppressed groups. Hartsock's theory is grounded in the assumption that contemporary society is characterized by a fundamental power imbalance that gives men far greater cultural, economic, and political capital than women (what feminists commonly refer to as "patriarchy"). She contends, therefore, that in order to achieve a more humane balance, feminist standpoint theory enables scholars to reveal unequal divisions of labor and cultural representations that marginalize and oppress women. One prominent theme in feminist studies of sport is the concern that women athletes are too often defined as "women" (with the assumption that they should be "attractive" and "feminine") first and "athletes" second. Shugart's (2003) study of the 1999 U.S. Women's World Cup team illustrates precisely this concern. Because so much of the media's attention was on the physical appearance of the team members, their historic World Cup victory was at risk of becoming an afterthought. Similar concerns have been expressed about athletes such as Danica Patrick, Maria Sharapova, and Hope Solo. Feminist standpoint theory, therefore, facilitates more open discussions about communication practices that, intentionally or not, subordinate women to men and men's interests.

GENDERED COVERAGE OF SPORT

Regarding media exposure, the amount of women's sports coverage on local news and on flagship programming such as ESPN's *SportsCenter* is at an all-time low. Cooky, Messner, and Musto (2015) found that a 2014 sample of *SportsCenter* had just 2.0% of all coverage devoted to women's sports. Even elements such as scrolling sports "tickers" doubled that total to only 5% to 6%, leading to the conclusion that such tickers become "a kind of visual and textual ghetto" for women's sports (Cooky, Messner, & Musto, 2015, p. 8). Billings and Young (2015) found that this was not merely an ESPN problem, as FOX Sports Live (on FOX Sports 1) showed women at an even lower proportion. Table 6.2 indicates the breakdown between the two networks over two different 1-month periods:

The authors found that it wasn't merely the amount of coverage, but that the number of stories were smaller for women athletes and, moreover, were much less comprehensive, as highlighted in Table 6.3.

TABLE 6.2 ■ Clock-Time by Program (in Seconds)

	Men	Women	Mixed	TOTAL
ESPN	144,989 (97.5%)	1,445 (1.0%)	2,308 (1.5%)	148,742
FOX1	168,885 (97.4%)	970 (0.6%)	3,498 (2.0%)	173,353
TOTAL	313,874 (97.4%)	2,415 (0.8%)	5,806 (1.8%)	322,095

Source: Billings, A. C., & Young, B. D. (2015). Comparing flagship news programs: Women's sport coverage in ESPN's *SportsCenter* and FOX Sports 1's *FOX Sports Live. Electronic News, 9*(1), 3–16.

TABLE 6.3 ■ Average Length of Story by Program (in Minutes: Seconds)

	Men	Women	Mixed	TOTAL
ESPN	1:28:95	1:02:83	1:32:32	1:28:64
FOX1	1:17:72	53:89	1:32:05	1:17:77
TOTAL	1:22:53	58:90	1:32:16	1:22:44

Source: Billings, A. C., & Young, B. D. (2015). Comparing flagship news programs: Women's sport coverage in ESPN's *SportsCenter* and FOX Sports 1's *FOX Sports Live. Electronic News, 9*(1), 3–16.

Such findings echo concerns previously found within ESPN's flagship program, where the National Spelling Bee received more coverage than an entire week's nightly coverage of women's sports (Eastman & Billings, 2000). Such lack of focus on women's athletics is found in print media as well; Weber and Carini (2013) found that women athletes received more exposure from *Sports Illustrated* covers in the years 1954 to 1965 than in the years 2000 to 2011, where just 4.9% of all covers featured a woman athlete. Such trends were found in the United Kingdom press as well, leading Godoy-Pressland (2014, p. 595) to conclude that the embodied attitude was that there was "nothing to report" in regard to women's sports. As Kane (2013) explained, "The better sportswomen get, the more the media ignore them" (p. 231).

While existing power structures tell a major part of the story, the relative lack of women viewers and readers of sports products is a mitigating factor. Women argue they do not consume as much sports media product as men do because so little of it focuses on women's athletics, yet others counter that women fans do not support their athletes and teams in substantial doses in instances when they are shown. The 2012 folding of Women's Professional Soccer (WPS) is a case in which the majority of the admittedly small viewership was men, a trend found in many other televised women's sports, including women's professional tennis and basketball. Scholars have found that women consume sports differently than men because of issues such as leisure time choices and familial commitments, making them consume less sports media than their male counterparts (Whiteside & Hardin, 2011). In fact, the only two major sporting events that draw more women than men viewers are the Olympics and the Kentucky Derby (Helm, 2009). Women's sports are frequently offered on fringe or secondary cable networks, making the events difficult to find, yet more men than women are seeking out these sports media offerings.

Given that women represent the majority of U.S. Olympic viewers, one must wonder whether the coverage highlights women in equal measures or if it is conversely diminished, following the trends previously outlined in *SportsCenter,* local television news, and *Sports Illustrated.* A composite of the findings from Billings (2008); Billings, Angelini, and Duke (2010); and Angelini, MacArthur, and Billings (2012) were reported on the gendered clock-time differences in six Olympic telecasts (see Figures 6.1 and 6.2).

A rudimentary glance at the data shows several key trends. First, the Summer Olympics telecast has consistently shown more women athletes than men. One explanation for this trend derives from the fact that there are fewer events in the Winter Games, meaning more preliminary rounds are aired and making the fact that there are more male athletes competing at the Games more meaningful. Another is that the Summer Games features athletes in attire that is considered appealing for the at-home male viewer, with many highlighted events showing women athletes in swimsuits and leotards. Another key trend worthy of note is that for the first time in Olympic media analyses, women received more media coverage than men (in the 2012 London Games). Although the fact that

U.S. Gymnast Simone Biles

American women won more medals than the American men may have facilitated this result, and one analysis does not necessarily represent an overarching trend, one conclusion that can be fairly drawn is that the increased focus on women Olympians did not hinder ratings, as NBC's telecast averaged 31.1 nightly viewers (International Olympic Committee, 2012), often quadrupling the rating of any other show on any network during the time period. The Olympics demonstrates that media outlets can draw a very high viewership while featuring women athletes, something underscored long ago in the largely surprising 13.3 rating of the 1999 Women's World Cup final between the United States and China and then surpassed with a 15.2 rating for the United States

FIGURE 6.1 ■ Proportion of Men's and Women's Olympic Coverage in the 1996–2008 Summer Olympics

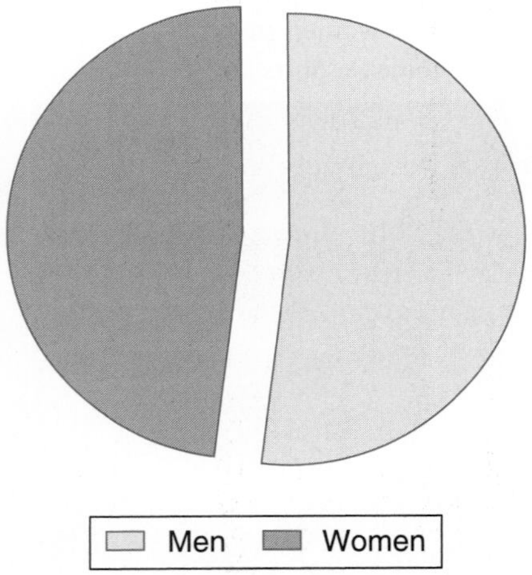

FIGURE 6.2 ■ Proportion of Men's and Women's Olympic Coverage in the 1998–2010 Winter Olympics

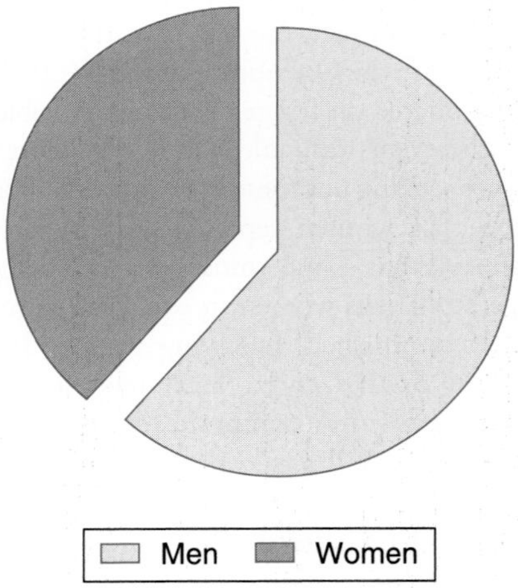

Sources: Billings, 2008; Angelini, MacArthur, & Billings, 2012.

versus Japan Women's World Cup final 16 years later, a rating higher than for the NBA Finals earlier in the same summer.

GENDERED LANGUAGE IN SPORT

Males and females may do similar things and even play the same sports, but the notion that they do so in overwhelmingly different ways is still quite prevalent in modern society. As explained in Messner (2002), beliefs that "men are from Mars, and women are from Venus" are "depressing evidence of how a renewed essentialism—the belief that women and men are so naturally and categorically different that they might as well be from different planets" (p. 1) remains. When former Wimbledon Gentlemen's Singles champion Pat Cash said that women's tennis is to men's tennis what horse manure is to thoroughbred racing (Spice Girls of Centre Court, 1999), he received more laughs than admonishment, a sign that women can play sports but are not exempt from being mocked by this decision. In terms of language, the result for women in sport is the diminishment or mitigation of their participation and accomplishments.

Naming Practices

One action that serves to diminish women's sports involves naming practices (see Halbert & Latimer, 1994). To wit, team sports employ qualifiers to women's teams to differentiate them from the "standard" men's teams. For example, a high school may have two basketball teams: the boy's team, called the Lakers, and the girl's team, called the Lady Lakers. The use of the feminine qualifier (especially in the absence of a men's equivalent) is a form of naming practice. In a similar vein, women athletes are more likely to be referenced by their first names, while men are most often referred to by their last names. Thus, we know that "Annika" was a great women's golfer, but "Watson" was a great men's golfer. In tennis, rivalries persisted, matching "Serena" and "Maria" (rather than Williams versus Sharapova), while men's rivalries pitted Sampras versus Agassi. It is fair to counter that these practices are occasionally used because women's last names can change when they get married, yet most modern athletes retain their last names, making this impact negligible. Other than the anomaly that occurs when the Williams sisters play tennis (making first names critical for clarification), naming practices impart no gender division that would innately occur, and yet they do. The impact on women who play sport below the professional level can be felt, as women often believe that naming practices relegate them to second-class status.

Gender Marking

The feeling that women's sport is substandard to men's is often felt in gender marking, a practice of qualifying which gender is participating in a given sport. Such marking becomes problematic when it is employed for women far more frequently than for men. For instance, one often sees media outlets that refer to two sports: basketball and women's basketball. When the qualifier is not used, the presumed gender is almost always male. Some associations reinforce these markings largely because the men's association was founded first, making the women's organization adopt a new gendered tag. Thus, we have the Ladies Professional Golf Association (LPGA) because the Professional Golf Association (PGA) had already been established for the men; similarly, we have the National Basketball Association (NBA) and then the gender-marked Women's National Basketball Association (WNBA). These qualifiers are then used to ascribe limiting assessments of women's achievement, such as referencing a person as the "best *women's* player in the conference" or "playing well enough to enjoy success on the *women's* tour." One could argue that the qualifier is necessary because men tend to be bigger, faster, and stronger than women at the highest levels of virtually all sports. Still, the notion that we appreciate only the fastest does not appear to apply in car racing, for instance, when the people regarded as the best drivers are ones driving for National Association for Stock Car Auto Racing (NASCAR), not Indy Car, which offers substantially more powerful cars. The inverse also doesn't seem to apply in athletics when agility makes women perhaps more innately capable, such as with certain flexibility requirements in gymnastics. Instead, such size and flexibility is sometimes couched as an unfair advantage, such as when Kacy Catanzaro became the first woman to qualify for the *American Ninja Warrior* finals, yet received criticism that her small size and flexibility diminished this accomplishment.

A MATTER OF ETHICS

STRIKING A POSE

As mixed martial arts (MMA) continues to gain in popularity, women have slowly become more visible in the sport—none more so than Ronda Rousey, largely considered one of the elite female competitors in MMA. You may also know about Rousey because she meets the standards of conventional beauty in American culture. In part to raise both her own profile and the profile of her sport, Rousey has featured that beauty in provocative magazine photo shoots and covers, including *ESPN The Magazine*'s 2012 Body Issue and the September 2013 issue of *Maxim*.

In this chapter, you've seen that many female athletes still face either overt discrimination or more subtle forms of sexism, including the expectation that they should remain "feminine" or "pretty" while competing in sports. Increasingly, however, athletes such as Anna Kournikova, Natalie Gulbis, and Danica Patrick *choose* to emphasize their physical appearance as a means to increase their marketability. The outcome of these choices is undeniable: Attractive female athletes who pose for publications such as *Maxim* or *Playboy* (predominantly read by heterosexual men) generally raise their profiles and collect more and more lucrative endorsements.

Critics of these athletes counter that while these overtly sexual images may benefit individual women, they do harm to countless other women who are not able to conform to conventional standards of beauty. In addition, their decision to pose nude (or nearly nude) for an overwhelmingly male audience risks reducing women to simple objects of sexual pleasure, which minimizes the actual *achievements* of women athletes.

Do women who pose for these publications have a responsibility to other women? Should an appearance in *Maxim* be understood primarily as a business decision? Why is it still important for female athletes to demonstrate their "femininity?" Are men held to the same expectations as women when they choose to exploit their own appearance and sexuality?

Sexual Disparagement

Gendered language also is used to presumably stigmatize a people through the mislabeling and denunciation of sexual orientations. Female athletes continually battle being labeled as "butch" or lesbian (Anderson, 2005) when excelling at sports, while homosexual slurs are heaped on males when they fail to perform adequately in sports. Griffin (2007) delineates six ways in which homophobia is manifest in sport: (1) silence—such as the lack of overwhelming outrage when Penn State women's basketball coach Rene Portland enacted a no-lesbian policy (see Hardin, 2009); (2) denial—either claiming not to be gay or claiming that one's private life is not for public discussion; (3) apology—a performance of proper gender roles, particularly in public roles other than during sport; (4) promotion of heterosexy image—the LPGA using attractive photo shoots and calendars for promotion (see Hundley & Billings, 2010); (5) attacks on lesbians—bad-mouthing in recruiting, arguing that other teams have a disproportionate number of gay players; and (6) preferences for male coaches—hiding homosexuality in women's sports through the presence of a male coach. Chapter 8 reveals much more about how athletes feel pressures to perform in certain ways that match not only their own identity characteristics but also the identity characteristics that they presume are most desirable in society.

Categorical Differences in Gendered Media Dialogue

Decades of study (see Billings, 2009; Blinde, Greendorfer, & Sankner, 1991; Daddario, 1998) have led to a longitudinal understanding of how men and women athletes are depicted, using divergent dialogues within the media. One should note that stereotyping is still a notion that is studied within communication scholarship, but the understanding of difference and bias has largely trumped the search for stereotypical behavior. This is largely because both social scientists and critical/cultural scholars have uncovered dialogic differences in sports commentary that may not fit traditional gendered power structures or overt sexism yet nonetheless represent difference in the manner in which we understand men and women athletes. Given that there are biological (e.g., pregnancy or the presence of testosterone) and sociological differences (e.g., unequal opportunities for men and women to compete in youth sports) between the genders that impact athletic performance, some difference is to be expected. Still, one must temper these anticipated

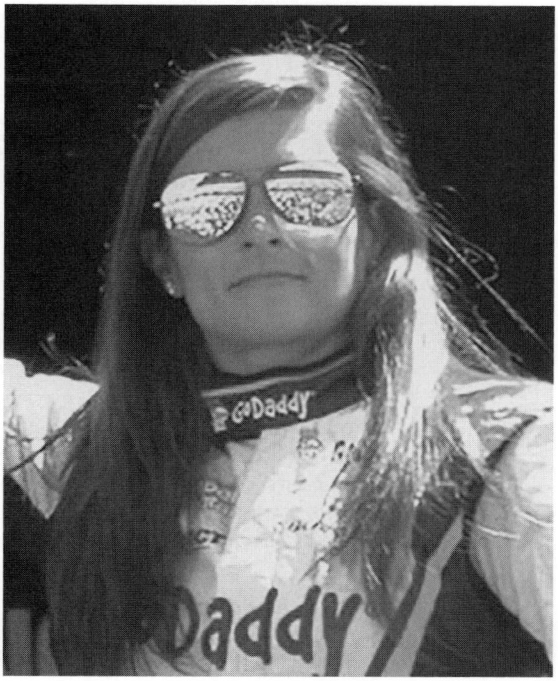

Source: By Sarah Stierch. https://commons.wikimedia.org/wiki/File:TSM350_-_2015_-_Danica_Patrick_-_3_-_Stierch.jpg. [CC By 4.0]. https://creativecommons.org/licenses/by/4.0/deed.en

NASCAR driver Danica Patrick

differences with notions of dominance and power that also inevitably percolate within these media dialogues. Consider commentary within the 2009 U.S. Open Tennis Tournament, wherein Kim Clijsters was asked over and over again, "How does it feel to win . . . *as a mom?*"

The following are some terms more likely to be attributed to a male athlete:

Powerful

Conquering

Best in the world

Fearless

Incredible

The following are some terms more likely to be attributed to a female athlete:

Talented

Dedicated

Best woman in the world

Emotional

Nice

OFF THE BEATEN PATH

GYMNASTICS

While the female gymnast's career could be over by the age of 20, the typical age of male Olympic gymnasts ranges between 19 and 26. This is largely due to the discrepancies between the nature of the events in which male and female gymnasts participate. The apparatuses differ between men's and women's gymnastics. Both sexes compete on the vault and floor exercises; the other men's events include the pommel horse, still rings, parallel bars, and high bar, and the women's events include the balance beam and uneven bars. Men's gymnastic events require a great deal of upper-body strength and muscular endurance, which men gain as their bodies develop into their mid-20s. Women's gymnastics focus more on grace and flexibility, which are easier to develop at a young age and more difficult to maintain postpubescence. Male and female gymnasts are ultimately judged differently based on physical attributes, which is reflected not only on scorecards but in the eyes of spectators as well. Female gymnasts garner more media attention and are often more celebrated by fans than their male counterparts.

Thus, there are some forms of comments that are more often attributed to men than women athletes. For instance, the most basic trend that has been consistently detected involves the notion that men are inherently superior in terms of athletic skill. This belief has been broken down into subcategories including superior power ("like a runaway locomotive"), touch ("incredible precision in his turns"), and finesse ("one of a handful of people in the world who could perform that dunk").

Beyond this hardwired trend, male athletes are also more likely to be considered superiorly experienced at their sport of choice. Some of these types of comments may be founded in logic and the sociological differences discussed earlier. For example, sports such as gymnastics typically involve teenaged female gymnasts but men in their 20s. Also, men athletes may truly have more experience (as measured in years rather than amount of practice time) because boys are encouraged to play more organized sports at earlier ages. Even when taking these mitigating factors into account, however, there is still a disproportionate focus on the experience of men athletes when compared to women of similar expertise and backgrounds.

A final trend that is likely to favor men involves perception of superior composure. Media analyses have found that commentary can sometimes regard men athletes as more "ready for the moment." Winners of men's sports events are more likely than winners of women's sports events to have their success attributed to mental toughness and the ability to be unrelenting when faced with an emotional moment.

There are also several areas in which women athletes are more likely to receive comments than men. Perhaps the most unsurprising trend involves a tendency for sports media outlets to concentrate on the overall attractiveness of women athletes. When one considers that the overwhelming majority of sportscasters are male and presumably heterosexual, this may not be much of a shock. However, the types of comments can nonetheless diminish the accomplishments of women athletes (and a discussion of the overt sexualization of women athletes can be found in Chapter 9). Consider the ramifications of watching a telecast where a female gymnast is referred to as an "adorable pixie" or perhaps the official FIFA's language in 2015, describing Alex Morgan as "a talented goal scorer with a style that is very easy on the eye and good looks to match." Some studies have found that in terms of sheer counts of comments about men's and women's bodies, the numbers could be considered to be relatively equivalent. However, the comments surrounding men athletes tend to be more apt to fall into references to physique ("built like Superman") than the same comments about attractiveness that women players more often receive.

Beyond an increased focus on looks, women receive more comments than men do about being emotional. Some members of society still argue that women are "too emotional" and "take things personally" in all circumstances, which is then used to argue that women cannot perform effectively at the highest level of the workplace. These same misguided notions have been found to seep into sports media commentary. This is perhaps a corollary to the trend to perceive men's superior composure—men athletes are depicted as succeeding because they do not let emotions override their athletic desires, and women athletes are perceived as failing for succumbing to these same obstacles.

A final type of commentary that women athletes are more likely to receive than men athletes involves attributions of luck. When a woman succeeds in sport, commentators may attempt to temper these achievements by noting that the player had some breaks go her way. This is often unpacked in communication scholarship as "consonance" or the notion that everything simply comes together at a moment in time to impact the athletic moment. Thus, positive consonance can exact victory (a basketball player who "couldn't miss tonight" or was "on fire") just as negative consonance can result in defeat ("just wasn't his night"). In terms of gender, women are more likely to receive comments about positive consonance than are men. This is especially true when women compete against men in the same competition. For instance, urban legends persist surrounding the Billie Jean King/Bobby Riggs Battle of the Sexes, arguing that King must have won because of luck. When the result couldn't be directly attributable to luck, false claims were made that Riggs received only one serve per point and that King was allowed to hit into the doubles court (both are absolutely untrue). In a similar vein, when Annika Sorenstam competed in a sanctioned PGA tournament, a commentator witnessed a man's shot bouncing from the rough onto the green and noted that it was an "Annika bounce," potentially implying that Sorenstam had a better-than-anticipated score earlier that day because of superior luck.

In all, it is abundantly clear that men and women athletes are described in a variety of media outlets in substantially different manners. Some differences are justified, some are explainable, and others could be judged to arise from personal ignorance. Regardless, the astute communication scholar must understand the dialogic differences involved in the conversations that surround sport at all levels of society.

OPPORTUNITIES FOR MEN AND WOMEN IN SPORT

Mark Twain once observed that "rumors of my demise have been greatly exaggerated," and this appears to be the case when talking about the old-boy network of sports. One cannot talk about opportunities in sport—whether involving jobs or mere access—without talking about power. Social class certainly is a contributing factor, yet gender is critical to the discussion, as men have possessed entrenched power roles throughout the inception and evolution of modern sport (see Oates, 2012). Female sports team owners are still regarded more as anomalies than as trends toward equality. Debates once circled over whether any Division I men's basketball program would offer a head coaching position to prominent former Tennessee women's coaching legend Pat Summitt, who amassed 1,098 victories and eight national championships. Women's access to sportscasting jobs is almost universally relegated to that of sideline reporter or weather prognosticator, with the sports industry still harboring less than progressive gender stances (see Genovese, 2015). These cases are hardly indications that sports structures are providing more access for women, yet instances such as the aforementioned hiring of women into key men's team coaching positions provide some glimpses of progress for women.

In terms of sheer numbers of jobs, the opportunities for women in sport are growing but at a very slow rate. The Women's Sports Foundation (2009) admits that sport is still highly male dominated but argues that five trends are leading to more opportunities for women within the sports marketplace:

1. *The active female consumer.* Women now out-purchase men for items such as athletic shoes and clothing.
2. *Females as spectators of men's and women's sports.* While we have already established that women rarely outnumber men when watching sportscasts, they do represent 40% of all sports consumers—and that proportion is increasing.
3. *Males and females as spectators of women's sports.* Women's professional leagues are struggling financially, yet their mere existence represents progress when compared to past opportunities.
4. *Women's sports being accepted by the sports media.* One should not equate the lower amount of media coverage to women's sports as being less acceptance of athletic talents; the fact that Dallas Mavericks owner Mark Cuban even publicly commented about former Baylor standout Brittney Griner playing in the NBA should be considered a positive harbinger.
5. *Corporations using sports to sell to women.* "Athletic" looks are desired within a significant segment of the women consumer population, often more than "sexy" looks. Organizations are hiring women athletes as spokespersons and sponsoring women's sporting events because of this trend.

Some of these postulates could be assessed as mere spin, trying to create a self-fulfilling prophecy, yet all of these trends are, indeed, pointing in the direction of more opportunities for women, even if the scale of these chances is not remotely equivalent to that of men.

Nonetheless, even when given the right to earn a job in sports media, women face many additional hurdles. Hardin and Shain (2005) report that half of women in sports journalism report being verbally abused in conjunction with their jobs. This ranged from sexual comments at the workplace to berating voicemails from readers who belittled their knowledge to locker room hassles with male athletes. Such comments appeared to be part of the evolution of the ESPN workplace as well, evidenced by Miller and Shales (2011). The presumptions were that (a) women did not know as much as their men counterparts about the sports they were covering and that (b) they received their jobs either because of their looks or the organizational desire for gender diversity. Women also cited lack of advancement as their top reason for leaving sports journalism, and more women than men dropped out of the field at the early stages of their careers. Schmidt (2013) studied university newspapers, finding that women were underrepresented specifically within sports reporting and also noting that university student journalists were not cognizant of the degree of gender disproportionality. New opportunities have arisen, such as the establishment of espnW, whose coverage is "by women, for women" while covering both women's and men's sport.

GLOBALIZATION AND CHANGE AGENCY

Given the established tendencies that can diminish women in terms of opportunities, representation, and depiction in sport, one could determine that women will always remain in the margins within a larger sporting landscape. Sport can certainly function as a vehicle for social change, and women athletes are particularly in the position of influencing societal perceptions, political realities, and the overall global treatment of women. As Wulf (2009) writes,

> If anything, XX-chromosome games are a truer, more meaningful calling than their XY counterparts. Women often have to compete for nothing more than the joy and the love of sport, not the fame and fortune we heap on the men. They usually have to play for their own rewards. [Consider] Yemeni students, running a relay in Sanaa recently. They're not just girls with exotic wardrobes battling heat and aerodynamics. They're literally racing against time, trying to bring their Islamic traditions of modesty into the modern world of gender equality. (p. 16)

We hope this chapter has underscored more than the negatives for women interested in sport, offering the positive trends and relatively newfound recognition of not just women athletes but also women fans, executives, and consumers that represent a newer and broader way of thinking about sport in society (see Walker & Melton, 2015). Gender certainly impacts our understanding of sport at virtually every level, and it is fair to conclude that it remains the most hardwired and perhaps last bastion of the old-boy network. One could see this as discouraging or could, instead, decide that sport is the venue in which the biggest social change could happen for women in the next generation. Regardless of one's standpoint, gender differences and advancements will continue to be negotiated largely from a communication perspective, whether that is through communication-based media, organizations, or social networks.

Suggested Additional Reading

Cahn, S. (2015). *Coming on strong: Gender and sexuality in women's sport* (2nd ed.). Urbana: University of Illinois Press.

Creedon, P. (2014). Women, social media, and sport: Global digital communication weaves a web. *Television & New Media, 15*, 711–716.

Jones, A., & Greer, J. (2012). Go "heavy" or go home: An examination of audience attitudes and their relationship to gender cues in the 2010 Olympic snowboarding coverage. *Mass Communication & Society, 15*(4), 598–621.

Mastro, D., Seate, A. A., Blecha, E., & Gallegos, M. (2012). The wide world of sports reporting: The influence of gender- and race-based expectations on evaluations of sports reporters. *Journalism & Mass Communication Quarterly, 89*(3), 458–474.

Messner, M. (2009). *It's all for the kids: Gender, families, and youth sports*. Berkeley: University of California Press.

7

RACE AND ETHNICITY IN SPORT

Bryant Gumbel once called the combination of race and sport the "third rail of polite discourse . . . a subject sure to burn those who try to deal with it honestly or speak of it truthfully," emphasizing that this combination can be perhaps the most difficult of all sports communicative terrain. Ridiculous comments have been offered for years; in 1998, the late NFL player Reggie White spoke to the Wisconsin legislature, stating that, for instance, Native Americans excel at "sneaking up on people" and Asians can "turn a television into a watch" (Ford, 2004, p. S6). The ignorance has continued in recent years, including incidents such as ESPN's Rob Parker labeling Black Washington Redskins quarterback Robert Griffin III a "cornball brother" (an African American who eschews racial stereotypes) for marrying a White woman and having conservative views, as well as golf's Sergio Garcia saying that he'll have Tiger Woods come for dinner and "we'll have fried chicken." The most recent years have featured much less tolerance for perceived racism within the sports world; for instance, ESPN baseball analyst Curt Schilling was suspended in 2015 for making comparisons between Muslims and Nazis. Moreover, a 2015 University of Oklahoma fraternity video that included members singing that there will "never be a n***er in SAE," resulted in the loss of a highly ranked football recruit and the creation of a social media campaign by head coach Bob Stoops called #NotOUrCampus.

Thus, activism now characterizes modern understandings of race and sport (see Lavelle, 2017), with sport being used for social change or awareness for issues ranging from the 2012 killing of Trayvon Martin (which prompted a "hoodie" protest from LeBron James and the Miami Heat) to the 2015 controversial remarks from Los Angeles Clippers owner Donald Sterling (which resulted in his being forced to sell the team), to the 2015 racial unrest at the University of Missouri (which resulted in the football team demanding the resignation of the university president or risk their not playing any remaining games). Clearly, most discussions of race are complex, with the communication surrounding them being less about the overtly racist and more about heritage, culture, and power. Race itself is not a Black/White binary; while the majority of professional athletes fall into one of these two racial classifications, small but noticeable increases in participation from other ethnicities are emerging, and amateur sport in America is played by all races in all forms. Moreover, the number of people who identify as being mixed race or don't identify with a racial group at all continues to increase. The discussion of race in sport is equally complex and changing. As a result, media gatekeepers, athletes, fans, and followers of sport rarely know how to discuss race in sport, resulting in a dropped conversation in which the vast majority finds the issue compelling yet not intriguing enough to risk the penalties of communicating about race in a manner dubbed inappropriate by another person or entity. This chapter attempts to discuss the presumed dangerous communication cocktail of race, ethnicity, and sport by (a) outlining a history of race and ethnicity in sport, (b) uncovering differences in participation and sport selection rates, (c) identifying the impact of race and ethnicity on sports culture, (d) analyzing differences in media exposure and "stacking" practices, and (e) articulating the ways in which media dialogues differ depending on the race and ethnicity of the athlete being described. We are not pretending to solve racial discord in one simple chapter but rather hoping to clarify the current state of the continued debate regarding the impact of this form of identity on a heavily involved sporting society.

HISTORY OF ETHNICITY IN AMERICAN SPORT

Before we begin this discussion, we must note that race and ethnicity are closely related issues, yet *race* and *ethnicity* should not be regarded as interchangeable synonyms. Debate continues about the ways in which the terms are unpacked, but a general consensus (although hardly a settled one) refers to ethnicity as a person's heritage and culture (e.g., Hispanic) and race as something that can be socially constructed (e.g., hairstyle and dress). Race often gets unpacked by much of the general society as simply a referent of skin color (e.g., Black), which can add to the confusion. As Coakley (2009) contrasts it, ethnicity refers to "a cultural heritage that people use to identify a particular population while race is when that population of people are *believed to be* [emphasis added] naturally or biologically distinct from other populations" (p. 276). Ways in which ethnicity can be performed are discussed in more detail in Chapter 9; however, the distinction between the two is worthy of a formative note here with media often referring to race (skin pigment) because it is somewhat easier to explain than a person's detailed cultural heritage. Thus, President Obama becomes "Black" rather than of mixed ethnic backgrounds, and the same is true for athletes, whether it be Derek Jeter who is often described as mixed race or tennis player Madison Keys, who is often described as Black even though she has mixed ethnic background.

Almost completely unique to American culture is the ethnic notion of the "one drop rule" (see Sweet, 2005), which posits that if a person has any level of non-White heritage, he or she is regarded as a minority. Most discussions in sports media do not focus on any notion of one drop or percentages of ethnic backgrounds, instead relying on the visual to provide a streamlined yet ultimately limiting view of race. Regarding race in the media, *Chicago Tribune* journalist Clarence Page (2009) stated that "we are geared toward the visual, not toward the conceptual. We are geared toward conflict, not Kumbaya moments."

We also limit the discussion of race and ethnicity to American sport because a person's human experience varies wildly depending on the nation in which one resides. One's ethnicity, heritage, or skin color is impacted, for instance, by whether one resides in Finland, Argentina, or Saudi Arabia. Notions of nationalism, religion, history, hegemony, and culture can enter the equation, making ethnicity in sport quite dynamic.

In terms of history in the United States, ties between sport and ethnicity began—and remained for quite some time—largely as a White versus Black dynamic. This was, at least in part, because most other races were just nominally represented in the country's population in the 18th and 19th centuries. Even within the two races with significant populations, participation in sport was highly segregated. Blacks played organized sports very rarely but possessed a deep desire to compete. Slaves were given the very occasional day off and, when this occurred, many opted to play sports from morning to nightfall. The 1834 *Book of Sports* by Robin Carver notes that Blacks were playing all sports imaginable during the pre–Civil War time period.

In the past century, advancements for Blacks in sports can often be measured by connections with groundbreaking performances and breaking of color barriers. Boxing became one of the earliest places where races competed in the same competitions. Legendary boxer Jack Johnson became the first Black heavyweight champion in 1908, albeit surrounded by riots and death threats and capsulated notions of a "Great White Hope" that could defeat him. In the 1936 Berlin Summer Olympics, Jesse Owens won four gold medals in front of the citizens of Nazi Germany, challenging Adolph Hitler's aspiration to showcase Aryan dominance. Blacks participated in organized sports leagues in the early part of the 1900s yet never were afforded the opportunity to move from Black leagues to White-established professional leagues until 1947, when

Source: Library of Congress [LC-USZ62-27663], https://en.wikipedia.org/wiki/Jesse_Owens#/media/File:Jesse_Owens3.jpg

Jesse Owens

Jackie Robinson joined the Brooklyn Dodgers. Despite a fair share of teammates and fans who felt racial integration was wrong, Robinson was able to largely win over critics. By 1948, several other Black players had joined the ranks of Major League Baseball (MLB); when Robinson won the National League Most Valuable Player (MVP) award a year later, it was clear that Black players would be a fixture in professional baseball from that point forward. Nevertheless, it took until 1959 before every MLB team was racially integrated.

University athletic programs were still exhibiting segregationist stances years later, but moments like Texas Western's (now the University of Texas at El Paso) 1966 national basketball championship team provided an impetus for changes. As dramatized in the 2006 film *Glory Road,* coach Don Haskins lacked the resources to recruit the top-ranked White high school players and instead opted to recruit players regardless of race. The result was a national basketball title as Haskins's all-Black starting lineup defeated the University of Kentucky's all-White starting lineup. While Hutchison (2016) identifies holes in that streamlined heart-warming narrative, the decision is still seen as a forebear for a much more integrated set of basketball teams in the decades that followed.

Activism became increasingly prominent in athletics of the 1960s and 1970s. The most resonant example remains the Black Power salute in the 1968 Olympics (see Bass, 2002). After winning medals in the 200 meters in the 1968 Mexico City Games, Americans Tommie Smith and John Carlos received their medals in atypical fashion to bring attention to Black heritage (and related American repression of it), including wearing no shoes but black socks (to recognize Black poverty), a scarf around Smith's neck (to recognize Black pride), and beads around Carlos's neck (to recognize Black lynchings). In addition, each wore a black glove and raised his arm (symbolizing Black power in America) during the playing of the U.S. national anthem. At the time of the protest, many key Olympic figures reacted quite negatively, but decades later, the image grew in stature to the point that the two men received the 2008 Arthur Ashe Courage Award—even though they have a fair amount of hostility toward each other.

Increasingly, organized sports became integrated with not just Whites and Blacks participating together but with a myriad of other ethnicities represented on the athletic field. The debate shifted to the ability of non-White athletes to advocate for broader social change using their visibility and status within professional sport. Considerable criticism has been levied against more recent prominent athletes of color, such as Michael Jordan, Tiger Woods, and Steph Curry who have not been nearly as openly activist about racial issues as their predecessors, people such as legendary Cleveland Browns' running back Jim Brown and 11-time National Basketball Association (NBA) champion Bill Russell. Jordan opted not to take public stances on political and social issues, perhaps most famously when he refused to endorse a Democratic candidate from North Carolina for the Senate by saying, "Republicans buy sneakers, too." Such considerable silence from basketball's biggest star led to surprise that eventually, in 2016, Jordan indicated he could stay silent no longer about racial inequities within the justice system while donating $2 million to the cause. Still, such stances are relatively low; *New York Times* columnist William C. Rhoden wrote of this dilemma in his book, *Forty Million Dollar Slaves* (2006), arguing,

Stephen Curry

> Occupants of two worlds—the world of the streets and the world of wealth—these athletes can speak from a perch of power and influence . . . [but] contemporary Black athletes have abdicated the responsibility to the community with treasonous vigor. They stand as living, active proof that it does not necessarily follow that if you make a man rich, you make him free. (p. 8)

Khan (2012) counters such notions, believing some of these writers are missing the point and that today's Black athletes are the logical by-products of the previous generation's activism. Regardless, many discussions are now reductionary, as some modern athletes are attached with "first" monikers related to race, such as speed skater Shani Davis becoming the first Black athlete to win individual gold in a Winter Olympics in 2006 or gymnast Gabby Douglas becoming the first Black winner of the women's all-around competition at the 2012 London Games.

INTERVIEW

KEVIN BLACKISTONE, ESPN AND THE SHIRLEY POVICH CENTER FOR SPORTS JOURNALISM, UNIVERSITY OF MARYLAND

Q: As we reflect on the two-term presidency of Barack Obama, some have argued we are living in a postracial world. Others are far more skeptical. What progress do you see in the sporting arena?

A: I'm not in the skeptics' camp. I'm in the nonbelievers' camp. I'll use my part of the sports arena, media, as evidence. Quantitatively and anecdotally, the bodies that collect and disseminate sports news are becoming less diverse with the growth of new media and shrinkage of traditional media. Diametrically, the sports they cover are being populated more and more by athletes of color, as is the audience seeking the information. And we know that the prism through which media controlled mostly by White men sees people of color is significantly different than that through which people of color see themselves. I'm hard pressed to see that as progress.

Q: While race and ethnicity used to be unpacked as a Black/White binary, that now seems woefully inadequate. How has this blurring of the lines changed discussions of race in sport?

A: I'm not certain that nuance has been realized. Take, for example, the continued discussion around Major League Baseball about the declining number of Black players in the game; it is myopic at best. Truth is, the number of Black baseball players has never been higher—we just don't recognize those from the Dominican Republic, which was the first stop on the trans-Atlantic slave trade, as part of the African diaspora. So, an otherwise intelligent Black baseball player Torii Hunter dismisses Spanish-speaking African descendants from the Domican Republic as "impostors."

Q: To what extent can race be discussed in terms of power—those who have it and those who don't?

A: Simply. There isn't a major U.S. sport predominated by labor of color that is also predominated by ownership and management of color. White men, by and large, control the professional and collegiate revenue-generating sports, while relying on labor pools of athletes of color, particularly Black athletes. While athletes have in the past couple of generations flexed more collective might, as a group they haven't overturned the power structure constructed by White men to mostly serve the entertainment desires of White men.

Q: What can be done to encourage athletes to play sports that are not typically associated with their cultural backgrounds?

A: One of the problems U.S. Soccer Federation President Sunil Gulati identified with the effort to produce better soccer talent in the United States was what he called a growing pay-to-play system for youth soccer. It depreciated the talent pool to those who could afford to participate, shutting out those in poorer communities, particularly in the innercity and ghettoized suburbs, who could not. That is not only happening in soccer but in baseball, hockey, swimming, and other sports where the club team phenomenon has taken hold. It appears as if economics, capitalism, has segregated and stratified youth sports in this country.

Q: Careers in sports journalism have been lost or derailed by inappropriate discussions of race, but is colorblindness and the omission of racial dimensions within sport the answer?

A: When Rob Parker, a friend of mine, was suspended by ESPN for questioning Robert Griffin III's political footing, I e-mailed my disagreement with the decision to a couple executives at ESPN, where I am also a contract employee. I asked what he said that required punishment. All Parker did was raise an intraracial discussion in an interracial arena. I would've hoped the reaction to the discussion spurred further examination rather than condemnation. But we as a society, perpetuated by such sophomoric reactions in the media, continue to be fearful of serious debate about the implications of race. In sports, we've so long heard ourselves talk about how meritocratic games are that we don't believe they could be any other way.

PARTICIPATION AND SPORT SELECTION

America's history of race in sport is one largely of privileging one race at the complete exclusion of others. This is largely not the case today within the majority of organized sports. Instead, races often segregate themselves in self-selected manners based on geography and post-emancipation influenced policies. Beliefs that certain races are naturally more gifted at one sport than the other have largely been debunked, yet there is no question that certain sports (and even some positions in a given sport) remain highly stereotyped to the point that it appears jarring for many members of society to see an athlete participate in a sport that is different from what is expected for his or her race. For instance, Venus and Serena Williams represented a heavy contrast to the typical racial profile of tennis players participating on the Women's Tennis Association (WTA) Tour. Relatedly, professional basketball became so heavily populated by Black players that Larry Bird was regarded by some journalists as the newest example of the mediated Great White Hope, and White wide receivers in football have their defenders who refute their characterizations as "deceptively fast" and "possession receivers" while Black quarterbacks are still expected to play the position in a demonstrably different manner than others.

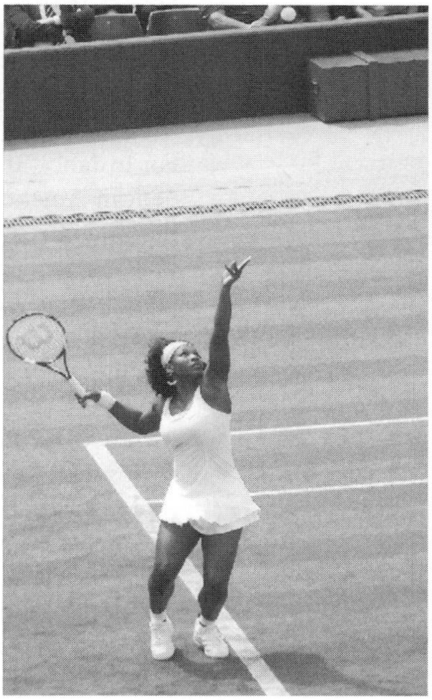

Source: By Tourism Victoria

Serena Williams

In sum, sports as a whole are popular for all ethnic groups, but each individual sport brings the reality of differential ethnic expectations. Witness the Summer Olympics, which is certainly ethnically diverse, yet it is hard to say we are witnessing ethnicities competing against one another when tuning into a swimming final that is predominantly White and then switching to a sprinting final that is predominantly Black. Such divisions are used to form stereotypes ("White people can't jump"; "Black people can't swim") when the realities are far more complex. Black swimmer Eric Moussambani was a rarity in the 2000 Summer Olympics because his country, Equatorial Guinea, had only two swimming pools at the time, and both were located inside luxury hotels; opportunity made his participation rare, not any limits arising from his race. In a similar vein, Black Americans are, on a whole, less likely to be skilled in swimming than White Americans, yet this is not because of any limitation of their race but rather the cultural implications of their racial history (Chen, 2010). For instance, decades ago, Blacks were banned from swimming in many pools, lakes, or oceans in the South, resulting in far fewer Black Americans with appropriate swimming skills. Older generations are less likely to teach younger generations skills like swimming when they have not been exposed to the activity themselves.

Table 7.1 shows how these expectations are manifested in sport selection rates within major American professional teams as well as Division I college basketball and football. The manner in which sports segregate athletes by race in the United States is less explainable than the international participation differences found in events like the Olympics. When faced with the opportunity to compete in multiple sports, today's modern athletes often opt for specialization. For instance, Latino players are more likely to opt for baseball; Blacks are more likely to choose basketball; Whites are more likely to choose golf. This is not because of some biological discrepancy between races that is often espoused by some of the people branded "celebrity racists" in the opening of this chapter. Rather, it is often the case that culture, geography, economics, and heritage jointly influence these choices. For instance, the racial makeup of MLB has changed substantially since the 1970s with African-American players constituting 28% of the professional baseball population in the mid-1970s but only 9% in 2012. African-American pitcher C. C. Sabathia notes that external influences like college scholarship structures impede African-American participation because, whereas basketball and football offer full scholarships, baseball rarely does (see Anderson, 2009). The athletes do not so much choose a given sport as much as a sport (through a confluence of interrelated variables) chooses them. When they do choose that sport as a means for entering college, the label "scholar-athlete" can be used detrimentally, as "some may disengage from education as a way to cope with their frustration" arising from such labels (Stone, 2012, p. 195).

In sports like football, different positions possess different athletic expectations. When these expectancies are violated, people often exhibit cognitive dissonance. In 2003, ESPN hired radio host Rush Limbaugh to participate in its studio show. Limbaugh's inappropriate comments about why the media tends to embrace Philadelphia Eagles quarterback Donovan McNabb (that the media has overplayed his quarterbacking skills because they have been "very desirous to see a Black quarterback do well") were indicative of a larger problem with the perception that McNabb and other Black quarterbacks were playing the "wrong" position (see Buffington, 2005).

TABLE 7.1 ■ 2011–2012 Athletic Participation Rates (Reported in Percentages From TIDES Racial Report Card)

	MLB	NBA	WNBA	NFL	MLS	CFB	MCB	WCB
White	61	18	16	31	49	47	31	39
African American	9	78	74	67	25	43	57	47
Latino	27	3	0	1	24	3	2	2
Asian	2	<1	0	2	1	1	<1	1
Other	0	<1	1	1	1	5	5	5
International	28	17	9	1	48	<1	6	4

Note: Percentages do not equal 100 because of rounding and multirace classifications. Abbreviations are as follows: The Institute for Diversity and Ethics in Sport (TIDES); Major League Baseball (MLB); National Basketball Association (NBA); Women's National Basketball Association (WNBA); National Football League (NFL); Major League Soccer (MLS); College Football (CFB); Men's College Basketball (MCB); Women's College Basketball (WCB).

We discuss the apology strategy surrounding these types of statements in Chapter 13. This notion is similar to what used to be the case in 1980s basketball, where the point guard was most likely expected to be occupied by a White player. Even the leader of the Philadelphia National Association for the Advancement of Colored People, J. Whyatt Mondesire, appeared to be ill at ease discussing McNabb. He went as far as to purport that McNabb's temporary decline in play was the result of his becoming a pocket-passer to avoid the image of being an athletic-running quarterback that would befit the Black football stereotype (Fitzgerald, 2005).

However, different racial structures are at play when analyzing the coaching rates highlighted in Table 7.2. Compared to the percentages in Table 7.1, it is clear that Whites are more likely to be selected for coaching or managerial positions. This is less the case in baseball, presumably because of a higher participation rate of White athletes in that sport in general. However, sports such as professional basketball, football, and soccer yield White coaching hires at rates approximately three times what participation rates would suggest would be equitable. Ross (2006) notes that "institutional racism continues to prevent African Americans from rising to various coaching, administrative, and ownership positions in sport" (p. x).

These variable participation rates are proving to be much more hardwired than many initially believed. When Tiger Woods emerged in the professional golf scene in the late 1990s, many presumed his success would inevitably lead to a more ethnically diverse professional golf membership. Thus far, this has not been the case, just as 1980s boxer Gerry Cooney did not lead a revival of White boxers, and the Williams sisters'

TABLE 7.2 ■ 2011–2012 Head Coaching Rates (Reported in Percentages From TIDES Racial Report Card)

	MLB	NBA	WNBA	NFL	MLS	CFB	MCB	WCB
White	69	47	67	81	89	89	80	83
African American	14	47	33	16	5	9	19	15
Latino	17	3	0	0	5	<1	1	1
Asian	1	3	0	3	0	1	0	<1
Other	0	0	0	0	0	1	1	1
Women	0	0	42	0	0	0	0	52

Note: Percentages do not equal 100 because of rounding and multirace classifications. Abbreviations are as follows: The Institute for Diversity and Ethics in Sport (TIDES); Major League Baseball (MLB); National Basketball Association (NBA); Women's National Basketball Association (WNBA); National Football League (NFL); Major League Soccer (MLS); College Football (CFB); Men's College Basketball (MCB); Women's College Basketball (WCB). Table represents just head coaches with the exception of MLB, which included the entire coaching staff.

participation has not resulted in a substantially more racially integrated professional tennis. People continue to select certain sports at the exclusion of others, and there is, no doubt, a racial component to these choices that is also largely impacted by economic status and facility (and membership) availability.

MEDIA EXPOSURE AND STACKING

Echoing a theme that is prevalent in this chapter, ethnic diversity in sports media has evolved from outright exclusion of non-White participants to selective exclusion of things that may appeal to minority audiences but not mainstream (read White) viewership. There has been a concerted effort to rework, revamp, and revise the cultures of sports that are currently played by a large number of minorities at the highest level. McDonald (2005) articulates the performance of Whiteness, which occurs in sports such as professional basketball. Through the use of enhanced dress codes, the NBA enforces a notion of how a "professional" should present himself. Similarly, when Allen Iverson's tattoos are airbrushed out of a cover photo for NBA's *Hoop* magazine, there was an attempt to reshape the game to make it more marketable for audiences who may not have related to Iverson's cultural background.

While not omitted from the sporting equation entirely, studies have continually found cases of underrepresentation of minority athletes when compared to their relative athletic successes. Longitudinal studies of magazines such as *Sports Illustrated (SI)* have found that minority athletes are not only shown less frequently than expected but that they are also more likely to be shown in ways that are violent, negative, and overtly physical in nature (see Goss, Tyler, & Billings, 2009). Lumpkin and Williams (1991) even found a 30-year gap between the first *SI* cover of an African American female and the second.

Sports on television have exhibited similar underrepresentation and disparities. For instance, college basketball features a majority of players who are Black, yet the coverage provides an environment in which they are not only usually orchestrated by a White coach but also are described by White announcers and surrounded by advertisements that feature Black characters only 9% of the time (Wonsek, 1992). As King, Leonard, and Kusz (2007) describe it, sports media aid the creation of narratives that are intended to present a postracial America, stifling any protest about lingering issues that still persist within race and sport. The legendary status of LeBron James is argued to be at least partly the result of clever marketing to make James racially "safe" for audiences to enjoy (Mocarski & Billings, 2014).

The concept of stacking enters this equation, although the way it has been unpacked has altered considerably over the years. In a nutshell, stacking relates to the placement of people in roles that closely fit social expectations of identity groups. Some studies have examined stacking from a sense of multiple races playing the same game yet being placed at different positions. For instance, baseball has been found to be racially stacked, with Black athletes more likely to play outfield positions, Latino athletes more likely to play in the middle infield, and White athletes more often positioned in corner-infield and catching positions (Margolis & Piliavin, 1999). Other instances of stacking can be viewed as the practice of self-selection mentioned previously in this chapter; athletes of a given race are covertly—and sometimes overtly—told that given sports are or are not for them. Media exposure influences these perceptions by the stacking of newspaper, magazine, television, and even Internet coverage so that White reporters are covering sports played by mostly White participants, while Black reporters cover sports that are occupied by largely Black athletes, and so forth. For instance, when a tennis sportscasting booth is exclusively filled with White sportscasters, a notion that this sport is for White people percolates within our psyches in the same manner that placing a Latino reporter on a soccer newspaper beat relays the subtle message that soccer is not for White people. Sports media become a reflection of sports that are already stacked ethnically, perpetuating differences that are based to a large extent on myth.

MEDIA DIALOGUES

Of course, the language surrounding linguistic choices in sport becomes strained when racial and ethnic difference becomes part of the discussion. Because there is largely a lack of open and honest discussion of perceived racial difference, reliance on embedded stereotypes can seep into media discussions, which then can transfer to everyday conversations about these same issues. Identifying inappropriate comments is relatively easy. When CBS NFL analyst Jimmy "the Greek" Snyder is quoted as saying Black athletes are bred to be better because of different bone structures, we know the comment is inappropriate. However, the linguistic choices embedded in dialogic assumptions are much more subtle, asking communication scholars to decipher the difference between stereotypes, biases, and actual demographic trends. Take, for instance, the 2015 comment from then-ESPN personality Colin Cowherd, who noted that baseball was not overly complex, which made it appealing to athletes from the Dominican Republic, which had "not been known, in my lifetime, as having, you know, world-class academic abilities." Within such comments, race is tied to issues of economics, class, and culture, making the unpacking of their meaning harder to interpret.

Such problems may be worsening, as Blackistone (2012) laments the paucity of non-White sports journalists, claiming that "the consequences of an increasingly less diverse or more White sports media . . . are concerns that will continue to heighten anxieties about Black males in society in particular" (p. 225). ESPN's recent response has been the creation of the website, The Undefeated, which focuses on intersections of race, sport, and culture—while featuring considerably more racial diversity of its journalists in the process. These general, monolithic media outlets often use skin color as a means for classifying race, indirectly implying that the camera can do the work of telling a full story. Part of the reason for this simplicity is because non-White athletes are typically afforded less opportunity to relay who they are. As Carrington (2010) argues, "Only rarely has the Black athlete spoken, or been allowed to speak. It is normally spoken for" (p. 2).

THEORETICALLY SPEAKING

CULTIVATION

Years ago, we had people who endorsed a hypodermic needle theory of media influence, also known as a "magic bullet" theory. At its core, the theory argued that people wholly accepted what media relayed to them, giving media tremendous persuasive sway. Of course, this theory is no longer the norm, and one of the reasons is the rise of cultivation theory. While framing was explored in Chapter 3, cultivation is different in that it pertains not to content but the effects of that content on society. Gerbner and his associates (1986, 2002) claimed that media sets the terms of the debate, cultivating certain social attitudes in the process. For instance, if someone watches *Law & Order* or *Bones* all day, they may feel the world is more violent than it actually is. Within race and sport, many stereotypes can be cultivated that can shape understandings. If ESPN's *SportsCenter* is more likely to show Chris Paul dunking the ball than it is to show Paul making a smart, precise pass, over time people could start to believe that this Black player is more athleticism than intelligence, when he appears to excel at both. When considering how much media the avid sports fan consumes, it appears something as benign as a football game could, over time, shape overall conceptions about race and ethnicity in America.

In many cases, such as that of Tiger Woods, skin pigment becomes a substitute for more complex ethnic backgrounds. Woods has a lineage that is Caucasian, Black, Indian, and Asian, but his skin is Black; therefore, he is, for all media intents and purposes, Black. The classification into larger groups of people dramatically simplifies race, yet communication scholars have found this is not only the case but that media descriptions of athletes diverge based on these essentialist categories of skin color.

One of the most prevalent assumptions in ethnic dialogues is that of the presumed athletic superiority of the Black athlete. As renowned sociologist Harry Edwards (1970) notes, so many people bought into this notion that "the White race thus becomes the chief victim of its own myth" (p. 197). Of course, this was decades ago, and times certainly have changed. Still, one finding in content analyses of sports media is that there is an increased emphasis on the notion of the innately talented Black athlete, the born achiever. In contrast to narratives surrounding other races that overcome great odds to excel through a great deal of hard work and effort, Black athletes can sometimes be perceived as succeeding out of a sense of destiny, having talents at an early age that quickly (and presumably easily) set these athletes apart from their peers. These types of embedded notions are employed to explain differential participation rates and sport selection. Sailes (1998) offers a history of Black athletic stereotypes in sport, ranging from the "dumb jock" to the "brute" or "sambo." Hoberman (2007) references this as the "hardiness doctrine" of sports, which involves the seemingly unrelenting belief that Black athletes are "a more primitive human type that is biologically distinct from and physiologically superior to that of civilized man" (p. 213).

In contrast, media dialogues must explain the existence of White athletes who succeed in mainstream sports, and they more often do so through an increased focus on the intellect, leadership, and hard work of a White athlete. Consider Peyton Manning. Consistent narratives exist about him in all of these areas. Without question, he is a tremendous quarterback, but rarely does overt athletic skill become the dominant focus of media discussions. Instead, Manning is discussed as the tactician, the player who is prepping for a game far beyond what others would opt to do. When you put these misguided concepts together, you find an undercurrent of a dialogue in which White athletes succeed through diligence—blood, sweat, and tears—while Black athletes have presumably been handed these athletic luxuries by the grace of God.

Black athletes are also expected to play sports in a more aggressive, hypermasculine way. When considering the sports Black players are socialized to select, many of the sports naturally lend themselves to power above finesse, strength over composure. Boxing is a classic example in which the hypermasculine Black athlete is expected to achieve. An interesting story line in regard to being somehow "true" to the African American ethnicity is in the 1975 epic "Thrilla in Manilla" between Muhammad Ali and Joe Frazier. Ali repeatedly called Frazier an "Uncle Tom" and a "White man's champion," and he also labeled him a "gorilla," a primal form of race baiting. Thus, a classic boxing match between two Black men still had racial overtones, pitting Ali's "float like a butterfly, sting like a bee" style against the presumably plodding but powerful Frazier. Decades later, media narratives still hearken back to the days in which Ali and Frazier represented contrasting notions of what being a "true" Black champion was supposed to be.

Again, in contrast to this aggressive style that is sometimes expected of Black athletes, White athletes have been depicted in the media as prototypically heroic. This sometimes occurs because White athletes are more likely to be placed in spotlight leadership roles, such as quarterbacking a football team or starting pitching for a baseball team. However, the notion of what we consider to be heroic is more than just the leader who produces victory. Butterworth (2007) used the 1998 home run chase between White player Mark McGwire and Latino player Sammy Sosa to illustrate the construction of what he termed a "mythological enactment of Whiteness" (p. 228). He notes that heroism in sport has always been connected to a notion of White enactment that rarely allows for other races to be considered prototypical heroes, even when, as was the case for Sosa, he proudly embraced notions of American exceptionalism and patriotism.

Another linguistic characterization that has been found to trend differently based on racial profiles is the notion of deviance. Given the immense White roots of most mainstream sports in America, discourses are often constructed with a sense of history that offers a notion of the "good old days" (which lacked racial diversity) and the current days (which have more racial diversity, coupled with sporting ills such as commercialism, greed, and corruption). The National Basketball Association has felt this tension when Black players failed to dress, perform, and talk in the same manners of great past heroes of the game (see Griffin & Calafell, 2011). Media dialogues then reflect that sports are changing largely because of demographic participation changes. ESPN used to have a segment on *SportsCenter* that illustrated this notion perfectly, titled Old School vs. Nu Skool; a White Skip Bayless debated the "old" way of looking at an issue while a Black Stephen A. Smith argued the "nu" way in which we should analyze a current event, embracing sports like the NBA with a veil of what some scholars call "ghettocentric" (Andrews & Silk, 2010). Similar dichotomies play out in other sports; Carolina quarterback Cam Newton was widely criticized not only for losing Super Bowl 50 but also for exhibiting what some deemed a lackadaisical effort, a form of criticism Peyton Manning did not receive 2 years earlier after an abysmal performance in the Super Bowl.

A MATTER OF ETHICS

RICHARD SHERMAN, THUG LIFE?

After the Seattle Seahawks won the 2014 National Football Conference (NFC) championship, defensive back Richard Sherman provided one of the more memorable post-game interviews in recent memory. While talking to FOX Sports' Erin Andrews, Sherman emphatically boasted, "I'm the best corner in the game! . . . Don't you open your mouth about the best, or I'll shut it for you real quick" (Boren, 2014, para 5). Sherman's over-the-top comments set off a flood of comments on Twitter and in mainstream sports media, with many observers being critical of his behavior. Much of the commentary was rooted in observations about Sherman's identity as African American.

Of the many names Sherman was called after the interview, one in particular stood out: "thug." Sherman himself took note of the term and, when asked whether he was bothered by it, replied, "The reason it bothers me is because it seems like it's an accepted way of calling someone the N-word now." He continued, "I know some 'thugs,' and they know I'm the furthest thing from a thug. . . . You fight it for so long, and to have it come back up and people start to use it again, it's frustrating" (Wilson, 2014). From this view, Sherman's postgame interview was less about the perceived excesses of African American self-expression and more about the perceived attitudes of mainstream (White) society.

Given this contrast of perceptions, how might the history of African American athletes presented in this chapter help explain the negative reactions to Sherman? Are there ways in which language choices such as "thug" function as code for less acceptable terms? Beyond Sherman, why are outspoken African American athletes at risk of being defined in negative terms?

Sources: Boren, C. (2014, January 19). Richard Sherman goes on postgame rant with Erin Andrews. *Washington Post*. Retrieved from https://www.washingtonpost.com/news/early-lead/wp/2014/01/19/richard-sherman-goes-on-postgame-rant-with-erin-andrews-video; Wilson, R. (2014, January 22). Richard Sherman: "Thug" is accepted way of calling someone N-word. *CBSSports.com*. Retrieved from http://www.cbssports.com/nfl/news/richard-sherman-thug-is-accepted-way-of-calling-someone-n-word

Such depictions are not meant to excuse cases in which minority athletes are arrested for crimes, such as Michael Vick's 2007 dog fighting crime or Greg Hardy's assault charges in 2014. Rather, it is important to note the framing of these stories, which is also constructed in a manner of presumed innocence of White athletes and presumed guilt of non-White athletes (see Baker & Boyd, 1997). Media have become so aware of this tendency to prejudge minorities that sometimes the presumption of guilt has swung to White defendants as well. The 2006 Duke lacrosse case documented in the 2016 ESPN 30 for 30 film *Fantastic Lies,* in which team members were presumed to be guilty of raping a Black exotic dancer, only to be later cleared of all crime and even declared innocent by the North Carolina Attorney General, is a case in point. The bottom line is that race now tinges discussion of social deviance and crime, altering media discourses in the process (Grano, 2010).

Dialogues become even more interesting (or, some would argue, convoluted) when race is not as simple to define. For instance, studies have found that attributions for Tiger Woods's successes most closely match that of other White attributions, such as composure and intellect but that his failures are described in ways more related to Black athletic attributions regarding innate skill (see Billings, 2003). Meanwhile, scholars continue to debate whether racial dialogues in the media are getting better (see Byrd & Utsler, 2007) or remain problematic (see Rada & Wulfemeyer, 2005).

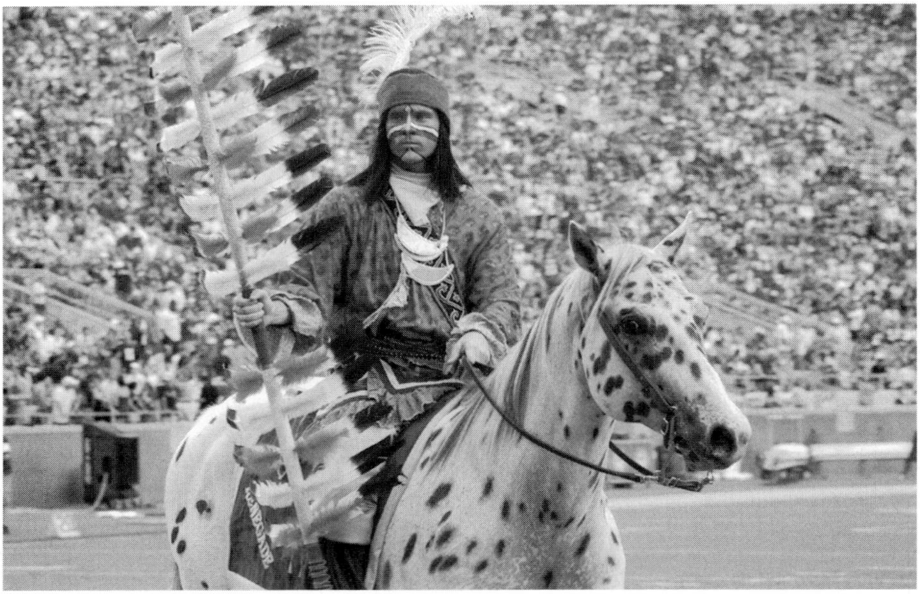

Source: Yomasta 12, https://commons.wikimedia.org/wiki/File:Chief_Osceola_Renegade.jpg

Florida State's Chief Osceola

Given all of these trends, one could presume that race is largely a Black/White binary in America, yet other races are either excluded from discussions at a disproportionate rate or are marginalized and even mocked in other communication portrayals. The clearest example of racial insensitivity conflicting with entrenched postulates about history is the consistently intense debate over offensive team mascots. As King (2016) argues, many find some mascot choices quite inflammatory, including the Washington Redskins, the Atlanta Braves' "tomahawk chop," and the Cleveland Indians' cartoonish representation of an American Indian. Some schools have changed nicknames in the wake of increased cultural sensitivity; for instance, the St. John's University Redmen became the Red Storm in 1995, and the University of Illinois eliminated Chief Illiniwek in 2007. Other teams have resisted such changes, citing close ties and even approval from Native American tribes (such as is the case with the Florida State Seminoles). A 2016 study (see Cox, Clement, & Vargas, 2016) finding that only 9% of Native Americans find the name Redskins offensive is a case in point of where some find this issue to be overblown, while others argue that the acceptability of such issues cannot be determined via national poll. Others cite branding issues that are too valuable to eliminate in an increasingly commercial sports culture. This subject will be covered at greater length in Chapter 9.

In sum, the language that is implemented to describe sport is inevitably shaded by race. This is not all bad as neglecting race as a subject and treating all athletes in a monolithic manner would be to eliminate a sense of narrative, watering down rich stories of heritage and background. Nonetheless, treatment of athletic accomplishments with an equal amount of respect should be the aim of anyone attempting to discuss race and sport in a literate and responsible manner.

CASE STUDY

RACIAL SOLIDARITY IN MISSOURI

During the Fall 2015 semester, students on the University of Missouri campus were engaged in open protest resulting from a number of racial incidents that had occurred during the previous year. A graduate student, Jonathan Butler, began a hunger strike seeking the removal of the Missouri System President Tim Wolfe due to the lack of responsiveness from the university administration. These protests resulted in little action on the part of campus leadership until Saturday, November 7, when 30 members of the Missouri Tigers football team bonded in solidarity behind the protests and posted the following on Twitter: "The athletes of color on the University of Missouri football team truly believe 'Injustice Anywhere is a threat to Justice Everywhere.' We will no longer participate in any football related activities until President Tim Wolfe resigns or is removed due to his negligence toward marginalized students' experience." (Pearson & Sutton, 2015, para 3). The players refused to compete in the football game against Brigham Young University that was scheduled for the upcoming week, forcing the institutions to determine whether the game should be cancelled, postponed, or forfeited. The lost revenue to both institutions was estimated at $1 million.

In addition to the team members seeking the ouster of their system president was the affirmation from the team's head coach Gary Pinkel, who supported the actions of his players after releasing a message that noted, "The Mizzou Family stands as one. We are united. We are behind our players" (para 9). The position of the team and the coaching staff produced widespread support from many, while others called for their scholarships to be pulled and the head coach be fired for positioning the team against the administration. In the days that followed, the actions of these individuals were heavily debated with many recognizing the significance the unwillingness to compete could have in the sport arena. Of significance for college athletics was the fact that athletes from the primary revenue generating sport at the University of Missouri reinforced the power they did have. Just 2 days later, on November 9, President Wolfe announced his immediate resignation, and hours later, Chancellor of the University of Missouri, R. Bowen Loftin, indicated he would be stepping down from his position at the end of the academic year.

1. Do you feel it was appropriate for the athletes on the Missouri team to use their positions at the university to call upon the resignation of a system president? What about Coach Pinkel?
2. What are the potential long-term ramifications from the outcome of the team's protest against the administration?
3. What similarities do you see with a number of the other examples provided in this chapter for how athletes have used their status in an attempt to influence change? How might the approach employed here be unique?

CONCLUSION

If there is one lesson to learn from this chapter, it is that there is a responsible way to talk about race and ethnicity in the United States, yet most shy away from doing so because of the ramifications of irresponsible talk. Ignoring differences in participation, media coverage, or language does not ultimately solve the problem. NBC News anchor Tom Brokaw once collaborated with author Jon Entine to examine the facts and fictions about Black athletes; he felt it was one of the most complicated and difficult processes of his life. In 2000, Entine went on to write a controversial book on the subject: *Taboo: Why Black Athletes Dominate Sports and Why We're Afraid to Talk About It.* He argues that there is a reason why, for instance, Kenyan runners do so well in distance events but not in sprints. The attributions are not about skin color but rather about the combination of science and culture. Some saw this reasoning as an advancement; others saw it still lacking a great deal of nuance.

Regardless of where one falls out on these subjects, this chapter, hopefully, provides avenues for conversing about stereotyping versus bias, self-selection, and stacking and linguistic attribution differences versus linguistic racism. Understanding the roles of race and ethnicity in sport is vital to gaining a full sense of perspective on issues such as class, sociology, and individual and collective politics. At its core, it helps to explain who plays what sport, why they do so, and to what effect.

Suggested Additional Reading

Andrews, D. L. (2013). Reflections on communication and sport: On celebrity and race. *Communication & Sport, 1*(1), 151–163.

Birrell, S. (1989). Racial relations theories and sport: Suggestions for a more critical analysis. *Sociology of Sport Journal, 6*(3), 212–227.

Carrington, B. (2007). Sport and race. In G. Ritzer (Ed.), *The Blackwell encyclopedia of sociology* (pp. 4686–4690). Oxford, UK: Blackwell.

Colas, Y. (2016). 'Ball don't lie': Rasheed Wallace and the politics of protest in the National Basketball Association. *Communication & Sport, 4*(2), 123–144.

McDonald, M., & King, S. (2012). A different contender? Barack Obama, the 2008 presidential campaign, and the racial politics of sport. *Ethnic and Racial Studies, 35,* 1023–1039.

Thompkins, J. (2015). 'A postgame interview for the ages': Richard Sherman and the dialectical rhetoric of racial neoliberalism. *Journal of Sport & Social Issues* (Online First).

8

POLITICS AND NATIONALISM IN SPORT

The death of Muhammad Ali in 2016 prompted numerous reflections on a boxer known popularly as "The Greatest." Ali was unquestionably a great champion, but his nickname was as much a product of his persona outside the ring as it was based on his success inside it. Ali first rose to prominence—with his given name Cassius Clay—as a gold medalist in the 1960 Olympics in Rome. He was young, attractive, and charismatic, making him enormously popular in the early 1960s. After winning the heavyweight title, however, Clay announced he would no longer be known by his "slave name"; from then on he was Muhammad Ali.

Source: By Ira Rosenberg

Muhammad Ali in 1967

The name change followed from Ali's association with the Nation of Islam, a religious and Black nationalist organization that played a key role in the Civil Rights Movement. Many "mainstream" observers viewed Ali's politics with suspicion, and some insisted on referring to him by his given name. The name change, then, became symbolic of more than Ali's shifting identity. It also spoke to the political climate of the 1960s, especially with respect to racial politics. Later in the decade, Ali again invited controversy when he spoke against the American war in Vietnam and refused to accept the terms of the military draft. Consequently, he was convicted by a federal court, fined $10,000, and stripped of his heavyweight title. Although the U.S. Supreme Court eventually exonerated him, Ali lost substantial income and 3 years of his prime.

Ali's fight outside the ring with the U.S. military also made him one of the most prominent figures of the antiwar movement and one of the most controversial figures in American culture. In the half-century since this moment Ali's legacy has been reinvented, with many heralding him as one of the most courageous figures of his time. As journalist Dave Zirin reminds us, too often this legacy has been softened, turning a once-radical figure into little more than a safe spokesperson for an allegedly postracial, postwar society. Beyond his titles and his flair for sport as theater, Ali was fundamentally a *political* figure, both in his time and now. As Zirin suggested after Ali's death, the celebration of his life offered a poignant counterpoint to the contemporary politics of 2016, in which the United States experienced the presidential candidacy of Donald Trump and wrestled with ongoing military conflicts abroad. In Zirin's words, Ali's funeral pushed "the country to come together to honor the most famous Muslim in the world at a time when a presidential candidate is running on a program of abject bigotry against the Muslim people, and the other presidential candidate is somebody who has proudly stood with the wars in the Middle East and the suppression of Palestinian rights" ("Dave Zirin," 2016, para 1).

The circumstances of Muhammad Ali's life and death are obviously unique. Nevertheless, the ranges of political meanings assigned to Ali and his actions illustrate the complex political terrain of sport. International sporting events, such as the Olympic Games or golf's Ryder Cup, are largely interpreted as competitions between nations. Political figures routinely appeal to audiences by trying to show their affinities with local and national sports teams. City leaders allocate financial resources to stadium development projects that sometimes exceed costs of $1 billion. For instance, in 2012 the state of Minnesota approved what would become a $1.1 billion football stadium for the National Football League's (NFL's) Vikings. Despite a historic budget deficit that affected Minnesota at the time of the proposal, state and local taxpayers ended up providing nearly $500 million of support (Olson, 2016). In 2015 in Wisconsin, the state approved $250 million public funding for a $500 million arena project for the Milwaukee Bucks, at a time when the state facilitated highly publicized cutbacks in higher education funding (Benjamin, 2015). In spite of these, and other, examples, many sports fans remain hesitant to acknowledge any presence of politics in sport. They prefer to think of sport as a *diversion*, a place for *escape* from "real world" issues.

On the one hand, this makes sense, for it can indeed be a distraction to go to a game or forget about the world's problems while analyzing fantasy statistics. Yet, on the other hand, such a view ignores that sport is a cultural *institution*, one that is inextricably linked with larger economic, political, and social structures. Writing specifically about international sporting events but commenting on sport more broadly, Nauright (2014) contends,

> Even in the face of readily available evidence demonstrating horrible living and working conditions of most workers who produce the goods consumed in and around sports and sporting events and in the face of forced removals, cost overruns, increase [*sic*] taxation, the suppression of democratic rights and freedoms, we enjoy our festivals of nationalist celebration, stories of triumph against adversity, and consume the products proclaiming loyalty to the nation and the brand of sport/event on offer. (p. 284)

Such commentary should not discourage us from celebrating the virtues of sport, but it does compel us to consider its political substance. In this chapter, we examine five specific relationships between sport and politics: (1) how sport has been used by elected officials as a political resource; (2) how sport has worked its way into the language of politics, including war; (3) how sport becomes a means of fostering national identity; (4) how sport has dramatized the effects of globalization; and (5) how sport has been used as a site of political resistance. In this chapter, we examine not only how these functions are political but also how they are expressed communicatively.

Before we move forward it is important that we define what we mean by *politics*. You may have specific images in mind: elected officials, campaign commercials, voting, and so on. Although these certainly are components of politics, it is important to think more broadly. Political theorist Chantal Mouffe (2000) argues that there is an important distinction between the terms *political* and *politics*. The "political," she maintains, reflects the unavoidable conflicts that are inherent in human relations. "Politics," meanwhile, encompasses the practices, discourses, and institutions in and through

THEORETICALLY SPEAKING

HEGEMONY

Scholars in a variety of disciplines have sought to understand how "power" is acquired, maintained, or lost. Hegemony theory addresses these concerns, as it is interested in determining the cultural and social practices that enable political institutions to hold power. The term *hegemony* comes from the writings of Italian theorist Antonio Gramsci (1971), who in the 1930s defined hegemony as the "spontaneous consent" given by the public to the interests of the dominant social order (p. 12). This definition is in contrast to power gained through means of violence—military dictatorships, for example—and focuses more on cultural practices that endorse a dominant ideology. As an institution, sport rarely resists dominant practices and instead favors rituals and symbols that provide "consent." Butterworth's (2010) book, *Baseball and Rhetorics of Purity*, provides an example of communication scholarship that is influenced by hegemony theory. He argues that in the years after the 9/11 terrorist attacks, baseball's symbolic role as the "national pastime" was enacted and performed through multiple rituals and discourses, including memorial ceremonies, museum exhibits, congressional hearings, and more. He concludes that "baseball as rhetoric articulated with a political order that justified preemptive military action, dictated the terms of democratic governance around the world, and restricted democratic practice within the United States" (p. 3). Such a critique is designed to identify symbols of power and to consider alternative ways of communicating about political issues.

- Butterworth, M. L. (2010). *Baseball and rhetorics of purity: The national pastime and American identity during the war on terror.* Tuscaloosa: University of Alabama Press.
- Gramsci, A. (1971). *Selections from the prison notebooks of Antonio Gramsci* (Q. Hoale & G. N. Smith, Trans.). New York, NY: International.

which we seek to address those conflicts and establish order. Politics, therefore, is the means by which we come to terms with conflict and construct collective identities.

Another term that helps us understand the relationship between sport and politics is *ideology*. Ideology can be defined in various ways, but it generally refers to the "system of ideas" of a given class of people (Eagleton, 1991, p. 63). In other words, ideology incorporates the dominant ideas, values, rituals, and history of a group. The more homogeneous a population, the more acceptance there is of a shared ideology. In a populous and diverse country like the United States, there are numerous groups and, thus, numerous ideologies that coexist. Accordingly, many political conflicts are the result of competing ideologies. But not all ideologies operate equally, and it is typically the case that some form of *dominant* ideology exercises greater control. That control might be exercised through formal political institutions such as government, but it also can be found in cultural institutions such as Hollywood cinema or sport. As will become clear, sport is indeed a prominent institution through which ideology is communicated and politics is engaged and enacted. As we proceed, we want to remind you that our focus in this textbook is on American sport. This does not mean that we believe the relationship between sport and politics is relevant only to a U.S. audience, but this chapter is restricted primarily to an American context or an international context featuring U.S. athletes or teams.

SPORT AS POLITICAL RESOURCE

In 1971, the American table tennis team unexpectedly received an invitation to visit China and compete against the Chinese team. Since formal relations between the two countries had long been antagonistic, the subsequent trip to China was seen as a positive development for each government. The moment was popularly described as "ping-pong diplomacy," and President Richard Nixon eagerly capitalized on the new spirit of cooperation by using sport as a springboard for his own subsequent visit to the People's Republic. In this way, the U.S. president recognized that sport could be a valuable political resource.

Nixon was, in fact, acutely aware of sport's significance. His CIA codename at one point, after all, was "Quarterback." Moreover, he was the president who began the tradition of phoning victorious coaches and players after major championship victories. Decades later, presidents and other elected officials continue to recognize the symbolic importance of sport. It is commonplace for candidates for elected office to attend live sporting events in the effort to connect with voters. President Barack Obama, for example, has used his love of sports to build identification with fans, through things such as ESPN's annual feature that reveals the president's picks for the NCAA basketball tournament, commenting on whether or not college athletes should be compensated, or throwing out the first pitch at the 2009 Major League Baseball (MLB) All-Star Game.

The use of sport by politicians is risky, however, for fans are quick to interpret such actions either as manipulations of the sporting context or as awkward attempts to invent a likeable persona. As for the former case, President George W. Bush is yet again a suitable example. When the Iraqi National Soccer team qualified for the 2004 Summer Olympic Games and later experienced unexpected success, the American president claimed that the team's victories were a direct result of U.S. military actions in the Middle East. As Butterworth (2007) demonstrates, this claim was highly controversial, and the majority of the Iraqi players themselves disapproved of Bush's efforts to communicate the triumph of American ideology. Rather than helping to advance American foreign policy, therefore, Bush's use of the Iraqi team instead intensified international criticisms of the president and the U.S. war in Iraq.

Observers generally are unenthusiastic about presidential interventions in international sporting events. President Jimmy Carter was heavily criticized when he decided the United States would boycott the 1980 Summer Olympics in Moscow. The decision was motivated by the Soviet Union's invasion of Afghanistan, but many believed the boycott harmed American athletes more than anyone. A similar debate emerged in 2013 as athletes prepared for the 2014 Winter Olympics in Sochi, Russia. Various groups called for a boycott in response to two politically charged issues: first, Russia passed oppressive legislation authorizing the persecution of gays and lesbians; and second, the Russian government provided asylum to Edward Snowden, an American citizen who leaked information about the U.S. government's surveillance programs. The strongest voices opposed to the boycott were those who drew upon the memories of 1980 and worried that American athletes would be unfairly punished. In both cases, sports media contributed to public perceptions of the boycott threats, framing the stories in terms of a "press nationalism" that affirmed the wisdom of U.S. political leaders (Moretti, 2013).

A different kind of moment from 2004 shows the awkwardness that can emerge from politicians' efforts to reach the public through sports. President Bush's challenger in the presidential election was Massachusetts Senator John Kerry. When Kerry attended a Boston Red Sox game that summer, he was asked to name his favorite player. Stammering through his answer, the senator replied with a hybrid of superstars David Ortiz and Manny Ramirez: "Manny Ortez." The gaffe was perceived as more than a mere slip of the tongue. Rather, it suggested to many observers that Kerry lacked the necessary authenticity to *communicate* effectively about sports. As you will recall from Chapter 2, sport generates an important sense of *community*. By making such an obvious communicative error, then, Kerry marked himself as an outsider to the community of sport and, given the role sport plays in the country more broadly, as a person out of touch with American culture.

Baseball's symbolic importance to the presidency is a product of several rituals, most notable of which is the presidential first pitch. At Game 3 of the 2001 World Series, played in the aftermath of 9/11 at New York's Yankee Stadium, President George W. Bush was able to communicate strength and resolve by standing at the center of the diamond in a time of national crisis. The symbolic importance of that moment has become a part of contemporary baseball folklore, documented by the 2015 short ESPN documentary, *First Pitch* ("About," n.d.). More than responding to the needs of the American public, President Bush was calling upon a history dating back to 1910, when William Howard Taft became the first president to toss a ceremonial pitch from the stands of Washington's National Park. Since that time, nearly every president has

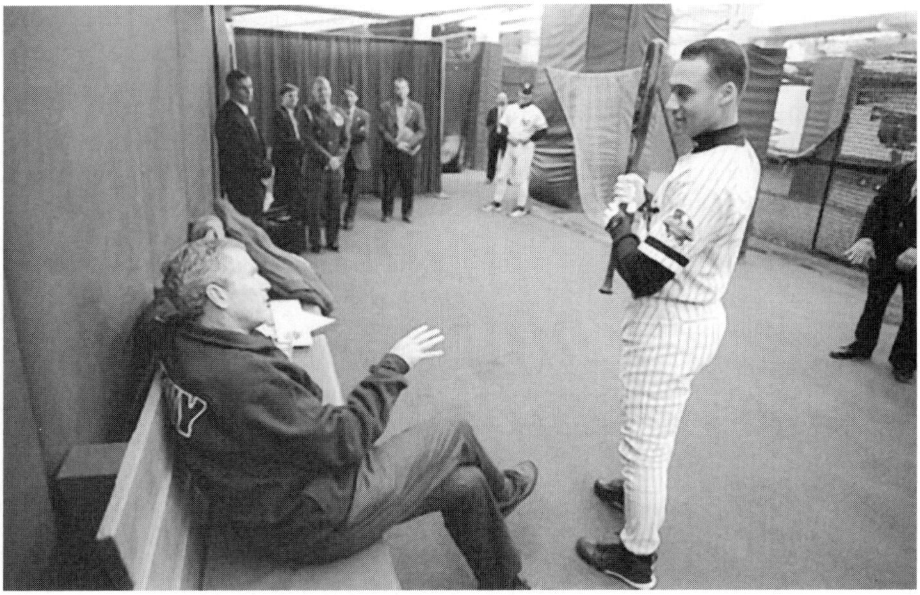

Source: By Office of Management and Administration

President Bush talks with New York Yankees shortstop Derek Jeter before throwing out the first pitch at Game 3 of the 2001 World Series

thrown at least one ceremonial first pitch. Given that baseball has a long history as the "national pastime," these presidential appearances are important communicative rituals that reinforce baseball's mythological connection to essential American values (as we discussed in Chapter 5).

These values are often most important at times of crisis, especially when the nation is at war. After the 1941 bombing of Pearl Harbor, MLB Commissioner Kenesaw Mountain Landis wrote to President Franklin D. Roosevelt to ask if the president wanted the league to suspend play during the 1942 season. "I honestly feel," Roosevelt responded, "it would be best for the country to keep baseball going." These words demonstrated the president's belief that playing baseball *communicated* important messages about strength and community. Years later, in the wake of 9/11, President Bush's campaign echoed this theme during the 2004 election. At the Republican National Convention, the party presented a video demonstrating the president's leadership. The most dramatic storyline in the video was the retelling of Bush's first pitch in 2001, a gesture that the convention audience was told encouraged Americans to "keep pitching, keep pitching."

Presidents also use sport to communicate values when they invite championship teams to visit the White House. Hester (2005) terms these visits "presidential sports encomia," through which presidents "draw attention to examples of athletic achievement that they claim support their visions of national unity and American values" (p. 52). The *encomium* is a classical rhetorical gesture of praise, which points to the fundamentally *communicative* nature of these White House visits. As Hester notes, presidents invite an average of seven sports teams to Washington, D.C., each

Source: By Executive Office of the POTUS

Abby Wambach takes a selfie with the U.S. Women's National Team and President Barack Obama after winning the 2015 World Cup

CASE STUDY

A POLITICAL SLAM DUNK?

As we have noted in this chapter, it is common for the American people to expect candidates to connect with the "common people," and sport serves as an important opportunity for meeting these expectations. As a recent example, during the 2016 Presidential race, Senator Ted Cruz organized a rally at the Hoosier Gym Community Center in Kingstown, Indiana, in an attempt to recreate a famous scene from the movie *Hoosiers*. In the movie, the head coach, played by Gene Hackman, has his players measure the dimensions of the court and hoop in an attempt to signal that, despite playing in a bigger arena and against one of the largest schools in Indiana, they are still playing a familiar game under familiar conditions.

Struggling in the polls at the time, Ted Cruz sought to use his presence in Indiana to draw a parallel between his campaign and the team depicted in *Hoosiers*, showing that despite overwhelming odds, the American people should continue to support his candidacy for President. However, during his presentation to the media and supporters, Cruz made a reference to the basketball hoop being measured as a "basketball ring," which many took to signal his lack of understanding and engagement with the sport of basketball (and by default the American people). Twitter erupted with many referencing the awkwardness of the moment. One Twitter feed noted, "No one has ever called it a 'basketball ring' before Cruz just now in the history of basketball, politics, or words" (Joseph, 2016).

1. Should the average American make any assumptions about a presidential candidate based on a lack of connection to sports?
2. What do you think of Cruz's attempt to draw similarities between his campaign and the fictional depiction of the team in Hoosiers?
3. In what type of situations would a presidential candidate be warranted to draw upon his or her connection with sport in garnering support?

Source: Joseph, A. (2016). Ted Cruz called a basketball hoop a "basketball ring" while recreating a scene from "Hoosiers." *USA Today*. Retrieved from http://ftw.usatoday.com/2016/04/ted-cruz-basketball-ring-hoosiers-indiana-gop-primary

year, demonstrating the extent to which elected officials recognize sport's symbolic power in American culture.

SPORT AND THE LANGUAGE OF POLITICS AND WAR

Even when sport is not being used overtly by politicians, it is often seen as a metaphor for politics itself. Sport and politics share some obvious features: They involve contests, and they usually produce "winners" and "losers." Using sport as a metaphor for politics is problematic, however, as it runs the risk of trivializing serious political issues or short-circuiting substantive debate. Communication scholars, therefore, have focused considerable attention on investigating whether sports metaphors are simply *descriptive* or if they have the capacity to *shape* our understandings of political issues themselves.

At one level, sport is used as a description in order to give language added vitality and force. As Segrave (2000) identifies, boxing metaphors have allowed politicians to embody toughness and determination through their language, while baseball metaphors depend on the familiarity of Americans with their "national pastime." Meanwhile, media often refer to political campaigns as a "horse race" by emphasizing candidates' positions in the race—that is, "front runner," "long shot," and so on. Yet with the rise of the NFL as the nation's most popular sport, it is football that has become "the root metaphor of American political discourse" (p. 51).

Football plays a vital role in political language for at least two reasons, Segrave (2000) maintains. First, it is grounded in a set of values that make teamwork, unity, and respect for authority central to success. The emphasis on "team" is especially important for politicians who seek loyalty and wish to reinforce hierarchy (Bineham, 1991). Second, especially through its mediated production, football cultivates heroic mythologies wherein great men perform great deeds for the benefits of their fellow citizens/fans. These men are great, at least in part, because they are highly specialized at what they do. Thus, the increased specialization found on the football field serves as a metaphor for the technical expertise required of politics and governance.

Left at the level of description, these metaphors provide communicators with colorful figures of speech. Yet, communication scholars have noted that metaphors commonly work on a deeper level, at which they are capable of shaping how we come to see the world. As Beer and de Landtsheer (2004) contend, "The power of metaphor is the power to understand and impose forms of political order. Metaphors reflect, interpret, and construct politics" (p. 30). Consequently, we should reconsider some of the metaphors noted above to examine how they may construct politics in problematic ways.

Let's begin with the "horse race" metaphor. The idea that journalists reduce political campaigns to a "play-by-play" account of who's winning and losing at any given moment has received considerable attention. In a study spanning nearly half a century, for example, Benoit, Stein, and Hansen (2005) discovered that the horse race metaphor was *the most common* topic of newspaper coverage of political campaigns. Although it is important to understand where candidates stand in relation to one another during a campaign, the overemphasis on the race comes at the expense of discussions of substantive issues. Thus, when viewers tuned in to the 2008 presidential debates between Barack Obama and John McCain, rather than hearing about policy differences between the two candidates, they were more likely to hear that McCain needed a "game-changing" performance because he was trailing in the polls. In this way, the use of sport as a political metaphor may actually do damage to the political process, reducing any discussion to "Red Team vs. Blue Team" and any policy stance to the role of a game tactic.

Another concern arises when we revisit the football metaphor. In addition to communicating values of toughness and teamwork, football also is commonly used to describe the military or war. Football's emphasis on territorial control, offense and defense, and militaristic language—such as "bombs," "trenches," and "blitzes"—has produced an almost seamless relationship between the game and warfare. This metaphor is obvious to anyone familiar with the highlight reels of NFL Films or the pregame narratives that hype big games. Yet if it is familiar to you that war is an apt descriptor for football, you may be surprised to see how often football is used to describe warfare. Therein lies another potential problem.

Especially since the first Persian Gulf War (1991), communication and sport scholars have attended to the use of football language to describe war. Perhaps the most famous reference came from U.S. General Norman Schwarzkopf, who referred to a specific military strategy as an attempt to throw a "Hail Mary pass." Not only does this language choice unwittingly position the strategy as one of desperation—a "Hail Mary" is an attempt to complete a deep pass for a touchdown as time expires, a play with a very low percentage of success—it also makes the consequences of military action seem no more significant than the outcome of a football play. The idea that sports metaphors trivialize the seriousness of war is one of the strongest criticisms against using this kind of language.

Sports metaphors also risk equating good citizenship with good fanship. If good fans wear their team's colors and root for their favorite players in good times and bad, and despite any questionable decision making, then the language of sport in politics may also position citizens to acquiesce to the decisions of their elected leaders, whether or not these decisions are in the best interests of the people. Writing about the Persian Gulf War, for example, Herbeck (2004) worries that "football metaphors discouraged substantive discussion of alternatives by casting the American public in the subservient role of the fans" (p. 129). Once again, efforts to use sport as a dramatic figure of speech may end up limiting, or even eliminating, the open discussions of policy that are essential to a democratic society.

Butterworth (2012) argues that such limits on democratic deliberation have become commonplace in highly commercialized sports. In his essay about an exhibit called, "Pro Football and the American Spirit," on display at the Pro Football Hall of Fame in 2008 and 2009, he considers how the valorization of wars from the past reduces Americans'

A MATTER OF ETHICS

POLITICS, SPORT, AND SPONSORSHIP

In the wake of the horrific December, 2012 shootings at Sandy Hook Elementary School in Newtown, Connecticut, American citizens and lawmakers vigorously debated the virtues of gun control. Although most agreed that child safety was crucially important, there was little agreement as to what, if any, laws were needed to prevent future acts of mass violence. Beyond public discussions, then, the debate was waged between lawmakers, including President Barack Obama and the U.S. Congress, and public organizations, such as the National Rifle Association (NRA). The president and the NRA were understood to have deep disagreements that reflected profound divisions among members of the American public.

Sports played a role in helping people in the Newtown area feel they were supported by others around the country. In particular, the National Football League held ceremonies to honor the memories of the children whose lives were lost. In March of 2013, as the public debate about guns and "gun culture" continued, the NRA announced that it would sponsor its first sporting event, a NASCAR race at the Texas Motor Speedway. With that announcement, NRA CEO Wayne LaPierre stated, "NRA members and NASCAR fans love their country and everything that is good and right about America. We salute our flag . . . volunteer in our churches and communities . . . cherish our families . . . and we love racing!"

In light of the Sandy Hook incident and the subsequent debate, the NRA's timing raises important questions. Should a political organization (the NRA lobbies for legislation on behalf of its constituents) sponsor a sporting event? Was the NRA's timing insensitive? What kind of politics does LaPierre suggest is shared between the NRA and fans of NASCAR? Is such a worldview consistent with your understanding of sport's role in American culture?

willingness to contemplate the role of war in the present. He especially focuses on the display about Pat Tillman, the former NFL player who gave up his career to join the Army Rangers after the terrorist attacks of 9/11. Tillman's death in 2004 became a rallying cry for heroic sacrifice, but later details revealed not only that he had been accidentally killed by one of his fellow Rangers but also that Tillman's own feelings about the war in Afghanistan were complicated. Nevertheless, Tillman's memory was routinely used by the NFL and the broadcast networks to tap into feelings of patriotism and nationalism. By presenting a sanitized narrative about Tillman's sacrifice alongside other memorials to professional football players who served in the military, and by completing omitting any reference to resistance or dissent from war, the Hall of Fame exhibit "reduced citizenship to flags and anthems and foreclosed honoring dissent as a critical democratic function" (Butterworth, 2012, p. 254).

Meanwhile, although militarism has largely been understood as an *American* phenomenon, it is clear that alignments between sport and the military have gained favor elsewhere. Scherer and Koch (2010), for example, explain that practices from the United States have influenced Canadian sport. They argue that the "Ticket for Troops" event, sponsored by the NHL and broadcast on national television, provides symbolic support for a war (Afghanistan) that was highly controversial among Canadian citizens. The high-profile platform of the most popular sport in Canada, therefore, provided "high-ranking military officials, Canadian soldiers, and Conservative political leaders . . . an uncontested platform to speak to a national audience and promote Canada's role in Afghanistan as a matter of national interest for *both* countries" (p. 16). Studies such as these thus remind us that although sport can be a form of diversion it often participates in the very problems and issues from which we wish to escape.

SPORT AND NATIONAL IDENTITY

One manifestation of politics is the ability to cultivate and maintain a national identity. Indeed, because it is often seen as an idealized symbol of a collective identity, sport's relationship to nations and nationalism has attracted the considerable attention of communication and sport scholars. What is a "nation?" Your initial response may be to think in terms of a "country," a place governed by a shared economic and political system with discrete physical borders. In fact, this is the conventional understanding of the "nation-state," a concept that finds its origins in the 17th and 18th centuries. Upon further reflection, however, it may occur to you that the term *nation* is often used to describe alliances of sports fans—for example, "Red Sox Nation," or "NASCAR Nation." Can we understand each use of the word in similar terms? Perhaps, in part because the concept of nationalism is more fluid and dynamic than traditional definitions might allow.

One influential theory of nationalism comes from Anderson (1991), who argues that a nation is a symbolic construct, what he calls an "imagined community." This suggests that national identity is less a product of geography or government and more a product

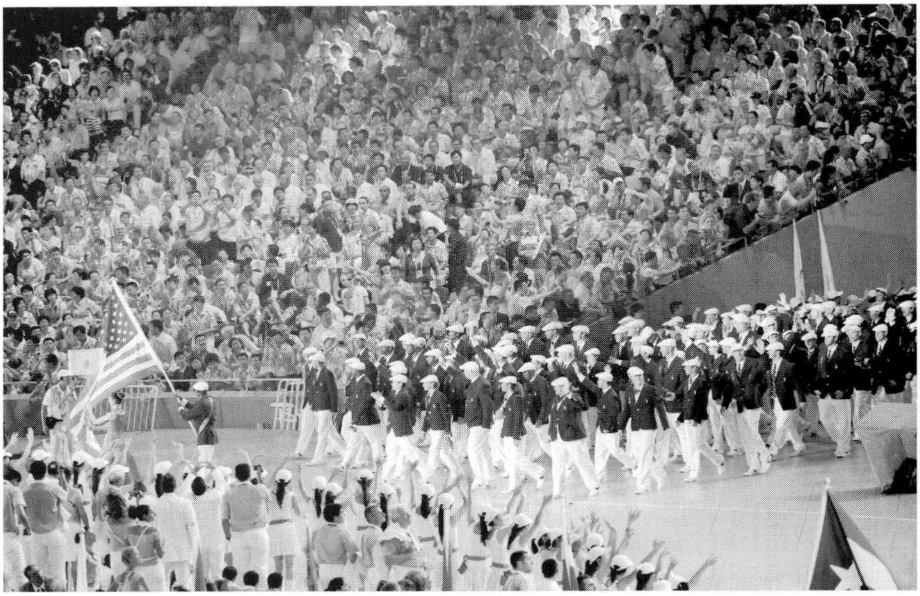

Source: Tim Hipps, U.S. Army [Public domain], via Wikimedia Commons

Team USA at 2008 Beijing Summer Olympic Opening Ceremony

of shared histories, myths, and ideology. You may recall from Chapter 5 that mythology plays a large role in communicating values shared by many Americans. For instance, the idea that the United States is a place where freedom and opportunity are available to an extent that has no precedent in history contributes greatly to the collective identity of its citizenry. In other words, by *imagining* that America fosters a particular kind of *community*, a national identity begins to emerge. Sport is especially important in this process because its shared experience makes it one of the few institutions capable of developing a "collective consciousness" (Rowe, 1999, p. 22).

Allison (2000) argues that "national identity is the most marketable product in sport" (p. 346). A primary reason for this is that when a sporting event has a national appeal, it draws much higher ratings for television. Consequently, when communication scholars examine the relationship between sport and nationalism, they often do so by studying mass media. The Olympic Games provide arguably the most obvious site for researching how television influences our understanding of national identity. As Billings and Eastman (2003) state, "the Olympics represents a mix of nationalism, internationalism, sport, and human drama unmatched by any other event" (p. 569). Their study examined the National Broadcasting Company's (NBC) coverage of the 2002 Winter Olympics in Salt Lake City, Utah. Particularly because the Games followed so soon after 9/11, "NBC created an unabashedly patriotic telecast" (p. 570). Even with 9/11 now more than 15 years in the past, Olympic coverage continues to emphasize these themes, as Billings, Brown, and Brown (2013) conclude that heavy viewers of the 2012 London Games were likely to express more nationalistic, patriotic, or even smug attitudes. Subsequent research affirms this conclusion, especially when applied to a large, highly successful nation like the United States (Billings et al., 2013). It may not be that Olympic coverage causes

INTERVIEW

CHRISTINE BRENNAN, *USA TODAY* SPORTS COLUMNIST

Q: George Orwell argued that sport is like "war minus the shooting." How true is this statement in international sporting competitions?

A: Pretty true, but I say that with a smile—most of the time. In 1994, Sweden won the Olympic gold medal in men's ice hockey. I was in the press center, and we would hear this roar from the offices of Swedish newspapers and news organizations when Sweden would score a goal. For smaller countries that don't win that often, that is one of the great charms of the Olympics.

For me, it was the 1980 Miracle on Ice hockey game. That's the metaphor—war minus the shooting—in this case, Mike Eruzione scoring the winning goal. All of our nation's problems melted away for a few hours, and we celebrated as a country. Years later, I was discussing the game with a Russian figure skating coach, and she didn't know what I was talking about. The loss didn't resonate for them the same way the win did with us. It's about context.

Q: If assessing nationalism within sports media, to what degree is it still "us versus them"?

A: Certainly in print and on air, the U.S. press never uses *us* or *we*. For me, it may slip in casual conversation, but anything for the record—never. Many other nations don't make the distinction, but the United States is so big and wins so many medals, plus, most important, our press is not run by our government, so we avoid it. I understand why South Africa or Nigeria would use *us* or *we*.

The other big point is that major rivalries no longer exist since the fall of the Soviet Union and, to a lesser extent, East Germany. We're glad it's gone; nobody's lamenting the loss of the Soviet Union. Still, we all love the concept of "your team versus the hated enemy." You live for that. China wants to be a player but will never mean to the United States what the Soviet Union did. No U.S. citizen can muster the immense dislike and even hatred toward China that we had then.

Q: What role does politics play in events such as the World Cup and the Olympics?

A: I'm amused when people or commentators say there is no place for politics in sports. It's never *just* about sports in international competition. Flags and anthems make it special. Watching such events even helps children learn about geography and other global issues. At the Ryder Cup in 1999, there is a prickly memory because the American golfers celebrated too early before a match was over, but no war started, obviously. If the big battle is who jumped around on the 17th green in Brookline, we're OK.

Q: For women, what impact does an athlete's citizenship have on the opportunities she has within sport?

A: It's about creating role models. For me growing up, I had my own personal Title IX—my father and mother—but for many others, it was about watching your countrywomen and cheering for them. President Obama recently said, "My girls look at the TV when I'm

(Continued)

INTERVIEW (Continued)

watching *SportsCenter*, and they see women staring back. That shows them that they can be champions, too." I can imagine this is even truer for women from other countries.

Q: Thomas Friedman argues that "the world is flat." How true is this in sports?

A: It's true but with way more advantages than disadvantages. There will be growing pains. We've seen that in the LPGA as they took a lot of criticism for how they were insisting their international players speak English. It was handled poorly, but you need a common language. You can't just go on hand signals; communication is essential.

You also run into this at the U.S. college level, where many international athletes are now taking scholarships at NCAA institutions that could have gone to American student-athletes. Still, the university is a place to come and learn, and this is another moment for that. I can see the concern, but are we opening up our world to others, or are we not? So, it's not just the world that is flattening, it's also the field of play.

these outcomes so much as it provides an outlet for people to express already held beliefs (Brown, Billings, Schallhorn, Schramm, & Brown-Devlin, 2016; Devlin & Billings, 2016). Nevertheless, few media events provide more opportunities than the Olympics for fans to channel feelings of patriotism and nationalism.

A component of these studies is the use of *framing theory*, an approach to media studies that examines how print and broadcast journalists tell stories so that particular themes or values are featured over others. Delgado (2003) also uses this theory in his study of newspaper coverage of a match between the United States and Iran during the 1998 World Cup finals. Because the two countries had a poor relationship, many sportswriters positioned the match as a symbolic contest over competing ideologies. Even as most players and coaches insisted that they were not interested (or even aware of) the match's politics, newspaper accounts used political terms to create a dominant frame. Some stories interpreted the match as a diplomatic effort between the United States and Iran not unlike the "ping-pong diplomacy" we discussed at the outset of the chapter. Thus, as Delgado argues, this narrative frame used politics and nationalism as rhetorical strategies to make this sporting event seem important to American sports fans who otherwise largely ignore soccer.

Narrative cinema also is a prominent site for expressing national identity. Movies such as *Seabiscuit* (2003) and *Cinderella Man* (2005) are popular largely because they use historical events to celebrate the core values that comprise American ideology. *Seabiscuit* recalls the story of a thoroughbred race horse who became a symbol of hope for Americans in the midst of the Great Depression. *Cinderella Man*, meanwhile, is the story of boxer Jim Braddock, who also became a depression-era symbol of triumph over adversity. In the case of these films, the celebrated values are those of individualism, hard work, and perseverance. The 2008 film, *The Express*, meanwhile, highlights Ernie Davis as the first African American Heisman Trophy winner; the 2013 film, *42*, dramatizes Jackie Robinson's story as the first African American to play Major League Baseball in the modern era; and the 2016 film *Race*, recalls Jesse Owens's triumph at the 1936 Berlin Olympics. Each of the films use historic sporting moments to affirm the democratic virtues of inclusion and social progress that are prominent components of identity in the United States.

There is a fine line between fostering national unity and cultivating an attitude that either stereotypes or denigrates other identities. Too often, sports narratives overemphasize the "us" versus "them" storyline to the point of influencing political attitudes (Jhally, 1989). Once again, reactions to 9/11 in the United States provide a useful example for communication scholars. When sports leagues returned to action after the terrorist attacks, they each used their games as a means to show resolve, patriotism, and unity. Brown (2004) notes that "sport can be seen as providing solemn opportunities to mourn the dead, patriotic messages to inspire, salutes to honor the life-saving efforts of all involved, messages to re-enforce unity amongst Americans and remind everyone that life must go on" (p. 41). Yet he also points out that the emphasis on military imagery brought risks of positively associating sport with war. Butterworth (2005) extends this theme by arguing that patriotic ceremonies at baseball games quickly moved from rituals of healing to expressions of militarism and an endorsement of war. The transition was perhaps best illustrated by the inclusion of "God Bless America" as a mandatory performance during the 7th-inning stretch of all baseball games. The song not only guaranteed a nationalistic element would be present at games but also conflated national unity with the military because it was commonly performed by members of the United States Armed Forces. As a result, Butterworth maintains that sport communicated a hostile and belligerent attitude at a time when the United States was engaged in controversial military actions in the Middle East. In each case, these scholars emphasize that sport, far from being a distraction from matters of politics, served the political function of affirming national identity at a time of crisis.

SPORT AND GLOBALIZATION

Because nationalism is frequently on display during international sporting events such as the Olympics, World Cup, or a Grand Slam tennis tournament, it is also important to think about politics and national identity in the context of ***globalization***. Maguire (2006) concludes that globalization can be understood as "the growing network of interdependencies—political, economic, cultural, and social—that bind human beings together, for better and for worse" (p. 436). Although globalization is not a new phenomenon, it has intensified in recent decades. Among the consequences of this development is that individuals are exposed to multiple forms of media, politics, and economics, thus calling their "national identity" into question. Globalization is affected by numerous institutions, including sport. Rowe (2013) acknowledges the importance of *sport* and connects globalization specifically to *communication*. As he notes, "Communication is central here not only because it is through the wide-ranging, mediated circulation of symbols that the nation can be made easily recognizable to the large, dispersed, and heterogeneous audiences that comprise it, but because sport is unquestionably one of the most potent sources of vibrant, compressed national symbolism" (p. 22).

One of the central debates regarding globalization has to do with the extent of American influence around the world. Perhaps you are familiar with Barber's (1995) *Jihad vs. McWorld*, in which he describes the global influence of American corporations such as McDonald's and Disney. Critics of such influences are likely to worry that the United States is engaged in a project of "cultural imperialism," wherein the integrity of national identity is threatened by the penetration of U.S. popular culture and ideology into native cultures. The presence of a LeBron James jersey in Spain may sound like good marketing to the National Basketball Association (NBA), but to some Spanish citizens it could feel invasive. For an example of how Americans react to the "intrusion" of an unpopular domestic sport, consider the outpouring of criticism against soccer each time it appears the sport may gain exposure in the United States. Perhaps the most dramatic example of this was the attention given to British superstar David Beckham's arrival in the United States to play for Major League Soccer (MLS). Much of the American sporting public felt it was much ado about nothing, while many international fans mocked Beckham's choice to play in a lesser league. Meanwhile, many fans and players have grown resentful of the NFL playing regular season games in England or MLB playing regular season games in Japan because these decisions appear to destabilize these sports' central place in the nation. The LPGA has been trying to adapt to a "Korean invasion" in which the Tour is deemed less palatable by some because of the unfamiliar names at the top of the leaderboard. The point here is that globalization does not operate in only one direction. Indeed, the United States *feels* its effects as much as it *produces* them.

Regardless of direction, globalization is seen by some as a threat to national identity. The increase of Japanese ownership of American businesses in the 1980s and 1990s produced cultural anxieties about a perceived loss of identity. When this trend affected ownership of baseball's Seattle Mariners, those anxieties were expressed through a fear that "America's pastime" was under siege from "foreign" interests (Ono, 1997). Similarly, in 2010, Russian businessman Mikhail Prokhorov became the owner of the NBA's Brooklyn Nets, prompting some anxieties reminiscent of the U.S.-Soviet Cold War. Across the ocean, British football (soccer) fans were upset when American millionaire Malcolm Glazer purchased the storied Manchester United franchise in 2005. Such moments are reminders that our imagined communities place great emphasis on their sports teams as symbols of their identities.

Part of the outcry in these incidents is surely the concerns about commercialization (for more on this, see Chapter 14). Globalization facilitates the exchange of capital and, because sport is a valuable commodity, leagues and players alike seek new opportunities across increasingly fluid geographical, economic, and political borders. An exemplary case of this occurred in 2002, when the New York Yankees reached an agreement with Manchester United to cross-market their franchises. As Miller (2004) explains, "The Yankees are world-renowned but world-unwatched, and Manchester United is no doubt covetous of opening up the wealthiest and most protected market in the world—sport in the United States" (p. 244). Although the agreement ultimately produced little of note, it is indicative of the cross-promotion and synergy strategies that characterize contemporary capitalism.

More than ever, sport is a truly international affair. Nearly 30% of Major League Baseball rosters are made up of players born outside the United States. The NBA is wildly popular around the world. The FOX and NBC networks televise European football (soccer). The biggest stars in tennis come from nearly every corner of the world. Meanwhile, 1.5 billion will watch the World Cup finals and the Olympics remain the "biggest show on television" (Billings, 2008). All of which makes the ideas of *nation* and *nationalism* particularly interesting phenomena for communication and sport scholars. Perhaps most important is to keep in mind that the relationship between sport and globalization reveals important dimensions of international cooperation. As Jarvie (2003) suggests, "the choice between global and local sport" is a false one (p. 549). Instead, contemporary sport is scene of a developing sense of *internationalism* and *cosmopolitanism*.

SPORT AND RESISTANCE

Even in a democracy, politics entails power. Power may be defined in various ways, but our most common understanding assumes that individuals possess power, with which they make decisions about access, opportunity, and resources. Because not everyone will have equal access to power, there will be those who are placed on the margins or even excluded from mainstream society. Consequently, the opposing side to power is *resistance*. More specifically, resistance can be understood in dynamic tension with power, for the ability to resist is itself a form of power (Tomlinson, 1998). Resistance can take many forms, some of which we examine in Chapter 9. In this chapter, we address the ways in which athletes have used sport as a means for resisting governments or formal political policies. In particular, we look to exemplars of participation in social movements, through which we can better understand the communicative role of sport in the resistance to power and dominant ideology.

Because sport is public and popular, it can become a site for productive political struggle and social change. For example, consider the legacy of Jackie Robinson, who, in 1947, became the first African American to play major league baseball in the modern era. Robinson's presence on the Brooklyn Dodgers—one of MLB's signature franchises—embodied a form of resistance to the social and cultural inequities of the era. Remember that this moment occurred nearly a decade before the advent of the Civil Rights movement. Given baseball's cultural significance at the time, it is difficult to overestimate the impact Robinson had on affecting American attitudes about race. Thus, sportswriter Bob Ryan (2002) calls the moment "the single most important social happening in American sports history."

As we discussed earlier, during the Civil Rights movement of the 1950s and 1960s, Muhammad Ali used his boxing celebrity as a platform to resist racism and war. Other athletes of the time embraced similar convictions. Arthur Ashe critiqued the apartheid

Source: Photo by Bob Sandberg Look photographer [Public domain], via Wikimedia Commons

Jackie Robinson

government of South Africa while his fellow tennis star Billie Jean King fought for women's equality. Yet perhaps the signature image of protest came from two Americans at the 1968 Olympic Games in Mexico City. After winning the gold and bronze medals in the 200m sprint, Tommie Smith and John Carlos used the medal ceremony to protest racial inequalities within the United States. As the national anthem played, the two men bowed their heads and raised fists clad in black gloves. The protest was largely interpreted as a sign of "Black power," and it resulted in both sprinters' dismissal from the Olympics. Nevertheless, it was fundamentally a *communicative* gesture, one that "created a moment of resistance and confrontation with dominant and existing forms of racial identity" (Bass, 2002, p. 239). As Hartmann (2003) details, despite the negative impression the protest made on many Americans at the time, people who see the image now typically associate positive values with it. In other words, it was a moment of resistance that has retained significant communicative power, even as social and political conditions have changed over the decades.

The 1960s and 1970s are often remembered as especially turbulent years in American history. During that time, sport was a site for challenging some of the political injustices that had too often been left unexamined. As a result, athletes such as Ali and King were able to use sport as a platform to advocate and advance social movements such as the civil rights movement or second-wave feminism. In the years since, however, fewer athletes have used sport as an outlet for political resistance. The explanation for this, at least in part, likely has something to do with the explosion of electronic sports media and the incredible rise in player income. In the words of sportswriter Robert Lipsyte (2002), "Forget about expressing yourself politically or socially; just wear the shoes; take the money and run" (p. 28).

The so-called decline of the "activist-athlete" is the subject of a book by Khan (2012), who uses the case of baseball player Curt Flood to argue that contemporary athletes are, in many cases, simply fulfilling the ambitions of the politically engaged athletes of previous generations. When Flood refused to accept a trade from the St. Louis Cardinals to the Philadelphia Phillies prior to the 1969 season, he issued a challenge to MLB's infamous "reserve clause," a policy that gave teams almost complete authority over player contracts. Flood ultimately lost his legal battle in a 1972 Supreme Court decision, but his actions made possible the move to free agency that became institutionalized in professional sports in the mid-to-late 1970s. Khan argues that critics of contemporary athletes who are apolitical often miss that the very thing Curt Flood fought for was the right to personal and economic self-determination. This is precisely what our political system values, and Khan therefore concludes, "Instead of demanding more from the framework of our political culture, we take our shots at Michael [Jordan] and Tiger [Woods] for their refusal to be Jackie [Robinson] and Curt [Flood], when perhaps who they are is exactly who liberalism hoped they would be" (p. 25)

Even if it is less common to see athletes model political resistance that was characteristic of earlier eras, there are those who feel compelled to express themselves politically. Steve Nash of the NBA responded to the American invasion in Iraq in 2003 by wearing a "No War" t-shirt. Carlos Delgado of MLB refused to participate in the orchestrated "God Bless America" ritual in 2004. In 2009, Andy Roddick withdrew from a prominent tennis tournament in the United Arab Emirates because officials refused to allow Israeli player Shahar Peer to enter the women's competition. In 2012, NHL goaltender Tim Thomas refused to accept the invitation from President Obama to celebrate the Boston Bruins' Stanley Cup championship at the White House. In 2013, Dwayne Wade posed for an *Ebony* cover with his sons wearing "hoodies" to continue a pattern of protest from members of the Miami Heat who objected to shooting death in Florida of Trayvon Martin and the subsequent acquittal of his killer, George Zimmerman. Although these moments may lack the dramatic effect of Ali's defiance or the visual impact of Smith and Carlos's protest, they nevertheless serve as reminders that, like people in all walks of life, athletes do have the capacity and, at times, opportunity to challenge political power.

The Trayvon Martin incident is symptomatic of renewed racial tensions in American society. In recent years, his death, alongside the deaths of other young African American males, such as Michael Brown (Ferguson, MO), Tamir Rice (Cleveland, OH), Eric Garner (New York City), and Alton Sterling (Baton Rouge, LA), has spotlighted issues of racial inequality and police violence. As the incidents mount, so too has the willingness of athletes to speak out in ways that echo the social movements of the 1960s and 1970s. For example, several college and professional basketball teams wore shirts displaying "ICan'tBreathe," the last words spoken by Eric Garner when he died while being placed in a police choke hold. Several members of the St. Louis Rams football team entered the field with their hands up in a symbol echo of Michael Brown's alleged plea, "Hands up, don't shoot!" And, after police killed Alton Sterling and Philando Castile (Falcon Heights, MN) in 2016, the NBA's Carmelo Anthony placed an ad in the *New York Daily News* calling for his fellow players to speak out against what he believed to be racially motivated violence (Florio, 2016). Later in 2016, political expression about racial justice coalesced around the actions of San Francisco 49ers quarterback, Colin Kaepernick, who sought to bring attention to ongoing concerns by refusing to stand during the national anthem ritual prior to each game. Although he received substantial criticism from those inside and outside of sports, Kaepernick also earned praise and saw other athletes follow his lead (Keown, 2016). Political activism from athletes certainly is not restricted to issues concerning race; however, the persistence of racial tensions and the prominent participation of African American athletes in the highest profile sports in the United States provides a compelling context for understanding the relationship between politics and sport.

Meanwhile, sport organizations may also begin to play a greater role in political resistance. For example, in 2010 the State of Arizona passed new legislation to curtail illegal immigration. Many argued that the law's language encouraged police to profile Latinos and, as a result, was racist. In response to the controversy, Phoenix Suns owner Robert Sarver had his team suit up for a Cinco de Mayo playoff game in jerseys stitched with "Los Suns." Sarver acknowledged his decision was not only to honor the holiday but also as a protest against "a flawed state law." The "Los Suns" jerseys provoked considerable discussion in the community of sport, making it a significant communicative moment both for those in support of and those opposed to the decision. Moreover, the decision overlapped with efforts from national lawmakers to pressure Major League Baseball Commissioner Bud Selig to move the site of the 2011 All-Star Game from Phoenix (the game was not moved). While these efforts may or may not become a model for other franchises and players to follow, it is nevertheless a compelling moment that makes real the relationship between politics and sport so often believed not to exist.

CONCLUSION

In this chapter, we have reviewed some of the major contributions of communication scholars interested in sport and politics. The symbolic use of sport by politicians, the interplay of sporting and political language, the cultivation of sporting nationalisms, the relationship between sport and globalization, and the necessity for resistance within sport are key features of this relationship. Despite the common claims that sport and politics should be separate, it should be clear that this is impossible. Indeed, if politics are about managing conflict and constituting identities, the question isn't about whether or not sport *is* political, it is about *how* sport is political. In the words of sportswriter Dave Zirin, "However you slice and dice it, politics are an enduring, constant, and historic presence in sports" (King, 2008, p. 335).

Suggested Additional Readings

Butterworth, M. L. (2014). Nate Silver and campaign 2012: Sport, the statistical frame, and the rhetoric of electoral forecasting. *Journal of Communication, 64*, 895–914.

Butterworth, M. L. (2014). Public memorializing in the stadium: Mediated sport, the 10th anniversary of 9/11, and the illusion of democracy. *Communication & Sport, 2*, 203–224.

Gorsevski, E. W., & Butterworth, M. L. (2011). Muhammad Ali's fighting words: The paradox of violence in nonviolent rhetoric. *Quarterly Journal of Speech, 97*, 50–73.

Fischer, M. (2014). Commemorating 9/11 NFL style: Insights into America's culture of militarism. *Journal of Sport & Social Issues, 38*, 199–221.

Jansen, S. C., & Sabo, D. (1994). The sport/war metaphor: Hegemonic masculinity, the Persian Gulf War, and the new world order. *Sociology of Sport Journal, 11*, 1–17.

Riggs, K. E., Eastman, S. T., & Golobic, T. S. (1993). Manufactured conflict in the 1992 Olympics: The discourse of television and politics. *Critical Studies in Mass Communication, 10*, 253–272.

Silk, M. L. (2011). *The cultural politics of post-9/11 American sport: Power, pedagogy, and the popular*. London, UK: Routledge.

Silk, M. L., Andrews, D. L., & Cole, C. L. (Eds.). (2005). *Sport and corporate nationalisms*. Oxford, UK: Berg.

9

PERFORMING IDENTITY IN SPORT

When we look at athletes, what do we see? Do we see strength and power? Grit and determination? Or, perhaps we see the markers of identity—the skin color that we associate with race or the hair length that signals gender? Although much public and media commentary celebrates the athleticism of sports figures, it is often done without a conscious awareness of the foundation of that athleticism. In other words, when we look at athletes, we see *bodies*. These are bodies sculpted and molded for highly specialized activities, and the fact that they are used in the pursuit of victory means that we inordinately value the bodies of athletes. As Houck (2006a) notes, "What sorts of public and commodified bodies showcase health, success, physical desirability, and relational bliss? Almost without exception they are athletic bodies—toned, fit, in control, and active" (p. 545). Thus, as a culture, we take a great interest in how bodies *perform* and what those performances *communicate*.

Our idea of performance probably means something different than what you have in mind. When you think of athletic performance, you likely are evaluating whether or not an athlete is successful. In communication scholarship, however, performance takes on additional levels of meaning. The visual attention given to bodies, athletic or otherwise, generally operates at the level of *representation*. Thus, our attention to gender (Chapter 6) or race and ethnicity (Chapter 7) in this textbook focuses mostly on how athletes are represented in and by the media. This approach is valuable, yet it does not account fully for the *presentation of self* that comes through bodily performances. Fenske (2007), drawing from the foundational work of theorist Judith Butler, suggests that focusing *only* on representation limits the ability of individual people, including athletes, to shape their own identities in accordance with their values and self-concepts.

With this in mind, we turn our attention in this chapter to the performances of identity that occur in and through sport. More specifically, we concentrate on the relationship between sport and the body, which we interpret as a "site of cultural inscription, self-regulation, and resistance" (Patterson & Corning, 1997, p. 7). This demands that we think of athletic performances as having an influence over interpretations of identity categories such as gender or race. Thus, to some extent, this chapter revisits some of the themes discussed elsewhere in this book. However, our focus here is on *performance* rather than *representation*, which allows us to examine additional dimensions of identity. These performative dimensions are significant because they communicate the willingness either to accept or resist the norms and dominant expectations of bodies in our culture. We proceed, then, with discussions of the (a) performance of gender and sexuality; (b) performance of race and ethnicity; and (c) performance of disability.

PERFORMANCE OF GENDER AND SEXUALITY

In the summer of 2009, a little-known South African sprinter won the women's 800-meter event at the track and field world championships. Caster Semenya not only won, she destroyed the field by nearly two and a half seconds (an enormous margin in elite track competition). Almost as soon as she crossed the finish line, she was confronted by accusations that she was not really a woman. To be sure, her physique resembles characteristics typically understood as "masculine"—thick muscles, a deep voice, and so on. Moreover, Semenya *performs* masculinity by eschewing conventional displays of femininity—she wears baggy clothing, avoids make-up, and so on. In the midst of growing controversy about her "sex," the International Association of Athletics Federations (IAAF) ordered a "gender test" in order to determine Semenya's eligibility for women's events. In response, media outlets fueled rampant speculation about the test's results, and one tabloid went so far as to discern that an anagram of Caster Semenya is "Yes, a secret man." Meanwhile, Semenya herself replied with an appearance on the cover of a South African magazine called *You*. The photo, accompanied by the headline, "Wow, Look at Caster Now," presented her in full make-up and a dress. The message was clear: In order for Semenya to be accepted as a woman, she needed to *perform* like one. The effort to reinvent her image largely failed, primarily because her initial success had been framed by cultural assumptions about race and gender (Young, 2015).

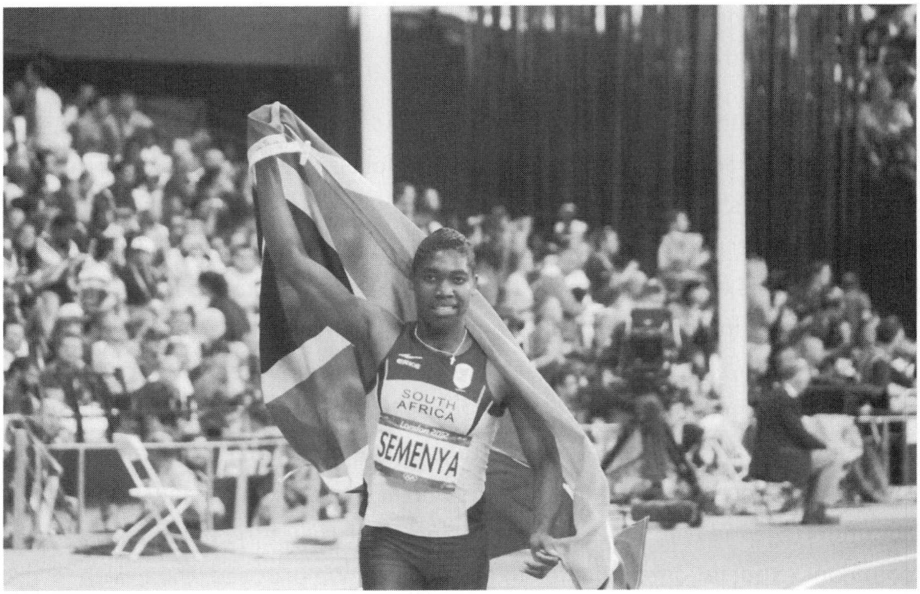

Caster Semenya

The Caster Semenya case recalls the controversy precipitated by the appearance in 1976 of Renee Richards, a male-to-female transsexual who participated in a professional tennis tournament. Once discovered, Richards indicated her desire to participate in the U.S. Open (one of tennis's four major tournaments). In response, the United States Tennis Association and the Women's Tennis Association (WTA) mandated she take a sex test, which she refused. A 1977 Supreme Court ruling subsequently allowed Richards to play on the WTA tour, which included her participation in the 1977 U.S. Open. Richards lost in the first round, but she continued to play on the tour until 1981. Although she had relatively little success on the court, she provoked significant anxiety in the tennis community, primarily because her performance of gender disrupted cultural expectations about how we communicate what it means to be a man or woman. More specifically, she threatened to cast doubt on the conventional wisdom that insists there are "two apparently natural, mutually exclusive, 'opposite' sexes" (Birrell & Cole, 1990, p. 2).

Semenya and Richards reveal a great deal about how we understand sex and gender, especially as they relate to sport. As you'll recall from Chapter 6, *sex* is most commonly understood as the biological difference between men and women. *Gender*, meanwhile, is a social category, one that emerges and develops in a given culture. Wood (2009) adds that gender "is defined by society and expressed by individuals as they interact with others and media in their society. Further, gender changes over time" (p. 23). As is evident by the IAAF's use of a "gender test" when attempting to determine Semenya's biological attributes—that is, her sex—there is much confusion about how these terms relate to one another. Moreover, because gendered norms change over time, there is additional confusion over what constitutes being a "man" or "woman." This is why Semenya's choice to perform her gender by defaulting to conventional markers of femininity—that is, dresses and make-up—is so revealing, especially given long-standing fears leading some to conclude that "the better [athlete] one is as a woman, the more likely that one is, in fact, a man" (Sloop, 2012, p. 85). It also is why the physical transformation of Richards from a man to a woman complicates the natural assumptions that one is *either* a man *or* a woman. At a moment when former Olympic hero Bruce Jenner is hailed for her transformation to Caitlyn, and various transgender athletes struggle to find a place in competitive athletics (Kahrl, 2016), we are reminded that sport is a particularly important site for examining how gender identity is performed and what implications those performances may have on our culture at large.

The idea of gender performance—or, more accurately, performativity—derives from the work of Judith Butler. Butler (1999) contends that gender is not something we *are*, it is something we *do*. In addition, for our actions to be understood as performative, they must be repeated so that they become naturalized. In American culture, for example, women commonly greet one another with a hug using both arms. Men, meanwhile, often opt for a half-hug and slap on the back that serves as an extension of a handshake. It is safe to conclude, then, that if two (heterosexual) men in the United States were to greet each other with a full embrace, they would immediately be seen as performing (if only temporarily) a feminine identity. Thus, the norms of gender are highly regulated by social expectations. In part, those expectations emerge from the institutions of popular culture, including sport. Because sport features such ritualized performances of gender, it is arguably "the most important public arena for the performance of gender as an asymmetrical, oppositional relation based on natural sex differences" (Disch & Kane, 2000, p. 126).

There is considerable support for the idea that sport reinforces a male/female, masculine/feminine essentialism. Accordingly, it is in the moments when gender norms are disrupted or challenged that we often find them reinforced most vigorously. Sloop (2005), for example, evaluates the performative dimensions of Deborah Renshaw's presence in auto racing. In 2002, Renshaw was a rising star in the lower division of NASCAR, someone viewed as both a skilled driver inside the car and a marketable personality outside of it. On the one hand, her participation as a professional driver helped redraw the boundaries of what is considered to be properly feminine. However, racing promoters and Renshaw herself were careful to emphasize her attractive appearance and conventional feminine performances when she was not behind the wheel (not unlike the far more famous Danica Patrick). Even more significantly, when she was involved in a crash that led to the death of another driver, many within the racing community argued that Renshaw should never have been allowed on the circuit in the first place. Her intrusion, then, was met with a vigorous "preservation of male space" that sought to re-establish auto racing as a uniquely masculine domain (Sloop, 2005, p. 206).

A similar reaction followed Katie Hnida when she joined the University of Colorado football team as a walk-on place-kicker in 1999. Butterworth (2008) notes that Hnida's presence on the team constituted an embodied argument that potentially blurred the lines between masculinity and femininity. Like Renshaw, Hnida was largely viewed as

CASE STUDY

PERFORMING MATERNITY IN THE WNBA

As this chapter attests, men and women are asked to perform their sport identities in unique and different ways under an unusual set of standards. For example, male soccer players commonly remove their shirts after scoring a goal, yet Brandi Chastain was heavily criticized for performing a similar act during the 1999 Women's World Cup. Most viewed it as an explicit sexual act rather than an individual celebration commonly performed by male athletes in the sport. In women's basketball, Sheryl Swoopes had been a standout collegiate player winning the Sportswoman of the Year honors and a gold medal as a member of the USA women's basketball team during the 1996 Olympic Games. Her appeal to women's basketball led Nike to develop the Nike Swoopes line of shoes and featured her as the prominent female basketball equivalent to Michael Jordan.

Shortly after the Women's National Basketball Association (WNBA) was formed, Swoopes was logically selected as the first-round draft pick by the Houston Comets. Shortly afterward, the league and the team faced a potential setback as it was reported that its premier player would miss the first half of the season because she was pregnant. Female athletes are often confronted with the challenge of childbirth in ways that do not interfere with male athletes' ability to perform in sports. Although many female athletes have become pregnant during the course of their athletic careers, Swoopes was required to sit out the first 6 weeks as she recovered from the birth of her first son at a crucial time for a sport league in its infancy. At the time, she felt legitimate concerns that the pregnancy would adversely affect her commercial appeal and that the contract with Nike might be in jeopardy. However, the WNBA saw this as a potential marketing strategy as it embraced her maternity and the distinction that it helped make between the WNBA and the NBA. The notion of performing motherhood on the court aligned with the league's early marketing campaign "We got next," which targeted female sport enthusiasts. The premiere issue of *Sports Illustrated/Women Sports* even displayed her on the cover at the peak of her pregnancy, further establishing the balance between her dual maternal and athletic qualities. After returning to the league, Swoopes went on to win three MVP awards and two additional Olympic gold medals. In 2005, she publicly acknowledged that she was a lesbian after two other prominent WNBA players had also made similar disclosures, noting that in the end, sexuality or motherhood have little to no effect on her on-court performance.

1. Was it appropriate for the WNBA to use Swoopes's pregnancy as a marketing campaign for the league?
2. Why would you suspect that public backlash is less for female athletes who acknowledge they are gay when compared to male athletes?
3. How might male and female athletes overcome the performance standards placed on them for the sports they find themselves engaged in?

conventionally attractive and feminine away from her sport but as an unnatural intruder within it. Hnida's case made national headlines when it became the focal point in a series of accusations that the football program at Colorado fostered a culture of violence and discrimination toward women. Although Hnida became an eloquent spokesperson on behalf of gender equity, her disruption of acceptable gendered performance led to a substantial amount of hostility that caused her to leave the university. Thus, even though Hnida "provided a model by which we may reconsider what it means to have 'male' or 'female' bodies" (Butterworth, 2008, p. 270), her resistance came with considerable risk to her own well-being.

We should also point out that athletes are not the only ones attempting to challenge gender norms. In 1988, Pam Postema became the first woman to umpire a Major League Baseball game (but only in spring training). After being fired despite a well-regarded minor league umpiring career, Postema filed a lawsuit for sexual discrimination and wrote a book, *You've Gotta Have Balls to Make It in This League* (1992). Postema faced criticisms that women did not belong on the field with men, a recurring theme for other officials such as Violet Palmer, who became the National Basketball Association's (NBA) first female referee in 2006 and Sarah Thomas, who became the first permanent female official in the NFL. In 2014, the NBA's San Antonio Spurs hired former WNBA all-star Becky Hammon as an assistant coach and, in 2015, the NFL's Arizona Cardinals hired Jen Welter as a training camp intern, demonstrating that previous barriers continue to fall (Markazi, 2015).

Communication scholars note that gender is fluid, and social expectations about gender performance change over time. Mozisek (2013), for example, reminds us that although it is now commonplace to see young girls play Little League, in the 1970s, the idea of girls playing with boys prompted an intense cultural and legal debate. Despite progress, such as the widely heralded performance of 13-year-old Mo'ne Davis in the 2014 Little League World Series, remnants of the debate from four decades ago linger, given that adolescent boys are encouraged to continue with baseball while adolescent girls are funneled into softball. Decades later, some similar changes have occurred with youth wrestling, a sport that now features mixed-sex competition. Miller (2010) details his experience as both a wrestling coach and father of a young girl who competes against boys. His essay draws on extensive field notes and reveals that children both adhere to and challenge identity norms in complex ways. His daughter both contests the perception that wrestling is only for boys—"I like [wrestling]. I like it because it shows I can do the same things as they can" (p. 168)—and embraces traditional performances of gender—"I like being pretty, but I don't get to be pretty when I wrestle, so it was fun to have [the boys] see me when I was dressed pretty and nice" (p. 175). As Miller notes, his daughter's ability to move along the gender continuum reflects how "female youth use both the performance of their athleticism and the performance of their gender to craft a dynamic and fluid gendered identity" (p. 164).

What is true for women challenging gender norms in sport may be doubly true for gay and lesbian athletes. Until very recently, there had been remarkably few openly gay athletes in the United States. Perhaps the most high-profile athlete to come out while still playing is the WNBA's Sheryl Swoopes, who revealed her sexuality in 2005. In 2013,

INTERVIEW

CYD ZEIGLER, COFOUNDER, OUTSPORTS

Q: With Jason Collins and Michael Sam in 2013, many thought the floodgates were about to come open for many more athletes to come out publicly. To what extent has that happened?

A: It's been a lot slower for the last few years than I thought it was going to be. Organizations are not helping people come out. They're not focused on the coming out process; they've been told by other activists that it's not anybody's role to convince people to come out. That's how we change things.

Q: Some athletes claim they waited to come out until they retired because they didn't want to be a distraction for their team. Is that a fair concern?

A: I call it the Big Lie of the Big Five. The big five sports leagues buy into this nonsense about distractions. That we have to avoid distractions at any turn, because it might sabotage our season or our team. But what they're really saying is, my leadership skills suck so badly that a gay person entering into our locker room could all of a sudden scuttle the entire season and destroy the whole team. They don't understand homosexuality; they also don't understand the tenor of sports and what a locker room is like. Every single athlete who has told their story at Outsports says the same thing: When they finally came out, they were totally embraced by their team and coaches, the people who they thought would be the most homophobic were the first ones to hug them and tell them it was going to be okay. Their only regret was they didn't do it sooner. Every single one.

Q: The locker room seems to be a big issue, particularly for men's sports. Is that the result on the male gaze—the focus on the visual and the performativity of masculinity?

A: We hear this all the time that if a straight man was plopped into a women's locker room he wouldn't be able to contain himself. Actually, yes you would. In a locker room of 20 women and one straight guy, does this person think he's going to be able to suddenly start raping women in the showers? It's insane. Will a gay man look at his teammates? There is a study out in England showing that essentially straight athletes act gayer than gay athletes in the locker room.

Q: You've argued that all the media sensitivity training in the world doesn't replace actually interacting with openly LGBTQ athletes. What does that interaction do that other actions can't?

A: Homophobia will end before racism does. With race, I can pick and choose whether I associate with Black people or Asian people or Hispanic people. I can *see*. Gay people just pop up in the middle of your family, your workplace, your team. You don't even know it until you've had an existing set of values and judgments on that person and you like that person in your life. Now they're gay, and you like a gay person, and you didn't even realize it.

the NBA's Jason Collins became the first active member of a male team sport to come out as gay. His open letter published in *Sports Illustrated* (Collins, 2013) was relatively well-received (Billings, Moscowitz, Rae, & Brown, 2015). However, already a marginal player in the league, Collins struggled as a free agent to sign a new contract. Because gendered expectations are so rigorously reinforced, gay and lesbian athletes most often "pass" as straight in order to avoid being ostracized by their teammates. Former baseball player Billy Bean (Bean & Bull, 2003), for example, writes about the difficulties he faced while hiding his identity within a culture that so openly derided homosexuals. Bean understood that in order to preserve a roster spot in Major League Baseball, he needed to *perform* an acceptable form of masculinity. Similarly, former basketball player John Amaechi (2007) describes the years during which he concealed his identity as a gay man for fear that he would be denied the opportunity of playing in the NBA.

Even in cases where athletes do not feel their playing time is at risk, the pressure to abide by cultural expectations can lead them to make compromises. When Brittney Griner spoke publicly about her sexuality in 2013, for example, she indicated her previous silence was in accordance with an unwritten policy on Baylor University's basketball team not to speak about it. In her words, "It was a recruiting thing. The coaches thought that if it seemed like they condoned it, people wouldn't let their kids come play for Baylor" (Fagan, 2013, para 2). Griner was also abiding by norms of a highly religious institution, and she did not speak about Baylor with any resentment. It is telling, however, that only once she became eligible to become a professional player did she feel comfortable talking about her sexuality openly.

The athlete whose coming out story has likely garnered the most attention is Michael Sam, the former defensive end for the Missouri Tigers who, in 2014, became the first openly gay player to be drafted by an NFL team. As an African American gay male playing the most conventionally masculine of American sports, Sam evoked a range of reactions. While many observers equated the declaration of his sexuality with the courage of Jackie Robinson (when he broke MLB's color barrier in 1947), others saw his status as a threat to locker room cohesion, specifically by suggesting the media attention he received would be a "distraction" (Khan, 2016). Ultimately, Sam did not make an NFL roster. He was later signed to play for the Canadian Football League's Montreal Alouettes, but, for reasons that remain unclear, he left the team shortly thereafter. Although Sam was unable to pursue an NFL career, his story unquestionably provided important visibility for LGBTQ athletes. Khan (2016) notes that ESPN's willingness to show—and, later, reproduce—Sam kissing his (White)

Brittney Griner

boyfriend as he celebrated being drafted to an NFL team provides evidence that the performance of gay identity in sport is no longer unimaginable. Nevertheless, the circulation of this image prompted significant criticism of the network from some fans and athletes. Consequently, Khan also cautions against overcelebrating this narrative, noting both the backlash and that Sam's intersectional identity as a gay, Black male was subordinated to discourses about whether or not he would be a marketable commodity. Especially as framed by sports media, LGBTQ identity can too easily be reduced to a brand identity.

Part of the issue is perhaps a preoccupation with the "coming out" narrative. Media speculation about whether or not (male) professional sport is ready for a gay athlete is common, but too often coming out is assumed to be the only means of performing a gay or lesbian identity. Iannotta and Kane (2002) argue that an overemphasis on public declarations of identity risks "marginalizing other, more subtle forms of identity performance" (p. 349). In their study of college coaches who are lesbian, they discover that women have multiple options when it comes to performing their gender. For example, interviews revealed that coaches were often "out" without ever explicitly telling anyone. Rather, they simply made their partners a part of their daily lives so that it would be obvious to others around them. Iannotta and Kane emphasize that these more subtle behaviors are just as, if not more, effective than public statements about sexual identity. Most importantly, they demonstrate that gender and gender performance are fluid, dynamic, and everchanging.

PERFORMANCE OF RACE AND ETHNICITY

In Chapter 7, we referenced the dress code installed by the NBA in 2005. Many critics have suggested that this policy was a means of curtailing the performances of African American identity perceived to be excessive, commonly marked by baggy clothing, cornrows, and exposed tattoos (Griffin & Calafell, 2011). Grano (2007) argues that especially in the aftermath of the infamous brawl between the Detroit Pistons and Indiana Pacers—and the fans in Detroit—the NBA wanted to "restore order and a veneer of professionalism by bringing players' dress into conformity with corporate tastes" (p. 460). The dress policy reveals a tension between interests in the NBA—management and players—and the corresponding attitudes about racial identity. No one in the league office admitted that race was a factor in installing the policy, of course. Yet few could argue that the effect of the dress code was to limit forms of expression that were specifically associated with African American players.

The NBA dress policy illustrates the performative dimensions of racial or ethnic identity that are located in sport. Just as gender identity is dynamic, so too is racial identity. Think no further than golfer Tiger Woods, an athlete often referred to as "African American," despite a heritage that includes African, Asian, and Caucasian ancestry. In an effort to avoid being reduced to a particular identity category, Woods has referred to himself as "Cablanasian"—a merging of multiple categories—or denied the relevance of race altogether (Houck, 2006b). Woods's insistence that he not be reduced to an essential identity speaks to the communicative power of identity performance.

By avoiding conventional racial labels, Woods seeks to communicate the importance of valuing people for their character and merit as opposed to race or ethnicity. Critics, meanwhile, suggest that by denying the persistence of racism, Woods's "postracial" identity further marginalizes those who continue to experience racial discrimination and oppression, consequently squelching any hope for a "Tiger Woods effect" that could have resulted in greater racial diversity on the PGA Tour.

As the Woods example demonstrates, performances of racial identity entail risks because of a troubling legacy of racism that associates certain attributes with observable markers of race. Thus, as we discussed in Chapter 7, conventional stereotypes hold that African Americans are physically dominant while White athletes are mentally superior. Similarly, certain performances become associated with different racial and ethnic groups: African American football players make outlandish displays when scoring a touchdown; Latin American baseball players have large swings with little plate discipline; White basketball players are fundamentally sound even if they lack spectacular athleticism, and so on. These characterizations become especially pronounced when an athlete deviates from the expected norm. For example, Larry Fitzgerald is an elite wide receiver in the NFL. He is also African American. It is common to hear television announcers praise Fitzgerald, in near disbelief, for his understated demeanor when he scores a touchdown. Rather than perform an elaborate prescripted celebration, he simply hands the ball to the nearest official. Fitzgerald is seen as the exception to the rule, and as Cunningham (2009) points out, much like the NBA's dress policy, the NFL has responded to the excesses of African American players by enacting harsher fines for their touchdown performances.

The assumption that players of a particular race or ethnicity will all behave similarly is problematic in other ways. Carrington (2008) describes his own experiences as a Black man raised in London, where soccer (football as it is called in England) and cricket are popular. As both an athlete and a then-aspiring academic, he was seen simultaneously as an insider and outsider to the members of a cricket club for whom he began playing. Because the club was predominantly Black and working class, Carrington's shared background allowed him to be accepted. However, his pursuit of a college education also marked him as different and prevented him from fully fitting in. Carrington thus emphasizes that although he was able to perform his racial identity in a manner that was consistent with his teammates, he was never quite an insider. As he notes, "This highlights one of the problems . . . with much of the [academic] work on race, namely the failure to fully interrogate and deconstruct what we might term the internal hierarchies of racial identity and the porous fault lines of racial boundaries" (p. 436).

Carrington's biographical example is echoed by scholarship that reveals the simultaneously complementary and contradictory nature of racial performance. For example, Schultz (2005) describes how Serena Williams's decision to wear a skin-tight "cat suit" during the 2002 U.S. Open gave voice to common stereotypes about the "animalistic" nature of African American athletes while at the same time challenging conventional thinking about femininity in tennis. After all, in a sport long dominated by images of players such as Chris Evert and Maria Sharapova, Williams's muscular and curvaceous physique provides a striking alternative. Meanwhile, others have noted that racial and ethnic performances can also be enacted when sport is fictionalized.

The popular movie, *Bend It Like Beckham*, which is about a young Indian woman in London who seeks the approval of her family to play soccer, was widely praised for its portrayal of British-Indian culture. Giardina (2003) expresses concern, however, that the stylized portrayal of a cultural group on the big screen can mislead an audience into believing that they have witnessed some form of "authentic" cultural expression. Because those outside of England will be exposed to so few images of British-Indian culture beyond a film like *Bend It Like Beckham*, the risk is that popular portrayals of sport limit, rather than expand, the acceptable range of racial or ethnic performance.

We also want to point out that performance may be a means of resisting the dominant or oppressive conceptions of racial and ethnic identity. An illustrative example of this can be found among those who object to the use of Native American mascots and imagery for sports teams. Miller (1999) argues that controversies about such mascots are a product of competing versions of how to perform "Indian." As he notes, "While the names and symbols that sports teams adopt are upsetting to many protesters, the primary concern is how those symbols get used or embodied" (p. 189). Thus, when fans of the Atlanta Braves perform the "Tomahawk Chop," or fans of the Washington Redskins come to the game wearing a feathered headdress, actual Native Americans see elements of their culture being taken out of context at best and outright disrespected at worst. Sport is crucial not only because it is a site where Native American imagery is used but because it has the power to shape our understanding of race and ethnicity. "Viewing sports as cultural performances," Miller writes, "means acknowledging the power of sporting events to *create* culturally shared beliefs and values" (p. 189).

Protests against Native American mascots must therefore be understood as performances designed to change those beliefs and values. In some cases, they have been

A MATTER OF ETHICS

HAIL TO THE REDSKINS?

The use of Native American imagery in sports has been contested over the years both by Native American groups and others advocating on their behalf. Although many high school and collegiate team mascots have been changed, professional franchises—including the Atlanta Braves (MLB), Cleveland Indians (MLB), Kansas City Chiefs (NFL), and Washington Redskins (NFL)—have refused to consider changes to their names, mascots, or logos. The Redskins are a particularly complicated case because the term *redskin* is not descriptive; rather, it is historically a racial slur, roughly equivalent to the "n-word" used to demean African Americans.

In 2013, renewed efforts to have Washington's owner, Daniel Snyder, change the team's name met with resistance both from him and NFL Commissioner Roger Goodell. When asked about a potential lawsuit against the team, Snyder replied, "We'll never change the name. It's that simple.

NEVER—you can use caps." Meanwhile, Goodell responded to a letter jointly written by 10 members of the U.S. Congress calling for the NFL to acknowledge the insensitivity of the term by insisting that the team's name is a "unifying force that stands for strength, courage, pride and respect." By contrast, former Redskins and Hall of Fame wide receiver Art Monk declared, "If Native Americans feel like Redskins or the Chiefs or another name is offensive to them, then who are we to say to them, 'No, it's not?'"

A name change does not appear likely, but that does not mean the disagreements about its meaning will disappear. Is it fair for a relatively small minority group (just over 1% of the U.S. population is Native American, according to the Census) to ask for a professional sports franchise to change its name? Is it reasonable to defend the name as a "unifying force?" What possible compromises could be reached that might allow an agreement between these opposing viewpoints?

successful, especially at the high school or collegiate level. Stanford University was the first to change its name, when it went from the "Indians" to the "Cardinal" in 1972. Since then, dozens of others have followed suit, either with entirely new names or with accommodations designed to minimize ongoing controversy. Some changes have sparked significant disagreement, perhaps most notably the retirement of "Chief Illiniwek" as the unofficial mascot of the University of Illinois. Opponents of "The Chief" expressed concern that his identity was a patchwork of Native American performances, none of which were particularly authentic. Supporters, meanwhile, countered that he was an irreplaceable part of the university's history. As Chidester (2012) summarizes the debate, "For Chief proponents, the moment has become a statement of resistance against what they see as the theft of a cherished university symbol by the forces of political correctness. For anti-Chief factions, it is nothing more than the perpetuation of hostile and demeaning culture depictions, albeit ones that have shifted from the field of play to the stands" (p. 59).

The performative complexities on display at the University of Illinois are paralleled by other conflicts. The University of North Dakota, for example, finally resolved a 15-year dispute in 2016 by changing its mascot from the "Fighting Sioux" to the "Fighting Hawks." One creative attempt to resist Native American mascots came from a group of intramural basketball players at the University of Northern Colorado. In an effort to call attention to a local high school team's mascot and logo, these players formed a team called the "Fightin' Whities." The name, which was supported by complementary merchandise, was an attempt to use parody as form of social protest. By "humorously positioning Whites in the marginalized role of sports mascot" (Carmack, 2011, p. 36), the Fightin' Whities hoped to show how and why racial representations could be damaging. Although the parody did receive considerable attention, it did not do much to change the mascot landscape. Meanwhile, no professional teams have seriously considered a name change and, in 2009, the United States Supreme Court refused to hear a case that might have led to a change of name of the Washington Redskins. Similar efforts in 2013 also met with minimal success (see A Matter of Ethics). Some fans and team

Chief Illiniwek performs in 2006 with the University of Illinois marching band

officials are reluctant to change, at least in part, because "the stereotypical views of how one performs Indian in mainstream American culture closely parallel the cultural rules about how one performs 'sports fan'" (Miller, 1999, p. 189).

Nevertheless, public sentiment and media coverage seem to be shifting to a more skeptical stance. For example, Cleveland's baseball team has preserved its "Indians" name but retired the imagery of "Chief Wahoo" that many found insensitive. In the case of Washington, a federal judge ruled in 2015 that the Redskins logo was offensive to Native Americans and the name's trademark was therefore canceled (Martin & Tatum, 2015). The ruling does not make the name illegal, but it places additional pressure on the franchise to adapt to evolving cultural norms. The ongoing debate about names such as "Redskins" highlights why the performance of identity is, and will continue to be, contested in the arena of sport.

PERFORMANCE OF DISABILITY

Disability studies is a growing area of research across academic disciplines. Because sport features the body in such prominent ways, disability scholars have increasingly turned to sport as a means of examining the practices of *ableism*. As Duncan (2001) explains, ableism is an ideology that assumes "the world should be tailored to those without disabilities" (p. 1). Such a worldview results in diminished visibility and opportunity for people with disabilities. Cherney (2003) adds that the spectacular performances within sport reinforce this ableist thinking by "locating ability in the body. [Sport] assumes an ideal of the stable and controllable body as the foundation of ability and as the essential characteristic from which ability derives" (p. 82). As a result, he argues, sport ironically rewards "certain freakish bodies" (p. 84)—those trained "to perfection" (p. 95)—while it marginalizes others—those that are disabled.

Communication scholars of sport and disability recognize that sport provides a space through which ableist practices might be challenged (Cherney, Lindemann, & Hardin, 2015). Drawing an intellectual parallel to queer theory's efforts to challenge what is considered "normal" in terms of gender, Cherney and Lindemann (2014) examine the character Jason Street, from the television show *Friday Night Lights*, to suggest that communicative studies of sport and disability have the potential to challenge the discourse of ableism. Over the years, several high-profile examples of athletes with disabilities have given fans the opportunity to reconsider what counts as "able-bodied." Former MLB pitcher Jim Abbott, for example, had a lengthy and productive career despite being born without a right hand. More recently, South African runner Oscar Pistorius, who had both lower legs amputated when he was just 1 year of age, competed in the 2012 London Summer Olympics. The most familiar case, however, is likely that of golfer Casey Martin, who successfully sued the Professional Golf Association (PGA) Tour to use a cart during tournaments. Because the case made its way to the Supreme Court, it has arguably generated the most attention and controversy about the Americans with Disabilities Act, which was enacted in 1990 (Cherney, 2003). At the heart of the matter was which bodies were allowed to perform in professional sport and a recognition that "certain bodies enjoy unwarranted privileges created by [sport's] rules, and that the resulting disparity discriminates" (Cherney, 2003, p. 97).

Despite the discrimination that athletes with disabilities face, there are also opportunities to resist ableist thinking. One of the more dramatic performances of ability, then, occurs through wheelchair rugby, which is often termed "murderball." Wheelchair rugby began as a form of therapy for individuals who are paralyzed but quickly evolved into a highly competitive sport. Because they take place within sport, the "performances of disability . . . can subvert the stigma associated with physical disability in surprisingly effective ways" (Lindemann & Cherney, 2008, p. 113). These performances

Source: By [WFR Eron, http://commons.wikimedia.org/wiki/File:Wheelchair_rugby_game_2.jpg. [CC-BY-SA-2.5], https://creativecommons.org/licenses/by-sa/2.5/deed.en

Wheelchair Rugby

OFF THE BEATEN PATH

PARA TABLE TENNIS

Table tennis is one of the most popular Paralympic sports. It has been embraced throughout the world, and the International Table Tennis Federation (ITTF) has set classifications in place that allow disabled athletes to participate at levels based on their abilities. The classifications include five classes for athletes in wheelchairs (Classes 1–5), five classes for standing athletes (Classes 6–10), and an additional class to accommodate athletes with intellectual disabilities. Only athletes with visual disabilities are unable to participate in para table tennis. The rules for Olympic table tennis are in place. Therefore, quickness, finesse, and strategy remain the key skills for all classes, while some rules have been modified for the wheelchair classes. For example, there is a rule that the serve for wheelchair classes must bounce off the back of the table to allow athletes to reach as opposed to serving off the sides where they would encounter difficulties. In all classes, para table tennis provides athletes the opportunity to compete at a high level, regardless of their disability.

were brought to life in the critically acclaimed documentary film, *Murderball* (2005). As Cherney and Lindemann (2010) suggest, "*Murderball* presents the point of view of the disabled athlete so that the audience views from a perspective that sees the players as powerful and heroic instead of lacking ability and pitiable" (p. 207). In addition, the documentary mostly avoids the common practice of oversentimentalizing these athletes for overcoming physical adversity.

Yet, even as *Murderball* recasts popular conceptions of disability, Lindemann and Cherney (2008) caution that wheelchair rugby depends on other forms of identity performance that might reinforce ableist thinking. In particular, because the athletes default to conventional performances of aggressive masculinity, murderball could reaffirm "ableist notions of competitiveness, athleticism, and the body" (p. 99). This point reminds us that identity performances are complex, often revealing multiple and, at times, competing visions of the athletic body. What should be clear, however, is that the performances of disability in sport open up new possibilities for how people with disabilities can be seen and understood in public. Such performances redefine commonplace "inspirational" narratives that hail the accomplishments of the so-called "supercrip" (Smith, 2015) and also make visible the range of athletic participation, from "murderball" to "blind football" (de Haan, Osborne, & Sherry, 2015). Given these possibilities, what has been a relatively recent area of interest in communication and sport scholarship is likely to generate increased interest in the years ahead.

Source: Photograph by Mb.matt

2003 Special Olympics opening ceremony

CONCLUSION

As we conclude this chapter, we want to be clear that we have not covered every possible variation of identity. Our discussion of diversity, for example, is limited to examples of athletes with *physical* disabilities. Equally important, however, would be to explore the performative dimensions of athletes with *mental* disabilities. For instance, the Special Olympics provides a showcase for these athletes to challenge stereotypes that restrict the range of activities that are accessible to those with mental disabilities. Not only can the Special Olympics help redefine common perceptions of mental disability, it also provides outlets for athletes to alter their perceptions of themselves or even improve communication skills (Lord & Lord, 2000). In addition to disability, we should also acknowledge that identity may be performed through categories such as age or religion. Consider, for example, how assumptions about age were undermined by the performance of 41-year-old swimmer Dara Torres, who won three silver medals during the 2008 Summer Olympic Games in Beijing. Or, think about how unexpected affirmations of religious faith—such Husain Abdullah's Islamic prayer in the endzone during an NFL game in 2014 (Palmer, 2014)—call into question the more traditional practice of keeping religious beliefs private. The willingness of an "old" swimmer to compete or a committed

Muslim to speak publicly about his faith are important communicative moments, and they remind us of how much of our identities are produced by our performances of them.

In this chapter, we have demonstrated that identity in sport is not always what it appears to be or what it is represented to be. Indeed, through the performances of athletes who challenge dominant expectations of gender, sexuality, race, ethnicity, and physical ability, sports fans are invited to consider the dynamic and multifaceted nature of identity. With this in mind, what will you see when you look at athletes in the future? Will you question norms of masculinity that are enacted in mixed martial arts fights? Will you wonder whether or not it is appropriate that a White man beats a drum to simulate a Native American ritual during a baseball game in Cleveland? Or, will you reconsider what counts as "able-bodied" when watching the performance of an athlete with a disability? Not all athletic performances of identity are designed to challenge norms or promote social change, of course. Nevertheless, the examples from this chapter should demonstrate that such possibilities help make sport a dramatic part of American life.

Suggested Readings

Butler, S., & Bissell, K. (2015). "The best I can be": Framing disability through the mascots of the 2012 Summer Olympics and Paralympics. *Communication & Sport, 3,* 123–141.

Butterworth, M. L. (2006). Pitchers and catchers: Mike Piazza and the discourse of gay identity in the national pastime. *Journal of Sport & Social Issues, 30,* 138–157.

Clayton, B., & Harris, J. (2009). Sport and metrosexual identity: Sports media and emergent sexualities. In J. Harris & A. Parker (Eds.), *Sport and social identities* (pp. 132–140). New York, NY: Palgrave Macmillan.

Cooky, C., Dycus, R., & Dworkin, S. L. (2013). "What makes a woman a woman?" versus "our first lady of sport": A comparative analysis of the United States and the South African media coverage of Caster Semenya. *Journal of Sport & Social Issues, 37,* 31–56.

Gieseler, C. M. (2014). Pranking Peter Pans: Performing playground masculinities in extreme sports. *Text and Performance Quarterly, 34,* 334–353.

Grindstaff, L., & West, E. (2010). "Hands on hips, smiles on lips!" Gender, race, and the performance of spirit in cheerleading. *Text and Performance Quarterly, 30,* 143–162.

Kian, E. M. (2015). A case study on message-board and media framing of gay male athletes on a politically liberal web site. *International Journal of Sport Communication, 8,* 500–518.

Lamb, M. D., & Hillman, C. (2015). Whiners go home: Tough mudder, conspicuous consumption, and the rhetorical proof of "fitness." *Communication & Sport, 3,* 81–99.

Trujillo, N. (1991). Hegemonic masculinity on the mound: Media representations of Nolan Ryan and American sports culture. *Critical Studies in Mass Communication, 8,* 290–308.

Whiteside, E. (2016). Politics in the toy box: Sports, reporters, Native American mascots, and the roadblocks preventing change. *International Journal of Sport Communication, 9,* 63–78.

10

COMMUNICATION AND SPORT IN PARENT–CHILD INTERACTIONS

Parent:	Brandon, get on the damn bag.
Spectator 1:	Brandon, maybe you should listen to your father and get on the bag, partner.
Spectator 2:	You know what I always tell my son, Nathan, is to go out there and try to have fun.
Parent:	Well, you know, having fun is the name of the game. Hey, son. You trying to make an ass out of me? Get on the bag!
Spectator 1:	Brandon, everything is going to be okay. Just do what your father tells you, please.
Parent:	Hey, little crybaby, I will downsize your face with a shovel if you don't get on the bag. By the way, does anyone know who I talk to about being a coach next year?

During his time on *Saturday Night Live,* Will Ferrell's performance as a vocal spectator at his son's youth baseball game resulted in a frightening portrayal of a verbally abusive parent. The scene depicts the competing orientations between "having fun" and the ego involvement that many parents confront as they cope with a child's performance in sports. During sport competition, there are numerous opportunities for parents to interact with their children to produce a range of constructive (i.e., encouragement during events, shared experience) and destructive outcomes (i.e., verbal abuse, obscene behavior). For many families, sport consumes a significant portion of their leisure activities, including the enactment, consumption, and performance of sports (Kassing et al., 2004). For larger families with multiple youth athletes, it is not uncommon for sport to constitute a central role in parent–child interaction (i.e., talk about practice and competitive experiences), parent–child time together (i.e., transporting to practice, coaching), and family leisure time (i.e., multiple family members assuming spectator roles). Feller (2014) recently noted that "We've gone from 'Friday Night Lights' to 'Every Night Lights'" in a recent commentary on the time commitments that are being forced through sport participation.

Also included is the financial investment on the part of the parents (club dues, purchasing equipment and uniforms, admissions), which can consume anywhere from 3% to 12% of a family's annual income (Baxter-Jones & Maffulli, 2003). For example, families that travel from state to state to compete in youth soccer can spend as much as $30,000 when factoring in expenses associated with traveling to games, hotel costs for weekend tournaments, payment to elite coaches, and everyday expenditures associated with being on the road (Wagner, Jones, & Riepenhoff, 2010). The desire to become and remain competitive can also divert significant family resources. For instance, the IMG Golf Academy assesses a yearly fee of $55,000 for participation in its program, and it isn't uncommon for wealthy families to pay up to $600 to $700 an hour for the individual attention from a quarterback, pitching, or shooting coach (Glanville, 2012). Staggering numbers like this further solidify that the youth sports enterprise is beginning to model collegiate and professional sports. This trend can be detrimental for many families that do not have the financial means to ensure a competitive advantage for their young athletes. Research has shown that single parent or reconstituted families were less likely to participate in organized sports, and the lack of participation was further mediated by perceived family wealth (McMillian, McIsaac, & Janssen, 2016).

Parents seek to encourage sports participation because of the valuable socialization function it serves (promoting teamwork, leadership, and sport-specific skills), and fostering such skills represents a direct communicative function that can be fulfilled as a result of a child's sports participation. Unfortunately, a number of underlying motives also exist to foster a heightened level of pressure for athletes at all ages. For instance, a number of parents are likely to push sports on their children as a way to live vicariously or determine their own "moral worth" through their sons' and daughters' accomplishments (Trussell & Shaw, 2012). Parents failing to achieve their own sports-related dreams and goals are likely to find themselves pressuring their children to meet goals they were unable to attain themselves. In these situations, it becomes difficult for a parent to separate the child's sports identity from his or her own. We can point you to a number of prominent sports families where a parent's identity is inextricably linked with his or her child's athletic prowess. For example, Peyton and Eli Manning's accomplishments in the National Football League (NFL) are often compared in contrast with the success of their father, Archie Manning. After a successful college career at the University of Mississippi, Archie had a mediocre career in the NFL because of the fact that he had been drafted in 1971 by the New Orleans Saints, a franchise that never had a winning season with Manning at quarterback and only in recent years has experienced sustained success (including a victory in Super Bowl XLIV). Eli's decision to reject a contract from the San Diego Chargers after his graduation in 2004 was perceived by many to be inspired by his father's experience in the NFL. The resulting trade to the New York Giants helped secure a Super Bowl win in 2008, through which the success of both Eli and Peyton have altered the Manning family's identity.

Despite such examples, the sporting world is filled with many instances where overzealous parents place significant pressure on their children to be professional athletes. Armour (2015) recently reported on a website that parents created for their sixth-grade football player, which described his ability as a "pro-style quarterback."

The website went as far as including reviews from coaches and scouts who had seen him in action with comments describing him to the likes of Tom Brady and Peyton Manning before he had ever competed in middle or high school. Consider the case of Ty Tryon, who, at a young age, was considered to be a golf prodigy with an illustrious career predicted for his future. At the age of 16 in 2001, he turned professional after choosing to forgo the opportunity to golf in college, where many outstanding professional golfers had the opportunity to further develop their skills in the amateur ranks. Tryon earned an exempt status in 2001 that allowed him to qualify for the PGA Tour, which ultimately led to a lucrative endorsement deal with Callaway. However, despite his early success during his first year as a professional, Tryon has failed to maintain any consistent success on the Professional Golfers Association (PGA) Tour, and he has spent time on a variety of other tours (National Golf Association [NGA] Hooters Tour, Gateway Tour) as he has continued playing professionally.

Peyton Manning

The culture of youth sports in our society continues to evolve in ways that further necessitate the potential for parent–child sports interaction. We open this chapter with a historical overview of the role of parents in the lives of their children's sporting experience as society has shifted from a *game-* to a *sport-*based culture. This transition has further extended what impact factors such as sports rage and socialization are having, as well as the competing perspectives toward sport involvement that have evolved over time. The body of sport socialization research stems more from research conducted in the fields of sports sociology and psychology, yet it emphasizes the important communicative distinctions between parental support and pressure. We introduce you to these two forms for parental sport communication (which emphasizes noticeable gender differences) as we examine the discursive behavior of parents in the private family setting and as spectators at sporting events. This chapter includes discussions of (a) changing sports culture, (b) sport socialization, (c) parent–child sports interaction, and (d) sex difference in parental influence.

CASE STUDY

THE RIDE HOME

If you were asked to reflect back on your worst experience as a youth or high school athlete, what might it be? Losing an important game? Early morning workouts or being yelled at by a demanding coach? When asking successful college athletes these very questions, Henson (2012) found a surprising response, "The ride home from games with my parents" (para. 2). Many athletes described that these trips (after both wins and losses) turned into critique sessions where every detail of the game or match was replayed. "Why didn't you throw a curve ball to the second batter in the 4th inning," or "Why didn't you take the last second shot at the end of the game," became recurring questions that forced young athletes to relive different aspects of the competition.

This feature of parental pressure was exemplified in the experience of Elena Delle Donne, who was depicted at an early age as the LeBron James of women's basketball. Her athletic abilities on the basketball court were so outstanding that she was heavily recruited by almost every major Division I basketball team in the country. During her senior year, Elena verbally committed to play for legendary Connecticut Huskies coach Geno Auriemma, even leaving home after graduation to get a head start on her collegiate career by moving to campus to take part in summer school and begin workouts with the team. However, 2 days later, Elena returned home and informed her teammates and Auriemma that she intended to give up her basketball career. In follow-up interviews, Elena confessed to the fact that she had lost the passion for the game of basketball at the age of 13 and that she was "living a lie."

Parental pressure is an underlying issue that many young athletes are forced to deal with, even talented athletes. For Elena, the subliminal pressure that her parents placed on her to compete caused her to reject the lack of passion she was experiencing for basketball. When this occurs, it is only a matter of time before an athlete finds a way to change his or her course. Some fake injuries, lash out, or in Elena's case, simply walk away. After a short break from basketball, Elena continued with her basketball career and was eventually drafted in the first round of the Women's National Basketball Association (WNBA) in 2012 and has continued to develop into one of the top WNBA players, earning the league MVP in 2015 and earning a spot on the USA Women's Olympic Basketball team.

1. What drives the parents of successful young athletes to focus so much on their performance at a young age? What percentage of talent athletes are likely lost each year to the tension that builds from these types of interactions?
2. How is it that Elena's parents were unable to see that she had lost the passion to play basketball?
3. What about our society makes it so hard for people to accept that a talented athlete would not want to compete?

CHANGING SPORTS CULTURE: GAME VERSUS SPORT

When considering the prevalence of sport in our society today, it is evident that sport and competition will continue to evolve. For instance, youth sports are at a crossroads as our society has shifted from a *game culture* (in which children were responsible for the design, maintenance, and development of the games they took part in), to a *sport culture* primarily organized by adults, especially parents. For example, there was a time at the turn of the 21st century when there were no organized youth baseball activities in the United States. Kids who enjoyed watching professional teams compete were responsible for organizing their own games as a way to further develop their own skills. This slowly transitioned into the creation of youth baseball leagues with drafts, practice and game schedules, and adult coaches and managers. In our opening chapter, we noted that sports participation in our society has been on the rise, with recent evidence suggesting that 36 million children aged 5 to 17 play some form of organized sport(s) each year (Minnesota Amateur Sports Commission, 2015). As parents have become more involved, the number of youth participants has increased dramatically, yet this has come at a cost. Adult models have been applied to the youth sports enterprises, where skill development and competitiveness have become the norm. For example, traditional youth baseball, soccer, and basketball programs intended to simply introduce athletes to a broad range of opportunities have transitioned into a collection of traveling teams that are becoming more selective. In 2012, the Amateur Athletic Union (AAU) began to sponsor a national basketball tournament, which results in the crowning of national championship teams that include second graders (Gregory, 2013). Additionally, to take advantage of this growing reliance on traveling teams, an entrepreneur in Cincinnati created "Youthletic" to serve as the equivalent of a dating site where parents could explore travel team options for their young athletes (Kane, 2014). The site seeks to match child interest and sport capacity with other children in the company's database to allow the creation of competitive travel teams as well as opportunities to practice and compete.

Elena Delle Donne

There was a time when athletes would make a decision about specializing in a sport to increase their chances of competing at collegiate and professional levels; however, more and more athletes are now required to specialize to ensure a spot at even the junior high school level. This specialization has resulted in youth coaches pushing the limits of young athletes at an early age, and it has caused many to become wary of the capabilities of preteen athletes. Many marveled at the athletic prowess of basketball star Johnathan Nicola, who competed for the Catholic Central Secondary School in Windsor, Canada. Johnathan was born in South Sudan but was arrested and detained at the border by immigration officials when his fingerprints appeared to match those of an individual who had sought refugee status in the United States years earlier. It was ultimately determined that rather than being born in 1998 as was reported to school officials, Nicola had actually been born in 1986 making him 29 years of age at the time (Brown, 2016). According to police reports, it was noted that his mother had refrained from informing him of his real age to provide an opportunity for the full scholarship to the private school. He noted, "I was always keep asking [*sic*] what is the specific age that I was born, and she has told me that she could not remember" (para. 5). The push to be successful should make you consider for a moment your own experiences as an adolescent. How far might your parents have gone to allow you to be successful? Have the lines blurred too much from the important developmental period in youth sports, to win at any cost necessary? Were you encouraged to participate in a variety of sports, or were you pushed into selecting one particular sport to be more competitive? A basketball season used to just be in the winter, but now the game is played year round; if you drop out at any point so you can play another sport, you are perceived as falling behind or lacking commitment. This transformation has taken hold and is beginning to produce a variety of unintended consequences that carry over into the increased likelihood of parents placing a stronger emphasis on athletic competition, which has increased the potential for sports rage.

Source: Reprinted with permission by Matt Judson

A father providing support to a young wrestler before his match

INTERVIEW

DARRELL BURNETT, CLINICAL PSYCHOLOGIST AND BOARD MEMBER FOR LITTLE LEAGUE OF AMERICA

Q: In a sporting context, what is the most important aspect of the parent–child relationship?

A: If I see my child as an *athlete* who happens to be a kid, I may tend to overreact emotionally to situations involving my child at a youth sports event (not enough playing time, not playing the "right" position, making an error, striking out, losing a game, etc.). My overreactions may also run the risk of communicating to my child that his or her self-worth is somehow tied in solely with his or her athleticism. If I see my child as a *kid* who happens to be playing sports, I can keep youth sports in perspective. I will not allow my child's athleticism (or lack thereof) to become the definition of my child's self-worth. I will maintain a solid, supportive, positive relationship with my child, and situations involving my child in youth sports (not enough playing time, etc.) will not be seen as "catastrophic" or "horrible."

Q: What is unique about a parent who takes a supportive rather than competitive approach toward his or her child's sport participation?

A: It is possible to be both supportive and competitive, provided the emphasis is on *process* (skill development) rather than *end product* (winning, statistics, etc.). Parents who see youth sports participation as an ongoing process of learning skills and having fun can be supportive of their children as they continue to participate in the process of playing sports. They can teach their children to compete against themselves, to become the best athletes they can be.

Q: Some parents are concerned that youth coaches wield too much influence on children. Is this a problem for the Little League of America?

A: The term "positive coaching" is common in youth sports. Little League International takes pride in making sure that "everybody plays" and that each player, regardless of his or her skill, has a positive experience. Managers and coaches are required to attend coaching workshops with an emphasis on positive coaching. The Positive Coaching Alliance works hand in hand with Little League International to assist the Little League managers and coaches in their efforts to be a positive influence on the players. Managers and coaches are monitored; there are always exceptions (and these exceptions tend to make the 6:00 p.m. news). However, the vast majority emphasizes fun and skill development.

Q: What trends are you currently experiencing regarding the pressure parents place on their children to compete? Are there particular approaches that are becoming more detrimental?

A: There seems to be a movement away from the "carousel" (youth sports as a process with friendly competition) and more movement toward the "brass ring" (youth sports as "big business," with an emphasis on the "prize"). The result is an increase in parents' decisions to spend more money on their child's sports development (specializing in one sport, individual training, equipment, travel ball, etc.) and a tendency for parents to put the emphasis on the win-at-all-costs competition.

(Continued)

INTERVIEW (Continued)

Q: In a recent study, 55% of parents reported that their children dropped out of sports because of hypercompetitiveness. How can this be counteracted?

A: When children see themselves as competing against *others,* they start comparing themselves to other players on the team ("I can't run as fast as . . ."), and the tendency is to drop out. However, if they can be taught to compete with *themselves,* they may continue to participate. If a child can be taught to measure his or her progress in terms of *frequency* (how often), *duration* (how long), and *intensity* (how much energy), and, if parents and coaches help the child to see the progress, an emphasis on process overcomes focusing on end product.

Q: What would you say is different about parental involvement today than it was 20 years ago? Are there benefits in regard to how things have changed?

A: It's mixed. The good news is that more positive parental involvement creates a sense of validation, especially in younger children. When a child repeatedly yells, "Watch me! watch me!" to his or her parents while trying a trick dive in the swimming pool, it is as though the dive doesn't "count" unless the parents see it. Likewise, if the parents and family "see" the hit, playing time, catch, et cetera, it "counts" more in the eyes of the child. The bad news is that with more parental involvement comes the possibility of overinvolvement and overreaction.

Sports Rage

Recent statistical accounts indicate that children involved in youth sports find themselves the focus of increasing incidents of pressure and abuse from parents, coaches, and fans (Lord, 2000). In addition, dramatic anecdotes further illustrate the problem. For example, on July 5, 2000, the father of a 10-year-old boy fatally beat another hockey player's father over a disagreement about body checking. A week earlier, a disgruntled parent coach in Florida broke the jaw of a 13-year-old umpire; and in 1999 in Virginia, a mother slapped a 14-year-old official when she disagreed with a call (Butterfield, 2000). Many have used the term *sports rage* (offensive behavior, both verbal and physical, that results from unfavorable sport outcomes) to describe a host of instances that have included both verbal and physical assault on players, coaches, or officials. But perhaps the best definition comes from Heinzmann (2002), who described it as "any physical attack upon another person such as striking, wounding, or otherwise touching in an offensive manner, or any malicious verbal abuse or sustained harassment which threatens subsequent violence or bodily harm" (p. 67). These incidents have even extended onto the playing field. For example, after being issued a yellow card at a high school soccer match, Ricardo Portillo punched the referee in the head. The official died 7 days later, resulting from the injuries incurred during the altercation (Segura, 2013).

Heckling players is not a new phenomenon in many sporting events, but there are still instances where the use of profanity and verbal abuse from fans fall outside the boundaries of what is considered appropriate. Arizona State University has drawn considerable attention in recent years due to their "Curtain of Distraction" used to deter opposing basketball teams during free throw attempts. The routine noise from the fan section has been replaced with a curtain meant to add an element of surprise intent on causing a loss of concentration while at the line. Richard Simmons impersonators, Michael Phelps in his Team USA Speedo, or diaper clad students are just a few of the many innovative techniques employed by this student body. The inappropriate levels of aggression, competitiveness, and overinvolvement appear related to the ways in which it has become culturally and communicatively normative to do sport. These practices appear to have spilled over into youth settings, not simply through wider discourses and influences but as coaches, parents, and fans communicatively enact their own sporting ambitions and identities in highly competitive and aggressive ways.

Most important to our discussion is the rise of vulgar behavior on the part of parents that commonly occurs at events designed for 4- to 5-year-old participants. More moderate forms of sports rage have occurred as parents' unsportsmanlike conduct has become more aggressive. Data suggest that 15% of parents or spectators will embarrass their children at a sporting event (Vandenabeele, 2004), and Lord (2000) notes that an informal survey conducted by the Minnesota Amateur Sports Commission found that 45% of sport participants had experienced being yelled at by adults, called names, or insulted during competitive events; 17% had even reported instances of physical abuse (hitting or slapping), with a handful of the athletes surveyed even reporting that they preferred that their parents not attend their events or practices. Much of this behavior has been linked to the fact that sports attrition rates are on the rise, with most youth participants dropping out by age 13, leading many organized sports associations to

Source: AP Photo/Matt York

Michael Phelps joins ASU students in the Curtain of Distraction require all parents to either complete sportsmanship training or sign a code of conduct statement before their children can participate. Family communication scholars argue that the family is an important socializing agent for children and that the way children view their athletic experience is dependent on the way their parents communicate to them about the importance of sports and what occurs while participating.

SPORT SOCIALIZATION

Each society, culture, or subculture has an innate need to train its members for the roles and norms necessary for its survival. This socialization process involves a society's ability to transfer its norms, practices, routines, traditions, and general knowledge to its next generation. Sport has been viewed as a legitimate source for this socialization process. Roberts, Treasure, and Hall (1994) argue that "in play, games, and sport, children are brought into contact with social order and the values inherent in society, and are provided a context within which desirable social behaviors are developed" (p. 631). Grounded in a family socialization model (Mead, 1934), the sport socialization movement argues that learning would occur from two important sources: (1) through athletes' exposure to the sport (e.g., the actual enactment of sport, interacting with other athletes, following rules and procedures developed for the sport) and (2) the reinforcement that is received from others (e.g., role models, peers, parents, coaches) while engaged in those sporting activities. Much of the sport socialization literature stems from research that views interaction with others as an effective method for internalizing appropriate and expected behavior.

Sport involvement at a young age is mostly unidirectional as parents make the initial, primary decision to enroll the child, and proper motivation on the part of the parent will produce the best likelihood for athletic success and continued performance. Parents with an active interest in sports are more likely to expose their children to sports at an early age and allow sports to become an important part of the family's leisure time (Baxter-Jones & Maffulli, 2003). For example, consider the level of success Venus and Serena Williams would have experienced if their father had not introduced them to tennis at an early age. The same could be said for our previous examples, raising the question, "Where would Eli and Payton Manning be without Archie?," or "Where would Tiger Woods be without Earl?"

Parents are likely to encourage sports participation because of the perceived benefits they anticipate their child will receive, as well as personal benefits that come as by-products of their participation (Na, 2015). These *parental benefits* include learning life skills, engagement with other children, and health promotion. Parents also experience a sense of community as they interact with other parents. Practice becomes an outlet allowing parents to interact with other like-minded adults as well as serve on organizing boards that further perpetuate the cycle of sport competition. In their analysis of parental changes resulting from child participation in sports, Dorsch, Smith, and McDonough (2009) observed four major impacts, including a change in parent behavior (becoming a coach, family sacrifices), cognition (stronger self-awareness, new goals, and knowledge), affect (emotional connection, pride), and relationships (parent–child, parent–parent, parent–family). *Child benefits* include the potential for participating in a competitive environment that allows one to experience winning and losing in addition to learning valuable lessons about sportsmanship, teamwork, and handling adversity. Teammates over time become close friends, even overlapping boundaries beyond the field, court, and/or mat as they integrate into things such as family rituals, birthday parties, social gatherings, and even holiday activities. Many parents noted their child's benefits because sport also serves as an important alternative to nonphysical activities, most notably video games. Brustad (1988) argues that an athlete can experience a number of emotions toward the sports he or she competes in, and these emotions facilitate motives such as affiliation, achievement, release, power, and independence (see Table 10.1). Finally, there is evidence that *family benefits* also exist from sport participation with evidence to suggest that those families who engage in recreational sports experience

OFF THE BEATEN PATH

VOLLEYBALL

Volleyball is a sport that can be challenging for youth. For example, elementary students are considerably shorter than the net. However, there are developmental skills that can be beneficial for children. Volleyball, at the youth level, provides a safe, fun, and supervised environment for playing a sport. It also provides players with an opportunity to learn by observation and through drills.

Drills such as catching, throwing, serving, and returning help children build confidence in their ability, and playing games helps build their self-esteem. Another important benefit of playing volleyball is learning the importance of teamwork. In addition to social benefits, volleyball offers physical benefits, including increased flexibility, balance, and coordination, which can be applied to other sports.

Playing volleyball allows children to be involved without having to perfect skills. Volleyball is also a sport that can be played with people of different ages, which presents an opportunity for parents to play with their children.

TABLE 10.1 ■ Young Athlete Motives for Sports Participation

Athlete Motive	Description
Affiliation	The potential to establish an association with a particular team or sport and be a part of something bigger than themselves
Achievement	The ability to obtain success in sports and work toward a level of excellence or skill acquisition
Release	An avenue for expending energy or aggressive behavior
Power	The perceived sense of clout obtained outside the sport or the ability to exert authority over teammates
Independence	The liberty to perform in an environment free from anxiety and pressure

higher levels of family resilience allowing them to overcome crisis situations. Sport appears to foster the necessary cooperation skills that apply to the family setting that do not emerge through other group interactions (Cho, 2014).

Sports offer the potential for creating a context not only where positive developmental characteristics are fostered; yet the benefits noted above are often contradicted by a variety of challenges for both parents and children. *Parental challenges* include the considerable expense required for competing at high levels (traveling clubs, camps, training materials). The time commitment is also significant, which potentially detracts from other forms of family time, causing parents to make difficult choices between competition, other leisure activities, or even academics. Hardy, Kelly, Chapman, King, and Farrell (2010) found that traveling time (to and from practice and events) was not a factor that influenced their decision to have their kids compete. In this investigation, cost appeared to be the strongest factor reported. It will be interesting in the future to see how the impact of the "pay to play" movement in many states (e.g., Ohio, Michigan) will become a significant barrier for parents as they make participation decisions for their children. *Child challenges* include finding a balance between being a child and an adult as the seriousness of sports has increased. Parents also note the growing emphasis toward sports that detracts from academic commitments that could have otherwise been fulfilled. Mostly, they note the intensity that comes from coaches and other parents. Although such by-products of the youth sporting environment have resulted in a number of unintended consequences from this shift to a sport culture in our society, many parents find themselves encouraging sports participation because of the important family-based socialization function it serves. As more family time and resources are devoted to sports, there is an increased opportunity for parent–child interaction that serves as feedback (both support and pressure) to encourage or discourage ongoing participation.

PARENT–CHILD SPORTS INTERACTION

Parents not only encourage young athletes, but also they assist in interpreting their child's experiences, which are then used to shape perceptions about abilities, establish expectations, and foster a valence structure about the sport itself (LaVoi & Stellino, 2008). Parents have an opportunity to provide support or pressure through their verbal or nonverbal behavior on the sidelines or in private family settings. When assessing techniques for encouraging sports participation, Roberts and colleagues (1994) found parents most commonly emphasize reaching goals, followed by pointing out the child's personal improvement or growth, importance of trying, and providing rewards for hard work and overcoming difficulties. These findings also indicate that children perceive two conceptually different types of parental involvement, one that represents *parental facilitation* (paying fees, purchasing equipment, providing transportation, attending games) of the children's activity participation and one that suggests *parental control* by imposing performance standards.

Encouragement in the form of *parental support* consists of behaviors or comments that athletes perceive to foster athletic participation, with evidence suggesting that supportive parents (noninterfering with a focus on effort rather than winning) used more open communication and encouraged children to develop at their own pace. When feedback is provided in a positive light, the support perceived by athletes can increase their enjoyment, perceived sport importance, increased involvement in a range of sports, and general self-esteem. Recent evaluations to assess models for youth physical activity have established strong relationships between perceived support and enjoyment that comes from being physically active. Recent work by Starcher (2015) sought to evaluate the memorable messages that athletes recalled from their engagement with parents during their time in organized youth sports. The analysis revealed five memorable message types that emphasized *Effort* by encouraging athletes to try their best or never give up. *Character Traits* included statements about displaying proper sportsmanship and displaying loyalty to the team or coach. Parents also emphasized *Physical Skill* through encouragement to remain in shape and perform at a high level. *Attention to Others* and *Having Fun* were the final two message types which drew attention to the importance of being a teammate and that winning was not the only benefit from competing.

Parental influence can also produce detrimental results when *parental pressure* involves messages continually focusing on success and foster improbable and impossible expectations of a child. Ego building involves instances where parents' natural instinct is to wish for their children's success in their respective sport, often producing a curvilinear relationship with a child's stress and parental involvement. Examination of the negative repercussions of parental involvement reveals that messages continually focusing on success and performance-based outcomes establish an expectation in children that

Source: By United States Marine Corps (090213-M-4913M-001). http://commons.wikimedia.org/wiki/File:USMC-090213-M-4913M-001.jpg

Youth basketball players prepare to compete

A MATTER OF ETHICS

PARENTAL PROTECTION

We all have had moments of frustration during a sporting event, perhaps because we think an official made a bad call or an opposing player isn't playing by the rules. While we might imagine translating these frustrations into actions, most of us will vent in indirect ways—that is, we'll shout at a referee or simply mutter to ourselves about how our team never gets the breaks. What happens, though, when someone tries to intervene in the action?

In 2012, Gina O'Toole took matters into her own hands during her teenage son's hockey game in a Boston area youth league. When an on-ice fight broke out, O'Toole felt that referees were not doing enough to protect the players. Fearing that her son could be injured, she left the stands and rushed onto the ice, yelling at the officials to stop the fight. According to O'Toole, the referee told her to "get off the ice and I said, 'You need to do your job'" (Kindelan, 2012, para 7). Shortly after her outburst, the fight ended, and play resumed. Video of the incident quickly showed up on YouTube, and O'Toole was later interviewed on ABC's *Good Morning America*.

O'Toole's morning talk show appearance focused primarily on the novelty of her actions; indeed, it is rare to see a parent confront a game official in this manner. Although there were no serious consequences from this incident, do you think it is appropriate for a parent to intervene in a game in this way? O'Toole claims that the officials had lost control of the game. Does that affect your interpretation? Would it have mattered if her son was 6, instead of 16? Under what, if any, conditions would it be ethical for a parent to confront an official?

Source: Kindelan, K. (2012, June 18). Hockey mom reveals why she stormed the ice mid-fight. *Good Morning America.* Retrieved from http://abcnews.go.com/blogs/headlines/2012/06/hockey-mom-reveals-why-she-stormed-ice-mid-fight

winning is the only relevant sports outcome. Parental pressure has been related to athletes' fear of failure, guilt, anxiety stress, and dropout rates and is inversely related to athlete enjoyment. Parents have an opportunity to provide support or pressure through their verbal or nonverbal behavior in private family settings and as spectators at sporting events. Meân and Kassing's (2007) work exploring statements made by parents at youth sporting events demonstrates the integration of both support and pressure displays by parents depicting a set of conflicting and overlapping identities. Their analysis highlights parental identities affiliated with "success, prowess and winning," with little to no references to having fun or enjoyment (p. 62). Actual parent statements during sport participation run counter to the underlying justifications that parents traditionally articulate when describing the benefits of competition.

Private Family Settings

The type of parental pressure or support an athlete receives will often depend on the level of involvement the family has in sports. For example, parents with moderate levels of involvement create the ideal sporting experience because they are able to find a balance between the competitive and enjoyment objectives from sport participation. When parents demonstrate low involvement, the athlete is likely to experience heightened uncertainty, which can be an anxiety-provoking experience. It is difficult for a young athlete to develop a commitment to a sport when parents demonstrate limited interest (i.e., "I can drop you off at the game, and then, I'll pick you up afterward"). Stress is likely to emerge when highly involved parents exert pressure on their children and occurs when athletes reflect on comments about their performance for fear of letting the parents down.

Turman (2007) conducted interviews with parents of young athletes to explore the factors that necessitated a talk with the child about the nature of his or her sports participation in the private family setting. Four prominent themes were identified, beginning with *playing time,* which included instances where parents confronted their child's frustration about playing time by interpreting the situation from the coaches' perspective. Such positive encouragement was found to help focus athlete attention on many of the factors the athlete controlled, including working to do his or her best and using the time on the bench to learn from teammates. Parents also emphasized athlete behavior that extended beyond the athletic ability of the child, suggesting that making contributions to the team and having the right attitude were the biggest determining factors for deciding playing time.

Sport politics was the second most common topic of talk focusing on factors outside the control of the child's athletic ability and resting on the subjective decision making of the coach. A wide range of issues were addressed by parents, including the perception that coaches showed considerable favoritism to their own children or older athletes and athletes who attended camps or extra practices, as well as overreliance on star athletes. When such behaviors were perceived, parents reported a need to talk about the politics of sports with their children. In these instances, parents reminded athletes that they must work harder to sway the political aspects in their favor. *Negative coaching behaviors* are actions whereby parents questioned the coaches' objectivity and ethical practices with their child or the team. In these instances, parents learned about coaches' behavior through their child's firsthand account of practice and locker-room behavior, requiring them to explain to their child(ren) how coaches' behavior was inappropriate. When faced with coaches displaying behaviors within this classification, parents used the private family setting as a place to interpret the coaches' behavior for the child.

Sport competitiveness was the final topic of talk, including instances where parents perceived sports had become too competitive by placing an overemphasis on winning. A majority of these utterances focused on the role of parents and sports organizations, which either pushed kids or established policies that eliminated athlete enjoyment. These parents perceived that winning was promoted as more important than learning to play the sport, and that overbearing parents inadvertently discouraged their own desire to have their children participate. As a result, parents indicated a need to address this topic

Youth hockey players in Canada

Source: Photo shot by Derek Jensen (Tysto), 2006-January-13 via Wikimedia Commons

with their children as a way to encourage continued participation by deemphasizing such inappropriate behavior.

Sport spectators, and parents in particular, feel an innate need to provide public disclosures at sporting events, yet this type of interaction highlights the harmful nature of such parental comments and behaviors. Bigelow (2005) noted that 45% of sport fans felt that parent sideline behavior was a legitimate problem, while 46% felt it was the most significant problem facing youth sport programs. How a child reacts to the sport environment will be a direct reflection of what he or she observes from parents and coaches. Much of this occurs through modeling as children develop the positive (congratulating players, supportive comments) and negative sport behaviors (failing to shake hands, questioning officials) by observing parents and coaches in this environment. Positive spectator behaviors have been found to be a strong predictor of player positive sportsmanship, just as negative behavior on behalf of the spectator predicts negative behavior from athletes. Interestingly enough, negative coach behavior does not appear to influence negative modeling by players, suggesting the "perception might exist that one of the coaches' roles is to argue with referees so when they do, players are less likely to notice. When parents, however, argue with referees, it is more noticeable because it is outside the expected role of the spectator" (Arthur-Banning, Wells, Baker, & Hegreness, 2008, p. 13).

The feedback young athletes receive from parents in the stands has been categorized into three general types (positive, negative, and neutral). Observations at a variety of basketball, soccer, and baseball games indicate that 51% of the parents' comments were

TABLE 10.2 ■ Types of Sport Talk in the Family Setting

Family Sport Talk	Definition	Example
Playing Time	Conversations about the extent that an athlete is obtaining adequate participation levels	"If you don't see an increase in playing time then maybe you need to reconsider going out for swimming next year."
Sport Politics	Discussion about the decision-making practices employed by the coach to determine participation levels or player positions	"It always seems that your coach puts in his own daughter at the end of the game even though the seniors should be getting an opportunity to play."
Negative Coaching Behavior	Interaction to discuss or question the coaching practices or behavior used to guide a team	"I don't think it is useful for your coach to discipline the entire team because of what one of your teammates did."
Sport Competitiveness	Conversation about the heightened levels of competitiveness generated from sport participation	"I accept that winning is important, but are there ways to still be competitive and make the experience enjoyable for the kids?"

Source: Photo by Staff Sgt. Jes Smith. https://www.dvidshub.net/image/787861/meet-your-mentor-part-2-devoted-mother

Mother teaching young soccer players fundamentals

positive, followed by negative (32%) and neutral (16%) comments (Blom & Drane, 2009). *Positive comments* include statements that reinforce or support athlete performance and include encouraging comments like "nice play," "go Kevin," or "good work." *Negative comments* represent statements made toward their own team or athletes that attempt to correct or scold behavior, such as "Don't take that shot," "You need to put in more effort," or "Did you even show up to play?" *Neutral comments* include important remarks that reinforce coaching strategies or features of the sport, such as "Keep your eye on the time," or "Talk with your teammates." A classification of such comments is found in Table 10.2.

There is the possibility that in "receiving multiple cues from several adults, children may be confused and distracted. If athletes receive this information while focusing on performing a new skill . . . their level of frustration and confusion may be multiplied" (Blom & Drane, 2009, p. 12). For instance, parents offering their child erroneous appraisals of her or his athletic ability are often thought to create a level of self-esteem dissonance (Mach, 1994). This self-esteem dissonance (the need to seek similarity between an individual's self-judgment and that of significant others) makes it difficult for young athletes to determine which messages are genuine. Unfortunately, a strong positive relationship has been observed between the judgments parents provide and an athlete's perceived physical ability (after controlling for actual ability), whereby parent messages about athletic ability have the capacity to override environmental cues that may come from the coach (McCullagh, Matzkanin, Shaw, & Maldanado, 1993). When young athletes rely solely on the reinforcement provided by parents, they are likely to have psychological development issues.

Some may recall the 2008 case of Kevin Hart, an offensive lineman in Nevada who believed so strongly in his athletic ability to play Division I football that he went so far as to schedule a fake announcement session for his commitment to play for the University of California (UC). Despite having his family and head coach at his side during the announcement, it was later confirmed that he had never been recruited by California or any other Division I program. In an interview after the incident, UC head coach Jeff Tedford noted, "I've talked to other coaches who have had people saying they've committed to their program who they've never recruited, and it just seems like this thing is getting so big and egos are getting so involved" (Wojciechowski, 2008, para. 15). The unfortunate feature of this story was that Kevin was skilled enough to play college football, but his pronouncements throughout his high school career led to his need to stage such an elaborate event. Hart later committed to playing football at a Division II school in Missouri.

SEX DIFFERENCE IN PARENTAL INFLUENCE

Early research in the area of sport socialization affirms that a variety of factors determine how parents will decide to influence their child's sports involvement. Often parents encourage children to participate for a number of reasons (e.g., values of physical activity, discipline), and differences have been found that are reflective of both the parents' and child's sex. Communication research argues that children are often socialized into either masculine or feminine communication cultures through their participation in a variety of sex-segregated games and sports as they mature. Wood (1996) argued that "games socialize children into understandings of how, when, and why to talk" (p. 150). As a result, specific communication behaviors are learned early in a child's life and are influential in determining how children communicate throughout their life span. This is important to note when considering that such masculine and feminine communication cultures appear to be a function of the parental support that young athletes receive to participate in various athletic activities. For instance, research in the early 1980s showed that fathers had the most influence over the behavior of male children, while mothers were more likely to serve the same function for girls. Traditionally, research on family sport socialization supported the notion that parental pressure and support were provided by the male parent, yet trends in youth sports involvement suggest equal levels of support from male and female parents regardless of the athletes' sex.

In Chapter 6, we discussed the role that Title IX has had for balancing the role of male and female participation, and it appears realistic that parental approaches to encouraging this participation would evolve and increase the likelihood that female parents may begin to perform a central role in their child's sports participation. For instance, Trussell and Shaw (2012) contend that highly organized youth sport settings provide a viable avenue for fathers in particular to become actively involved in the lives of their children compared to other socialization activities. Their analysis observed that self-perception as being a "good parent" was influenced by both the level of investment (time and financial) and the ultimate success of the child. This desire to epitomize what is believed to be a good parent then has the potential to influence the way parents interact with both male and female children athletes. Blom and Drane (2009) observed no difference in the disposition of mother and father comments at sporting events, yet there were more positive comments at girls' events and more neutral comments at boys' events. Leff and Hoyle (1995) found that male athletes viewed their fathers as using more forms of pressure when compared to their mothers, while female athletes in their investigation perceived similar amounts of pressure from both parents. This transformation over the past 20 to 30 years suggests a number of possible implications for the way masculine and feminine communication styles are likely to form in future generations. Hardy et al. (2010) observed a distinction between parents' willingness to have their male or female children participate, with most being disinterested when they had female athletes.

CONCLUSION

The parent–child relationship can be influenced dramatically when sport enters into the family equation. As we have noted throughout this chapter, sport is a continually evolving phenomenon that appears to be making parent–child interaction increasingly complex. The transition from a game to a sport culture has further facilitated things such as sport rage, the emphasis toward greater sport socialization, and discourse in the public and private settings. This also bridges the boundary between parents and coaches, with alarming consequences. Although our focus in this chapter has been on the potential consequences of increased parental participation, we would be performing a disservice if we didn't end this chapter by also demonstrating the role that sports can have for fostering positive parent and family relationships. For example, our society is rife with examples of parents like Dick Hoyt, whose son Rick was born with significant brain damage after complications during birth left him unable to control the use of his limbs. Despite these difficulties, Rick became an avid sports fan who eventually asked his father to help him participate in a charity run for a high school classmate who had become paralyzed. Dick responded by pushing his son in the 5-mile run, and the event was such a life-changing experience for the two that Dick began to enter them both in more races, ultimately qualifying for the Boston Marathon in 1984. As if that were not enough, they soon took on the challenge of competing in a variety of triathlons, where Dick pulled or pushed his son in a small dinghy or cart during the swimming, bicycling, and running portions of the event. To date, they have participated in more than 200 triathlons and competed in more than 20 Boston Marathons. This example is one of a thousand different stories that reinforce the importance that sport can have in the parent–child relationship as sport becomes a central contextual environment where parents interact with their children. As sport and family continue to intersect in meaningful ways, the evolution of this important interpersonal relationship will also continue.

Suggested Additional Reading

De Lench, B. (2006). *Home team advantage: The critical role of mothers in youth sports.* New York, NY: HarperPerennial.

Engh, F. (2002). *Why Johnny hates sports: Why organized youth sports are failing our children and what we can do about it.* Garden City Park, NY: Square One.

Kay, T. (2009). The landscape of fathering. In T. Kay (Ed.), *Fathering through sport and leisure* (pp. 6–22). New York, NY: Routledge.

Wheeler, S., & Green, K. (2014). Parenting in relation to children's sports participation: Generational changes and potential implications. *Leisure Studies, 33,* 267–284.

Shields, D. L., Bredemier, B. L., LaVoi, N. M., & Power, F. C. (2005). The sport behavior of youth, parents, and coaches: The good, the bad, and the ugly. *Journal of Research in Character Education, 3*(1), 43–59.

11

PLAYER–COACH RELATIONSHIPS IN SPORT

Many people operate under the assumption that athletic ability will translate well into possessing the critical skills necessary for effective coaching, yet there is so much more to coaching than athletic ability. The capacities to develop a vision for a team, foster athletic skill, and build relationships with players are essential attributes that can escape even the most talented athletes who seek to transition into the instructional side of sports once their competitive cycles have ended. We can point you to a number of highly successful coaches who have never been able to compete at the highest levels of their sports. For instance, Joe Gibbs, the famed coach for the Washington Redskins, had an insignificant college career before he emerged through the coaching ranks to lead them to three Super Bowl victories. Surprisingly, when compared against the ranks of the current NFL coaches, only a handful ever advanced to play professionally. Despite this track record, there are also numerous examples of talented athletes who failed to make successful transitions into coaching (Wayne Gretzky, Michael Irvin, etc.). Such examples are fairly common in sports as less tangible characteristics often mark the difference between a skilled technician and a successful coach. The success of brothers Jim and John Harbaugh has often been attributed to their experiences with their father, who coached them in high school and served as a head college coach at numerous colleges and universities. Despite Jim's success as a National Football League (NFL) quarterback, John's lack of professional experience didn't put him at a disadvantage when his Baltimore Ravens defeated Jim's San Francisco 49ers in Super Bowl XLVII. Effective communication, when leveraged with knowledge of the technical skills in the sport, work together to establish the difference between successful and unsuccessful coaching. Jowett (2009) recently noted that "while an athlete may have a chance in sport by going it alone, the athlete and the coach in partnership have more and better chances of success" (p. 34).

Sport success can be tied to a number of factors: athletic talent, team financial resources, fan support, luck, and so on. Regardless of the impact these factors have in determining success or failure in sports, the coach can be a central catalyst in this equation; as a result, coaches often receive the praise or blame for athletes' or teams' accomplishments. The way our society conceptualizes leadership places a significant emphasis on the coach to manage athletes (at all levels) to perform at optimal levels. This is never more evident than when we consider the importance of the coach in bonding a collection of individual athletes in team-based sports. For example, try to identify one highly recognizable coach for an individual sport. Name the coach for Olympic gold medal wrestler Jordan Burroughs, Ladies Professional Golf Association (LPGA) champion Annika Sorenstam, Women's Tennis Association (WTA) champion Steffi Graf, or seven-time Tour de France winner Lance Armstrong. Do the names Mark Manning, Henri Reis, Heine Gunthard, or Chris Carmichael sound familiar? If given these names in advance, you then might be able to link one of these athletes to his or her coach. What if we were to ask you to identify the coach for the Pittsburgh Steelers during the 1970s, current National Collegiate Athletic Association (NCAA) women's basketball coach for the Connecticut Huskies, the U.S. hockey team during the 1980 Olympics, or the Chicago Bulls in the 1990s? Even if you couldn't name them off the top of your head, it is likely that you have heard of Chuck Noll, Geno Auriemma, Herb Brooks, and Phil Jackson.

Source: Keith Allison from Owings Mills, USA (John Harbaugh) [CC-BY-SA]

John Harbaugh

Our tendency to attribute team success to the coach has its benefits for coaches who are fortunate to work with highly skilled athletes, but the desire to blame coaches for poor team performance can be detrimental for coaches to overcome. Because the coach–athlete relationship is challenged by the fact that winning is such an important outcome in sports, we begin this chapter by exploring the influence such expectations have on the need for coaches to win at all levels. In Chapter 10, we discussed the important role that parents play in fostering sports participation, and we extend this discussion in this chapter by briefly uncovering the parent–coach relationship as an ever-evolving feature of how sport is enacted. The remainder of the chapter shifts to the important role that communication serves in the coach–athlete relationship as we explore the range of styles that coaches draw upon as they interact with their athletes to prepare them for competition.

INTERVIEW

DEANE WEBB, HEAD VOLLEYBALL COACH, OHIO UNIVERSITY

Q: You've coached at the junior level and at multiple collegiate levels. What similarities and differences are there for you when communicating with players at these different levels?

A: The differences are the amount of time you are able to share together, which sometimes can limit the depth or volume of communication. At the junior level, video sessions and in-depth scouting reports are the exception, not the norm. Collegiately, practices happen more frequently and there is a great deal of time available to communicate, whether in the office or on the road while traveling. The biggest similarity is the desire to be totally and brutally honest when communicating with our players. While it looks different when communicating to a 15 year-old versus a 21 year-old, the goal remains the same.

Q: What is your approach with student-athletes you recruit to play at Ohio University? What values do you want your players to share and communicate?

A: We truly are a family, and we want potential athletes to see as much about us as possible. We ask our players to be very honest with recruits on both the good and bad things in our program. I tell our players that the worst thing that can happen is not that someone says 'no.' The worst thing that can happen is that someone says 'yes' and then finds out our school isn't what they thought it would be. We want every player to understand the work required to be a successful D1 athlete, and if they aren't willing to do that, we want to find that out on the front end.

Q: People who haven't watched much volleyball in person might be surprised by how vocal the players are and how supportive the culture appears to be. What do you think accounts for this, especially since it appears to characterize the sport as a whole (and not only your team)?

A: If you consider the density of players per square footage of surface area that they play on, I can't think of another team sport that keeps more players in such a small space. Football begins each play that way, but when each play begins, they spread out considerably. Because of the proximity that continues in our sport throughout each play, communication opportunities are frequent and ongoing. Since there are many communications that happen in every match, the quality and tone of the communication become very important in helping build team chemistry and winning matches.

Q: Scholarship in communication and sport about player–coach relationships indicates that affirmative communication behaviors tend to be more successful. Yet many of the images the public sees of coaches (across sports) show them modeling more negative communication behaviors (yelling, etc.). Why is this, do you think? When, if at all, do you take a more assertive approach with your players?

A: I do believe there are many more coaches that communicate in positive ways than there are negative. The negative stories oftentimes get the most interest, as is the case with many types of news stories. For my own coaching, if I get very assertive with

(Continued)

INTERVIEW (Continued)

a player, it usually has to do with their effort. If the process isn't good, I may push hard in the moment to change that, either verbally or by removing her from the match. If the process is good but the product isn't, then I usually try to offer small positive pieces of information to help her change the product. I am also much more likely to be verbally negative with a team away from the match either in the locker room or in our next practice, as this gets them away from the stresses that happen in a match-like situation. Matches are about adjustments and managing player emotions. Practices are about learning, increasing effort levels, and processing new information. If quite a few things happen in the match setting that we haven't already covered with our team, then I've done a poor job preparing my team.

Q: What are the biggest communication challenges you face as a head coach? How do you try to address those challenges?

A: There is one of me and usually 15–16 players. I never get as much time with each player as I would like. This is especially true for non-starters, who inevitably get less of my time in season than those that are getting more feedback in practice and match situations. I feel a disconnect with some players because of that, and I can't imagine how hard it is for coaches with larger squad sizes.

Here, we emphasize how the positive coaching movement has produced surprising results for coaches who embrace an athlete-oriented approach when seeking the appropriate balance between positive and negative comments to increase performance and general orientation toward competition. When this orientation is transferred into a competitive context, the interaction that coaches have with players has been found to produce positive results. When these positive statements or messages are examined within the context of competitive interaction, there are a variety of opportunities to motivate, foster team cohesion, and provide a broader perspective for the importance of sport beyond the athletic context. For you to gain a deeper appreciation for the communication-based complexities that coaches face as they develop relationships with their athletes, we include discussions of (a) sport outcomes and coaching, (b) parent–coach relationships in sports, (c) leadership orientations, (d) positive coaching, and (e) communication contexts. We begin by examining the pressure coaches have to win.

SPORT OUTCOMES AND COACHING

Vince Lombardi is often criticized for allegedly suggesting that "winning isn't everything, it's the only thing." While many coaches might be unwilling to acknowledge the fact publicly, the outcome for every contest does matter. Many youth sports leagues have even established policies that restrict keeping score to emphasize participation over winning. This has caused many to openly debate the departure from fostering a competitive environment for young athletes. For instance, James Harrison, middle linebacker for the Pittsburgh Steelers, was criticized (and praised) by many when he returned his young sons' participation awards at a school field day events. Harrison was quoted on Instagram following his observation, "I'm not about to raise two boys to be men by making them believe that they are entitled to something just because they tried their best . . . cause sometimes your best is not enough, and that should drive you to want to do better." His rationale was that rewarding just participation removes the motivation for kids to exceed and improve their athletic performance. Despite this new focus on participation, it's quite common to hear 4-year-olds talking after their games, saying, "If we would have been keeping score, we would have won!" Scoreboards, "most valuable player" titles, and team and player rankings were created for this purpose, as we are predisposed to consider our achievements in relation to those around us. Ask high school coaches if winning matters when they arrive home after a loss to a collection of "For Sale" signs in their lawn. Supporters and boosters place significant pressure on coaches to achieve, and as a result, school boards, athletic directors, and team owners are under considerable pressure to fire coaches who can't achieve as expected. The Monday after the end of the NFL season is referred to as Black Monday because so many teams fire their coaches after subpar seasons. The Los Angeles Lakers fired Mike Brown just five games into the 2012–2013 season, while the Cleveland Cavaliers fired head coach David Blatt midway through the 2015–2016 season, despite the fact that the Cavs were atop the Eastern Conference standings at the time.

Operationally, coaches serve two important roles for their teams (teacher and game manager), which equally contribute to a team's ability to win. At all levels of play, these competing roles have the ability to force coaches to make decisions about what's best for the team versus what's best for the athlete. Roberts (1984) argued that sport offers a "forum" in which athletes learn a great number of skills, including "responsibility, conformity, subordination of the self to the greater good . . . effort, persistence, and delay of gratification" (p. 251). However, coaches are constantly confronted with the "win at any cost" mentality in sports that requires them to do more than simply educate athletes. Sagar and Jowett (2012) evaluated coach reactions to athletes after a loss and when mistakes had been made to assess their feelings and well-being. Although both positive and negative reactions were identified, it was common for coaches to express negative emotions through aggressive behavior and punish athletes when mistakes resulted in a loss. These displays resulted in low perceptions of self and decreased affect toward the sport. We are taught at a young age to win, and winning at all costs becomes an ethical issue that coaches and athletes alike are expected to overcome. It seems that even when coaches violate rules, this practice can be validated if done to maintain competitiveness. Bart Starr, NFL Hall of Fame quarterback and former coach of the Green Bay Packers, was reprimanded by the league early in his coaching career for violating NFL recruiting policies. In his apology to Packer fans, he noted that he was only doing what was expected to ensure a competitive advantage for the team, causing Kruse (1981) to observe that in sport rhetoric, the very ethic of sport suggests it's a coach's duty to bend the rules if it aids in his or her team's ability to win. Players and coaches in all sports often joke that "if you ain't cheating, you ain't trying." With the number of recruitment violations on the rise in college sports, one might consider that this statement might hold true at least when it comes to public opinion. While the NCAA has held universities accountable for such violations once they emerged, there is seldom overwhelming public outcry about such behavior.

Despite these examples, it is foreseeable that such a breach can go only so far, as fans and leagues have drawn the line when it comes to specific intent to cause physical harm to other players. More recent accounts surfaced at the conclusion of the 2011 NFL season when New Orleans Saints' coaching staffers were reprimanded by the NFL for the creation of a slush fund offering bonuses to defensive players when they inflicted injuries on opposing players. The term *Bountygate* was used to describe the scandal, and head coach Sean Peyton and members of the coaching staff were suspended for the entire 2012 NFL season.

This mounting pressure to win increasingly impacts the coach–athlete relationship as coaches are required to make decisions that are less about athlete development (character, skill, etc.). Even in developmental leagues, coaches are accused of playing to win versus playing to learn, and parents have added to the complexity of this issue, as our section on sport rage in the previous chapter attests. The rare exception might be coaches for minor league baseball teams who are less concerned about wins and losses than they are about the development of their potential major league talent. Because sports have become more specialized, coaches are now granted even more exposure to their athletes at levels never before seen. This year-round access has the potential for coaches to understand the styles that are most appropriate for fulfilling both features of the coach–athlete relationship (development and winning). Making this even more difficult is the fact that as the avenues for competitive sports have grown, so have the general athletic abilities of young athletes. However, just because young athletes can perform feats traditionally set for adults doesn't mean they are both cognitively and emotionally ready to cope with the pressures that coaches might put on them for their effort. Cote's (1999) research on Olympic athletes found that it was not until at least 10 years of age that participation becomes important

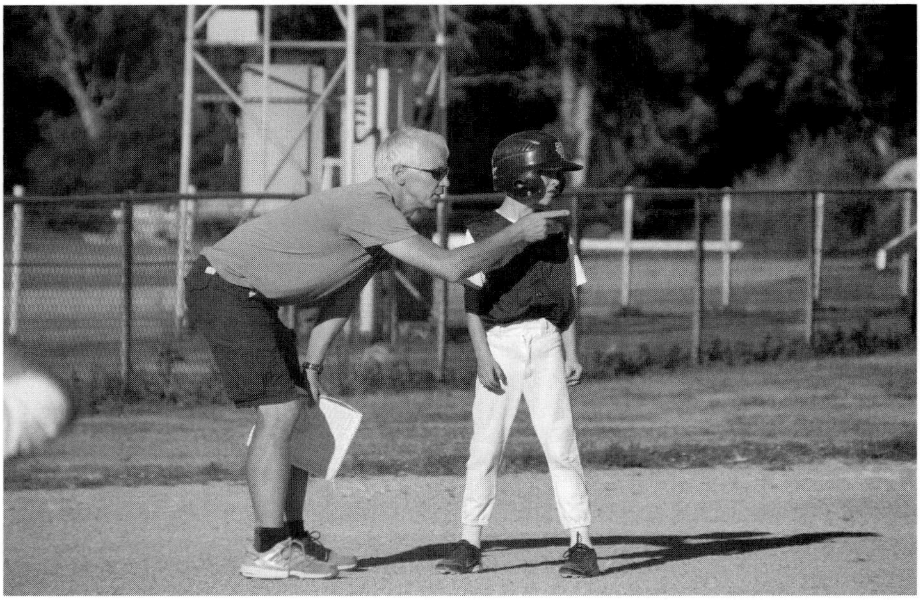

Source: Reprinted with permission by Jim Edman

A youth coach provides instruction to a young baseball player for an athlete to be competitive at the international level. This suggests that a coach who is making developmental-based decisions for athletes at young ages is unlikely to assist in the long-term performance for these players. This further supports the notion that athletes' win and loss rates at an early age are irrelevant beyond the psychological awareness that young athletes might have. In spite of his statement about winning early in his career, Lombardi was later quoted as saying, "I wish to hell I'd never said that damned thing (that winning is everything). What really counts is the effort (having a goal). That sure as hell doesn't mean for people to crush human values and morality" (Masin, 2007, p. 5). Despite Lombardi's retraction, parents continue to make the coach–athlete relationship difficult because of the overreliance on winning. Face it: More people remember Lombardi's first assertion than his second one.

PARENT–COACH RELATIONSHIPS IN SPORTS

In Chapter 10, we spent considerable time providing an overview of the parent–child relationship in sports, demonstrating the significant role that parents play in encouraging sports participation. This relationship also carries over into the coach–athlete relationship as sports participation often necessitates the need for parent–coach interaction, making the coaches' jobs increasingly difficult. Many coaches have observed that parents serve as primary obstacles in their attempt to coach young athletes. Mach (1994) noted that "misunderstandings between the coach and the parent later lead to clashes of opinion between the parent and the child and then between the coach and the child" (p. 5). Coaching clichés, such as "The best coaching jobs are in orphanages because there are no parents there," or "If it isn't one thing, it's a mother," add credence to the fact that coaches struggle with the interaction they have with parents. The competing notions of "everyone should be allowed to play" and "win at all costs" provide opportunities for conflict between parents and coaches. For example, in 1999, Rodney Carrol, a volunteer youth baseball coach in Brunswick, Ohio, was sued by the father of one of his players after the team went 0–15. The parent complained that the ineffective coaching cost his son a chance to participate in a tournament in Florida. A mother in Canada sued the coach of her 14-year-old's hockey team for the cost of league registration, camps, and mental anguish after her son was benched in what she considered to be a crucial game. The fact that more than 1,300 lawsuits were filed during a 5-year period this past decade, ranging in violations from game strategies and starting status to instructional approaches, further exemplifies the difficult environment that coaches at all levels are expected to navigate. Coaches have even been forced to react to increasing parent pressure. For instance, in 2014, Rob Bloom, high school varsity basketball coach in California, sued parents for defamation for their repeated attempts to have him fired from his coaching position (Blidner, 2014). Despite a coach's attempt to establish rigid boundaries for communicating with parents, playing status appears to be a unique factor necessitating that parents establish direct and indirect contact with coaches.

Kirk and MacPhail (2003) found that coaches believe a significant number of parents were *antagonists* who overemphasized the skills of their children and demanded that much of the coach's time and effort be devoted to their children. Assessment of parent types classified parental positioning into several categories. *Nonattenders* were likely to drop off children at practice or games but never stayed to watch. *Spectators* were parents that attended all practices but took no part in helping with practice or the management of the team. The *helpers* were described as parents who contributed time and effort to assist the coach. These parents typically begin as spectators who transitioned into assisting after their children had been properly introduced to the sport. Their final parent classification was the *committed member,* who assisted the coaches, maintained contact with other parents, and helped manage the sports organization.

A MATTER OF ETHICS

COACHES AND THE KIDS

We are familiar with the image of the football coach as a no-nonsense, tough-love authority figure. Legendary figures such as Vince Lombardi and Bo Schembechler are celebrated, years after their deaths, for using this authority to mold winning football teams and disciplined citizens. Although the model of the football coach has evolved—think of personalities such as Pete Carroll and Urban Meyer—the idealized image of coaching authority remains persuasive for many coaches at all levels, including youth football.

A dramatic example of this authoritarian model can be found in the reality television series, *Friday Night Tykes*. Debuting in 2014 on the Esquire network, *Friday Night Tykes* follows 8- and 9-year-olds in a San Antonio area youth football league. The show depicts coaches yelling at the players ("You have the opportunity today to rip their freakin' heads off and let them bleed!"), forcing them to engage in physically demanding drills and imploring them to feel no compassion for their opponents ("There should be no reason why y'all don't make other teams cry!"). The show immediately drew criticisms from a range of observers, including the National Football League. Critics felt the show communicated unhealthy attitudes about competition and revealed youth coaches who had lost perspective about the virtues of their sport.

In response to the criticisms, an Esquire spokeswoman claimed the show provides "an authentic and provocative glimpse into an independent youth football league in Texas. . . . [It] brings up important and serious questions about parenting and safety in youth sports, and we encourage Americans to watch, debate and discuss these issues" (Nesbitt, 2014, para 13). Do you think the coaches' behaviors are appropriate for a league of 8- and 9-year-olds? Is the responsibility more with the coaches or the parents? Is Esquire's response adequate? How else might a television show try to address the issues noted in the Esquire statement?

Source: Nesbitt, A. (2014, January 15). Friday Night Tykes is the most depressing show on television. *Fox Sports*. Retrieved from http://www.foxsports.com/buzzer/story/friday-night-tykes-is-the-most-depressing-show-on-television-011514

Source: Photo by Lance Cpl. Paul Peterson

Youth football players compete in an organized game in full pads

Turman, Zimmerman, and Dobesh (2009) extended this research to explore the techniques parents used to develop relationships with their child's coach and what drove the perceived need for those relationships. The lowest level relationship was classified as the *spectators* and included parents who maximized their distance from the coach but made conscious efforts to ensure the coach recognized their presence and level of support. These parents attended a number of practice sessions and supported their child's athletic involvement by attending all games, volunteering to provide team meals, or providing snacks or refreshments. The second level was classified as the *enthusiasts,* representing those parents who made a point to offer insight or encouragement to the coach but also made a conscious effort to establish only a surface-level relationship. Their interaction focused mainly on the accomplishments or actions of the team as a whole and excluded recognition of individual children's accomplishments. One key distinction between the enthusiast and the spectator relationship was the motive behind the interaction with the coach. Enthusiast parents appeared to use these opportunities to demonstrate their level of knowledge about the particular sport as a way to establish a level of status or influence over coaching decisions. These parents worked to demonstrate a high level of interest and subject knowledge in the sport beyond what a spectator would attempt. The third level relationship is characterized as the *fanatic,* consisting of parents who perceived permeable boundaries between themselves and the coach. These parents were willing to address issues and topics directly, either face-to-face or over the phone. This interaction was seldom described in a negative manner by parents and was more common in smaller communities, where parents and coaches often associated away from the sport. When this occurred, parents often used external interests as a logical excuse for talking about sports.

Coaches are faced with a number of challenges as they establish boundaries that negotiate the extent of the interaction they need to have with external stakeholders in the sport experience. As they attempt to orient more directly toward the internal consistencies, coaches are faced with a number of choices as they select the appropriate style, or orientation, for best leading their athletes.

LEADERSHIP ORIENTATIONS

For those not familiar with the sport of wrestling, there is no coach more revered than Dan Gable. After an undefeated record as high school wrestler, three NCAA individual championship wins, and an Olympic gold medal, Gable began coaching the Hawkeye wrestling program at the University of Iowa. During his career, his teams won 21 consecutive Big Ten Championships. Many of his athletes have gone on to fill the coaching ranks of current NCAA wrestling programs at institutions like Minnesota, Ohio State, Illinois, Indiana, Wisconsin, as well as the current Iowa program. Gable coached the current Hawkeye team coach (Tom Brands) to win three individual NCAA titles, as well as an Olympic gold medal. As the head coach at Iowa, Brands now has two NCAA titles under his belt, and when he talks about his experience with Gable, he

THEORETICALLY SPEAKING

COACH IMMEDIACY

Mehrabian (1967) grounded immediacy behaviors in approach-avoidance theory suggesting that they represent behaviors that diminish psychological and physiological distance. Its central premise is that individuals would be attracted to and willing to approach those they liked, while avoiding those they disliked. When first applied to the classroom context, Andersen (1979) conceptualized immediacy behaviors nonverbally to determine the connection between such behaviors and student cognitive learning. Andersen described nonverbal immediate behaviors as "communication behaviors engaged in when a person maintains closer physical distance" (p. 545) and included behaviors such as touching others, use of gestures and eye contact, length of interaction, informal dress, and relaxed body position. When evaluating coach immediacy behaviors, Turman (2008) observed that verbal immediacy emerged as the only significant predictor of athletes' satisfaction in their sport, after accounting for athletes' playing status and team success. Likewise, the results indicated that coaches' verbal immediacy behaviors were significant predictors of three of the four measures of team cohesion, while perceived nonverbal immediacy behaviors emerged as a predictor for social attraction to group and were the only significant predictor of task group integration.

emphasizes the authoritarian styles that Gable often employed. Brands recently noted, "He [Gable] ran some guys out of town. He was a hard guy to wrestle for. You had to be tough to wrestle for him" (Hamilton, 2011, p. 7).

The above narrative about Gable is used as a lead in to our discussion about coach communication styles, because it emphasizes the impact that a coach with the right style can have on his or her athletes. Coach–athlete relationships are fostered differently among athletes based on the style(s) the coach decides to employ. The multidimensional leadership theory (MLT) proposed by Chelladurai and Saleh (1978) operationalizes effective sport leadership by examining the way coaches understand member characteristics (e.g., the athlete's need for achievement or affiliation in the sport), situational characteristics (e.g., size of the team, amount of formal structure involved in the sport, task), and required leader behavior. To examine how coaches used these three variables in determining appropriate behaviors, a five-dimensional representation of leadership strategies in athletics has been proposed. These dimensions include (1) *autocratic behaviors,* or the extent to which coaches create a separation among athletes by establishing their position and authority over the team; (2) *democratic behaviors* used by coaches to foster participation by the athletes when making decisions related to the sport; (3) *social support* to satisfy interpersonal needs of the athletes; (4) displays of *positive feedback* to motivate athletes and demonstrate appreciation; and (5) *training and instruction* to foster the development of athletes' skill and knowledge aimed at improving performance in the sport (see Table 11.1).

MLT is premised on an assumption that a coach must be cognizant of the leadership preferences of his or her athletes, as well as understand their maturity level, to adjust to the leadership style that is most appropriate for the time. Overall, a number of team and athlete characteristics have been found to influence preferences for coaching styles, with collegiate and professional athletes preferring more autocratic behaviors, youth and high school athletes preferring training and instruction, and athletes with limited performance expectations having a stronger preference for positive feedback. In particular, when examining autocratic behaviors displayed by coaches, a small number of communication researchers have sought to understand the impact that coach verbal aggression has on athlete perceptions toward the sport. Negative behavior alternation techniques (punishment and guilt) have been found to be negatively associated with athlete motivation and affect toward the coach (Martin, Rocca, Cayanus, & Weber, 2009), and high verbal aggression has been found to decrease perceived coach credibility and competence (Mazer, Barnes, Grevious, & Boger, 2013). Coaching experience has also been found to impact the style a coach draws upon, with older coaches relying more on autocratic behaviors but having also mastered the ability to employ a strong mixture of democratic skills than younger coaches (Dimec & Kajtna, 2009).

When collapsing four of the five styles (democratic, training and instruction, social support, and positive feedback) into one general prosocial style, studies have found that this type of behavior is positively associated with athletes' affective learning toward sports (Turman & Schrodt, 2004). Contrary to prosocial behaviors enacted by coaches, an autocratic leadership style (e.g., antisocial or custodial behaviors enacted by coaches) is inversely correlated with athletes' affective learning, suggesting that coaches who rely solely on autocratic leadership behaviors may find their athletes demonstrating less appreciation for the sport, their teammates, and, most important, their coach. Even when accounting for success, it has been found that autocratic leadership in the presence of moderate to high levels of positive feedback may actually increase an athlete's developmental learning, whereas the sole use of autocratic leadership behaviors may lead to a decline. This tends to support "traditional," anecdotal notions that effective coaching is inherently a form of "tough love." In other words, coaches can enact autocratic leadership as long as athletes know that their coaches have their best interests in mind and can occasionally communicate some form of positive feedback. Butterworth's (2013) evaluation of media coverage of inappropriate behavior by coaches Mike Leach, Jim Leavitt, and Mark Mangino (college coaches terminated because of inappropriate behavior toward players) demonstrated a tendency to embrace the authoritative behaviors that reinforced "rugged individualism, fierce competitiveness, and moral courage" (p. 294). At the very least, coaches who rely solely on the use of autocratic leadership may find that the deleterious effects of such behavior greatly outweigh athletes' need for positive feedback (consider the Mike Rice incident at Rutgers that led to his removal as the head basketball coach in 2013). Such behaviors on the part of the coach also increase the potential for dissent within a team. Organizational research has shown that when confronted with unpleasant situations or behavior, individuals are likely to seek out familiar audiences to voice their dissent. When this occurs between employees and managers it is referred to as upward dissent, and it is called lateral dissent when between coworkers. When explored in the sport context (Kassing & Anderson, 2014), research has found that an athlete's position of power (i.e., starter) increases his or her likelihood of upward dissent when confronted with anxiety-provoking situations. Lateral dissent tended to be present more for high school athletes than any other sport type with the perceived openness of the coach to discuss issues resulting in dissent when compared to other sport levels.

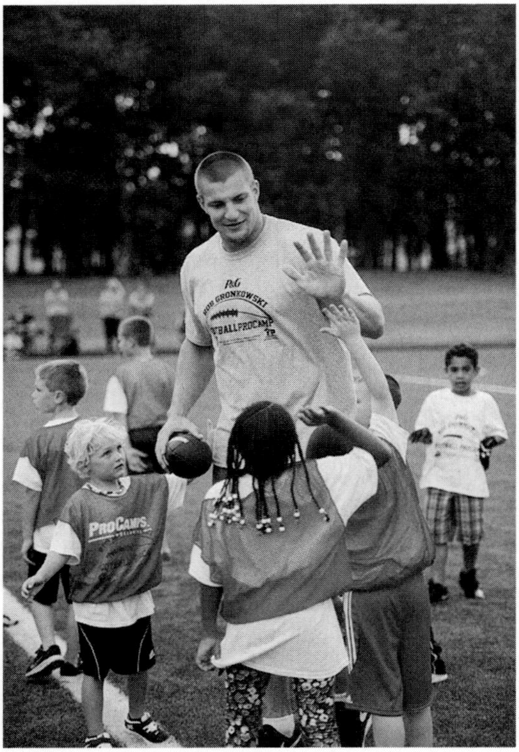

Source: Photo by Tech. Sgt. Robert Cloys from Joint Base Andrews, MD US

Rob Gronkowski provides positive instruction to young players

This brings us back to the example about Dan Gable that was used at the beginning of this section. The quotation given by Tom Brands (about his former coach) reinforced the authoritative style that Gable used with his wrestlers. Yet, consistent with the research on coach communication styles, Gable tended to embody an uncanny ability to use varying styles depending on which approach he felt would work best with his wrestlers. After a series of in-depth interviews with three of Gable's most prolific wrestlers, Hamilton (2011) noted,

TABLE 11.1 ■ Multidimensional Leadership Behaviors Used by Coaches

Leadership Types	Definition	Example
Autocratic	Direct and controlling approach where the coach has the final decision-making authority for the team	"If you want to make this team, then you will do what I ask without question."
Democratic	Egalitarian approach where the coach encourages athletes to be involved in the decision-making process for the team	"For this last play, do you think it will work best if we give Jennifer a chance to make the last shot?"
Social Support	Encouraging approach that allows the coach to demonstrate a level of caring for athletes	"I'm proud of what you have accomplished even if we weren't able to win this game."
Positive Feedback	Providing constructive statements that help to provide positive reinforcement for what occurs during practice and competition	"Keep up the good work, and it will pay off at the end of the season."
Training and Instruction	Feedback that focuses on athlete and team skill development	"Kicking the ball toward the center of the field at this point in time will set up the clear shot for your teammates."

> There are dozens of other stories, but the one these three tell describe Gable as a man who was overtly demanding yet compassionate, a coach who had the elasticity to serve the individual needs of his roster without sacrificing the standards of the team, a leader who could see the brightest characteristics in his athletes during the darkest times. Gable's best trait may have been his uncanny ability to push the right motivational button. He knew who needed a pat on the back and who could handle a kick in the pants. (pp. 7–8)

Although it is difficult to attribute the overall success of the teams Gable produced solely to his coaching style, the heightened need for positive feedback at the right time from coaches is one of the central premises set forth by those involved in a new approach to coaching referred to as the positive coaching movement.

POSITIVE COACHING

In the opening section of this chapter, we discussed the constant tension that coaches face because of the importance our society places on winning. Recognizing this tension, a group of coaches from various sports throughout the United States has joined together to form the Positive Coaching Alliance. The mission of this organization is to engage coaches in encouraging athletes to enjoy sports as a positive character-building experience. This movement has been geared toward youth sport organizations, but the efforts of this organization carry over into both the collegiate and professional levels. Phil Jackson, coach of 11 National Basketball Association (NBA) championship teams, has been an avid supporter of the program since its inception in 1998. He affirms that his coaching philosophy centers around the ability to use positive feedback with his players by ensuring that approximately 75% of his comments to players focus on positive rather than negative statements and messages. Sport psychologists have supported these findings, as athlete self-efficacy and motivation are highly correlated with positive coach behavior. This also extends to coaching ability within the practice setting, as athletes report (Felton & Jowett, 2013) greater satisfaction when they are afforded the opportunity to be involved in the decisions surrounding training sessions. Taking this approach improves athletes' sense of autonomy by providing them with choices and options. As they are required to make their own choices, their potential for skill development and decision making is further increased (Craig & Lynn, 2011).

This orientation toward an emphasis on positive messages is reflected in recent work by Cranmer, Anzur, and Sollitto (2016) that identifies memorable messages used by coaches with their players. Drawing from interpersonal research on memorable messages in romantic and family relationships Cranmer identified coach messages that offered both esteem and emotional support. *Esteem messages* emerged across three different instances that included coaches emphasizing an athlete's ability to be successful, highlighting features about his or her ability that could improve success, and maintaining teammate relationships. Four types of *emotional support* emerged from this work that included an emphasis on athlete well-being beyond the sport, messages that praised effort, performance and personalities, and interaction that sought to assist athlete performance while also communicating about poor performance. These two general categories of memorable messages emerged as athletes were asked to reflect upon advice or support message that signified their relationship with the coach. These forms of sport support highly correlate with athlete satisfaction toward the coach and the sport experience (Cranmer & Sollitto, 2015). Additionally, these forms of social and emotional support align nicely with research exploring how coaches communicate power to their athletes. Cranmer and Goodboy (2015) observed a strong relationship between coaches' reward, referent, and expert power and an athlete's communication satisfaction. In their observation of college athletes they noted that "when coaches have task-related knowledge that could aid in athletes' development, those athletes likely feel more satisfaction in their communication with coaches because their task-related goals are being addressed" (p. 626).

Although positive coaching is considered to be a new movement, many coaches have found success using this approach, even at the collegiate level (Austin, 2011). For example, John Gagliardi, football coach at the Division III program at St. John's in Minnesota for almost 8 decades, amassed 484 wins during his career. Gagliardi didn't use whistles during practices, nor did his players engage in live contact outside of game situations. His soft-spoken approach, which included no profanity, was effective for fostering strong bonds with his players, who interacted with him on a first-name basis (even his players all called him John). When evaluating the role of the coaching in fostering positive development for athletes, Vella, Oades, and Crowe (2011) identified eight key themes that reflect how coaches communicate with athletes to produce positive outcomes. These included messages that emphasized *competence, confidence,* and *character* while also reinforcing *connection* among players and positive *team climate.* When these five were also reinforced with increased *life skills, psychological capacities,* and *positive affect,* the end results were coaches who viewed themselves as responsible for the positive development of their athletes.

In 2014, after being indicted on charges of reckless endangerment of his young son, NFL running back Adrian Peterson's high school football coach publicly noted his frequent use of corporal punishment by striking Peterson routinely with a wooden paddle (Katzowitz, 2014). When coaches draw upon punitive actions—or what Peterson's coach referred to as "tough love"—to influence their athletes, they invite stress, yet positive feedback and reinforcement strategies have been found to have a greater impact on athletes' optimal performance, satisfaction levels, enjoyment, and self-esteem. Jowett (2007, 2009) notes that the most appropriate way to view the coach–athlete relationship is through four interrelated constructs that include closeness, commitment, complementarity, and co-orientation. *Closeness* includes the affective ties that form between a player and coach as an aspect such as a sense of liking and respect develops. *Commitment* emerges in this relationship when a cognitive attachment is created, and the athletes begin to sense a long- rather than short-term orientation toward the coach. *Complementarity* occurs as the athlete and coach begin to communicate from a perspective of cooperation and affiliation. Lastly, *co-orientation* represents athletes' and coaches' abilities to understand the duality of their relationship by recognizing a division between mutual friendships while also existing in a relationship that reflects superior–subordinate behaviors. Each of these dimensions has been found to positively influence the depth of a coach–athlete relationship.

Coaches' positive orientation toward players also has an impact on the self-fulfilling prophecies for their players. A self-fulfilling prophecy occurs in sports when coaches view athletes differently (based on gender, ability, level of enthusiasm) and provide differential treatment. Solomon, DiMarco, Ohlson, and Reece (1998) state, "When coaches' perceptions of an athlete are consistently communicated and understood by the athlete, they can impact the athlete's future performance and psychological growth in a positive or negative manner" (p. 445). Athletes with limited performance expectations are said to receive more technical instruction from their coaches, while those with high expectations are reinforced or encouraged at greater levels. As a result, these low-expectancy athletes are likely to view their experience more negatively when compared to high-achieving athletes. *High-expectancy* athletes have been shown to prefer more instruction and positive feedback, encouragement, and positive reinforcement. *Low-expectancy* athletes are asked fewer questions by their coaches and receive fewer skill practice opportunities, fewer constructive comments, and higher levels of criticism. A cyclical effect is likely to occur in these situations. Coaches interact in a more negative fashion, which then causes the low-expectancy athlete to withdraw and experience decreased motivation; this is then recognized by the coach, who then provides feedback that can then cause athletes to completely withdraw.

Positive coaching or support-based communication aids in reducing uncertainty that athletes might be experiencing with their sport. When uncertainty is eliminated, the relationships have been found to be less ambiguous, complex, and unpredictable. Naylor (2007) noted,

> The role of teacher is to educate, nurture, and empower athletes providing opportunities for personal growth and development. These are objectives that are easily accomplished in practice, yet decisions and behaviors of coaches during competitive situations are often at odds with educational ideals. (p. 32)

In the section that follows, we attempt to explore this dichotomy within the context of coach–athlete interaction during competitive situations.

CASE STUDY

WINNING ISN'T THE ONLY THING AFTER ALL

In the first section of this chapter, we explored the "win at all cost" model represented in sport today, but there are stories that emerge every so often that demonstrate how coaches and athletes can still embrace the honorable side of competition. Such was the case in 2008 when the Central Washington University Wildcats softball team played host to Western Oregon University. Before the start of their double-header, Western Oregon was one game ahead of Central Washington in the standings for the Great Northwest Athletic Conference race. After losing the first matchup, Central Washington needed to win the second game to ensure that their playoff hopes remained intact. When Sara Tucholsky stepped up to the plate in the second inning for what could be her final at-bat as a college athlete, she performed a feat that she had never achieved in her 4 years of collegiate ball. A 0.153 hitter for the year, Tucholsky hit a three-run home run and began sprinting toward first base. In her excitement, she strode to first base as she looked up to watch the ball clear the center field fence, causing her to miss the bag and tear her anterior cruciate ligament in her right knee. She was able to crawl back to first base, but because rules specify that a player must be able to advance around the bases unassisted from teammates, Tucholsky was at risk of having a substitute runner replace her at first causing her home run to be replaced.

As the head coach and umpire considered the team's options, Mallory Holtman, the first baseman for the Western Oregon team, offered to have her teammates carry Tucholsky around the bases for the score. The rules specified that a player must be unassisted by teammates to advance, but there appeared to be no such stipulation when it came to the opposing team assisting an injured player. Holtman recruited her shortstop teammate Liz Wallace to assist her, and together they picked up Tucholsky and advanced her around the diamond, pausing at each base to ensure that she was able to touch the bag as specified in the rules. After the game, Holtman was quoted as saying, "In the end, it is not about winning and losing so much. . . . It was about this girl. She hit it over the fence and was in pain, and she deserved a home run." Western Oregon went on to win the game 4–2 and eliminated Central Washington from playoff contention, but both teams learned a valuable lesson about the integrity that sport can produce.

Acts of sportsmanship like this are often overshadowed by more unsavory acts by coaches and players. For example, at the conclusion of the final track event that cost his team the conference title, a head coach recently approached the officials, noting that the athlete had been wearing a friendship bracelet thus violating established rules prohibiting jewelry. The athlete was disqualified, and team points were stripped, causing the team to lose its conference title.

1. How difficult would it be for you to perform a similar act for an opponent?
2. Take yourself out of the context of a softball team. Would any of your coaches have allowed you to perform such an act if it meant the possibility of losing?
3. What do the actions of these players say about the coach–athlete relationships?

COMMUNICATION CONTEXTS

The coach–athlete relationship can occur in a variety of contexts, giving coaches a range of options for communicating with players. For instance, coaches are no longer limited by the confines of the athletic season, as many sports have become year-round activities for youth, high school, collegiate, and professional athletes. In many instances, coaches attempt to begin building this relationship before an athlete has even joined the team. For example, text messaging has become such a powerful tool employed by college coaches in their recruiting efforts that the NCAA has recently established limits on when these messages can be sent to players. Kelvin Sampson (head basketball coach at Indiana University) was even fired for violating these text messaging policies. Such limits are not placed on recruiting letters, resulting in cases such as five-star football recruit Matt Elam receiving 182 letters from the University of Kentucky—in a single day.

When placed within the window of the traditional season, coaches are most likely to communicate with players during practice or competitive events. Performance feedback is an important feature of any instructional process whereby coaches are afforded the opportunity to provide an assessment of athletes' overall performance. As the positive coaching movement might attest, the messages coaches select to frame their feedback can directly influence the attributions athletes make about their athletic experience. For example, a coach's decision to place the blame on the team's star athlete after a loss is quite different from a decision to encourage the player who missed the final shot that marked the end of the season. The coach may also place the blame on himself or herself or even make a point of building up players who have been struggling by using the pregame speech to challenge them to perform beyond their means. Gallmeier (1987) followed a

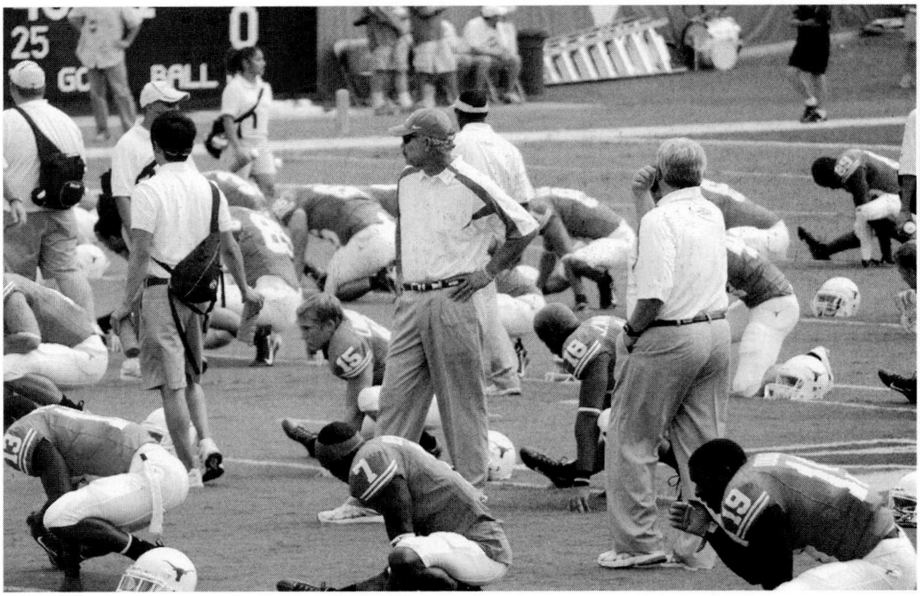

The Texas Longhorn coaching staff watches over players during warm-ups

professional hockey team throughout the season, noting that the coach relied upon the pregame speech to "psych up" players, especially in situations where the coach didn't have access to the players throughout the day. Players exposed to these speeches were found to have higher levels of self-efficacy and larger margins of victory. Not only are athlete outcomes influenced, but they self-report also that the pregame speech is an important function that the coach fulfills for the team, with most athletes noting a strong desire for an emotional response from their coach.

The messages coaches select can be powerful predictors of how athletes view their athletic experiences, and most individuals are predisposed to interpret behaviors, actions, and events that occur around them in connection with their causes. People have an innate need to find an explanation for why an event occurred, allowing for better control of their surroundings; when they are unable to understand the reason why, the world is rendered unpredictable. The messages that coaches employ during these competitive situations have also been found to produce feelings of regret as athletes are called upon to reflect on what could have or should have happened. *Regret* is defined as a complex emotion causing individuals to make judgments about events they take part in, and they have the ability to feel regretful not only about their participation in past experiences but also about how decisions concerning future events are made.

The need to use messages that connect antecedents and outcomes is likely to increase as individuals or groups are faced with winning and losing situations. For instance,

Turman (2005) identified six types of regret messages used by coaches during their pregame, halftime, and postgame speeches. The most predominant was *accountability regret,* which represented coaches' need to assign blame or praise following their team's first-half performance. By focusing their players' attention on factors that reduced the team's ability to win, coaches were able to implicitly demonstrate that if these antecedents were addressed by the team, a more positive outcome would result at the end of the contest ("If we just would have gone for it on fourth down, we could have won the game"). *Individual performance regret* messages were used to help magnify the potential self-regret felt by athletes after a poor performance and outcome. A majority of these messages occurred during the coaches' pregame comments to the team and included a combination of counterfactual antecedents (e.g., "If you play hard") and upward counterfactual outcomes (e.g., "You will feel satisfied"). Third, *collective failure regret* signified messages that demonstrated how athlete performance was potentially linked to the disappointment of their teammates or coach ("If you don't give 100% on every play, you will be letting this team down"). *Social significance regret* was derived from the coaches' efforts to construct the game as socially significant for their players. For instance, as the season began to draw to a close, a number of coaches began to call attention to the fact that athletes in their senior year were drawing closer to their final game or would direct their athletes' attention toward the significance of the upcoming event for both the team and their school ("Letting them come in here and push you around isn't something our fans will accept"). Fifth, coaches relied on *regret reduction* primarily during the postgame interaction; it characterized coaches' attempts to reduce the potential regret felt by athletes after a loss ("If we hadn't tried for that long pass, we still would have lost the game"). Finally, as the season drew to a close, a number of coaches relied on regret messages that described the *future regret* players would experience as a result of a team loss. It appeared that coaches used this foreshadowing of events and the potential emotional response athletes would feel afterward to identify antecedents that athletes could employ to control their future outcome ("Lose this game, and you'll take it to the grave").

Turman (2007) further explored the impact of regret on a variety of athlete outcomes and found that success and status determine the extent to which athletes will perceive increases in coach performance and future regret messages. Hastie (1999) explored coach–athlete interaction during time-outs, observing a positive relationship with athlete performance for the team calling the time-out. He noted that messages fell within three categories, including (1) *technical statements*—messages that correct the behaviors of players both positively and negatively; (2) *tactical statements*—proactive or reactive statements that use a combination of questions or focus on consequences; and (3) *psychological statements*—general encouragement or reasoning statements that attempt to draw attention or focus athletes. The messages or statements employed in each of these contexts (pregame, time-outs, halftime, and postgame interaction) provide a brief glimpse into the nature of the coach–athlete relationship during competitive situations (see Table 11.2).

TABLE 11.2 ■ Coach Regret Message Types Employed During Competitive Situations

Message Type	Definition	Example
Accountability Regret	Statements that emphasize the factors that contributed to a team's unsuccessful performance	"When you fail to pass the puck around to your teammates, it's difficult to score points."
Individual Performance Regret	Messages that place specific blame on an individual occurrence or event that signaled a team's loss	"If we just would have tried for a two-point conversion, we wouldn't have lost in overtime."
Collective Failure Regret	Statements geared toward reinforcing the need for the team to work together to ensure success	"Despite losing Jackie to an ankle injury, we can all pull together in the second half to win."
Social Significance Regret	Messages that reinforce the broader impact of sport beyond just the outcome for the event	"The people of this town are expecting you to win this game, so don't hold back anything tonight."
Regret Reduction	Statements that are used by the coach to reduce the feelings of regret that players might be experiencing after a contest	"I know that winning is important, but I would hope that you have learned from this experience and can use it to get better as we move forward as a team."
Future Regret	Emphasis on the significance of the team's outcome as an approach to help reinforce a team's desire to win	"When you get to a championship game, either you give it everything you have, or it will haunt you for the rest of your life."

Bob Knight during his time as the head coach for Texas Tech

CONCLUSION

In this chapter, we have introduced you to a number of factors directly influencing the coach–athlete relationship. As one considers the tension that coaches face when making decisions about winning versus the developmental needs of their players, a number of styles are likely to emerge. The rhetorical and communicative resources that a coach draws upon determine not only a team's success but also how athletes view and interpret their sport experience. Having a coach who emphasizes a positive orientation toward coaching could be important for young athletes who are seeking an enjoyable experience from their sport participation.

On the other hand, collegiate or professional athletes are more inclined to have coaches who draw upon the authority of their position to ensure the highest levels of success. This does not mean that coaches have to take a punitive approach to obtain the desired response from their athletes, as even professional coaches must understand the emotional turmoil that athletes can experience in the "just business" model for professional and collegiate athletics. Although he was often vilified by the media for his antics during games and harsh treatment of players, Bob Knight (former NCAA basketball coach who once held the all-time record for most career wins in NCAA men's basketball) is often described by his former players in affectionate terms. His autocratic behavior was a function of the competitive nature of NCAA basketball, but he also possessed skills for teaching the fundamentals of the sport while producing some of the highest player graduation rates in the nation. Vince Lombardi was viewed in a similar fashion by his players. Many describe him as a coach who was intent on winning but who could also connect with players on a personal level in one-on-one situations. Developing a suitable balance in one's communication style is what marks the difference between coaches who effectively foster positive relationships with their athletes and those who don't.

SUGGESTED ADDITIONAL READING

Kassing, J. W., & Infante, D. A. (1999). Aggressive communication in the coach–athlete relationship. *Communication Research Reports, 16,* 110–120.

Llewellyn, J. (2003). Coachtalk: Good reasons for winning and losing. In R. S. Brown & D. O'Rourke (Eds.), *Case studies in sport communication* (pp. 141–158). Westport, CT: Praeger.

Turman, P. (2007). Coach regret messages: The influence of athlete sex, context, and performance on high school basketball coaches' use of regret messages during competition. *Communication Education, 56,* 333–353.

Cranmer, G. A., & Brann, M. (2015). "It makes me feel like I am an important part of this team": An exploratory study of coach confirmation. *International Journal of Sport Communication, 8,* 193–211.

Wooden, J. (1997). *Wooden: A lifetime of observation and reflection on and off the court.* Chicago, IL: Contemporary Books.

12

SMALL GROUPS/ TEAMS IN SPORT

Throughout this text we have emphasized the significant impact that sport can have for individuals at varying levels. Parents encourage sport participation because they view it as an important socializing agent, fans can feel transcendence through viewing or taking part in rituals central to sport spectatorship, and coaches help shape their players' mind-sets by emphasizing the important life lessons that can surface through the preparation for competition. Each of these contexts has one element in common: They all occur in groups. Groups and teams play a foundational role not only in how sport is enacted but also in how our society consumes and learns from the sport experience. For example, more than half of today's children are involved in some type of organized group sport, suggesting that many will reach maturity after acquiring much of their understanding about the nature and structure of small-group interaction from sports and games. We all learn from our group experiences, and because many of these groups are composed primarily of sport-type groups, it seems relevant that much of what we learn about group practices, norms, roles, and how to communicate would take place within a sport context. Furthermore, as we gain a stronger appreciation for the impact sport participation might have on the development of various communication behaviors, a stronger emphasis could be placed on sport as an important informal learning context with societal implications.

With this background in mind, this chapter is used to explore these issues by providing perspective on the influence of communication within the context of sport and games. Sport is overflowing with examples of teams filled with talented individuals who have failed to win team championships. For example, Steve Nash won the NBA Most Valuable Player award in 2004–2005 and 2005–2006 yet never was able to lead his team to an NBA title during his career. During the 2016 NBA finals, league MVP Stephen Curry eventually lost to MVP contender LeBron James despite a 3–1 lead early in the championship playoff series. It is not uncommon for the league MVP to not also win the eventual team title. Sport teams can easily be distinguished based on the level of interdependence required by athletes during competition, a function that is mediated by communication. *Independent teams* (wrestling, track and field, gymnastics, etc.) include those where the culmination of individual effort contributes to a team's performance, while *interdependent teams* (football, baseball, hockey, etc.) require that athletes collaborate to ensure victory (Bruner, Eys, Blair Evans, & Wilson, 2015). We begin this chapter by examining the complex communication events that contribute to team cohesion. Although variables including team performance and athlete inputs and outputs have been found to strongly influence cohesion, team interaction and coaching behaviors or strategies also contribute to ensuring a team's winning potential. Also, as your experience might attest, there are a number of group processes unique to sports. Sport teams often introduce coaches and players to an important set of group processes (e.g., norm development, power, leadership emergence) that are central to framing the team experience. We explore each of these processes through a communication lens in an effort to highlight unique group functions that occur in sport teams. Finally, we conclude this chapter by demonstrating the role that sport and games have for developing the unique communication behaviors that distinguish masculine and feminine communication cultures. Such gender differences become quite pronounced and have the potential for influencing one's future group interaction. As we explore each of these major themes throughout this chapter, we anticipate that you will develop a broader appreciation for the direct and indirect ways that participation in sport teams affects your everyday experiences.

Source: http://www.usmc.mil/marinelink/image1.nsf/lookup/20027121231338?opendocument via Wikimedia Commons

Dale Earnhardt, Jr.

TEAM/GROUP COHESION

Maximizing effort to win is an essential feature of sport, but to achieve this goal, it is critical that individual team members be equally invested in ensuring team success. For this to occur, team members must experience a sense of connection, which has been assessed in terms of team cohesion levels. *Cohesion* is an important sport

INTERVIEW

DALE EARNHARDT, JR., NATIONAL ASSOCIATION FOR STOCK CAR AUTO RACING (NASCAR) DRIVER

Q: To an outsider, NASCAR is an individual sport that is focused solely on the driver. NASCAR fans know differently. How important is assembling the right team?

A: It's extremely important. Each team consists of 10 to 15 people that work directly on the race car, and that's not counting your motor department or pit crew. They each have their own responsibility. Each one affects the way your car performs, and it doesn't have to be off by much to hinder the performance of the car. We measure things in hundredths-of-a-second and fractions of an inch, and so forth. So everything has to be clicking. If there is just one fracture in the overall makeup of the team, it jeopardizes the entire team.

Q: In many other team sports, players have little control over who else is on their team. How much control do you have, and how often do you exert it?

A: It probably varies for each team, but I would say the crew chief and maybe a team director or competition director handle most personnel decisions. They may ask for my input, or I may go to them and recommend someone occasionally, but for the most part, they have a lot better handle on who's good and who's not than I do.

Q: Describe the chain of command on race day.

A: We'll have a race strategy that we formulated over the previous 2 days based off practice speeds, qualifying, and team debriefings. The crew chief will implement that strategy and decide if we need to sway from it due to circumstances in the race. The crew chief is privy to a lot of information on top of the pit box, so he is the conductor, so to speak. He'll decide how to adjust the car, when to make pit stops, and so forth based off the information I'm giving him about the car. The driver is certainly important, especially when it comes to working with the crew chief. The spotter on the roof does most of the talking. I would say those are your top three, and then, pit crew and mechanics fall under that.

Q: Do roles on your team stay well defined, or do those roles get blurry, at least at certain points?

A: For the most part, they are well defined as far as the "road crew" and competition personnel go. You tend to see more utility-type players in administrative roles or front office positions. Take my company, JR Motorsports, for instance. My sister, Kelley, runs the company, and she covers many areas. I think the economic climate over the past 5 years forced us all to rethink how we do our jobs, because the sponsorship game changed. Their priorities changed. So it forced employees to put on a glove and become educated in other areas. For that reason, you see some situations of bleedover in responsibilities and roles.

Q: What qualities do you think comprise a winning team formula in NASCAR?

A: You've got to have a strong team leader for sure, and that starts at the very top—the owner. You've got to have clear and concise communication, especially between the driver and crew chief. And to be honest, I think you've got to have a work environment that is enjoyable to come to. Our industry is a grind. We race 38 weeks out of the year, and much of that is on the road. No other major sport has a schedule like that. It's important that the culture of the race shop is fun and enjoyable, because if it isn't, it becomes quite detrimental to the performance of the race team.

outcome—defined as the sense of belonging or sense of morale individuals experience as a function of their team membership. There has been some speculation that success and cohesion can be used interchangeably, as 83% of studies indicated a positive relationship between cohesion and performance (Widmeyer, Carron, & Brawley, 1993). Scholarly work on cohesion suggests that team cohesion is mediated by two dimensions reflecting the *task* (e.g., desire to achieve the group's goals) and *social* functions (e.g., desire to develop and maintain relationships) fulfilled by the group.

Much of this cohesive environment has been influenced by a number of factors driven by communication. Such feelings have been described as "we-ness" because members are more likely to use the term *we* than *I* when referring to the team (hence the saying that "there is no *I* in *team*"). Drawing attention to one's individual performance in team sports can be viewed as a detriment to the cohesive environment fans are likely to expect. For example, the National Collegiate Athletic Association (NCAA) implemented strict rules that prohibit football players from on-field celebrations that draw attention to the individual rather than the team. Significant backlash is also likely to occur when athletes present the impression they are not playing to peak potential. Johnny Manziel, the former 2014 first-round draft pick for the Cleveland Browns, was released from the team following a number of off-field incidents that management perceived as a distraction to the team. Despite earning the Heisman Trophy while playing college football for Texas A&M, his performance on the field and the detrimental impact for the team makes many teams hesitate to have him as a part of their future plans. Athletes are expected to place the needs of the team in front of their own, and, in many cases, to sacrifice their individual needs to benefit the team (Cronin, Arthur, Hardy, & Callow, 2015).

Athletes themselves often embrace and understand the impact that their own behavior can have on the cohesion that exists among team members. The tendency for gay and lesbian athletes to remain "in the closet" has often been attributed to the potential backlash that many expect from fans and the media; however, many athletes have feared the impact it might have on team dynamics. For instance, when Jason Collins was the first National Basketball Association (NBA) player to come out during an interview with *Sports Illustrated* in 2013, he noted that he didn't come out sooner because of the distraction it would cause for his teammates.

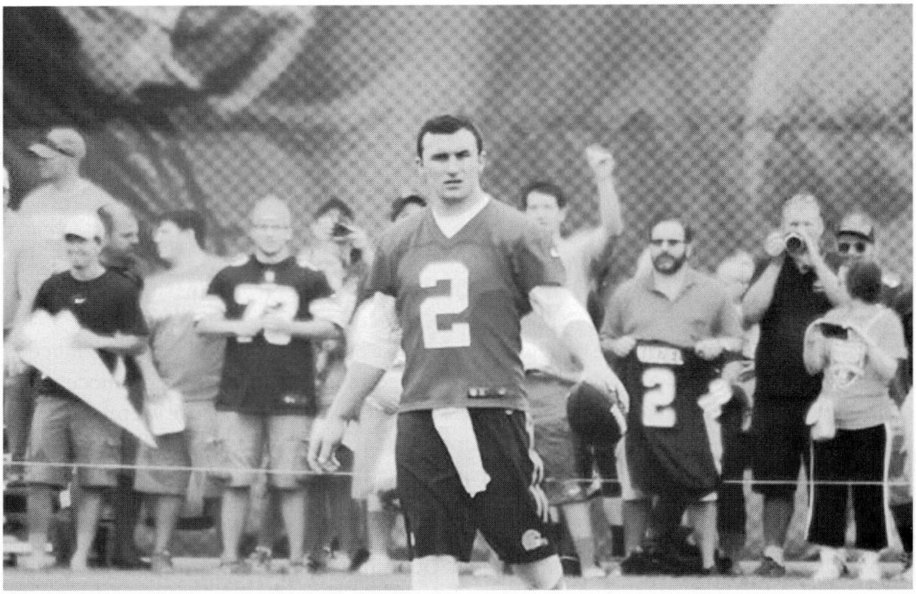

Source: By Erik Daniel Drost Morbeck (originally posted to Flickr as Johnny Manziel 2014 Browns training camp (3)

Johnny Manziel warms up during the Cleveland Browns training camp

Coaches' Impact on Cohesion

Teams at all levels of competition spend considerable time, energy, and resources to unravel factors that enhance team effectiveness, with much of this emphasis placed in the areas of cohesion. Because the team's cohesion level affects individual group member behavior, numerous scholars emphasize the important role of the coach in fostering cohesion to further enhance team performance (see Chapter 11). Research has even shown considerable need for cohesion among the members of the coaching staff (Martin, 2002). Recent investigations of coaching strategies suggest that positive relationships between coaches and athletes have the potential to positively influence team cohesion levels (Seyed-Mahmoud & Kwasi, 2009). For instance, Turman (2003) interviewed college athletes regarding the specific communication behaviors displayed by their coaches that deterred or promoted team cohesion. Two different behaviors were found to deter cohesion among athletes. Athletes described *inequity* as situations where coaches showed favoritism to a particular athlete or group within the team, use of poor communication skills, and/or bragging about the ability of other athletes. Favoritism included situations, such as allowing individual athletes to do less work or miss team functions (i.e., meetings, events, practices), without reprimands. This is consistent with other research that has explored jealousy in sports, where categories such as scholarship funding and attention from the coach were found to be negatively correlated with team cohesion levels (Schelling-Kamphoff & Huddleston, 1999). The second theme included *embarrassment and ridicule,* reflecting behaviors such as yelling at athletes or benching them for poor

CASE STUDY

MORE THAN TALENT REQUIRED

Although athletic talent of individual team members can be a significant predictor for team success, there is support for the fact that teammates need to develop a strong social connection to help coordinate their efforts. High school, collegiate, and professional sports are filled with instances where teams with unlimited potential have failed to achieve their anticipated outcomes because the sense of "we-ness" has been lacking from the group. At the start of the 1999–2000 NBA season, the Los Angeles Lakers hired Phil Jackson, who had recently retired after coaching the Chicago Bulls to six NBA titles. With two of the league's most talented players (Kobe Bryant and Shaquille O'Neal), Jackson was considered to be a pivotal piece in the puzzle as he helped lead the team to three titles during his first three seasons. The following year, they went 11–19 to start the season, ultimately recovering to finish with more than 50 wins. However, they were eventually eliminated from postseason play by the San Antonio Spurs at the conclusion of the 2003 season.

During the off-season, Jackson sought to further position the team to win his fourth championship with the Lakers. Management aggressively pursued a trade for Karl Malone from the Utah Jazz and Gary Payton from the Seattle SuperSonics. With a lineup that included Bryant, O'Neal, Malone, and Payton, many considered the Los Angeles Lakers team to be one of the most talented groups of players ever amassed on one team in NBA history. With four future Hall of Fame players taking the floor each night, the team appeared unstoppable on paper. However, the team faced early setbacks during the season resulting from a number of injuries to the starting lineup and tension between the team's two star players. Despite these difficulties, the Lakers ended the regular season with a 0.700 record and advanced into the 2004 NBA playoffs, where they were eventually eliminated in five games against the Detroit Pistons. Tension further escalated during the postseason between Bryant and O'Neal. Bryant even displayed considerable disagreement with Jackson's coaching style as he publicly criticized Jackson for employing a game strategy that did not fully use his talents. Jackson soon demanded that Bryant be traded. In response, the Lakers front office eventually sided with Bryant as they traded O'Neal and terminated their contract with Jackson. The Lakers failed to make the playoffs the next two seasons and were unable to return to championship form again until Jackson returned as the head coach for the 2007–2008 season.

1. To what factors would you attribute the team's inability to win a fourth championship with the talent it had amassed?
2. How might the presence of four superstar players inversely affect the team's ability to foster a cohesive environment conducive to winning?
3. Where might you fit Bormann's process of residues (1996, see p. 271) as a contributing factor in explaining the problems this team confronted?

performance. This type of behavior appeared to not only influence the athlete being reprimanded but also affect other players who witnessed the events.

Five behaviors or strategies were identified that have positive effects on promoting team cohesion. *Sarcasm and teasing* consisted of joking, mocking, and ridicule of athletes that allowed them to collectively laugh together. Athletes reported that forms of sarcasm drew them closer because coaches were able to show a nonsport side that worked to build relationships between players. *Motivational speeches* were influential because of the way they allowed athletes to interact as a team afterward while also stressing team over individual effort. Cohesion was further fostered when coaches focused on relinquishing personal agendas for the good of the team. When the team faced a *quality opponent,* the respect that coaches afforded the opposition increased cohesion as players bonded at higher levels. When coaches described opponents with respect, athletes perceived increased cohesion after accepting that no opponent should be taken lightly. Some alluded to the connection and focus of their teammates during weeks they played higher caliber opponents, as coaches often approached difficult games differently during pregame speeches. Matchups in college football between Ohio State and Michigan or the Red Sox and Yankees in Major League Baseball are just two examples of instances where significant rivalries assist to bond players at higher levels (Karmel, 2009). Focusing on the rivalry helped establish a clear "us" versus "them" quality threaded throughout a coach's behavior leading up to the contest. Coaches fostered *athlete-directed techniques* by encouraging teammates to develop their own connection, including spending time together off the field, lifting weights and studying together, or scheduling team picnics. Finally, athletes reported that the use of a *team prayer* during pregame and postgame interaction was a successful strategy because it emphasized that every team member must perform up to his or her maximum ability. Internal conflicts and tensions among athletes appeared to be eliminated, as the prayer would often bring the team together as a unit just prior to competition.

Each of these coaching strategies works to establish team rituals that not only foster team cohesion but also institute important norms, roles, and processes that determine appropriate behavior on the team. As participation in teams is an essential feature of sport, sport participants are likely to be exposed to a combination of both rewarding and detrimental grouping processes. We explore each of these areas in the following section.

GROUP/TEAM PROCESSES IN SPORT

As we discussed in the opening paragraph, there is evidence to suggest that much of what individuals learn about group behavior, norms, and roles can be traced to their sport participation. This can produce both positive and negative outcomes for individuals' future behavior.

Group Norms

Group norms serve as a standard for how group members begin to understand how they are expected to behave as members of the team. These acceptable forms of behavior evolve over time and become powerful determinants of how team members are socialized. While sometimes related, *group roles* often emerge over time and represent the individual expectations attributed to group member behaviors. For instance, team captains are often assigned and expected to fulfill specific types of roles (i.e., "When there is a problem, Karen will call a team meeting"), while some can emerge from routine behaviors from a particular team member (i.e., "We always expect Chantel to be late for practice"). Although one would expect that acceptable norms are reinforced, scholars have exposed a range of norm behaviors (cheating, aggression, and rule violations) that violate the underlying tenets of competition. For example, officials in the National Hockey League (NHL) were evaluated to determine rule accuracy and correctness, yet it was found they were less concerned with these two officiating norms than with emphasizing consistency and fairness during the game (Rains, 1984). For teams, a combination of competitive, practice, off-season, and social norms have been found to exist (Munroe, Estabrooks, Dennis, & Carron, 1999). *Competitive norms* include things such as the team's expected game preparedness and work ethic. Teammates are expected to be punctual and attend with a mind-set that results in productivity from other players. *Practice norms* include many of the same game expectations yet do not tie directly to team productivity. Players are expected to work hard and be prepared and punctual. Lack of attendance is frowned upon by teammates, indicating the direct perceived correlation between practices and team success during competition. During his time with the Philadelphia 76ers, Allen Iverson was heavily criticized by his coach, teammates, fans, and the media for routinely being late or absent from scheduled practice sessions. Many of you may have seen his infamous 2002 postgame tirade where he criticized his coach and the media after he had been suspended for violating this important team norm. In the interview he noted, "We're sitting here, and I'm supposed to be the franchise player, and we're talking about *practice*." His response went on for 4 minutes and used the term "practice" 14 times. *Off-season norms* include behaviors such as keeping in contact with teammates and sharing workout strategies that are developed in the off-season. Players also expect others to maintain a healthy lifestyle that would not adversely affect the team while continuing to train and compete in the sport during the off-season. In 2008, NFL Pro Bowl lineman Casey Hampton was heavily criticized by his coach and fellow teammates when he came back to training camp almost 30 pounds overweight and unable to perform very basic conditioning requirements. Finally, *social norms* represent the general atmosphere or climate teammates are expected to maintain, which include keeping others in high regard, avoiding physical conflicts, and remaining silent about internal matters of the team. Early in his NBA career, LeBron James was scrutinized for criticizing his coach's decision to bench a fellow player on the eve of him breaking a franchise record for games started. Munroe and her colleagues (1999) concluded that "the development of group norms for social situations and during the off-season inevitably ensures that the interpersonal

Allen Iverson

bonds within the team are characterized by stability, affective concern, and a sense of continuity" (p. 180). The findings depict favorable benefits for teammates, yet there are no guarantees that norm violation won't occur, especially when you consider that unproductive norms and rituals continue to exist in team sports. Despite these findings, there are instances where norm violation or dissention can be beneficial in team sports. In particular, Tauber and Sassenberg (2012) found that sports teams need dissention to ensure the welfare of the team, and that star players often show the greatest likelihood of sacrificing themselves and dissent when the team norm warrants conformity. Being willing to go against the edicts of an authoritative coach or not engage in conventional hazing activities is more likely to be accepted by the team when highly identified players are involved.

THEORETICALLY SPEAKING

SOCIAL LOAFING

At the turn of the 21st century, researchers attempted to uncover why people deliberately exerted less effort to achieve group goals when compared to what the combination of their individual efforts might achieve. Research in this area began with rope pulling experiments by Ringelmann (1913) who found that members of a group tended to exert less effort on pulling a rope than did individuals alone. Latané, Williams, and Harkins (1979) later coined the term "social loafing" to describe the phenomenon, noting that as the number of people in the group increase, people tend to feel deindividuation. Ultimately, as the size of the team increased, the potential for dissociation from individual achievement and the decrease of personal accountability resulted in lower exerted effort for individuals in collaborative environments. Hoigaard, Tofteland, and Ommundsen (2006) evaluated the presence of social loafing behaviors in team sports and found that this presence mediated cohesion among teammates. Specifically, they found that cohesive teams were less likely to experience social loafing, resulting in heightened team performance levels. They concluded that "one function of team cohesiveness may be that a sense of social attraction and integration to the team counteracts social loafing, and thereby enhances individual effort and team performance" (p. 70). More recently Backer, Boen, Cuyper, and Brock (2015) observed that coaching behaviors (in particular perceived fairness) were highly correlated with athlete social loafing behaviors. When a coach is viewed as fair by his or her players then they focus less on their personal interests and more on the overall success of the team.

Hazing in Sports

Hazing rituals are a common communicative norm (harassment, abuse, humiliation) that many consider to serve as important rites of passage for initiating new members into the group. As groups develop, there is a strong need for members to be socialized into the culture and history of the group, as members are commonly tested to determine their commitment to becoming a part of the team. Some even go as far as to suggest that hazing is an important team-building experience or even has a positive impact on team cohesion levels. When viewed as team member behavior toward new members, hazing can be a vicious tool for communicating power and team positioning. Hazing laws have been implemented in numerous states, with high schools and colleges imposing strict penalties on teams that still take part in this unproductive grouping experience. Often, you will see media reports of incidents such as when a high school football player filed charges against his coach and school officials after senior players taped him to a goal post and then took turns kicking soccer balls at his head. There have also been more graphic examples, such as video footage that surfaced in 2008 (Illinois's Glenbrook North High School girls' soccer team) showing teammates putting Tabasco sauce and vinegar in the eyes of freshmen players and covering them with fish guts, Spam, and pig intestines. More recently, 12 former Florida Agricultural and Mechanical (A&M) University band members were charged with manslaughter after a band member died due to injuries suffered from a beating resulting from a common hazing ritual following an away football game.

Despite the threat of stiff penalties, hazing continues to be a common occurrence that can depict an unconstructive feature of team sport participation. Despite this perception, it is difficult for many teams to curb this practice because of the customary recurring cycle of hazing; hazed underclassmen take out their frustrations on other underclassmen when they later find themselves in leadership positions. At the professional level, media often portray trivial forms of hazing such as having male rookie players dress up as women, expecting them to carry equipment for veteran players, or requiring them to sing at team meals. For example, Larry English (the San Diego Chargers' first-round pick during the 2009 NFL draft) was forced to pick up a $15,000 dinner bill for returning players as an annual hazing ritual veteran players engage in. Well-intended bonding occurrences of hazing such as this are likely to be found each year during the start of most professional seasons. The *Sporting News* reporter has also been known to ask a player from each team an embarrassing question at NFL training camps, which has been considered a mild form of hazing. However, the frequency and severity of such events are continuing to increase even in professional sports. Hazing or allegation of bullying emerged in 2013 when Jonathan Martin, tackle for the Miami Dolphins, walked off the team due to what he referred to as continuous abuse and harassment from fellow teammate Richard Incognito. Following investigations by the team, a series of text messages emerged that highlighted the extent of the harassment, and the NFL conducted a comprehensive workplace review of the organization and other NFL teams (Brennan, 2013).

While media reports often highlight various forms of hazing activity that might routinely emerge in professional sports, it has been difficult to obtain accurate data on hazing at the high school and collegiate levels, as only 12% of athletes report exposure to hazing (Hoover, 1999), yet more than 80% of these same athletes reported being involved in a range of specific hazing activities as a way of initiation. This suggests that athletes engage in hazing activities, while also recognizing the negative perception that society has of such activities in sport. One of the difficulties associated with hazing is that what constitutes *hazing* has been difficult to clearly articulate. Krzysztof and Craig (2010) observed high levels of hazing activity in their analysis of high school athletes, yet the types of behaviors that they defined as hazing further demonstrate that traditional team guidelines or coaching techniques could be obscured as mild forms of hazing. These included behaviors such as attending preseason training, keeping specific grade point averages, and participating in calisthenics not related to a sport. On the other hand, more extreme behaviors such as destroying or stealing property, engaging in or simulating sexual acts, or being kidnapped or transported and abandoned were much less frequently reported. Research connecting hazing to cohesion levels has been limited (Van Raalte, Cornelius, Linder, & Brewer, 2007), though findings indicate a strong negative correlation between hazing and an athlete's commitment to participating in the sport. In this analysis, they distinguished between unacceptable and acceptable team-building behaviors (see Table 12.1).

TABLE 12.1 ■ Unacceptable and Acceptable Team-Building Behaviors Linked to Hazing in Sports

Team-Building Types	Description
	Unacceptable
Passive Victim of Abuse	Instances where players have been kidnapped by fellow teammates, abandoned in isolated areas, tied up or taped without permission, or berated for nonsport-related behaviors.
Coerced Self-Abuse or Degradation	Forcing teammates to drink unknown substances or engaging in drinking contests. Coercion also includes food and water deprivation or using rookies as personal servants.
Coerced Abuse of Others	Requiring teammates to harass other players or nonteam members, destroy personal property, or engage in acts of vandalism or theft.
	Acceptable
Skill Development and Assessment	Requiring teammates to participate in nonmandatory preseason or early workouts or practices that might include physical exertion or tests of endurance unrelated to sport performance.
Coerced Deviant Behavior	Requiring teammates to engage in tattooing, piercing, or branding. It can also include public displays of embarrassing clothing and/or simulated sex acts.
Team Socialization	Involve teammates in public performances that include skits, singing, dressing up, or team roast.
Required Positive Behavior	Established team policies requiring grade point averages, study sessions, community service, or other behaviors that produce favorable public exposure.

Interestingly, researchers have documented the fact that hazing behaviors for male sports has tended to reinforce masculine traits, which has aided in fostering a homophobic culture. Following an extensive 7-year investigation, Anderson, McCormack, and Lee (2012) found that "hazing youth into homosexual activities served as a mechanism to prove allegiance to a team . . . reinforcing heterosexuality during rites of passage into masculine arenas" (p. 442). Despite this homophobic culture, the authors did note a gradual decline in "homoerotic" elements across time during the duration of the investigation. Whether acceptable or unacceptable forms of behaviors emerge, hazing is generally frowned upon. Individual acceptance of such norms and rituals can depend on the individuals who occupy leadership positions on the team and the way they prefer to establish their bases of power.

Leadership Emergence and Power

Leadership is one of the most widely studied phenomena, and the impact that formal leaders have on teams was explored in Chapter 11 as we discussed the coach–athlete relationship. Athletes and teammates can also serve as an important source of formal (e.g., team captain assigned and selected by the coach) and informal leadership (emerge as an inspirational figure for the team). Research supports that athletes who are assigned the role as captain for their team report more development as a leader than other players on the team, along with an increased desire to learn how to become a better leader (Grandzol, Perlis, & Draina, 2010). Additionally, interviews with team captains have uncovered that the "captain" designation results in increased influence over the attitudes and behaviors of other athletes on the team. In particular, this role assignment is likely to emerge in situations where task behaviors are necessary to enhance team norms and functioning (Dupuis, Bloom, & Loughead, 2006).

Some sports, such as hockey, have team captains wear a "C" on their uniform to signify this *formal leader* assignment. Team captains on a football team are asked to represent the team during the coin toss or communicate with officials when deciding to accept or decline penalties during the course of the game. *Informal leaders* assume a different set of behind-the-scenes roles for the team, which may include relationship building, fostering cohesion, or resolving team unrest during times of conflict. Having the appropriate composition of formal and informal leaders on team sports has been found to be important to a number of factors. Research supports that roughly 85% of team members should perform some leadership function for their team with the majority of that coming from behaviors and activities that would constitute informal leadership (Crozier, Loughead, Munroe-Chandler, 2013). However, it is important that the appropriate balance is established within the team so that a team isn't composed primarily of athletes who feel strongly about performing formal leadership roles.

Formal and informal leadership is important to consider in this section because group communication processes are essential to determining how leaders emerge in sport teams. Think about how you attempt to assess your place in the groups you encounter (decision-making group, intramural team, professional sport, etc.). It is not uncommon for you to assess others in relation to yourself by comparing strengths and faults. Through this process, you are able to determine who wishes to be a bystander on the team (determined to be a support player) and who seeks legitimate leadership positions. Those who fail to give 100% to the team or who are deemed to have limited contributions are quickly eliminated from consideration. You are then left with those whose contributions are of most interest to the team.

Bormann (1996) refers to this process as a method of *residues*, whereby we seek to eliminate individuals from contention until we are left with those we are most willing to consider. Burtis and Turman (2009) describe this as an informal and "interaction-based negotiation. It is usually not done in a particularly cruel or overt manner (except when children chose teams during recess). We just start paying more attention to people whose potential for giving direction we place closer to the center of our palate of choices" (p. 108). On sport teams, there are particular factors that seem to lend themselves to this emergence process. The most talented players (e.g., Abby Wambach, Brittney Griner), certain positions (goalie, point guard, etc.), or even veteran players are likely to remain standing after this process of residue has transpired. The extent to which teammates engage in interpersonal interaction in team sports appears to increase perceived leadership capacity. People who play central positions on a softball team that require *significant interactive tasks* (catcher and infielders) are more likely to emerge as informal or formal team leaders when compared to those in *low-interacting positions* (pitchers and outfielders).

As this process of residues unfolds, teams begin to operate under established bases of power inherent in the coach, captain, or informal positions. Bases of power (coercive, reward, legitimate, referent, and expert) can be traced to important communication attempts with team members (French & Raven, 1959). *Coercive*

A MATTER OF ETHICS

CHEMISTRY IN THE CLUBHOUSE

Athletes and coaches speak frequently about "team chemistry." Although there are examples of successful teams with players who did not get along well (the World Series championship Oakland A's teams of the early 1970s, for example), most will suggest that a successful team requires a degree of cohesion and a willingness to work together. In a sport such as baseball, which has a 162-game schedule that stretches over 6 months and through the "dog days of summer," team chemistry takes on an even greater significance.

Going into the 2015 season, the Washington Nationals were among the favorites to win the National League pennant and advance to the World Series. Led by young superstars Bryce Harper and Steven Strasburg, the Nationals later acquired Jonathan Papelbon, a pitcher who played an important role in the Boston Red Sox's 2007 World Series championship. Harper and Papelbon are two of the game's more notorious figures, both wildly talented but also frequently accused of lacking maturity. Washington's lofty expectations for the season were never reached, as the team missed the playoffs and barely finished with a winning record (83–79). Late in September, the disappointing season intersected with Harper's and Papelbon's volatile personalities. After Harper failed to hustle to first base on a ground ball, Papelbon shouted to him from the dugout, "Run that out!" When Harper returned to the dugout, the two players confronted each other, with cameras capturing the image of Papelbon's hand around Harper's neck.

By the time the incident took place, the Nationals already were going to miss the playoffs. Nevertheless, it offered visual evidence of a clubhouse that lacked chemistry and provided a partial explanation for Washington's poor play throughout the season. Some observers suggested that such confrontations are not uncommon during the course of a full season, but they usually happen out of sight of media and fans. Should Papelbon have called out Harper for his lack of hustle? Do you think it is appropriate for teammates to fight, even privately? What impact might such a confrontation have on team chemistry? Can players who dislike one another still cooperate during competition?

power is dependent on a player's belief that leaders will follow through with punishments. *Reward* power exists in the form of positive feedback from leaders, such as acknowledging achievements or offering words of praise. *Legitimate* power is more closely associated with formal leadership positions, warranting compliance due to the nature of the coaching position. This legitimate power can be distributed across assistant coaches who make playing status decisions or apply pressure on behalf of the coach. Informal leadership positions often rely on *referent* power, which is the capacity to garner compliance from others based on their desire to form and maintain positive relationships. Coaches have the ability to rely on referent power for rookie players who have a strong desire to identify and satisfy their coaches. At the start of each NFL season, HBO network follows a different team in the program *Hard Knocks,* which depicts players on the bubble for making the team whose primary concern is making a favorable impression on the coaching staff. Finally, *expert* power is derived from athletes' ability to perceive the competence of individuals in formal leadership positions. Lacking a clear understanding of the sport, previous success, or skill will be a detriment to one's ability to gain compliance from team members using this power base. Possessing a combination of referent and expert power is likely to stand out both internally and externally for the team. Group processes collectively work to determine how individuals reflect on their team experiences. However, these processes are not relegated to sport participants, as fans and spectators also take part in important grouping practices that further establish their sport identities (see Table 12.2).

TABLE 12.2 ■ Power Bases Employed in Small-Group Sports

Power Type	Description	Example
Coercive	Use of punishments by a team leader to obtain compliance from other team members.	"If you don't start passing the ball around, then I'm going to ask the coach to pull you from the game."
Reward	Providing resources (positive encouragement, playing time, etc.) to encourage compliance in achieving team outcomes.	"It's unselfish play from players like Sandra that has helped us to be the team that we are."
Legitimate	Relying on one's formal position to ensure compliance from players or teammates.	"As the team captain, I feel it's necessary that we stay after practice and run to improve our conditioning."
Referent	Using player or teammate desire for a strong relationship to gain compliance.	"If you expect me to respect you as a player, then you need to be willing to put in the additional effort that is necessary."
Expert	Drawing upon one's skill or knowledge to emphasize why compliance is necessary.	"Having coached five conference championships, I know that the best way to approach this season is to run extensively during practices each day."

Social Identity and Sport

Consider how you might respond to the question, "Who are you?" To answer this question, it wouldn't be uncommon for you to respond by making the connection you have to group or team affiliations, many of which are sport related ("I'm a Minnesota Lynx fan," or "I was a member of a high school state championship team"). In Chapter 9, we established the significance of performing identity in sport, as one's social identity is profoundly linked to the social groups and networks he or she aligns with, and one's personal identity is further advanced by maintaining membership in a highly valued social group. For example, if you find yourself in an environment where you are the sole supporter for your favorite team, you are likely to experience a decline in your social identity. A Dallas Cowboys fan transplanted to Philadelphia or a Boston Red Sox fan who is the only one cheering for his or her team in a bar filled with New York Yankees fans is likely to experience a significant decline in social identity because the familiar group network is no longer valued or recognized. As Wann (2006) noted,

> By identifying with a local sport team, an individual becomes attached to a larger social group. These associations to other fans form the basis for a valuable connection to society at large and serve as a buffer to loneliness, isolation, and so forth. (p. 80)

Research findings here suggest that team identification with a local team has a positive relationship with individual physiological health, more so than an individual's identification with distant teams.

The above line of thought has a legitimate connection to social identity theory, which suggests that individuals relate to others in relation to their social groups rather than as independent, isolated individuals. To maintain a positive self-image, we are predisposed to make our group affiliations based on the potential impact such affiliations might have on enhancing that image to others. There is evidence to suggest that such affiliations have a significant positive impact on one's psychological well-being (Wann, Keenan, & Page, 2009). In Chapter 4, we discussed how bandwagon fans have waning interest in a particular sport franchise until an affiliation has the potential to produce a positive impact. For example, few people may be likely to follow track and field, but the sport routinely increases in popularity as elite or dominant athletes emerge in national or international competition. The success of Usain Bolt during in the 2008 and 2012 Olympic Games followed giant celebrities such as Carl Lewis and Jackie Joyner-Kersee in drawing considerable attention to the sport during the late 1980s. If this is the case, then what would explain why individuals continue to support teams or sports with limited potential for producing positive social identity connections? Most likely, these individuals consider their commitment to their team as a more meaningful aspect of their self-concept ("My support has never waned even though the Cubs haven't won a World Series for more than a century"). Players may change, but the team is the bond, leading to Jerry Seinfeld's observation that we're really just cheering for the jersey.

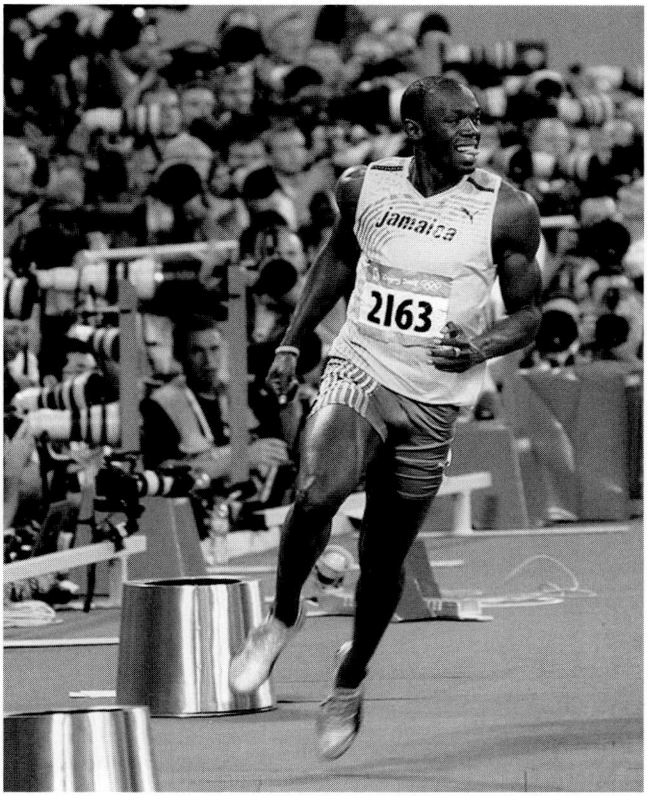

Source: By Richard Giles. https://commons.wikimedia.org/wiki/File:Usain_Bolt_Olympics_Celebration.jpg. [CC By-SA 2.0]. https://creativecommons.org/licenses/by-sa/2.0/deed.en

Usain Bolt celebrates following one of his Olympic victories

Four primary behaviors have been identified from group affiliation unique to teams (Jones, 2000). *In-group favoritism* includes preferential treatment given to members simply due to their association with the team. The belief appears to exist that only members possess positive behaviors or qualities due to the sense of team homogeneity that is fostered. For example, Nebraska Cornhusker fans have often considered themselves to be some of the most gracious fans in all of collegiate sports. They promote this assumption among themselves, ultimately forgetting that in times of considerable success, it is easier to be gracious to an opposing team after a win (Aden, 2007). The perception was one of the factors that contributed to the departure of their head football coach Bo Pelini after numerous on field instance of cursing, berating players, and criticizing fan support. In 2013 Pelini was recorded stating "Our crowd, what a bunch of f—ing fair-weathered f—ing—they can all kiss my ass on the way out the f—ing door" (Merrill, 2013, para 11). *Out-group derogation* occurs by assigning positive traits to group members and undesirable traits to individuals in the out-group. This often results in hostility to the out-group, which then provokes a reaction that is used to help reinforce these negative perceptions. This out-group derogation has been found to occur in two different forms: direct and general group affiliations. Members feel a strong connection to their team, in addition to the league, conference, and sport they participate in. Los Angeles Sparks fans are generally likely to experience derogation toward teams in their own conference (the Women's National Basketball Association [WNBA] Western Conference). However, they will also experience similar out-group derogation when considering fans who do not follow women's basketball. The perceived benefits individuals feel they obtained from their team affiliation reflect *unrealistic optimism*, as fans with a greater connection to the team are more likely to experience a state of euphoria toward their team. Here, fans are likely to promote an internal belief that success is always achievable despite the odds. Finally, fans noted a *sense of voice* that identification provides as they are able to overshadow unsuccessful performances by emphasizing athletic qualities the team possesses despite

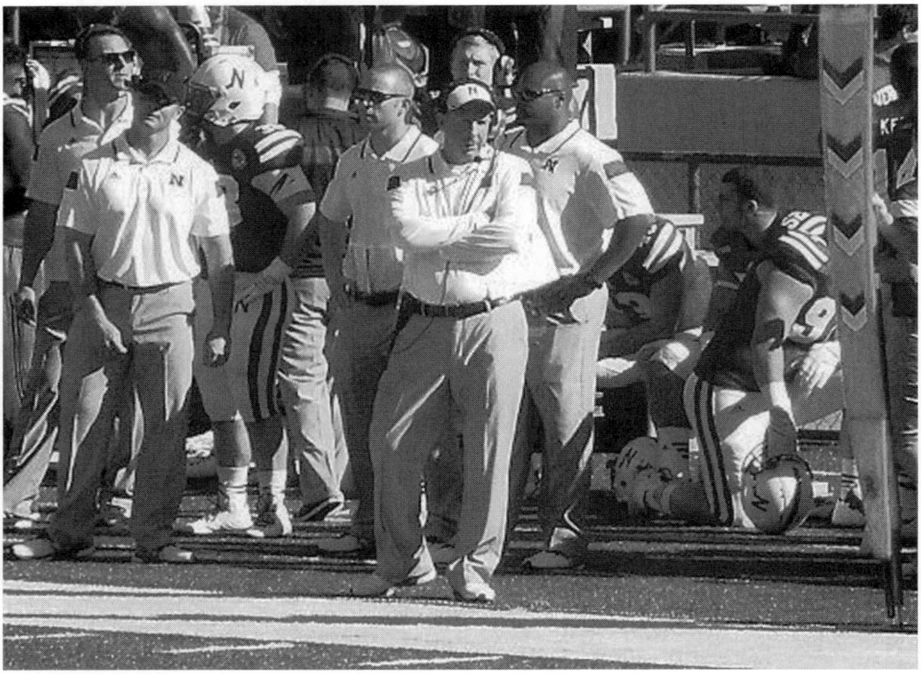

Former Nebraska football coach Bo Pelini looks on during one of his final games

a loss. "The team may lose, but that is only because they play the game fairly." External factors are likely to emerge here as the source of poor performance (player injury, bad call by an official, etc.), and the ability to articulate such concerns and demonstrate support for the team after a loss is an important part of being a fan.

These four categories identified in Jones's work depict the in-group orientation that is likely to occur based on one's membership or affiliation with sport teams. Although this particular type of orientation can be rather centralized (i.e., boxing fans are different from those who watch mixed martial arts), sport does have the potential for influencing larger cultural orientations. For instance, Deborah Tannen (1990), an established gender scholar at Georgetown University, noted that males bond because of a common sport language. This common language allows males to form a unique social network that promotes social bonding. Should you find yourself in the company of males with no identifiable similarities, the discussion most likely will turn to sports. Females, she contends, have no such common language, which might explain why it is not uncommon to find courses or seminars that provide women exposure to sport as a means of fitting into a sport culture. In the final section of this chapter, we explore how sport and games have the potential for establishing such cultures and also for contributing to the way we develop to one of two orientations toward communication.

SPORT AND COMMUNICATION CULTURES

Communication research argues that, at an early age, children become socialized into either masculine or feminine communication cultures (Maltz & Borker, 1982; Wood, 1996) through their participation in a variety of sex-segregated games and sports as they mature. Wood (1996) argued that "games socialize children into understanding how, when, and why to talk" (p. 150). As a result, specific communication behaviors are learned early, becoming influential in determining how children communicate throughout the course of their lives. Specifically, when examining the communicative influence of games, Maltz and Borker (1982) argue that games are influential in dividing individuals into a gender communication culture (masculine or feminine). They indicate that because children's games tended to be sex segregated during adolescence, boys (who play kill the carrier, tag, war, etc.) and girls (who play house, school, library, etc.) learn different appreciations for when, why, and with whom they should interact.

These differences can be distinguished in six unique ways, including the facts that (1) girls more often play indoors, (2) boys tend to play in larger groups, (3) boys' groups tend to include a wider age range of participants, (4) girls play in predominantly male games more often than vice versa, (5) boys more often play competitive games, and (6) girls' games tend to last a shorter period of time than boys' games. These differences lead boys and girls to rely on their social networks to learn their communication skills. Messner (1990) indicated that "the earliest studies of masculine identity suggested that boys were seen essentially as 'blank slates' who came to their athletic experiences to be socialized into 'male roles'" (p. 417). Boys are encouraged to participate in the outside environment and are seldom reprimanded for torn clothes, skinned knees, and dirty hands because this is considered a part of a masculine growth process. If girls participate in these same activities, it may be tolerated, but they are often classified or stereotyped because of their masculine qualities.

Wood (1996) uses the arguments set forth by these authors to suggest that those exposed to a masculine communication culture are more likely to use communication to achieve instrumental goals, assert individual status and authority, and ensure their status by using communication to establish individual positioning and power. Boys learn at an early age that exerting one's authority is a valued communication skill, and those deemed in highest regard during games include those with the greatest skill or knowledge of the game itself. The rules are clearly established, and the only changes to those rules can occur during situations where slight interpretations are available. Those who know the rules the best or use their communication skills to work around the rules can easily establish their status among the participants.

Those involved in a feminine communication culture are more likely to become skilled at using communication to "build connections with others," "include others," and "cooperate, respond, show interest, and support others" (Wood, 1996, pp. 152–153). Many of the sex-segregated games girls are exposed to have general tenets that assist in establishing the ground rules for play. As a result, each time a new game begins, they are required to communicate effectively and establish the rules for play that will be amenable to all those involved. Many of these games involve small groups

Source: © iStockphoto.com/ActionPics

Huddle at a fastpitch softball game

(sometimes just two or three players), requiring the development of relationship-building skills that are essential for ensuring that the game continues. Establishing power, authority, or status is a part of these games, but there is an underlying understanding that there must be a balance: "You can't always be the teacher, the librarian, or the mom every time we play." When players feel slighted, they are more likely to leave, and the game ends as a result. To ensure this doesn't occur, one must manage relationships effectively to ensure the longevity of the game. Group-based games are intended to provide children with enjoyment and skill development, yet indirectly they serve as activities that assist in building important communication skills. Ultimately, these skills developed at play in these groups transcend into the formation of masculine and feminine communication styles used in adulthood to listen, manage conversations, and resolve conflict.

With the advent of Title IX, it's hard to imagine a time when female athletes were believed to be naturally unsuited for sports. In fact, it wasn't until late in the last century when girls' basketball players in Iowa were allowed to play both offense and defense during high school games. However, Title IX has opened the floodgates to provide opportunities for female athletes, and Messner (2011) recently found that parents viewed sports participation as one of the most logical ways for their daughters to learn crucial masculine traits.

CONCLUSION

Because of the pervasiveness of sport, it is likely that your participation in activities surrounding sport and games will have a lasting impact on the way you communicate in group, organizational, and interpersonal contexts. With this in mind, we developed this chapter to expose you to the unique communication events that exist within team sports to demonstrate how group interaction in this context can influence numerous elements of our day-to-day activities. The sense of connection you have with group members can be traced back to team experiences, and it is understandable that you would expect other group activities to facilitate similar levels of cohesion. Just as coaches can manage cohesion levels, it is understandable to assume that leaders can positively or negatively impact your desire to achieve similar objectives with those around you. The same is true when considering the grouping processes that occur in team sports. Although sport teams can provide unique grouping experiences, the basic tenets surrounding norm development, socialization, leadership emergence, or social identity are reflected in a majority of the groups you come into contact with. Even something as detrimental as hazing is likely to occur in more cordial groups as members engage in acceptable team-building exercises that are an important socialization phase for group development. Last, we explored the impact of sex-segregated games that have been found to play an integral role in the development of our communication orientations. A greater appreciation for sport can be achieved as you consider how your participation in sport teams or group-based games shapes communicative approaches outside the sport context.

Suggested Additional Reading

Cranmer, G. A., & Myers, S. A. (2014). Sports teams as organizations: A leader-member exchange perspective of player communication with coaches and teammates. *Communication & Sport, 3*, 100–118.

Leo, F. M., Gonzalez-Ponce, L., Shanchez-Miguel, P. A., Ivarsson, A., & Garcia-Calvo, T. (2015). Role ambiguity, role conflict, team conflict, cohesion and collective efficacy in sport teams: A multilevel analysis. *Psychology of Sport & Exercise, 20*, 60–66.

Steinfeldt, J. A., Vaughan, L., LaFollette, J. R., & Steinfeldt, M. C. (2012). Bullying among adolescent football players: Role of masculinity and moral atmosphere. *Psychology of Men & Masculinity, 13*, 340–353.

Turman, P. (2008). Coaches' immediacy behaviors as predictors of athletes' perceptions of satisfaction and team cohesion. *Western Journal of Communication, 72*, 162–179.

Waldron, J. J., & Kowaiski, C. L. (2009). Crossing the line: Rites of passage, team aspects, and ambiguity of hazing. *Research Quarterly for Exercise & Sport, 80*, 291–300.

13

CRISIS COMMUNICATION IN SPORTS ORGANIZATIONS

At any given time, individuals within sport organizations can find themselves confronting a pending crisis that requires some form of response to help shape the reaction for those outside the organization. For example, in late 2011, Penn State football coach Joe Paterno came under scrutiny when his former defensive coordinator Jerry Sandusky was arrested on 40 counts of child sexual abuse, with allegations for some of the incidents occurring on the Penn State campus. As the scandal unfolded, evidence emerged suggesting that Paterno was aware of the incidents and had failed to intervene to ensure the safety of the children involved. Paterno offered his resignation prior to the end of the 2011 season; yet the Board of Trustees instead stripped him of his coaching duties. After a scathing report by former Federal Bureau of Investigation (FBI) director Louis Freeh was released almost 6 months later, the National Collegiate Athletic Association (NCAA) assessed $60 million in fines to Penn State and vacated Paterno's wins dating back to 1998, dropping him from the second all time winning coach to the 12th.

Albeit with much lesser severity, prior to the 2015 Super Bowl, the New England Patriots were accused of tampering with the air pressure in footballs during the AFC Championship Game against the Indianapolis Colts. The Patriots organization denied the allegations, which dominated the news coverage leading up to Super Bowl XLIX and for many tainted the eventual win by the Patriots 2 weeks following the AFC championship game. A few months after the Super Bowl, the NFL hired Ted Wells to investigate the allegations for what was then being referred to as "Deflategate," and the "Wells Report" that was released shortly afterward resulted in the suspension of the Patriots' star quarterback for four games during the 2015 regular season. The suspension was eventually vacated in federal court resulting from unfair due process;

however, in April 2016, a U.S. Circuit Court of Appeals reinstated the four game suspension for the beginning of the 2016 season.

These two examples reflect only a small handful of situations in sport that occur almost on a daily basis for players, coaches, owners, fans, organizations, and even leagues that are likely to face looming crises that can have an adverse effect on public perception. A crisis can result from a number of competitive situations (cheating, fighting, brawls, etc.), off-field occurrences (scandal, assault, player abuse, etc.), or reflections about sports (racial overtones, gender bias, press-conference outbursts, etc.) that require one to respond to the occurrence. Crisis in sport has a profound ability to require organizations to manage information in response to the fans' and spectators' need to make sense of what has occurred. As a crisis unfolds, individuals are confronted with a range of options for framing and responding that can be influential in shaping public opinion. Much of this involves communication processes that occur within the frameworks for (a) sensemaking and information management, (b) image repair and apologia, and (c) antapologia. We begin here by first exploring the role of communication in the sensemaking process. In this section, we highlight the major elements involved in sensemaking as it relates to fan dichotomies for winning and also the important influence that information management can have for shaping spectator reactions. The second major section in this chapter provides insight into the response to sport crises in two different forms. The first reflects individual responses to events in the form of an apology (or what communication scholars describe as *apologia* or a speech of self-defense) to facilitate image repair. After a public event, the resulting outcry often requires that individuals apologize for their part in the event, which can take a number of forms, and sport apologia has its own set of nuances that influence fan and spectator acceptance. As we discussed in Chapters 3 and 4, the growth of new media has had a significant influence not only on the way that fans consume sport but also on how they are able to contribute to that consumption. In the final section, we explore how this portal (talk radio, fan blogs, editorial comments, etc.) has further shaped *antapologia* (the response to an apology), as a greater number of fans are now afforded an opportunity to publicly react to perceived sport crises.

Tom Brady attempts a pass during a game against the Baltimore Colts

OFF THE BEATEN PATH

CYCLING

Lance Armstrong is undoubtedly the most well-known cyclist in the history of professional cycling. The world watched as he became a legend and stayed in tune as he slowly fell. In August 2012, after years of being accused of taking performance enhancing drugs, Armstrong was banned from cycling and stripped of all seven of his Tour de France medals.

Before he was banned from the sport, whose image he helped create, 2012 proved to be the busiest year for public relations (PR) professionals supporting Armstrong and USA Cycling, the governing body of cycling. Charges against Armstrong were dropped by U.S. federal prosecutors, Armstrong was then charged by the U.S. Anti-Doping Agency, and then Armstrong publicly decided to end the uphill battle of arbitration.

In January 2013, Lance Armstrong confessed to doping for the first time during an interview with Oprah Winfrey. After a series of accusations, investigations, and lawsuits, Armstrong ended a long cycle of denials and attempts to repair his image. Armstrong's confession follows confessions from his teammates and other involved parties, and America's professional cycling image has been tarnished.

SENSEMAKING AND INFORMATION MANAGEMENT

Sensemaking and information management can be viewed through a variety of lenses and serve important functions for the need to further communicate about sport crises. The first reflects the way we are programmed to accept sport outcomes, while the other is represented in the way media are able to frame our interpretation of the sporting events. While we explore this issue in greater depth in other chapters in this text, we provide a brief discussion here to emphasize the implication it has for shaping public opinion.

Sport participants and consumers constantly face a win or loss dichotomy in which ties are considered to be lose–lose situations for all involved (an internal crisis or tension). Torres and McLaughlin (2003) noted that as a society, we find it difficult to see resolution in events that end in a tie, as most sports require a winner be declared. Sport organizations have responded to such internal dichotomies for fans by employing the shoot-out in hockey and trading goal shots in soccer. High school and collegiate football provide each team an opportunity to score from the 25-yard line (even imposing that teams must attempt a two-point conversion in situations where a third overtime is required). Ties require all involved to engage in an internal sensemaking experience that is difficult to resolve when the dichotomy of sport necessitates the need for a winner and loser to be identified. For example, during the 1984 Orange Bowl, University of Nebraska football coach Tom

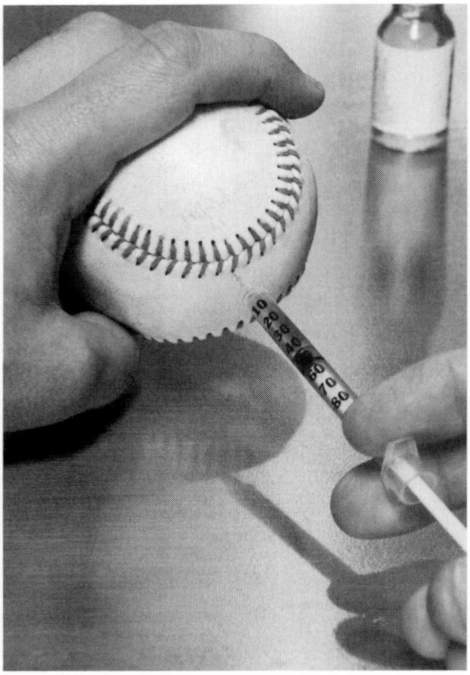
Source: © iStockphoto.com/sshepard

Baseball in the steroid era

Osborne decided to go for a two-point conversion to win rather than end the game in a tie. After failing to convert, Nebraska lost the game—costing Osborne his first national championship. When asked to explain his play calling during the postgame interview, Osborne noted that "I don't think you go for a tie in that case. You try to win the game."

Sport organizations are continually faced with managing the perceived crisis that emerges for fans as they attempt to fill a void left after a tie goes unresolved. Even in situations where winning isn't the ultimate goal, we expect a winner to emerge. Youth sport leagues establish rules to emphasize the developmental nature of the sport, yet that doesn't keep players, coaches, and parents from pronouncing a winner or loser at the end of a contest. The need for a definitive winner took center stage during the 2002 Major League Baseball (MLB) All-Star Game, when Bud Selig (MLB commissioner) decided to call the game after it went into extra innings and both teams were down to their final pitcher. Public outcry was so significant that the following season, MLB established that home field advantage for the World Series would be granted to the team whose league won the All-Star Game. Torres and McLaughlin (2003) argue that the distinction for fans may be influenced by the fact that they are either outcome or resolution seekers in their orientation toward sport. *Outcome seekers* are attracted to the basic elements of sport but are primarily motivated by the need to establish a clear winner or loser. *Resolution seekers* are more likely to view contests as a central point where athletic promise or superiority can be displayed over the quest for excellence. Consider for a moment where you might fall on this continuum. When you support your team, are you more concerned about ensuring their victory or hoping to see a good game or contest? If the latter is more accurate, then you would be a resolution seeker, and the conclusion of a contest that ends in a tie might be the ideal sports outcome.

With growing pressure to resolve the existing bowl structure, significant change was implemented in 1992 when the Bowl Coalition was established to further ensure a matchup between the top two teams in the country. Prior to this time, the number-one- and two-ranked teams had met in a bowl game only nine times since 1945. In its first year, the Bowl Coalition system worked effectively to match number-one-ranked Miami and number-two-ranked Alabama to produce what was described as a "true national champion." The same result occurred during the 4 succeeding years until a joint national championship was awarded to the University of Nebraska and the University of Michigan in 1997. The following year, the commissioner of the SEC established the Bowl Championship Series in an attempt to eliminate the likelihood of future ties. A computer ranking system was created that would ensure the number one and two teams in the country would play in a bowl game that would rotate across four different bowls: Fiesta, Orange, Sugar, and Rose. This practice produced a unanimous national champion until the 2003 season, when a split decision between the coaches and Associated Press polls awarded titles to both Louisiana State University and the University of Southern California. During the past few years, a number of teams from smaller conferences have gone undefeated (Boise State University, University of Utah) but have been unable to secure enough points in the computer ranking to warrant an opportunity to compete in the championship game. The system was again changed for 2013 when for the first time a playoff was used for determining the national champion from a pool of the top four teams in the country.

Connected to our internal disposition to making sense of sporting events in relation to the achievable outcome is the fact that the media can be influential in shaping our impressions of what occurs during the contest itself. This information-management process is reflected in the work of Billings (2008) regarding coverage of the Olympic Games, which relies heavily on backstory montages that assist in setting the stage for viewers as they watch what is believed to be live coverage of the events. This staging was also affirmed by Mullen and Mazzocco (2000) in their assessment of the methods used by television producers to portray head coaches during the Super Bowl. In an attempt to create a more compelling viewing experience, producers were found to use advances in technology between the 1969 and 1997 broadcasts to alter reality for the home viewer, whereby "they, in effect attempt to create a story with mythical qualities complete with plot, protagonist, antagonists, climax, and denouement" (p. 358). The coach was portrayed as a corporate leader, exemplifying both hero and villain roles at any given point during the game. When sport organizations and media outlets manage the flow of information and sport outcomes in these ways, consumer expectations are shaped, requiring responses when internal and external violations occur. Despite the fact that such occurrences have become common features for the way sport is produced and consumed, there are numerous instances when organizations, franchises, athletes, and coaches are required to engage in individual image repair after unanticipated events. This image-repair process involves a well-established line of research known as apologia, which we explore further in the following section.

A MATTER OF ETHICS

CRISIS ON CAMPUS

Unfortunately, several high-profile universities have found themselves in crisis because of improprieties in their revenue-generating sports programs (football and men's basketball, in particular). One of the most damning set of allegations to emerge has been at Baylor University, where several women have claimed they were sexually assaulted by members of the football team. Beyond those allegations, an ESPN *Outside the Lines* report further suggested that university officials failed to take the women seriously and instead protected athletes and athletic department officials.

As the scandal unfolded in the early months of 2016, more credible information suggested that university officials had enabled a culture that tolerated sexual assault. As noted by an independent investigation, "Institutional failures at

Baylor football coach Art Briles speaks at a press conference

every level of Baylor's administration impacted the response to individual cases and the Baylor community as a whole" (Smith, 2016, para 5). By the end of spring, Baylor fired head football coach Art Briles, accepted the resignation of Athletics Director Ian McCaw, and re-assigned Chancellor Ken Starr. Briles's firing, in particular, drew the ire of fans who not only appreciated the team's success under his leadership but also insisted he had no role in facilitating a negative culture on Baylor's campus.

This case affects a range of individuals at Baylor University, but at the center of the scandal is the role of football and the behaviors people are willing to tolerate in exchange for a competitive team. Under Briles, Baylor experienced unprecedented success, but did it also accept a culture of privilege and sexual violence? Allegations of sexual assault by athletes are not unique to Baylor; are athletic programs themselves to blame for these instances of violence? Did Baylor officials act appropriately by firing or re-assigning the leaders of the institution and the athletics department? How might it have intervened earlier in the crisis?

Source: Smith, J. B. (2016, May 26). Report shows systemic failure in sex crime response at Baylor. *Waco Tribune*. Retrieved from http://www.wacotrib.com/news/higher_education/report-shows-systemic-failure-in-sex-crime-response-at-baylor/article_432b820a-6e64-5864-92c2-f3081f020384.html

Image Repair and Apologia

Research on public apology making related to image has generated two important bodies of literature—apologia and image repair. Communication scholars have defined *apologia* as discourse that focuses on the "self-defense" needed to combat external personal attacks on one's character (Ware & Linkugel, 1973). The actual theory of *image restoration* is based on the assumption that maintaining a positive face is a primary communication goal (Benoit, 1995). Image itself is threatened when an act is perceived as reprehensible by a relevant audience. However, the most prominent extension to apologia stems from Benoit's (1995) work on image repair. Benoit sought to create a more complete theory of accounts, apologies, and image-repair strategies. He argues that human beings inevitably face situations of real or alleged wrongdoing, and these situations are recurring and damaging to reputations. Consequently, when one's actions are considered "reprehensible" to a "salient audience," that individual's image is damaged and must be repaired.

Benoit and McHale (1999) contend that "rhetors have five general options for self-defense: denial, evade responsibility, reduce offensiveness, corrective action, and mortification" (p. 267), yet much of the research on apologia has been rooted in political discourse. As you might recognize, sport figures routinely find themselves in the spotlight as they are required to engage in a practice of image repair similar to that employed by public officials. Kruse (1981) recognized this feature about sport and was one of the first to explore apologia in this context. She suggests that much as in political discourse, an underlying ethic of team sports (the team is greater than any individual members) warrants that sport participants embrace apologia differently. Within this general ethic of team sport, Kruse contends that the interests of the team must be placed above one's own ego or individual accomplishments. This assumption rests on a number of basic tenets, suggesting that one never (a) criticizes the game or sport while serving as a participant or ex-participant, (b) accepts defeat until the contest has concluded, or (c) takes part in activities or events (internally or externally to the sport) that can adversely affect the team's performance. In her examination of sport apologia, Kruse (1981) identified a number of situations requiring apology on the part of the athletes and successful strategies that resolved ethical violations, including (a) suggesting that the team would be unaffected by the ethical violation, (b) shifting responsibility to the sport organization, (c) stressing a desire to be a team player, and/or (d) placing the blame on the emotion of the situation.

Kruse (1981) also conceded that there are specific situations in sport that do not warrant an apology after a violation, as she noted that fans expect coaches and players to work within the framework of the rules to win games. "Consequently, sport personalities who cheat are unlikely to be called upon by the fans to make public apologies, even though the media and other teams' followers might label their conduct 'im-moral'" (p. 279). You might recall the incident that unfolded during the 2007 NFL season when Bill Belichick (head coach of the New England Patriots) was accused by a former assistant coach of videotaping defensive signals during the game. Although Belichick faced considerable fines by the NFL, there was substantial backlash from coaches and the media against the former assistant for airing what many considered to be inside information about coaching practices. As this example attests, the need for image repair is likely to occur in a number of situations occurring at both the organizational and individual levels. We explore the unique circumstances that surround the image-repair function for sport organizations, athletes, and coaches when faced with anticipated and unanticipated crises in sport (Harris, 1990).

Organizational Image Repair

Sport organizations at all levels can face considerable need to engage in image repair after events outside their control shake public confidence. There are numerous examples of sport crises that have been handled effectively, and while organizations are often faced with unanticipated events, the response to those events can be influential in determining public reaction. To handle such events effectively, organizations must take control of the situation and report facts in a consistent manner.

Over the past century, MLB has faced events, including the Black Sox scandal during the 1919 World Series, a player strike in 1994 that eventually canceled the World Series, and a betting scandal involving a one-time future Hall of Famer Pete Rose during the 1987 season. For almost 20 years, Rose refused to admit that he had bet on baseball, and his apology (primarily for not telling the truth rather than for betting) failed to adequately resolve what he had done in the eyes of many critics. The MLB response to the situation represented an indisputable need to demonstrate to the public that the integrity of the game was indeed intact, so much so that they imposed a lifetime ban on Pete Rose for his

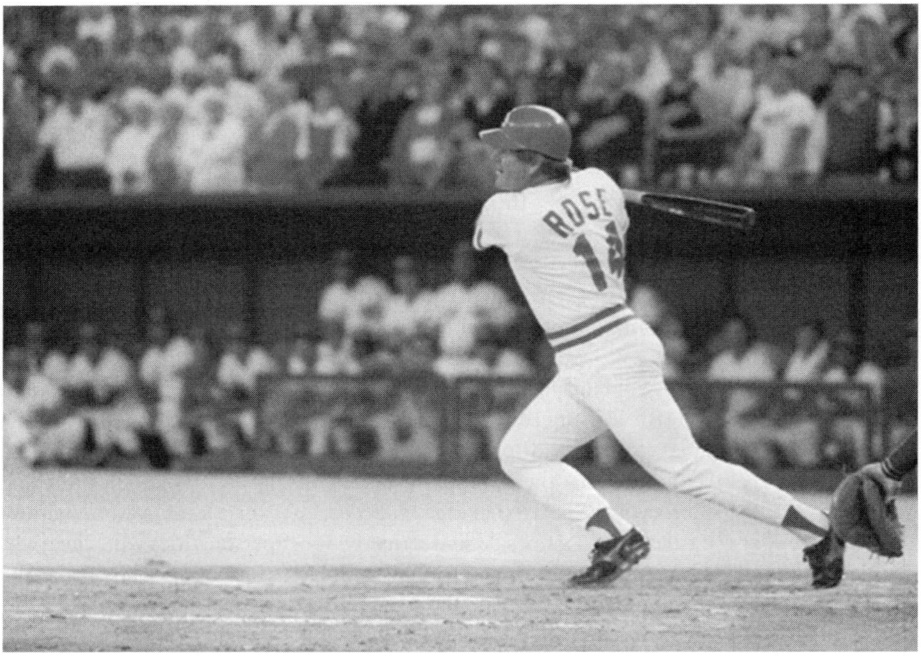

Pete Rose

involvement in gambling. Baseball Commissioner A. Bartlett Giamatti focused his decision to ban Rose on the issue of integrity, noting that "one of the game's greatest players has engaged in a variety of acts which have stained the game, and he must now live with the consequences of those acts. . . . Let it also be clear that no individual is superior to the game" (as cited in McDorman, 2003, p. 5). To eliminate the public impression that the "fix is in," such harsh consequences have been implemented in a number of sports. More recently, the National Basketball Association (NBA) faced a similar situation in 2008 after Tim Donaghy (a longtime official) pleaded guilty to betting on games in which he officiated and made calls affecting the point spread in those games. After an FBI investigation led to Donaghy's arrest, it was uncovered that he had been betting on games since the 2005 season and had strong ties to organized crime. NBA commissioner David Stern took control of the story when it initially broke, emphasizing terms like *betrayal* and *trust* as he assured fans that an internal investigation would demonstrate that this was an isolated incident.

In the opening paragraph, we briefly discussed the events of child abuse that came to light at Penn State in 2011. While many have emphasized the impact that these events had on Joe Paterno and his place in history as one of college football's top coaches, the impact on the institution was more significant. While Paterno did report the initial incidents that were witnessed by an assistant football coach in 1999, the university's administration failed to follow the necessary procedures to ensure the safety of children. The Freeh report highlighted the fact that administrators placed the university, and the potential impact on the football program specifically, in the forefront during internal discussions

INTERVIEW

KEVIN LONG, CEO, MVP SPORTS MEDIA TRAINING

Q: What was the impetus for creating MVP Sports Media Training with an emphasis on crisis communication?

A: I worked as a contractor for the Department of Defense. In 2004, I was in a bar in Bogota, Colombia, watching *SportsCenter.* Kevin Garnett came on and was talking about how he had all his guns at home and was "ready to go to war" in the NBA playoffs. It struck me that a lot of what we do in strategic communications would be useful for athletes who find themselves in situations like that. Over the years, social media became more prevalent, and it became clear that athletes may not be paying that much attention to what they say on Twitter or in other areas of the media. A lot of what we do is pretraining, so they know how to avoid being in those awkward types of situations.

Q: How much of what you do is about avoiding crisis situations as opposed to handling crisis situations once they occur?

A: About 95% of the work is preparing ahead of time. What do you do when the worst possible scenario happens? Do you have a plan in place? How do you handle traditional and social media when the worst possible thing happens? I stay as a resource for them to lean back on when a crisis occurs, but when I visit with them, I try to provide realistic scenarios that could be adapted to a given college or professional team.

Q: What is the best advice you give to people?

A: Don't lie. You don't have to answer every question they ask, or any questions at all, but don't lie when you do provide an answer.

Q: What is the biggest mistake people tend to make when trying to navigate a crisis?

A: There are two. One is a lack of preparation. The other is that they say too much. It's not that they can't be transparent, but you want them to speak in sound bites and controlled message releases. That requires you to think about what questions you most likely will be asked—*before* you step in front of the microphone. Often they find themselves in holes they didn't mean to get into. If they're prepared, they'll have a controlled message, and this will be less likely to occur.

Q: What is the impact of the media sound bite culture in which we now live?

A: What you say is not necessarily going to be taken in the context in which you said it. If you don't practice, it can become an issue. Your answer can become half or one third of what you intended, so you have to ask yourself how each part of your answer will be taken separately. It's an art form.

Q: How much of what you do involves the instantaneous nature of social media, which can drive a story from the onset in a way traditional media cannot?

A: Social media is as important if not more important than traditional media in the training I put forth. The great thing about social media is that you can easily get your message out; the bad thing about social media is also that you can easily get your message out. Once you have fired that bullet, you can't get it back. Even if you delete a post, someone likely will have screen-grabbed it. If you are not thinking through what you want to disseminate, social media can be a very bad experience.

about the appropriate course of action to take. While the Board of Trustees fired Paterno once the facts came to light, they also dismissed a number of top administrators. In 2013, three administrators in particular (Graham B. Spanier, the former president; Timothy M. Curley, the former athletics director; and Gary C. Schultz, the former senior vice president) were charged with perjury, obstruction, endangering the welfare of children, failure to properly report suspected abuse, and conspiracy. In 2016 additional reports surfaced that shed further light on who knew what and when, suggesting that Paterno knew of the allegations dating back as early as the late 1980s.

The two examples outlined above certainly reflect examples of sport organizations forced to react to unforeseen crisis that had a negative impact on the organization.

Although many would contend that sport currently walks a fine line with entertainment, the clear divide for fans is the uncertainty surrounding the outcome. These examples depict organizations faced with scandals that target the integrity of sport, as fans and spectators begin to question whether contest outcomes are fixed or administrators are providing the necessary oversight of their programs. Analysis of each of these organizational crises presents two different reactions to the events that necessitated image repair. While baseball may continue to experience unrest regarding the lifetime ban placed on Pete Rose, the commissioner's response at the time has been recognized by many as a necessary reaction to deter public perception surrounding the legitimacy behind baseball's outcome. Attempts by Penn State officials to cover up allegations that would harm their program cast further doubt on the role that Division I football programs serve in higher education. When image repair is required for athletes, they are faced with a set of challenges that are unique to the choices an organization is asked to confront.

Athlete Image Repair

Since Kruse's (1981) initial work on sport image repair, the need for athletes engage in image repair activities has increased significantly due to the value that has now been placed on an athlete's image (Brazeal, 2008). The financial value (in terms of potential endorsements and future performance earnings) and the increased news coverage of athletes has resulted in the need for image repair that positively employs the basic tenets of apologia. One such case is tennis legend Billie Jean King's comments surrounding her disclosure of an extramarital lesbian affair with her secretary. After the story broke, King made her official apology in three different settings, which included a press conference, an appearance on a television news program, and an interview in *People* magazine. During each of these interviews, King successfully *bolstered* (attempting to connect the accused with something positive) herself by having her husband at her side. Nelson (1984) noted that "they entered the news conference holding hands, and during the press meeting the tennis star occasionally rested her head on her husband's shoulder. Following the conference, the two kissed in front of the camera" (p. 93). Using this strategy, along with defense by her tennis peers, Nelson concluded that when an individual or supporters of the individual use *transcendence* (joining something to a larger context) as a strategy, it is possible to shift the situation into another context viewed favorably by the audience. In King's case, this was privacy and personal autonomy, and essential to this strategy was consistency in the presentation by King, her peers, and the media after the apology was performed (see Table 13.1 for a complete list of resolution strategies).

Source: By Kobe_Bryant_7144.jpg: Sgt. Joseph A. Lee derivative work: JoeJohnson2 [Kobe_Bryant_7144.jpg] [Public domain], via Wikimedia Commons

Kobe Bryant

Over the past decade, a number of events requiring image repair have involved sex scandals. Los Angeles Lakers guard Kobe Bryant was accused in 2003 of sexual assault against a front desk employee at a Colorado resort. During a press conference on July 18 of that year, Bryant (seated next to his wife) refuted the allegations, stating that "nothing that happened June 30th was against the will of the woman who now falsely accuses me. I made the mistake of adultery. I have to answer to my wife and my God for my actions that night." Rogers (2003) argues that Bryant's public apology encompassed elements of denial, differentiation, and mortification, taking on what Ware and Linkugel (1973) describe as an absolutive stance. When faced with an attack on one's image, the only response is to vehemently deny the allegations. The case was ultimately dropped after the accuser refused to testify at the trial, but Bryant's squeaky-clean image was tarnished as his endorsement contracts with a number of major companies were terminated. A similar stance was taken by Tiger Woods after a crash outside his Florida home in 2009 led to his formal apology for having multiple affairs that had lasted more than 2 years. Benoit (2013) noted that since the initial incident caused considerable backlash for Woods, his use of mortification and corrective action was highly effective in helping to turn public attention away from the acts themselves. Despite being dropped by a number of sponsors, Woods has recaptured public attention. Finally, in 2010 NFL quarterback Ben Roethlisberger was accused of sexual assault, and while the case did not lead to criminal charges, Roethlisberger did face a six game suspension by the NFL. In a review of the image restoration strategies employed by Roethlisberger, Meng and Pan (2013) observed instances of corrective action ("I'm happy to put this behind me and move forward") and bolstering strategies through attempts to build up public character.

Another case occurred in the aftermath of the events leading up to the 1994 Olympic Games after speculation mounted regarding Tonya Harding's involvement in an attack on U.S. teammate Nancy Kerrigan. During an interview with CBS reporter Connie Chung, Harding attempted to deny the allegation that she had helped plan the attack on Kerrigan at a practice facility in Detroit. Although Harding's husband was the actual perpetrator, she relied heavily on the technique of bolstering by suggesting that she had been abused by her exhusband, insisting she worked hard for a chance at the gold medal, and expressing concern and sorrow for the attack. She also employed denial strategies

TABLE 13.1 ■ Verbal Self-Defense Resolution Strategies Employed During Apologia

Resolution Type	Description	Example
Denial	An attempt by the perpetrator to change the meaning or connotation of the act being questioned	Kobe Bryant arguing that he is guilty of infidelity and a violation of the sanctity of his marriage but not rape
Bolstering	An attempt to link the perpetrator or the act itself with something positive	Billy Jean King sitting with her husband during interviews after she was accused of having a lesbian relationship
Differentiation	An attempt made by the perpetrator to disconnect the event from the larger context	Pete Rose suggesting that when he bet on baseball, it was solely about gambling and had nothing to do with his role as a manager
Transcendence	An attempt made by the perpetrator to connect the event to a larger context	Michael Vick suggesting that his involvement in a dogfighting ring was linked to his cultural upbringing and background as a youth

by rejecting the accusations that she had been involved and claimed she had no prior knowledge regarding her exhusband's involvement in the attack. She repeatedly attacked those committing the assault in an attempt to restore her image. Benoit and Hanczor (1994) concluded that Harding's use of bolstering, denial, and attacking the accuser were "clearly appropriate" because the past had shown them to be effective in situations where an individual has been "accused of heinous acts" (p. 425).

Similar to the circumstances surrounding the backlash that Harding experienced were the dogfighting allegations that resulted in 18 months of imprisonment for NFL quarterback Michael Vick (Smith, 2013). Following his release from prison in April 2009, the sitting NFL Commissioner Roger Goodell supported Vick's return if he could demonstrate what he referred to as "genuine remorse" for his behavior. Grano (2014) evaluated this notion of "genuine remorse" and the impact it had on public forgiveness; whereby Goodell exerted his power as NFL commissioner to "restore or deny social and economic status" resulting from his perceived belief that Vick was truly sorry for his actions (p. 96). Grano alluded to forgiveness on the part of Goodell and media figures responsible for commentating on the evaluation at the time as "gift-giving" with no form of reciprocity available. While King, Bryant, and Vick's images after their crises have been restored, many have failed to forgive Harding for the events that occurred prior to the 1994 Olympic Games. Why do you think this might be the case? What appears to be different about these situations that necessitated a formal public apology? Many considered this to be a unique situation in sport because of the fact that no Olympic athlete prior to this event had been accused of attempting to injure a teammate. Kruse (1981) contended that one of the essential principles guiding the ethic of sport is that one's behavior not have a detrimental impact on the team's performance. Had Kerrigan gone on to win the gold medal, public opinion for Harding might be considerably different. Additionally, Utsler and Epp (2013) argued that one feature of sport among all others seems to separate the distinction between successful and unsuccessful image repair strategies—winning. They contend that "An athlete's successful contribution to a winning team gives fans an excuse to forgive the athlete" (p. 159). As athletes are required to embrace the underlying ethic of sport, coaches are faced with a unique set of challenges influenced by both the need for apologia and rebuilding their teams in the wake of crisis.

Coach Image Repair

As our section on sport organizations might attest, organizations are required to respond to allegations of wrongdoing and often enforce strict penalties to ensure that unanticipated events are not likely to occur again. While this might account for the necessary organizational response for player behavior, coaches have been found to be just as likely to engage in acts that necessitate apology. For example, during the 2013 season, video footage surfaced of Rutgers basketball coach Mike Rice verbally and physically abusing his players during practice. When the video had been initially reviewed by Rutgers athletic director Tim Pernetti, Rice was suspended for three games, but he was allowed to resume his coaching duties until the footage was released to the general public. Rice was forced to make a formal apology for his actions, noting, "There's no explanation for what's on those films because there is no excuse for it. . . . I was wrong." Rice's contract was soon terminated by Rutgers, and Pernetti was also removed from his duties as athletic director due to his initial inaction. After numerous incidents (choking a player, throwing a chair onto the court, and berating university officials) as the head coach at Indiana University, Bob Knight was terminated in 2000 as the head men's basketball coach, as these incidents violated a no-tolerance policy implemented by the president.

Both of these examples represent instances that mark the departure of a high-profile coach. Yet in the wake of their departure, new personnel (namely, coaches and their staff) are often left with the daunting task of moving the team and organization forward in light of the series of events. For example, during the late 1990s, the University of Minnesota men's basketball program was heavily sanctioned by the NCAA for numerous violations of academic fraud by the head coach, his staff, and university academic counselors. After the corruption was exposed and new coaching staff was hired, they were then required to go about dealing with the stiff NCAA penalties that ensued, resulting in four primary consequences (Kihl & Richardson, 2009). First, *sanctions* placed considerable restrictions on the coaching staff to fulfill their responsibilities in the areas of recruitment. Using the uncertainty surrounding the extent of the sanctions, other institutions worked to create an attitude of paranoia as a way to draw away the institution's recruits. The heightened media speculation also required coaches to deal with the sensationalism that occurred and left negative connotations for the players who remained from the previous administration. Coaches were forced to manage as they dealt with the postscandal period, which basically stripped the program of its national prominence. They noted that recruits are most interested in playing for a team that "has national television exposure, consistently competes in the NCAA tournament, and is a successful major program" (p. 287). Without the potential for these three elements, it became difficult to draw recruits into the program.

Stakeholder separation was the second issue that emerged, as long-term stakeholders (players, boosters, academic community, administration, etc.) began to slowly disconnect from the program. Players who remained after the scandal found it difficult to connect with the new coaching staff, while shame and embarrassment were common themes displayed by the broader campus community. Even the coaching staff from other sports felt a need to isolate themselves from the men's basketball program, resulting from fear that public perception would be connected to all University of Minnesota athletics. The two final themes were the coaching staff's need to manage *reform policies* and *multiple roles*. The first here included the climate of suspicion that appeared to remain after the sanctions were imposed. Faculty and administrators felt a need to be more involved in the day-to-day administration of the athletic department and the men's team more specifically. The coaching staff was also required to wear numerous hats beyond traditional coaching responsibilities, as they were frequently required to respond to academic fraud and public scrutiny. In the end, each of these concerns suggests that "suffering is the core category that derives from the consequences and harmful outcomes related to academic corruption" (Kihl & Richardson, 2009, p. 300). What Kihl and Richardson describe here represents the way in which teams are asked to respond to the aftermath of unintended events. Just as a governing body has the potential to impose formal sanctions as they did with the Minnesota basketball team, there are a number of ways in which informal sanctions can be presented. As institutions have become more concerned about the potential impact that official NCAA sanctions might have on a program, they have become more likely to impose their own sanctions in the hope of getting to resolution earlier. Such was the case for the Duke lacrosse team after allegations surfaced that members had raped an exotic dancer. Duke University responded by canceling the season and firing the head coach before an official investigation was completed. Furthermore, the three accused athletes were eventually cleared.

SPORT ANTAPOLOGIA

As the above section suggests, defense of one's behavior to the media and fans represents an important feature of sport consumption in today's society. However, advancing forms of mediated technology have allowed fans a greater public platform on which they can articulate their reactions to what occurs in sport organizations. In Chapter 3, we discussed the significance that sport blogs have for allowing fans an opportunity to add their perspective to the dialogue of events that surround sport. A more traditional form of this environment has been sport talk radio, which continues to gain in popularity. Such programs "open a public space where the ideas and attitudes of ordinary people seem to matter, enabling the fans and broadcasters to share dramatic interpretations about the relationship between sport and society, whether or not these interpretations correspond to reality" (Zagacki & Grano, 2005, p. 46).

In their review of sport talk radio in Baton Rouge, Louisiana (home of the LSU Tigers football team), Zagacki and Grano (2005) demonstrated that this medium was influential in helping fans cope with perceived crises that surrounded team losses. Losses for many of these fans were perceived as a personal attack that resulted from the internal identity crises that stemmed from the strong sense of identification they had with their team. Sport talk radio provides these fans an opportunity to vocalize their frustration and overcome the imminent internal crisis they are experiencing. In a number of chapters in this text, we have introduced the conflict that fans faced with "The Decision" as LeBron James announced his transition to the Miami Heat organization once he became a free agent with the Cleveland Cavaliers in 2010. Brown, Dickhaus, and Long (2012) evaluated fan reaction and assessed how James may have best used image repair strategies based on the high or low involvement that the fans depicted, noting that mortification may be the most successful image repair strategy when high involved fans feel slighted. Brown, Billings, Mastro and Brown-Devlin (2015) observed similar findings when manipulating response strategies where mortification was found to be more effective when compared to evading responsibility. A number of scholars observed that failure to use mortification strategies in the initial response was detrimental. Examples include Serena Williams's attempts to apologize for her widely criticized outbursts during the 2009 U.S. Open (Brazeal, 2013) and Teresa Earnhardt's reaction to Dale Earnhardt, Jr.'s departure from the Dale Earnhardt, Inc. racing team in 2007 (Jerome, 2013).

One other unique feature of sport is the fact that athletes and coaches are often asked to provide commentary and reaction immediately after competition. Coaches take part in postgame interviews as they leave the field, athletes are confronted by media in the locker room, and sport organizations have increasingly mandated that coaches and players take part in press conferences to feed the sport fans' need for information. For losing coaches and players, this enhanced exposure also increases the need to engage in self-defense disclosure. Such self-defense discourse involves what Ryan (1982) described as the speech set of *kategoria* and *apologia* (attack and defense), whereby any critical focus on the apology should also examine the attack preceding it. Athletes', coaches', owners', and organizations' behavior clearly necessitated a defense of their actions, especially when such behaviors had the potential for dramatically impacting long-term image. However, focusing exclusively on the apologia itself ignores a third component, which Stein (2006) referred to as *antapologia* (response to apologia). Antapologia is an important feature of the apologetic situation because the rhetor may choose to construct the initial image repair based on what he or she perceives to be the likely response by the offended person(s). When the discourse addresses the account of the act, it constitutes an instance of antapologia.

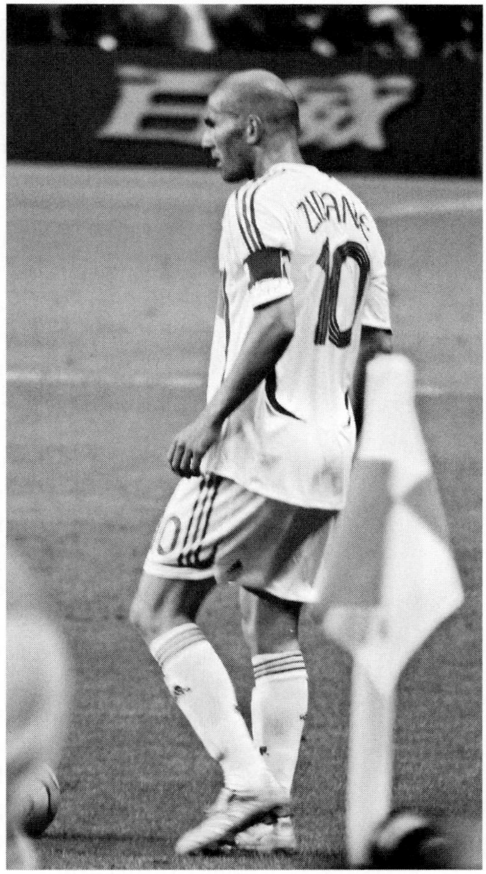

French soccer player Zinedine Zidane

Turman, Stein, and Barton (2008) evaluated the Zinedine Zidane headbutt incident during the 2006 World Cup championship game in which Zidane physically assaulted an opponent after he allegedly made a derogatory slur toward his sister. After the incident, Zidane made a formal response to the public, which many argued failed to adequately apologize for his behavior. Turman and company (2008) assessed blog responses from fans to the apology, noting four antapologia situations. First, the apologia represented *character flaws of the accused* as fans argued that a nonapology for one's actions is reflective of poor character, suggesting that the lack of apology became a greater reason for revoking Zidane's status as a role model than his actual on-field behavior. Other fans appeared to *attribute motives* to the apologia, and in this case, fans called into question the overall sincerity of Zidane's apologia. Here, fans identified potential motives behind the discourse, which included implications that Zidane's words were provided to him by other people and that the media may have played a role in allowing Zidane to account for his behavior more easily. Other fans argued that the *apologia is incomplete,* suggesting that the response was deficient because he expressed only regret and therefore did not offer a full mortification for his behavior. Fans are able to recognize the distinction between apologizing (or even regretting) harmful behavior and feeling sorry that consequences result from the act. The apologia was also perceived to be *untrue and dismissed,* as fans argued that portions of the apology were patently false, lacking in credibility, or devoid of evidentiary support. Here, the fans dismissed the idea that Materazzi, the victim, may have insulted Zidane during the course of the entire match, arguing that Materazzi did not have sufficient time within the video clip to provoke Zidane with three offensive remarks.

Although several antapologia strategies offered criticism in response to the apologia, many of them functioned to defend the apologia. During the World Cup incident, fans took on the role of surrogate apologizers in an effort to strengthen Zidane's defense. The strategy used by fans in defense of Zidane's apologia is similar to the image-repair strategy of bolstering, characterized by an attempt to offset the damage done to the player's image through the harmful act by emphasizing his positive characteristics. Fans counteracted the negative effects of the headbutt by emphasizing other aspects of Zidane's character. Stein, Turman, & Barton (2013) observed similar aspects of antapologia in the Mike Leach incident at Texas Tech in 2009.

The potential for antapologia does not rest solely on those participating in sports, but it can have an impact on those providing commentary for the events as they unfold. For example, in 2003, Rush Limbaugh commented during a segment on ESPN's *Game Day* that Philadelphia Eagles quarterback Donovan McNabb received considerable praise only because of society's desire to see a Black athlete succeed at the position. Considerable backlash ensued, and despite his apology for the statement, Limbaugh was subsequently released. Howard Cosell's departure from *Monday Night Football* came shortly after he used the term *monkey* to describe a Black player's performance on the field—something that resonated in Don Imus's comments about Rutgers University's women's basketball team when he referred to them as "nappy-headed hos" and "rough girls." In 2007, when the criticism for these comments began to mount, Imus set up a meeting to personally apologize for his comments about the Scarlet Knights. After a

CASE STUDY

LEACH VERSUS JAMES

Inappropriate behavior by coaches, players, owners, and even fans can occur during sporting events, and in most situations, sport organizations must react in some way to the public outcry that often emerges. At the end of the 2009 college football season, administrators at Texas Tech University were forced to react to allegations that surfaced about their head football coach. Hired just 9 years earlier, Mike Leach had led the team to 10 straight winning seasons, nine consecutive bowl appearances, and five bowl victories. Leach quickly became the program's winningest coach and signed a 3-year contract extension worth $2.5 million guaranteeing his position with the team through the 2013 season. However, just 5 days before his team was scheduled to play in the Alamo Bowl on New Year's Day, Leach was suspended indefinitely pending an investigation of inappropriate treatment of one of his players. During the second to last game of the season, senior wide receiver Adam James suffered a concussion and was unable to practice after examinations identified an abnormal heart rate. When James notified Leach that he would be unable to practice, he was ordered to report to a dark equipment shed where he was required to stand alone throughout the duration of the practice. Adding complexity to the situation was the fact that James's father was former NFL running back and current ESPN college football analyst Craig James, who approached university officials for the mistreatment of his son after being notified about the incident.

Campus administration asked Leach to apologize in writing to the James family by a December 28 deadline or face suspension by university officials. After refusing to apologize, Leach received a termination letter, and Texas Tech released a statement noting his "defiant act of insubordination" in the institution's attempts to resolve the complaint that had come forward from the James family. Assistant Coach Lincoln Riley noted in a letter to the administration prior to the suspension that "two practices before Adam James claimed he had a concussion[,] Coach Leach and I were forced to discipline him for poor effort," which was something that had become "a common theme about Adam's work ethic and attitude during his entire career." Despite these reports, Craig James used his position on ESPN to continually frame Leach as an abusive coach with limited disregard for his players. These events set the stage for a give-and-take between Leach, the Texas Tech administration, and the Jameses that continued months after the termination. Although fans were not directly impacted by the events that transpired between Leach and James, many felt connected to the situation because of their connection to the institution or the emotional attachment they felt for a father's desire to protect his son.

1. Did Leach's behavior warrant the need for a formal apology to the James family, the administration, and Texas Tech fans?
2. Are there times when a coach's behavior is justified when it comes to the discipline he or she chooses to use with athletes?
3. How much do you believe that Leach's unwillingness to apologize impacted the administration's response to his behavior as a coach?

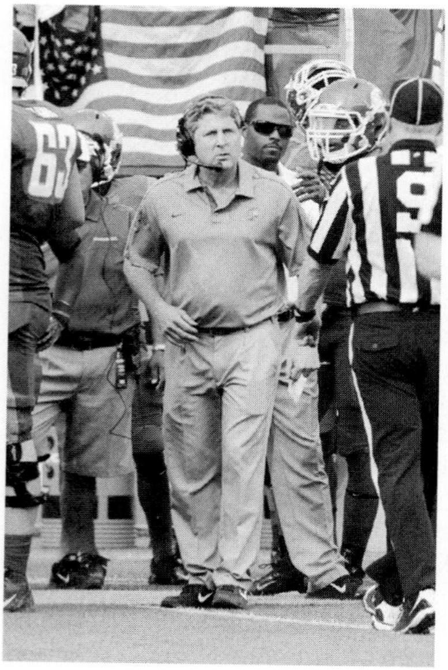

Mike Leach

lengthy private discussion, the team accepted his apology, yet they contended that the comments themselves were not the most egregious act they encountered during the situation. Ultimately, the comments overshadowed the fact that the team had made it to the national championship game, and Essence Carson (junior guard on the team) commented after the meeting with Imus, stating, "Where were these major networks when we were making history [on the court] for a prestigious university?" (Kinkhabwala, 2007, p. 18). In each of these situations, the act of apologizing was overshadowed by response from the Black community, negating the follow-up from these individuals in accounting for their statements.

CONCLUSION

Throughout this chapter, we have presented you with the scope of activities surrounding crises in sport. We defined crisis as the combination of intended and unintended events that necessitates a response on the part of athletes, coaches, commentators, or organizations and franchises to either account for the behaviors or further respond to consumer concerns that might arise. We hope that our discussion here provides you with a greater appreciation for the intricate dance that ensues when these events unfold. They can be as routine as the daily press conference where coaches and athletes are asked to account for their on-field performance or decision making. They also occur on a grander stage, as was the case for Ryan Braun, who was forced into making a formal apology after his suspension by the Milwaukee Brewers stemming from substance abuse violations. In his apology rests the need to apologize not just for his actions—many fans were most critical of his unequivocal denials in the months leading up to the announcement consistent with other athletes facing similar accusations (Smith, 2007; Utsler & Epps, 2013). He went so far as to blame the FedEx delivery man for possibly tainting the sample secured by MLB, placing this individual under significant public scrutiny despite Braun's full knowledge of his guilt. The public wanted to believe his denials so much that close friend Aaron Rodgers (quarterback for the Green Bay Packers) wagered an entire year's salary if the allegations for substance abuse were true. The most recent suspension of Maria Sharapova from the International Tennis Federation after testing positive for the banned drug meldonium suggests that these violations will continue to confront athletes and sport organizations. As opportunities for consuming sports continue to expand, it is likely that sport consumers and participants will be faced with a need for internal sensemaking as well as instances of crisis that require ongoing image repair.

Maria Sharapova

Suggested Additional Reading

Blaney, J., Lippert, L. R., & Smith J. C. (2013). *Repairing the athlete's image: Studies in sport image restoration.* Boulder, CO: Lexington Books.

Boyd, J. (2000). Selling home: Corporate stadium names and the destruction of commemoration. *Journal of Applied Communication Research, 28,* 330–346.

Brown, N., & Billings, A.C. (2013). Sports fans as crisis communicators on social media websites. *Public Relations Review, 39*(1), 74–81.

Hopwood, M. K. (2005). Applying the public relations function to the business of sport. *International Journal of Sports Marketing & Sponsorship, 1,*174–188.

Sanderson, J. (2008). "How do you prove a negative?" Roger Clemens's image-repair strategies in response to the Mitchell Report. *International Journal of Sport Communication, 1,* 246–262.

14

THE COMMODIFICATION OF SPORT

College football is among the most popular and profitable sports in the United States. It draws large television audiences, produces millions of dollars in revenue, and generates considerable enthusiasm on college and university campuses across the country. In spite of its presence, however, some have voiced concerns that treating college football as a commercial enterprise threatens the core values of higher education. In the words of one observer, college football "has become a business, carried on too often by professionals, supported by levies on the public, bringing in vast gate receipts, demoralizing student ethics, and confusing the ideals of sport, manliness, and decency" (quoted in Smith, 1988, p. 214). While this quotation comes from a book that is nearly 30 years old, you may be more surprised to learn that the words themselves actually come from the historian Frederick Jackson Turner, who said them in 1906. If college football was a commercial enterprise in the early 20th century, how do you suppose Turner would react to developments in the 21st century, such as ESPN's contracts with the University of Texas for $300 million and the Southeastern Conference for $2.2 billion? Indeed, in more recent years, critics have echoed Turner's lament, paying particular attention to the ways that money and sponsorship have negatively affected college and university educational missions (McAllister, 1998; McAllister, 2010; Sperber, 2001). In light of multimillion dollar salaries for coaches, numerous high-profile scandals involving illegal recruiting, debate about whether or not players should be paid, long-term contracts that dictate television programming decisions, constant talk about athletic conference expansion, the development of a playoff system that determines a "true" champion, and endless cross-promotions between networks and sponsors, it is easy to see why some fear that college football has become excessively commercial.

Source: © iStockphoto.com/J-Elgaard

Money, football, and America

CASE STUDY

COMMODIFICATION'S UNINTENDED CONSEQUENCES

In recent years, postsecondary institutions around the country have been faced with difficult decisions associated with funding high cost programs. In particular, over the past decade the number of universities choosing to eliminate football programs has increased, primarily with programs at the Division II or NAIA level forgoing football in order to shift resources to other more profitable sports. However, in 2014 the University of Alabama-Birmingham (UAB) became the first institution in more than 20 years to terminate their Division I football program. Although it is not uncommon for colleges and universities to eliminate sport teams, football has often been viewed as "sacred" on most campuses. Those that have eliminated these programs have often done so in response to meeting Title IX compliance and to address considerable shortfalls in endowments brought on by the recession. In the case of UAB, the primary driver appeared to be an unwillingness to invest the millions of dollars that would be needed to improve the team to meet the school's ambitions or remain competitive with programs with the resources to cover increased stipend amounts for athletes.

You might ask yourself why the situation facing this program fits into a chapter on commodification. This is because high-profile conferences are able to generate considerable revenue for even those teams with a history of unsatisfactory performance.

(Continued)

CASE STUDY (Continued)

For example, as we noted earlier, the Southeastern Conference has a 15-year, $2.2 billion contract with ESPN, and the Big 12 is currently in the middle of a 10-year, $100 million contact with Fox Sports to telecast conference games. This revenue assists in offsetting the costs for maintaining costly athletic programs, and those institutions that participate in peripheral conferences tend to experience limited television exposure. When considering the growing cost for coaching salaries and the need for luxurious stadiums to attract talented athletes and fans, it becomes increasingly difficult for a university to invest in a program in the hope that it will become commercially viable in the future. Institutions at this level are more likely to explore other priorities. For UAB, however, after making the decision to disband the football program in 2014, the administration reversed course in 2016 following significant outcry from alumni and program supporters.

1. How does the termination of football programs impact college football? What are the consequences for athletes?
2. How do you expect the continued commodification of collegiate sports to influence programs that may struggle to maintain their economic viability?
3. Is there a long-term future for athletic competition outside the Division I level when one considers the growing costs for institutional participation?

Although the perceived threat to higher education's integrity makes college football an appropriate target for some criticism, it is far from the only sport that is subject to commercialization and commodification. After all, the industry of sport in the United States alone is valued by *Street & Smith's* at $213 billion (Pegoraro, Ayer, & O'Reilly, 2010). With such money at stake, it is inevitable that sport will be affected by multiple and, at times, competing commercial interests. Although there is much to be said about the relationship between sport and commercialism in strictly economic terms, our purpose here is to examine the communicative impact of this relationship. As Wenner (2010) points out, "consumer culture infuses our sporting identities and explains much about how our communities are approached and how we think of, and talk amongst, ourselves" (p. 1).

Because commercial interests and consumption practices contribute to how sport functions communicatively, our aim in this chapter is to examine the significance of thinking of sport in terms of *commodification*. Commodification is a term derived from critical scholarly traditions, especially the work of the 19th-century German theorist, Karl Marx. It refers to the process by which capitalism transforms objects from their natural purpose to objects that are "for sale." We are not suggesting in this chapter that all commercial activities in sport are *bad*, for the very nature of sport entails a mixture of marketing and consumption. Moreover, it is important to acknowledge that commercialism does not always or necessarily produce commodification, as some sporting products, such as recreational equipment or memorabilia, are explicitly designed to be sold (Moor, 2007).

Nevertheless, the explosion of the sport industry in recent decades has produced various concerns about the consequences of an overly commercialized sport culture. The balance, so to speak, between commodification and other roles sport plays could be viewed as skewed, diminishing other potential noteworthy benefits of the enactment and consumption of sport. With this in mind, our attention in this chapter is on four dimensions of the commodification of sport: (1) the interdependent relationship of sport and media, which often depends on the production of "spectacle"; (2) the consequences of corporate interests in sport, especially through sponsorship and naming rights; (3) the effects of commodification on identity and the tendency to view cultural groups as objects of consumption; and (4) how overly commercial practices in sport have provoked a movement toward nostalgia.

THE SPORTS/MEDIA COMPLEX

It is nearly impossible to conceive of contemporary sport without the media. Yet it is almost equally the case that media industries in the United States look to sport as central to their success. So while sport depends on the media to be visible to large audiences, the media relies on sport to generate sales and advertising revenue (McChesney, 1989) and, in turn, sport relies on media for promotion and exposure. The relationship is mutually beneficial and, consequently, requires a level of integration and cooperation that one might equate with "a real life version of the movie *The Matrix*" (Jackson, 2013, p. 102). As an illustration, consider the story of Manti Te'o and his alleged girlfriend, Lennay Kukua. Te'o was a standout linebacker for the University of Notre Dame, one of the most decorated programs in college football history. Given its accomplishments and influential fan base, Notre Dame attracts a loyal following and substantial television ratings. As Te'o led the Fighting Irish toward a national championship appearance during the 2012 season, he received additional attention when his apparent girlfriend died of leukemia. Sports media, from ESPN to *Sports Illustrated*, reported the story and used it to frame a familiar sports narrative about inspiration and overcoming adversity. Especially for ESPN, which televised the national championship game between Notre Dame and another traditional power, the University of Alabama, there was much to gain from the sentiments of the story.

Despite the inspirational narrative, the death of Te'o's girlfriend turned out to be a hoax. An investigative report by *Deadspin.com*, long known as an irreverent counter to ESPN's sports media monopoly, revealed that Lennay Kukua never existed and that Te'o was either the victim of an elaborate scheme or complicit in an orchestrated effort to generate publicity (Burke & Dickey, 2013). ESPN, meanwhile, had received information about the hoax prior to *Deadspin*, yet opted against running the story. Although ESPN's news chief Vince Doria suggested that the network was trying to exercise journalistic caution, others speculated that they simply did not want to jeopardize their considerable investment in college football and the national championship game. That the information was shared within days of the title game only fueled such speculation (Sandomir & Miller, 2013).

It may not be possible to determine whether or not ESPN intentionally buried the story in order to protect its relationship with a major sporting organization. Other cases, however, suggest that such an explanation is entirely plausible. Defining the "ESPN effect," for example, Armfield and McGuire (2015) argue the network ceased production of its 2003 prime time drama, *Playmakers*, because it had been pressured by one of its primary partners, the National Football League (NFL). Subsequently, programming that challenges the image of the league appears to be viable only for networks without a direct connection to the sport, such as the series *Ballers*, which airs on HBO. In another case of conflict of interest, ESPN bowed out of its role in producing *League of Denial*, a PBS Frontline documentary that exposed the NFL's suppression of medical research on concussions and chronic traumatic encephalopathy (CTE) (Staton, 2015).

These examples do not tell the entire story, but they are representative of the *synergy* that exists between sport and the media. As Wenner (2004) notes, synergy "is a vertical-integration strategy aimed at maximizing the ways that complementary holdings can strengthen each other through cross-promotion and marketing to make the corporate whole stronger than the sum of its parts" (p. 316). Because it has become so commonplace, the synergy between sport and media organizations has been the subject of communication scholarship that examines what is often called the "sports/media complex" (Jhally, 1984). Communication scholars continue to adopt this perspective (Dart, 2009; Kidd, 2013) and express concern about the negative consequences of the sports/media complex, with particular attention to *accumulation* and *spectacle*.

INTERVIEW

LAWRENCE WENNER, VON DER AHE PROFESSOR OF COMMUNICATION AND ETHICS, LOYOLA MARYMOUNT UNIVERSITY

Q: We used to lament the commodification of sport; now we seemingly accept it as part and parcel of modern sport fandom. What resistance remains and in what forms?

A: You're right that some people lament the commodification of sport but certainly not everybody and certainly not those that profit from the depth of public fascination with sport. My hunch is that the "lamenting" being done by some stems from two main things. The first may be a little fallacious: the myth of the good old days when times were pure or better; in the instance of sport this was anchored in the notion that athletes played for the love of the game. The second part of the "lament" is that, increasingly, consuming sport is a pricey proposition; in the old days taking the family to a ballgame was cheap entertainment, and today a family outing to attend a major sport contest is a big dent in the household budget. Still, I agree that most people have made their peace with sport being expensive. And some fans are checking out due to hefty price tags and also on the sense that athletes are spoiled and overpaid. Unfortunately, I think this is a bit of a misnomer; indeed, the athletes, who have limited window careers, may now be paid at market rates, but the owners of professional sport are the much larger benefactors, just like the titans of any industry.

Q: Athletes have been used to sell brands for a long time, but now they increasingly are brands themselves. What is the impact of this trend?

A: This "branding" logic is pervasive in modern culture. On one hand, this is a good thing. Athletes have limited careers, and those engaged in team sports deserve to reap the benefits of their sport quite apart from the success (or not) of their teams. However, the broader impact of this is seen in the rise and impact of athletes as celebrities and the hero worship that comes in tandem with this rise. In today's culture, true heroes, known for noble action and deeds or for their character and contribution to the common good, are increasingly hard to find. In this void, come athletes, who are talented undoubtedly but in a very limited way, gifted for running fast or shooting a basketball or hitting a baseball, but that's a narrow band of human existence, and with the elevation of athletes to the heroic, we risk confusion about what it means to live a good and worthy life.

Q: To what extent can corruption at the highest levels of international sport organizations be attributed to the commodification of sport?

A: My short answer to this question is that the commodification of sport, with the large amounts of money and power at play, has been integral to virtually all corruption in the sporting culture and in its organizations. Does this mean that sport or money in sport is inherently evil? No, I think this would be a simplification. But the tolerances here are tricky. For sport to have market value, there has to be the appearance of a level playing field and to some extent that athletes "play" for the love of the game and the challenge of competition. But big money has not always been the driver of corruption in sport. Even when athletes were amateurs or poorly paid (in the era before collective bargaining in team sports), athletes took bribes to cheat. So here the lack of money in sport made money coming from outside sport seem appealing. But in today's world, with scandal rife in organizations such as the IOC and FIFA infrastructures, it is clear that the overlords have benefited the most from our compelling attraction to sport and "competition" for nations and locales to host mega-events with the high hopes of reaping economic benefit, which sometimes comes and sometimes does not, but even when it does, tends to benefit select people.

Q: What is the predominant impact of the overlap between capitalism and sport?

A: An answer here can be pretty simple. Capitalism is about the rise of commodities and the buying and selling of commodities. When capitalism comes to sport, sport becomes a commodity. In this, sport is not distinct from any other aspect of contemporary life that can be commoditized, and capitalism works to make sure that there is a market, ideally a robust one, for most things. There are a lot of reasons why sport is so marketable at this moment in history. The answers here range from the shift to an experiential economy, a search for the authentic amidst a world seemingly comprised of artifice, and increasingly watching the world through the eyes of media as spectators, whether that be watching a sporting contest, a feature film, or a news report on the latest act of terror.

Jhally (1984) maintains that sport should be understood *primarily* as an institution of capitalism. Although most fans would acknowledge that the sport industry generates millions of dollars in revenue, they would be reluctant to reduce its meaning only to profits and losses (wins and losses, perhaps). Rather, sport is more commonly viewed as a form of entertainment or escape. In other interpretations, sport provides community and a sense of belonging. Even though sport can be these things, Jhally insists that sport exists to make money. Thus, decisions that are made between sports leagues and television networks, for example, can be understood as efforts to maximize profits at the expense of any other concerns. Jhally (1984) argues that this focus on accumulation of wealth becomes not a product but the organizing logic of the sports/media complex. As a result, the human interests of those involved become secondary to the material interests of those who run sport and media organizations.

A MATTER OF ETHICS

PLAYING AT WHAT COST?

Despite significant evidence to the contrary, many sports fans still believe that NCAA athletes are "amateurs." In some ways this is true, but especially in the revenue-generating sports—that is, college football and men's basketball—the athletes are collectively helping to generate hundreds of millions of dollars for their universities and related institutions. The most common controversy associated with this issue involves whether or not athletes should be paid. But among the details lost in that controversy is the discussion about athletes and their health care. One high-profile case helps to dramatize this issue.

On March 31, 2013, in a regional final game during the annual NCAA Men's Basketball Tournament ("March Madness"), Louisville's Kevin Ware fell awkwardly on his foot and broke his leg in grotesque fashion. The injury stunned players and the crowd, and it received a tremendous amount of attention on sports media. An important aspect of the injury is that, although Ware's health costs were to be covered so long as he was at Louisville, any long-term health problems he may have with his leg will be his responsibility. This is this case for countless athletes who have competed for high-profile teams and universities and have suffered later because of serious injuries.

You may be thinking, "If I played hoops at my university's rec center and broke my leg, I wouldn't expect them to pay my long-term medical costs." Of course, you (most likely) aren't participating in a multimillion dollar enterprise (according to the *New York Times*, Louisville generated $40 million in 2012 through basketball alone). Given the extent to which college athletics have become commodified, is it fair that Ware will ultimately have to fend for himself? What medical benefits *should* players receive? Is a scholarship and a "free education" enough?

Two brief examples can illustrate Jhally's contention. For example, did the New York Yankees need to spend nearly $1.5 billion to construct a new Yankee Stadium, which opened in 2009? Surely, the stadium is designed to generate revenue for the franchise through its corporate sponsorships, luxury boxes, and entertainment amenities. However, these extra features inevitably mean that ticket prices will be higher, resulting in decreased opportunities for average fans to attend games in person (Ritzer & Stillman, 2001). Indeed, Yankee Stadium is representative of new forms of stadium excess. While the average ticket cost in Major League Baseball (MLB) is $31, it is $20 more than that for the Yankees, one of the highest in baseball. Even more striking is that some seats—given the glamorous name of "Legends Boxes"—sold for as high as $2,500 (face value) when the new stadium opened in 2009. Along with the high prices of actual tickets come the rising costs of parking, concessions, and souvenirs. Team Marketing Report provides an annual "Fan Cost Index," estimating the average cost for a family of four to purchase tickets, parking, concessions, and souvenirs at a big league baseball game ("Team Marketing Report," 2016). As you can see in Table 14.1, even for the most affordable of teams, attending a live game is no small investment!

Given that MLB teams host 81 home games each season, this cost is all the more alarming. Meanwhile, other professional events have even higher single game costs, to the point that 75% of American families cannot afford to attend a live professional sporting

TABLE 14.1 ■ 2016 Fan Cost Index for Major League Baseball

MLB Rank	Team	Average Ticket Cost	Fan Cost Index
1	Boston Red Sox	$54.79	$360.66
2	New York Yankees	$51.55	$337.20
3	Chicago Cubs	$51.33	$312.32
4	Philadelphia Phillies	$41.50	$258.50
5	San Francisco Giants	$35.76	$255.04
	MLB Average	**$31.00**	**$219.53**
26	Cleveland Indians	$25.61	$179.44
27	Atlanta Braves	$19.38	$178.02
28	Cincinnati Reds	$22.01	$166.54
29	Tampa Bay Rays	$21.04	$154.16
30	Arizona Diamondbacks	$18.53	$132.10

event (Thompson, 2009). Despite this sobering reality, high-cost arena construction projects are the norm, not the exception, in contemporary sport. Several new (or proposed) facilities make this point clear. In 2010, the Dallas Cowboys began play in Cowboys Stadium, which cost an estimated $1.2 billion. In 2013, the franchise announced that the stadium would thereafter be called AT&T Stadium after signing a deal that, according to team owner Jerry Jones, was for "the most dollars that there has been for naming rights" (quoted in "Cowboys Stadium," 2013, para 5). Also in 2010, MetLife Stadium, shared between the New York Giants and New York Jets, opened at the cost of $1.6 billion with a 25-year naming rights deal with MetLife (Kercheval & Novy-Williams, 2011). In 2016, MLB's Texas Rangers announced they would replace their existing ballpark—*only 22 years old*—with a new $1 billion facility in the same location (Caplan, 2016). Similarly, the Atlanta Braves began play in 2017 in a new ballpark in the city's suburbs at a total cost of $1.1 billion, including surrounding infrastructure and mixed-use development costs (Meltzer, 2015). Their previous home in downtown Atlanta had been built for the Summer Olympic Games in 1996, making it *less than 20 years old* when plans for the new facility were announced.

Other sports are not immune from these escalating expenses, evidenced by the $1 billion Barclay's Center, built primarily for the National Basketball Association's (NBA) Brooklyn Nets (McCarthy, 2012). And, even after declaring bankruptcy in 2013, the city of Detroit announced plans to subsidize the construction of a $444 million arena for the National Hockey League's (NHL) Red Wings (Isidore, 2013). By 2016, the proposed costs had risen to $627 million, $284.5 million of which would be supplied by public money (Thibodeau, 2016). Simply put, single-purpose facilities with elaborate

AT&T Stadium, home of the Dallas Cowboys

entertainment options are appealing both to fans and municipal officials who are excited by the spectacle of sport and the promise that modern arenas will boost local economies. Unfortunately, independent research consistently reveals that such promises are largely an illusion, as the primary economic benefits of new stadium construction go to local investors and team officials (Trumpbour, 2007). Meanwhile, the fans for whom these stadiums purportedly are built have fewer and fewer opportunities to experience and enjoy them and, even when they do, their experience is typically far from the luxurious options granted to the corporate world with the optimal seats.

Meanwhile, consider the controversy that has emerged regarding the use of performance-enhancing drugs in sport. For many observers, the primary reason that steroid use was widespread in MLB was that each of the major interests involved—ownership, players, and media alike—refused to interrogate suspicious practices because the increased productivity allegedly linked to steroids was also producing large gains in revenue (Bryant, 2005). In the case of Yankee Stadium, the process of accumulation compromises the ability of many fans to identify with the team; in the case of steroids, it compromises the integrity of the sport. In both cases, something is lost when the commercial logic of sport is reduced *only* to making a profit.

For Jhally and other critics, there is also a concern that the sports/media complex depends on the production of *spectacle*. As Kellner (1996) explains, "Spectacles are those phenomena of media culture that embody the society's basic values, serve to enculturate individuals into its way of life, and dramatize the society's conflicts and modes of conflict resolution" (p. 458). Events such as the Olympic Games or the Super Bowl can be understood as examples of the "ritualized spectacle" (Jhally, 1984, p. 53) that is produced by the sports/media complex. The problem with spectacle isn't necessarily the excess that seems to accompany such productions, although that might warrant criticism. Rather, it is that spectacles focus so persistently on elaborate productions and practices of consumption that audiences are conditioned to consume spectacular events passively. As a consequence, those who watch the Super Bowl, for example, may be more willing to accept problematic values embedded in the broadcast because they see them as components of the sport/media production.

Understanding the spectacle of sport is about more than identifying big, "mega-events" (Real, 2013; Roche, 2000). As Andrews (2006) argues, commercial sport is spectacular through a host of institutionalized arrangements that promote consumption. In his study of the NBA's transformation from "moribund anonymity to popular culture centrality" (p. 97), he draws parallels between the league and another purveyor of spectacular consumption, Disney. Key to the NBA's growth in the 1980s and 1990s was the substantial revenue generated through television contracts coupled with new marketing strategies featuring prominent superstars such as Magic Johnson and Larry Bird. Andrews argues that, much like corporations such as McDonald's and Disney, the NBA features a logic of branding, marketing, and consumption characterizing a "late capitalist" society. By branding its games as an experience—"I love this game!"—and equating its arenas with theme parks, the NBA became less about *sport* and more about *entertainment*. These patterns have only intensified in the past two decades, especially with the explosion of new forms of media. The concerns expressed by Andrews and others are that sport spectacle becomes an end unto itself, drained of its fundamental joy or any purpose other than ever more consumption.

CORPORATE SPONSORSHIP

One of the most obvious signs of commercialism in contemporary sport is the nearly ubiquitous presence of corporate sponsors. Sponsorship is about more than companies purchasing space or time to advertise their products and services. Indeed, sponsorship now includes naming rights for stadiums, events, and even segments during broadcasts. Thus, no longer do viewers watch the Rose Bowl, they watch the "Rose Bowl, presented by Northwestern Mutual." Meanwhile, corporate names introduce media segments from the "Chevrolet Pregame" to the "Budweiser Hot Seat." Although a commercial presence has always been a part of sport, critics are concerned that the breadth of sponsorship has negative effects on sporting events and those who watch them. This is especially the case with respect to the frequency of advertising content and the rise of corporate names for stadiums.

McAllister (1998) argues that college bowl games have become a representative illustration of the spectacle that we discussed earlier in this chapter. Yet he notes that the corporate sponsorship of these games, beginning in 1982 when the Tangerine Bowl was renamed the Florida Citrus Bowl, threatens the integrity of the sport. As he states, "the effects of this particular form of sponsored spectacle may serve to taint and devalue the essence of the event itself" (p. 366). Indeed, one would be hard pressed to dispute that the subject of his analysis—the 1996 Tostitos Fiesta Bowl—was anything but one "giant commercial" for Tostitos chips (p. 368). While McAllister is worried that an overemphasis on commercialism threatens the amateur ethos of college sports, he also emphasizes that too much influence has been given to the sponsors to affect sports events and broadcasts. As an example, he notes a $7.9 million contract between Reebok and the University of Wisconsin, which, had it been approved, would have prohibited any employee of the university from ever criticizing Reebok. In 2009, the University of Central Florida went one step further, dropping a shoe contract with Adidas because one of its players—the son of the legendary Michael Jordan—insisted the team wear Nike shoes. And in 2011, Adidas allegedly discouraged NBA center Dwight Howard from signing with the Chicago Bulls because they already had a major apparel contract with the Bulls' superstar guard, Derrick Rose (Wojnarowski, 2011).

Corporate sponsors clearly stand to benefit from such influence, and that influence continues to grow. In an updated study, McAllister (2010) notes that college football advertising revenue yields more than $450 million while professional football generates over $2 billion. As a result, through an analysis of the 2007 college football national championship game, he discovers that more than *80%* of the broadcast included some form of advertisement on screen. Consequently, he indicates at least six potential criticisms of this extensive presence:

1. Large college football programs benefit at the expense of small ones, while ticket prices limit accessibility to events.

2. Common promotion of products such as alcohol perpetuates dangerous behaviors.
3. Unethical corporate practices are left unexamined (thus tacitly accepted).
4. Commercials and actual content are increasingly blurred.
5. Athletic achievement itself is cheapened.
6. Encroachment of advertising into public arenas is legitimized.

The bottom line for McAllister is that "the continued acceptance and visibility of advertising activities in sports helps to normalize commercial intrusion not just in athletics, but in . . . other domains as well" (p. 1489).

The influence of commercialism is not restricted, however, to sports broadcasts. Another means by which corporations advertise within sport is through the purchase of stadium naming rights. As the cost of stadium construction has exploded in the past 20 to 30 years, sports franchises have increasingly partnered with corporations who spend billions of dollars to "name" an arena. Although some ballparks and stadiums retain names that reference their location or affiliation—Dodger Stadium in Los Angeles, for

THEORETICALLY SPEAKING

COMMUNICATIVE DIRT

Although you are likely to think of dirt as something that is unclean, anthropologist Mary Douglas (1966/2002) famously defines it as "matter out of place" (p. 44). She is thinking metaphorically here, as she theorizes dirt as a symbol of disorder that creates new forms of interaction and meaning. Building on this idea, Edmund Leach (1976) declares that "power is located in dirt" (p. 62). For communication scholars, what is useful here is the idea that "dirt" is a logic through which one idea can "rub off" on another. This is especially true of what Wenner (1994) calls "sports dirt," a metaphor for the ways that the values of sport rub off on and influence cultural values more broadly. In his analysis of sponsorship of the 1992 Olympic "Dream Team" (men's basketball), Wenner identifies three layers of sports dirt that promote nationalism, the myth of the American dream, and the athlete as a heroic figure. The key to these dirt narratives is the commercial interests—Gatorade, McDonald's, Nike, and so on.—that have made the Olympics one of the most commercialized events in the world. As Wenner (1994) summarizes, then, these commercial interests depend on the "naturalization of seeing sport as spectacle" (p. 45). If this is true, what other ways of "seeing sport" are being sacrificed?

- Douglas, M. (1966/2002). *Purity and danger: An analysis of concept of pollution and taboo.* London, UK: Routledge.
- Leach, E. (1976). *Culture and communication.* Cambridge, UK: Cambridge University Press.
- Wenner, L. A. (1994). The Dream Team, communicative dirt, and the marketing of synergy: USA basketball and cross-merchandising in television commercials. *Journal of Sport & Social Issues, 18*, 27–47.

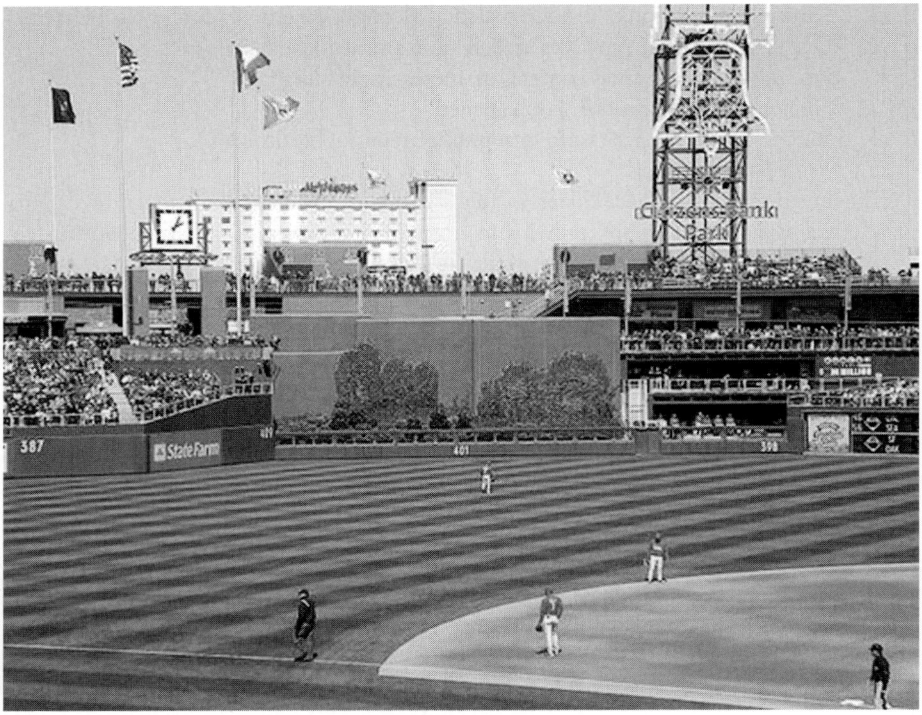

Corporate sponsorship is clearly present at Philadelphia's Citizens Banks Park

example—the majority of arenas have corporate sponsors. For example, imagine you live in or near Philadelphia and follow the four professional sports teams in that area. You would attend baseball games in *Citizens Bank Park*, football games in *Lincoln Financial Field*, and basketball and hockey games in the *Wells Fargo Center*. Of course, this trend is not restricted to professional sports, as more and more college teams play their games in corporate-named arenas, as well.

For some sports fans, stadium names are incidental. After all, does your experience at a San Francisco Giants game change if the ballpark is called "AT&T Park" instead of its previous names of "Pacific Bell Park" or "SBC Park?" Perhaps not, but communication scholars point out that the name of a stadium tells us something about the community in which it is located, and it affects the identification between fans and franchises. As Boyd (2000) asserts, the name of a sports arena is important because it anchors "the building as a memory place and [makes] an identity statement about the city and the fans" (p. 331). Moreover, he suggests that people identify with sport and sports franchises because they connect them to one another in ways that other cultural forms cannot. The risk, therefore, is that if sport is reduced to "just another business," then its unique communicative aspects are diminished (p. 341). What is lost is the sense of history and tradition that sport so often provides. The corporate sponsorship of sports arenas thus influences the feelings of nostalgia that we will return to later in this chapter.

Identity for Sale

We should clarify that it is not only the events or arenas that are for sale in the sports/media complex. As Meân, Kassing, and Sanderson (2010) contend, "sport comprises a site for commodification that is especially hard to resist due to its significance for identities and as a referent for meaning-making across a variety of interpretive communities" (p. 2). In other words, commodification in sport often functions to sell, if not actual people, *images* of people and cultures. As we discussed in Chapter 9, for example, those who object to the use of Native American mascots often do so on the grounds that such imagery presents Native American identity as a product to consume. Meanwhile, because high-profile athletes receive millions of dollars in endorsement money, they are often discouraged from acknowledging their race, gender, or class positions. Thus, it is important to examine the extent to which commercialism distracts us from substantive discussions of identity.

We discussed racial dynamics in sport in detail in Chapter 7. It is important to return to this topic because sport is one of the few arenas in which racial minorities achieve widespread exposure and praise. In particular, well-paid athletes of color are chastised if and when they suggest that race plays a role in the treatment they receive. The common conclusion is that no athlete can claim racism when he or she is making millions of dollars. Sportswriter William Rhoden (2006) uses this logic as a foil in his book, *Forty Million Dollar Slaves*, a title that points to the inherent tensions experienced by many African American athletes. Minnesota Vikings running back Adrian Peterson spotlighted those tensions in 2011, when he suggested that the NFL's exploitation of (largely African American) labor constituted "modern-day slavery." His comments were met with significant criticism, through which he was "called 'ungrateful,' 'out of touch,' 'an idiot,' and, in the darker recesses of the blogosphere, far worse" (Zirin, 2011, para 2). The gravity of the slavery analogy likely overstated his case, but Peterson's larger point warranted serious discussion. When fans object to such observations they demonstrate what Halone and Billings (2010) call "aversive racism" (p. 20), wherein dominant audiences reject the structures of racism even as they maintain negative views of individual minority athletes. Thus, the average basketball fan might decry racism at a social level but nevertheless lament that the NBA is too strongly influenced by "hip-hop culture."

Even as the visibility of race is often hidden in individual instances, it is simultaneously promoted at the collective level in practices of consumption. Ironically, then, White sports fans might lament what they perceive as the detrimental influence of Black culture even as they consume elements of that culture through products such as music and clothing. Perhaps no better example demonstrates this tendency than the explosion of "throwback jerseys" that were originally popularized in the hip-hop community and have since become highly desirable commodities for sports fans (Lane, 2007). The concern voiced by critics of these practices is that the identities, indeed the *bodies*, of racial minorities become objects of consumption. In a study of sports talk radio, Goldberg (1998) concludes that the practices of consumption that are so often tied to racial identity—rooting for a team, purchasing apparel, or imitating the behaviors of racial minorities—all but eliminate any serious discussions about race. Instead, the commodified athlete, especially the African American male, legitimizes "racist expression coded as race neutrality, racialized

Brendan Haywood in a Wizards "throwback" jersey

exclusions as color blindness, racist discrimination as market choices, as commodity preferences" (p. 220).

A more recent development in sport consumption is the rise of corporate social responsibility, often demonstrated by fans through "consumer activism." This idea has become commonplace in American culture, as corporations encourage citizens to purchase particular products with the knowledge that a portion of the profits will be donated to a worthy social cause. King (2006) refers to this as "cause-related marketing," and she uses the NFL's partnership with the Susan G. Komen Breast Cancer Foundation to argue that selling pink colored NFL gear "packages generosity as a lifestyle choice through which individuals can attain self-actualization and self-realization" (p. 2). Others raise similar concerns about the NIKE(RED) campaign, a corporate-sponsored effort to sell red-themed products to global soccer fans in order to raise awareness and money to fight the spread of HIV/AIDS. Although such an effort may have good intentions, Duvall and Guschwan (2013) worry that this form of "commodity activism" harms social causes because it minimizes important political issues and therefore "commodifies activist and fan identities to promote capitalism and consumerism as effortless and effective forms of social engagement" (p. 298).

It is clear that the various forms of sponsorship and commercialism have affected the ways fans interact with sport and think of their own fanship. In short, through advertising and other promotional influences in sport, "fans are both idealized as consumers and have become commodities themselves" (Wenner, 2013, p. 87).

NOSTALGIA

In the wake of constant sports media coverage, new stadium construction, free agency, and rising ticket prices, it is not uncommon to hear sports fans long for the "good old days." The idea that sports were once more pure, or that athletes simply played for the "love of the game," is common especially among those of older generations. These feelings are typically understood as *nostalgia*, a word that translates to "homesickness." Nostalgia, then, expresses a desire to regain something that has been lost or to return to a place that is no longer accessible. There are numerous cultural, political, and social changes that have provoked nostalgia in recent decades, and the commodification of culture, including sport, is surely among those changes. As Sobchack (1997) suggests, dramatic changes produce a feeling that something has come to an "end," a feeling that places the "purity" of a collective identity at risk. In the United States, "nostalgia for a 'pure' American identity is also satisfied by sports" (p. 179).

Sobchack especially focuses her attention on baseball in movies, and she points to the theme of "innocence" that is characteristic of a film like *Field of Dreams* (1989). To emphasize the point, think about some of the baseball films you have seen featuring children. It is likely that you will recall films such as *Angels in the Outfield* (1994), *Little Big League* (1993), *Rookie of the Year* (1993), and *The Sandlot* (1993). Each of these stories uses children in one way or another to reconnect audiences with the "purity" of baseball. Notice, also, that they all were released at relatively the same time, a time when fans and media alike were increasingly cynical about athletes who they perceived to be arrogant, overpaid, and disconnected with fans. These Hollywood films happened also to overlap with some notable documentary features, including *When It Was a Game* (1991) and *Baseball* (1994).

Ken Burns' nine-part documentary television series, *Baseball*, has received the majority of public attention, but Aden (1995) looks to *When It Was a Game* to examine the uses of nostalgia. The documentary is an assemblage of home movies taken by major leaguers who played from 1934 to 1957. It features rare footage of some of baseball's greatest legends, including Joe DiMaggio, Jackie Robinson, and Ted Williams. The homemade quality gives the film a kind of authenticity that allows viewers to reconnect to a previous era. From a historical perspective, the movies are a fascinating glimpse into what many view as baseball's "golden age." Yet Aden explains how *When It Was a Game* returns viewers to a time and place that no longer exists. This is effective, he argues, because for many baseball fans who grew up in the 1930s, 1940s, and 1950s, economic and social changes have left them longing for something they can find comfort in, what Aden terms a "secure place of opposition" (p. 23). Although such a place may provide a temporary escape, he warns that it also fails to help people accommodate and adjust to change. In addition, nostalgia tends to present an overly romanticized vision of the past. In the case of *When It Was a Game*, for instance, Aden notes that the "good old days" celebrated in the documentary mostly occurred prior to baseball's integration and thus were marred by racist and classist sentiments.

Nostalgia is not only an effort to return to a time before commercial interests (allegedly) ruined the sports we love. Indeed, nostalgia has itself become a commodity and a highly sought after one at that. The throw-back jerseys referred to earlier in this chapter, for example, serve as a simple illustration of how memories of the past become the commercial products of the present. Given the proliferation of "retro" days at sporting events, there can be little doubt that franchises use these promotions as opportunities to sell more merchandise. At a larger level, a sport like baseball explicitly draws upon its history (and mythology) in ways that use nostalgia as a marketing ploy. As the title of Springwood's (1996) study of baseball nostalgia indicates, there are marketing opportunities from *Cooperstown to Dyersville*. Cooperstown, New York, is the site of the National Baseball Hall of Fame and Museum, while Dyersville, Iowa, preserves the actual field used in *Field of Dreams*. While both sites are certainly about baseball, they are also about using baseball as a commodity.

The consumption of baseball nostalgia is also prevalent in the "retro ballpark" trend of the 1990s and early 2000s. Beginning with Oriole Park at Camden Yards, which opened in Baltimore in 1992, major league franchises increasingly drew upon architectural cues

The Field of Dreams in Dyersville, Iowa

from the past when designing their ballparks of the present (and future). Most of these ballparks, such as those found in Cleveland, Denver, Pittsburgh, and San Francisco, are located in urban centers and feature architecture heavy on brick and steel. Many of them provide spectacular venues for baseball, and throughout the 1990s, they generated widespread enthusiasm and praise. In particular, they have been hailed as a return to an urban community that had been lost in the post-World War II years. As many critics have demonstrated, however, the construction of these facilities has provided only an illusion of community, as more often than not these projects are pursued to the benefit of wealthy outsiders at the expense of local residents. As Rosensweig (2005) maintains, these retro ballparks are more "urbanesque" than "urban," meaning that "they are carefully controlled, relatively homogenous environments, sometimes barely resembling the areas around the ball parks after which they are modeled and lacking much in common with the landscapes they replaced" (p. 130). In this way, baseball nostalgia promises an escape from the present or a return to the past, even though the very means of that experience—the retro ballpark—is a product of the highly commodified culture in which sport presently operates.

CONCLUSION

In this chapter, we have examined some of the more controversial issues associated with sport commercialism and commodification. The development of the sports/media complex, the production of spectacle, the consumption of identities, and the repackaging of nostalgia each reveal how deeply embedded commercial practices are within sport. Sport is, and nearly always has been, a money-making enterprise. Nevertheless, there are consequences to the extensive marketing, sponsorship, and product placements that are ubiquitous in sport. Rather than taking these practices for granted, it is important to consider whether or not the form or the degree of commodification is healthy. This does not suggest that money should not play a role in sport, but that perhaps it should not be the only factor.

Suggested Readings

Aden, R. C. (1999). Integrating self and community as a means of finding homes: The shift from consumerism to altruism in *Field of Dreams*. In *Popular stories and promised lands: Fan cultures and symbolic pilgrimages* (pp. 219–249). Tuscaloosa: University of Alabama Press.

Ferrari, M. P. (2013). Sporting nature(s): Wildness, the primitive, and naturalizing imagery in MMA and sports advertising. *Environmental Communication, 7*, 277–296.

McAllister, M. P. (1999). Super Bowl advertising as commercial celebration. *The Communication Review, 3*, 403–428.

Schuck, R. I. (2010). The rhetorical lines on TV's poker face: Rhetorical constructions of poker as sport. *American Behavioral Scientist, 53*, 1610–1625.

Von Burg, R., & Johnson, P. E. (2009). Yearning for a past that never was: Baseball, steroids, and the American dream. *Critical Studies in Media Communication, 26*, 351–371.

Wenner, L. A. (1989). The Super Bowl pregame show: Cultural fantasies and political subtext. In L. A. Wenner (Ed.), *Media, sports, & society* (pp. 157–179). Newbury Park, CA: Sage.

Wenner, L. A., & Jackson, S. J. (2009). Sport, beer, and gender in promotional culture: On the dynamics of a holy trinity. In L. A. Wenner & S. J. Jackson (Eds.), *Sport, beer, and gender: Promotional culture and contemporary social life* (pp. 1–34). New York, NY: Peter Lang.

15

SPORTS GAMING

The majority of our attention thus far has focused on enacted sport, whether that involves communication within the enactment of participating in sport or the enactment that is embodied in sport fandom. However, a survey of communication and sport would not be complete without a study of the games within games that frequently occur. If the early part of the 21st century was defined as the information age, it appears we are entering the ludic age, where virtually anything one does has some element of play and personalized gaming becomes central. In terms of the sports world, gaming encompasses many activities, but this chapter focuses on three major games that collectively represent a massive and growing segment of the sporting experience. Specifically, this chapter will uncover communication trends as they relate to (1) fantasy sports, (2) sports video games, and (3) sports gambling. All three areas are supplemented by the overarching enacted sports media complex yet feature very specific offshoots of sport in the 21st Century.

FANTASY SPORTS

An Overview

Fantasy sports are one of the great dividers of modern sports fans: Some heavily committed sports fans mock the concept, not even understanding the basics, while others cannot imagine a world in which fantasy sport is not directly tied to the game at hand. What is beyond dispute is that the number of fantasy sport participants has reached critical mass. In 2013, 35 million North Americans played fantasy sports, with $3 billion spent annually on the activity (Fantasy Sports Trade Association, 2013); just 3 years later in 2016, 56.8 million North Americans participated, and the financial stakes had tripled (Fantasy Sports Trade Association, 2016). Consider many of the aspects of the "game within a game" nature of fantasy. Much of what makes fantasy sports a draw for millions of Americans are the ties to communication—the interpersonal interactions with their friends, the media outlets that increasingly offer minutiae on player performance, and the bombastic rhetoric that is often included in e-mails related to the good or bad performance of fantasy sports teams. The advent of the fantasy sport era is not only a trend in sport but also one worthy of very close examination within communication and sport.

Younger sports fans may have a difficult time comprehending a world before fantasy sports, but the evolution of the game has been relatively short, with its popularity particularly ascending since the 1990s. Harvard professor William Gamson is credited with creating the first form of fantasy sport (although he did not call it that) using professional baseball in 1960 (Schwartz, 2005). Several of his professor colleagues joined him in a fairly informal game in which each would score points based on how selected players performed in areas ranging from batting average to earned run average (ERA). The first documented form of fantasy football arose 3 years later when four people connected to the Oakland Raiders organization developed a fantasy league called the Greater Oakland Professional Pigskin Prognosticators League. Based on the same concept as Gamson's (selecting players from different professional teams and assigning points to them based on their performance), the league gradually developed, although it was never patented or sold to the masses. The first player selected was George Blanda, undoubtedly because of his ability to score points as both the quarterback and placekicker for the Houston Oilers.

A major turning point in the evolution of fantasy sports occurred in 1979, when a group of New Yorkers, led by writer Daniel Okrent, developed a more sophisticated form of fantasy baseball called rotisserie (based on where the group often met to eat, New York restaurant La Rotisserie Francaise). Ironically, it was the stoppage of baseball (the long strike of 1981) that hastened the growth of rotisserie baseball as journalists wrote about previously niche stories because of the dearth of things to cover during the stoppage. They found fantasy sport to be of interest in an offbeat sort of way. The strike—and labor unrest in sports more generally—generated a kind of cynicism that rotisserie baseball helped to counter, returning the "ownership" of the game to the fans.

For years, rotisserie resided largely in two forms (baseball and football) and was relegated mostly to fans who loved statistics and did not mind the time it necessitated to mine them from the local newspapers to determine fantasy winners. Participating in fantasy sport in the 1980s was a burdensome task, but the Internet dramatically altered that in the 1990s (see Felps, 2000, for an extended explanation). Suddenly, many more people who loved sports but did not previously play fantasy sports because of the legwork required opted to join online fantasy leagues because of the ease of statistical acquisition and league upkeep. Some leagues cost a modest amount of money while others were free and, as of the early 2010s, this format has largely stayed the same. People can now purchase online draft kits, receive injury updates, and follow virtually every aspect of a player's life both on and off the playing field. As is true with many other facets of society, players get what they pay for, as more money invested provides things such as real-time updates of scores and fantasy guru advice. As a result of the information age, many more forms of fantasy participation are now available including basketball, golf, hockey, cricket, bass fishing, and auto racing. There are even nonsporting forms of fantasy leagues, ranging from Fantasy Congress (where people draft House and Senate members and score points based on their actions) and the Hollywood Stock Exchange (in which players are handed millions in imaginary money to invest in upcoming film projects based on how they think they will perform at the box office). The concept in all forms of fantasy leagues is roughly the same: Take events that are already occurring naturally within society and find a way to reconstruct the people acting in the events to predict and perform new assimilated meanings to the existing actions.

Daily Fantasy Participation

Without question, the largest area of expansion for fantasy sport in recent years has been daily fantasy games. Instead of drafting a team and following it for the entire season, daily (or in the case of professional football, weekly) gaming changes the equation by having people redraft or reselect players continually throughout the season for minicompetitions. The amount of money entering the industry as a result has been staggering; FanDuel posted revenues of $200 million in 2015, representing a 300% increase from 2014; DraftKings had revenues of $150 million in 2015, representing a 500% increase from 2014 (Fisher, 2015). In direct response to the growth, major media entities embraced the new trend. ESPN bought a $250 million stake in DraftKings (Lefton & Ourand, 2015), while Time Warner (among many others) jointly invested $275 million in FanDuel the same year (Sacco, 2015). Major sports leagues such as the National Basketball Association (NBA) have partnered as well (Rovell, 2014).

Because of the large influx of money coming into the industry as the result of daily fantasy play, controversy has commenced as to whether such leagues constitute gambling. Those decisions are still being determined in state courts across the country with no key determining principle currently winning that debate. Arguments indicating that daily gaming constitutes gambling note that the fewer the repetitions (for instance, a single game—as opposed to a full season), the greater luck enters the equation; arguments against labelling it as gambling note that daily fantasy sports offer far from random odds of winning, as 1% of participants currently win over 90% of the money involved within the games. Without question, the rise of daily fantasy play offers a new angle in which to explore sports gaming.

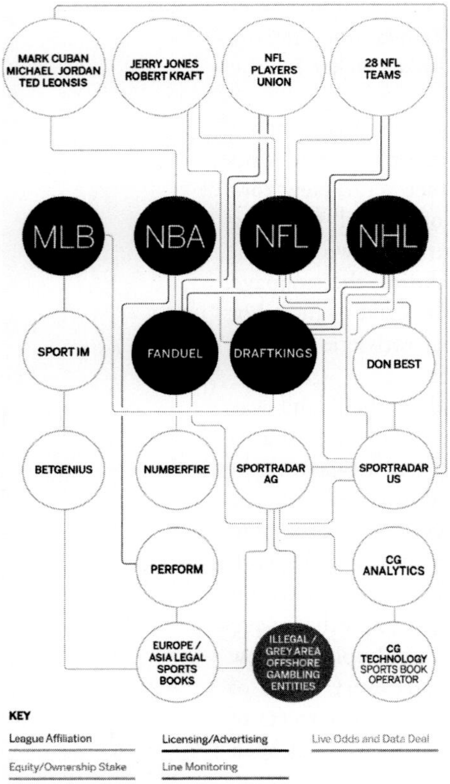

Intermingled interests of daily fantasy sports

INTERVIEW

MATTHEW BERRY, SENIOR FANTASY SPORT ANALYST, ESPN

Q: To what do you attribute the rapid growth of fantasy sport since the 1980s?

A: Technology is a big one. The games are much more easy to play thanks to the Internet. Thanks to mobile devices, you can play fantasy sports without ever getting onto a computer. You don't even have to have a smartphone; if your phone can access the web, you can access and manage your team. The second thing that has helped has been the embracing of fantasy by the professional sports leagues themselves and also from major media companies like ESPN. They realized it makes the average fan a passionate fan, a hardcore fan. The typical fantasy player watches twice as many hours of sports as other sports fans.

Q: Is the stereotype of the "stathead" or "fantasy geek" the best description to apply to players of fantasy sport within today's society?

A: One of the things we worked on here was to take it out of that stigma, that it was for nerds or something—that would take a lot of time and [be] hard to understand. You'[re] probably going to spend more time because you're going to get into it, but you can just spend 5 minutes a week updating your lineup. Now we have 5-year-olds to 85-year-olds playing. The fact that you have professional athletes and *SportsCenter* anchors drafting their own teams and referencing fantasy helped make it cool and outside of the "geek realm."

Q: How does fantasy impact sports culture and American culture as a whole?

A: It's changed the way a lot of people watch games. There's more of an emphasis on stats. The whole Sabermetric/*Moneyball* movement is facilitated by fantasy. I'm not saying it's the result of fantasy, but the mainstreaming of stats—and the way to interpret data through not just what we see on the field is a result of fantasy. It changes the way we watch, talk, and consume sports.

Q: Is fantasy sport coverage best when it is its own entity (such as Fantasy Football Now) or when it is integrated within mainstream sports news (such as SportsCenter)?

A: It depends on your goal. If you are trying to just serve the fantasy fan, something like *Fantasy Football Now* or a podcast devotes more time and depth to it. The things we do on *NFL Live* or *SportsCenter* are great because first, it gives information for the casual fantasy player. It gives a halo effect to the rest of it, anything you can get on *SportsCenter* relays the message that fantasy is important.

Q: What do you see as possible trends for the future of fantasy sport play?

A: For one, there will also be more people like me. I am paid to talk and analyze fantasy sports. That's my entire job. I'm lucky to have it, and you'll see more people paid by major media companies to analyze and discuss fantasy sports on their various platforms.

Motivations for Play

Various forms of fantasy sport communities exist, with their function largely stemming from the owners' motivation for participation in the league. Employing a uses and gratifications (see Rubin & Perse, 1987) framework for endorsing the belief that people select and use media for the fulfillment of personal needs, Farquhar and Meeds (2007) identified five needs that are satisfied through participation in fantasy sports, which parallel the motives for sport fandom discussed in Chapter 4. The first two, arousal and surveillance, were determined to be the primary motivations, while entertainment, escape, and social interaction functions were uncovered as well.

More recently, Billings and Ruihley (2013) explored whether the motivations for fantasy sport fandom were different than for traditional (nonfantasy) fandom. Table 15.1 illuminates these differences, showing that for all motivations but one, the fantasy player had higher motivations for sports media consumption. The sole exception was in the area of escape, with fantasy players feeling less escape motivations, likely because they play these fantasy games with friends, family, and coworkers, intermingling their sports desires with other aspects of their life. Still, the desires of traditional fans and fantasy sports players can sometimes conflict, as they did for Maurice Jones-Drew in 2009. Needing to run out the clock more than score a touchdown, the Jacksonville Jaguars running back "took a knee" rather than running into the end zone, making the smart decision for his team but infuriating fantasy sports fans in the process. Jones-Drew later issued a public apology to fantasy participants acknowledging the duality of fan desires in an era of fantasy sport. However, ancillary evidence such as the 2010 National Football League (NFL) "Pick Me" campaign (in which players make a case for being selected on a fantasy team) reinforces the importance leagues place on promoting fantasy sports, to transform the team to a more individual entity.

TABLE 15.1 ■ Motivation Differences Between Fantasy and Traditional Sport Fanship

Motivation (1 = low; 7 = high)	Fantasy Players	Traditional Fans	Total
Arousal	4.8	4.7	4.7
Entertainment	5.6	5.3	5.4
Enjoyment	5.6	5.3	5.4
Escape	3.9	4.2	4.1
Pass Time	5.1	4.7	4.9
Self-Esteem	5.0	4.5	4.7
Surveillance	5.5	4.8	5.1

Fantasy Sport Communities

Decades ago, one could stereotype the community of fantasy sport with a modicum of accuracy. The world was dominated by "stat geeks" who were more than willing to spend hours seeking out the data needed to play the games. The "ultra" fan was the prototypical fantasy sport player. That, without question, has changed in the mainstreaming of fantasy sport. As a result, many different types of communities exist that were analyzed and combined for this chapter.

First, there are still the statistical enthusiasts. They love crunching numbers to determine whether a middle infielder would rebound after a down year or to uncover the degree to which having the first pick offers owners intrinsic advantages or disadvantages. However, these players differ in the games they play, as the degree of detail is quite impressive. A basic fantasy baseball league may have four or five batting and pitching components, while these communities may be assessing as many as two dozen statistical categories to determine fantasy superiority. Playing games within this type of community requires astute observation, attention to detail, and a willingness to place fantasy value over value in the "real game."

A second community is the fan-first players. They enjoy and care about fantasy sport but will not care about it so much as to disregard the fate of their favorite "real" teams. They draft players that they think are the best for their fantasy team, simultaneously realizing that if given the choice between winning their fantasy championship and their

Source: © iStockphoto.com/Double_Vision

Fantasy sports are usually played online

favorite team winning a real championship, their loyalties will ultimately lie with the team with which they grew up.

A third group of players exists that is casually dubbed the "homers." Not only do they care about their favorite teams more than any fantasy game, but they will also actively select players from their favorite team to essentially be rooting for the same team in the fantasy and real worlds. An example would be a Sacramento Kings fan who selects Kings players in the first four rounds of the fantasy draft. He likely realizes his decisions will be a detriment to his fantasy performance (obviously, a Kings player was not always the best available selection) yet only desires fantasy sport glory if it is paired with the success of his favorite regular team.

A final fantasy sport community includes those players that opt for fantasy sports merely for the social aspects. They still have a desire to win, but, most importantly, they would like to be a part of the conversation. A prime case would be an office league in which many of a person's administrative superiors play; a newcomer may wish to join just to get to know people and have something to discuss over coffee in the morning. Some of these players would not even classify themselves as sports fans, much in the same way that millions of people who do not care about football nonetheless watch the Super Bowl for fear that they would otherwise be missing something.

Obviously, other forms of fantasy sports communities exist (as hybrids of the four listed above but also as uniquely separate organized entities). The important aspect to remember is that as the fantasy world expands, so does the breadth of fantasy sporting communities.

A MATTER OF ETHICS

TAKING A CHANCE ON DAILY FANTASY?

As we discuss in this chapter, there is a fine line between "games of chance" (gambling) and "games of skill" (fantasy). The advent of websites such as DraftKings and FanDuel has raised new questions about the differences between chance and skill. FanDuel was founded in 2009, and DraftKings debuted in 2011. Since that time, they have become the leaders in the daily fantasy sports industry, allowing millions of fans to pour millions of dollars into daily fantasy transactions.

While the Fantasy Sports Trade Association (FSTA) contends that the particulars of daily fantasy transactions require an appropriate level of skill, some lawmakers see them instead as obvious moments of chance. For example, in the spring of 2016, New York Attorney General Eric Schneiderman leveled gambling charges against DraftKings and FanDuel, both of which then agreed to stop accepting money in the state. Schneiderman's actions put a spotlight on the daily fantasy industry and jeopardized its future status. By August of 2016, however, New York Governor Andrew Cuomo had signed legislation that defined daily fantasy sports as "games of skill." The sites would still face regulations by the New York State Gaming Commission, yet the legal action ensured that the daily sports industry would remain viable.

The popularity of daily fantasy sites notwithstanding, do you think they are able to make a clear distinction between being games of "chance" and "skill?" Does this distinction make a difference? Should sites such as DraftKings and FanDuel be subjected to oversight by state agencies or governments?

Societal Impact

The advent (and subsequent mainstreaming) of fantasy sports impacts the communication and sport landscape at many levels ranging from fandom to social attitudes and interactions to media entities and even to deviant behaviors. This section expounds on each of these four influences.

Impacts abound but none more so than on the *role of the fan*. Fantasy sport changes fandom in the same way that gambling alters attitudes about winners and losers—it creates a game within a game. Walk into a packed sports bar in America, and you will see these often conflicting paradigms at play. All are watching the same game but for different reasons: Some are fans of the home team, others of the visiting team, others of certain players on either team as they relate to their potential fantasy sporting prowess, and still others care not as much about who wins but by how much in relation to a Las Vegas point spread. Many of these motivations for consumption converge and conflict because in fantasy sport, "allegiances to the real team and to other fans of the real team are frayed from the start," but we are drawn to it because "fantasy sports do not merely offer [a] point of transcendence through interaction; they are predicated on it and, in a way, necessitate it" (Serazio, 2008, p. 31). Sandomir (2002) states that fantasy sport causes people to "root, root, root for no team" (para. 1) which is at least somewhat true, as Billings, Ruihley, and Yang (2018, in press), found that 60% of all sports fans preferred a win by their favorite team, yet 31% preferred the fantasy victory (with the remainder having equivalent preference).

Social attitudes and interactions are influenced by fantasy sports as well. Consumption of sports media is at an all-time high (see Raney & Bryant, 2006), meaning that a family that used to adjust its weekend schedule around when its favorite team played (consider the family relationships outlined in Chapter 10) now may try to work around an entire sporting schedule, as each game may be of import in the fantasy sports world. It no longer matters if your favorite team is on; any game may feature a player in which you now have a rooting interest.

Fantasy sports interactions, though, inevitably occur after the games have been played, meaning that interactions surrounding sports can become a weeklong and (in extreme cases) even round-the-clock endeavor. Even with football, where games are contested only once per week, owners spend significant amounts of time determining starting lineups, brokering trades, and chatting (in person and virtually) about previous performances.

The downside is that an estimated $13.4 billion of workplace productivity is lost each year because of fantasy football play (Snyder, 2014).

Scholars have also found that fantasy sports can reinforce traditional aspects of sports culture, particularly masculinity (Davis & Duncan, 2006). Not surprisingly, the majority of fantasy sports owners is male, and along with that arise the predictable patterns of dominance and exclusion. Thus, fantasy sport becomes the new form of male sports club in which it becomes tacitly permissible for "boys to be boys" because little feminine resistance (or even participation) is present in the majority of fantasy sports leagues. A recent analysis (Ruihley & Billings, 2013) showed that while men consume more than 10 hours more sports media per week, fantasy sport play increases that figure for men and women in near-equal proportions: Men playing fantasy sport consumed 63% more media than nonfantasy sport playing men, with the figure being a 61% increase for fantasy sport-playing women as opposed to their nonfantasy playing counterparts. As ESPN's Matthew Berry (a.k.a., "The Talented Mr. Roto") offers, the fantasy sport industry caters to the masculine side of the sports universe:

> We wanted to change the perception of fantasy sports. We didn't want it to be geeky or nerdy; we wanted to make it just one of those things that guys do. What do guys like? Guys like movies where stuff blows up. They like fast cars. They like attractive women. They like cigars. They like going to Vegas. They like poker with the guys. They like pickup ball. Oh, and they like fantasy sports. Getting more people to play it and referencing it as something that everyone does helped move it more into the mainstream. (Berry quoted in Billings & Ruihley, 2014)

Fantasy sports have also changed the way *media entities* conduct their business. Pregame shows feature analysts drafting their own teams and fantasy sports experts advising owners who "start or sit" for a given game. National sports radio programs now routinely feature callers looking for fantasy advice. Major Internet entities, such as Yahoo, ESPN, and cbssportsline.com, make fantasy sport a heavy portion of their online sports offerings, as people are much more likely to become unique logged users for fantasy sports than merely seeking other forms of sports information.

Media also are influenced by fantasy sport in larger ways, perhaps most noticeably in featuring individual accomplishments to the detriment of team achievements. A sports fan following a Mets versus Phillies baseball game may be checking which pitcher got the win or who hit the home runs before noticing that the Mets actually won the game. In television, onscreen graphics have become more commonplace, partially because of the information age but also because the growing number of fantasy sports fans demand it. Perceptions of athlete worth are altered in the process. For example, a running back who leads the league in rushing may not be as valued as the person who always gets the ball at the goal line because of convoluted notions of fantasy sports worth. For example, Minnesota Viking running back Adrian Peterson was the league leading rusher in 2015 with 1,530 yards during the regular season while Jeremy Hill from the Cincinnati Bengals was 18th overall with just 844 yards. However, Hill's touchdown performance exceeded Peterson's by one that same year.

Lomax (2006) notes that media outlets have not yet uncovered ways to fully realize the profits fantasy sports can provide but that the future is clearly in determining how to capitalize on this avid and growing fan base. Media outlets are hoping that fantasy sports ultimately will provide insight into not only what fans want but also perhaps even in predicting whether the collective knowledge of millions of fans can aid the prediction of future sporting successes. This has already proved successful in the film industry, as the fantasy site Hollywood Stock Exchange (hsx.com) has proven to be a very reliable indicator of how a film will perform in its first 4 weeks at the box office (see Smith, Sharman, & Hooper, 2006, for more information on harnessing decision-making insights).

A final impact of fantasy sport lies in the area of *deviance,* particularly in the form of addiction and gambling. Consider the obsessiveness of the fantasy sports players within the fictional FX series *The League,* which debuted in the fall of 2009. Characters were depicted as placing fantasy sport success ahead of other fundamental obligations to family and career, once even having a character jokingly call FOX Sports broadcaster (and legendary former Pittsburgh Steelers quarterback) Terry Bradshaw to query the injury status of a player on his team. The ties between fantasy sport, addiction, and gambling are perhaps weak at the current moment, yet the obsession of fantasy sport players can certainly border on deviance and can make these connections quite clear on individual bases. Scholars are also attempting to determine whether fantasy sports participants are more or less likely to gamble money on games and also whether fantasy becomes a gateway to various forms of addictive and deviant behavior.

The Future of Fantasy Sport

Some roadblocks remain for fantasy sport, but other heavily argued debates such as intellectual property issues (see Bolitho, 2006) have been settled predominantly in favor of fantasy sporting outlets (Van Voris & St. Onge, 2007). In addition, fantasy sport should become more prevalent in more aspects of modern life, including the world of education. For instance, scholars already are arguing that the games can be quite beneficial in the understanding of sports marketing (Gillentine & Schulz, 2001), and the teaching of information literacy (Waelchli, 2008) as fantasy sport inherently provides demographic and behavioral information about the tendencies of millions of people.

Finally, it appears that the line between the real games played by professional (and potentially, in the future, collegiate) athletes and the fantasy games played with the statistics derived from the real games will continue to be blurred. The more media outlets and other gatekeepers report on fantasy sport, the more it enters the bloodstream of the modern sports athlete. Professional sports players already are asked questions about their fantasy performance and respond with a great deal of accuracy and specificity. This combination of real and fantasy sport is quite different than other forms of blurred realities presented in staged formats, such as professional wrestling. It is difficult to discern what the ultimate outcome of this collaboration of sporting worlds will be, but there is no question that fantasy sports are here to stay as a significant factor of modern sporting culture.

CASE STUDY

CHECK THE COVER BEFORE YOU DRAFT

As the NFL season approaches each fall, millions of football fans undertake the time and energy needed to draft the right combination of players that will lead them to a successful season in their fantasy leagues. Difficult decisions must be considered to ensure the right mixture of players are selected with the goal that they not only perform well during the season but also avoid injuries that can significantly hamper any chances of success. As fantasy leagues have developed over time, savvy players have come to understand that picking a team too early before the season, or the completion of the preseason games, can be detrimental. Consider those who conducted drafts for their league in 2003 when Michael Vick broke his leg in a meaningless scramble during a preseason game for the Atlanta Falcons. While few could have predicted such an event, it helped to further solidify what many had come to believe to be the "Madden Curse." Each year, the top selling Madden NFL football video game is released, and tradition holds that one of the top NFL players from the previous year will grace the cover. Running back Eddie George was the first player to do so in 2001, and he had a record setting performance that year for the Tennessee Titans. However, the following year, Minnesota Viking quarterback Daunte Culpeper followed up a stellar 2001 season by underperforming after being placed on the cover of Madden 2002. In the years that followed, a series of lackluster or controversial seasons awaited those athletes who were unfortunate to be featured on the cover. These include the following:

2007—Shaun Alexander—Fractured foot and just over 900 yards rushing
2008—Vince Young—Only nine touchdown passes and 17 interceptions
2009—Brett Favre—Threw 20 interceptions and suffered a torn bicep muscle
2010—Troy Polamalu and Larry Fitzgerald—Both players achieved personal bests at that point in their careers
2011—Drew Brees—Second highest passing total for his career
2012—Peyton Hills—Only three touchdowns and just over 700 yards rushing
2013—Calvin Johnson—Over 1,900 receiving yards
2014—Richard Sherman—Lost in Super Bowl following a last second interception on the goal line against New England Patriots
2015—Odell Beckham, Jr.—Suspended by the NFL late in the 2015 season following safety-related rule violations
2016—Rob Gronkowski—Missed half of regular season games with multiple injuries

Since Eddie George's performance during the 2001 season, only the combination of Troy Polamalu and Larry Fitzgerald, Drew Brees, and Calvin Johnson have been able to put up record-setting performances for that point in their careers. In addition to implications surrounding fantasy league player selection, the Madden NFL game has also generated considerable interest through the "Madden Bowl," which is a single elimination tournament held each year since 1995 in the Super Bowl host city. NFL players are invited to participate, and it has recently been televised by ESPN due to the increased fan interest the competition has generated.

1. What stock should fantasy football participants put into selecting a player who has been selected to be on the cover in a particular year?
2. Other than what many believe to be a curse associated with the Madden cover image, what might be a contributing factor to what has traditionally occurred to these athletes?

SPORTS VIDEO GAMES (SVGS)

Another major component of sports gaming involves the heavy use of sports video gaming (SVG's), particularly among males in younger demographics. As Brookey and Oates (2015) note,"sports simulation games have held an important place in the history of every sector of the video game market" (p. 2). Within gaming as a whole, a half billion people worldwide play an average of 1 hour or more per day. By age 21, the average person has spent more hours playing video games than they have spent in the classroom for all of their secondary education (McGonigal, 2011). While other forms of video games such as *Halo* and *Grand Theft Auto* receive a great deal of media attention, it is important to note that sport video games represented three of the top 10 most popular games in 2012, the most of any subgenre of gaming (Plunkett, 2012). As Crawford and Gosling

Source: © James Woodson/Digital Vision/Thinkstock

Playing sports video games

OFF THE BEATEN PATH

EXTREME GAMING

ESPN offers online games that allow users to play arcade games of their favorite sports. The X Games selection is free and includes *Epic Air, Rally & Super X, Rally Racing, Vert Star,* and *TG Motocross 4—X Games*. An additional online game is *Zoom: X Games 15*, which is a photo game. The arcade is equipped with monthly and all-time leader boards, tutorials of how to play the games, rating scales, video clips, photos, and other interactive features. Users are able to log-in to their Facebook accounts to view their friends' leader boards and access the ESPN Arcade page. Users have a customizable experience with the tricks they watch their favorite athletes perform during competitions, which adds to their personalized connection to the X Games. This selection of online games is included in the Fantasy and Games section on ESPN.com that provides users with an experience that extends beyond their interest in the X Games.

—Aisha Avery

Sports video games and personal fitness

(2009) argue, "Video games, for many, are an important component of their everyday lives . . . sports-themed video games provide an important resource and cross-over with associated sports fan interests and narratives" (p. 63).

The role SVGs play in the communication process is still being uncovered, yet we know several interesting components to this massive amount of game play. For instance, there is a positive correlation between playing video games and consuming sports media (Kim, Walsh, & Ross, 2008). Presumptions that playing SVGs takes time away from watching or listening to sports events appear unfounded, as gamers are more likely to be highly identified sports fans, finding time for sports in all facets of life, often consuming multiple forms of sports media simultaneously through second-screen options. Bonding with athletes and teams is more likely to take place as "in an electronic environment, sport fans can develop an emotional bond with a sport team or athlete by closely identifying with the cyber athlete on the video screen" (Kim, Walsh, & Ross, 2008, p. 45).

Electronic Arts (EA Sports) incorporates the tagline, "If it's in the game, it's in the game," in an attempt to highlight the degree of realism and accuracy that is found in modern video games. The result is that SVG players are more likely to feel engaged with all realms of sport, being more likely to connect sports video game experiences with sports experiences in real life (Kim & Ross, 2006). Such transfer is relatively unique, as most other video game studies have found little identity transference between the character one assumes on a video game and feeling more connected to those same people or roles in real life.

Sports video games also allow for a great deal of personalization, often allowing one to insert oneself into the game by physically and attributionally modifying a given player or character. Scholars have shown that when one becomes increasingly skilled at a sports video game, he or she is more likely to take advantage of these personalization options—and those who do personalize characters experience higher levels of enjoyment and game satisfaction (Kwak, Clavio, Eagleman, & Kim, 2010). Additionally, from a uses and gratifications perspective, SVGs appear to offer three components not traditionally found in other forms of media: knowledge application, identification with sport, and fantasy (Kim & Ross, 2006). All three of these factors mirror the first part of this chapter, unpacking fantasy sports with some of the same motivations; for instance, the fantasy notion of Schwabism could easily be equated with the knowledge application delineated here. As Kim and Ross (2006) note, "SVGs may be a unique and valuable outlet for needs that might not be fulfilled in a real life sporting context" (p. 43). Not surprisingly, marketers are finding ways to capitalize on this heavily identified group as playing an SVG is, for instance, more likely to increase brand awareness for advertisers within the gaming industry (Cianfrone, Zhang, Trail, & Lutz, 2008).

Of course, concerns and controversies are found within these billions of hours of game play. For instance, violent SVGs (e.g., NFL Blitz, NHL Hitz) are more likely than nonviolent simulation-based SVGs (e.g., MVP Baseball, FIFA Soccer) to make a player have increased levels of aggressive affect, aggressive cognition, aggressive behavior, and positive attitudes toward violent sports (Anderson & Carnagey, 2009). Given increased public focus on any potential relationship between violent video games and behaviors within society, such findings should be substantially and thoroughly studied.

Controversy also resides within the role of SVGs pertaining to college sports. Former University of California, Los Angeles (UCLA) basketball player Ed O'Bannon won an antitrust case (joined by many other prominent former and current players) for $42.3 million against the NCAA and EA Sports for using their likeness in SVGs without offering any compensation (Berkowitz, 2016). The case of *O'Bannon v. NCAA and EA Sports* is a harbinger of issues to come, as addendums have been added to the lawsuit that make issues like this a "pay for play" issue within college sports that could accelerate talks of whether college athletes should be paid or compensated in some way beyond the scholarships they receive.

Gaming as a family activity

All of these issues, both good and bad, underscore how sports video games are big business and are a major form of consumption for a substantial segment of both North America and the world. As such, sports video games are likely to receive increased focus as to their ramification on communication processes.

eGaming

One final largely unexplored—yet rapidly growing—area of SVGs pertains to egaming. These games are largely not sport-based but instead involve mass competitions of people playing fantasy-oriented games for competition, with world competitions for games such as League of Legends now generating millions of dollars and heavy investment. Gaudiosi (2015) reports that 179 million hours of the 2015 world championships were streamed, with 27 million streaming the final match, representing more viewership than for the NBA Finals or World Series. Media entities have noticed the massive potential; Turner Sports announced in 2015 that they would begin eLeague to televise esports competitions on their cable networks (Spangler, 2015), and *EGR* (*e-Gaming Review*) continues to thrive as an online magazine.

SPORTS GAMBLING

The third and final type of sports gaming addressed in this chapter involves the world of sports gambling. Betting on sports events has a history as long as the games themselves; the 1919 Black Sox scandal involving the intentional loss of World Series games will soon reach its centennial anniversary. However, the advent of the Internet has facilitated sports gambling at levels never before measured, both in terms of the number of people who bet and the amount of money wagered on the games. One in six Americans gamble on sporting events (Jones, 2008)—with Keating (2012) equating the amount of money wagered on sports in America as being roughly the equivalent of the U.S. defense budget. The most recent thorough research of the industry shows that online sports gaming is a particularly burgeoning business, with revenues (not to be confused with the overall amount wagered on sports, which would be a much larger number) increasing 252% from 2001 ($1.7 billion) to 2005 ($4.29 billion; American Gaming Association, 2012). Given such totals, it is not surprising that Rushin (2013) argues, "We are One Nation, Under an Over/Under" (p. 68).

Most Americans know that sports gambling is a massive industry and generally believe such betting is underreported and underestimated. Novices to the world of sports gambling may be surprised to hear that these bets are not relegated to casino towns; the entire state of Nevada handles just 1% of all sports bets (Rushin, 2013). Some of the other statistics about American sports betting (Jones, 2008, via Gallup poll) may be equally surprising for some:

- College graduates are nearly twice as likely (24%) as noncollege graduates (14%) to gamble on sports.
- Men (22%) are almost twice as likely as women (13%) to gamble on sports.

- Sports betting is massively positively correlated by annual income: 6% of people with a household income of less than $30,000 participate, while 17% of those with a household income of $30,000 to $75,000 and 28% of those with a household income of more than $75,000 gamble on sporting events.
- Frequency of sports betting decreases with age: 26% of those aged 18 to 34 gamble on sports, compared to 18% of those aged 35 to 54.

Consequently, one might be surprised to hear the typical U.S. sports bettor is a "42-year-old married guy living in the suburbs with a household income of $74,000 per year" (Keating, 2012, p. 23). And the numbers keep rising. Over three quarters of those betting on sports (78%) increased or maintained betting over previous years while 3.5 million adults admit to a gambling addiction. Of Americans, 56% find nothing wrong with betting on sports while just 20% label it a sin.

The figures are hard to pinpoint and appear to be in flux. The two most prominent events for sports wagering are the Super Bowl ($132.5 million legally bet on the 2016 Super Bowl) and NCAA basketball's March Madness ($100 million legally bet annually). However, this is a relative pittance compared to the amount illegally bet, which the American Gaming Association (2012) places at a total of above $2 billion on each of these cornerstone sporting events.

Regardless of the value judgments that could be attached to all of these statistics, the sports gambling industry (both organized and informal or local) portends shifts in the ways one communicates and consumes sport. Concerns about point shaving and other gambling ties already exist in college sports, particularly when 30% of college athletes bet on sports, and 92% of those gambling athletes were doing so before entering college (Millman, 2010). This fractured relationship between college sports and gambling is typified by cases such as the one of former University of Washington football coach Rick Neuheisel, who was fired from his job in the summer of 2003 for entering a local March Madness betting pool.

Recent court cases also could alter the overall landscape of what constitutes sports gambling as an industry. For instance, is betting money on fantasy sports leagues a form of sports betting? Bernhard and Earle (2005) believe that "if we broadly define gambling as an activity that risks something of value (substantial amounts of money) on an event whose outcome is undetermined (such as whims of a professional baseball season), fantasy [sport] clearly qualifies (p. 29)." Meanwhile, a 2012 Maryland court ruling paved the way for the legalization of everything from fantasy sports to poker, arguing that, unlike pulling a lever on a slot machine, such activities have greater ratio of skill to luck, making the activities less than random when determining winners and losers (see Katz, 2012). What does appear to be the case is that activities such as fantasy sports have positive correlations with sports betting and could be deemed as complementary activities (Mahan, Drayer, & Sparvero, 2012). Fantasy sports outcomes have also been linked to an increase in the amount of sports television viewing—particularly when money is involved—at least within professional football (Drayer, Shapiro, Dwyer, Morse, & White, 2010).

Debates about the role of gambling and arguments about its potential harm on professional and college sports continue to percolate. A high-profile case in 2013 involved a petition from the state of New Jersey to save its struggling casino industry by legalizing sports betting. A federal judge blocked the case, siding with the NCAA and four major sports leagues, yet New Jersey appealed. The crux of the case was the potential harm that could be done to the professional leagues with no one being able to establish such damages in a definitive manner. Such lack of direct causal harm seemingly led to additional decisions to worry less about sports gambling, such as the National Hockey League awarding an expansion team to Las Vegas in 2016.

CONCLUSION

The world of sports gaming is incredibly broad. As this chapter shows, it encompasses everything from the 13-year-old grinding to get another touchdown from a running back to defeat his uncle in a fantasy sports challenge to a bookie in Las Vegas checking the lines on international rugby to the intense video gamer who rarely plays sport but nonetheless finds the game interface appealing. The diversity of sports gaming options will continue to expand, but the offerings will also continue to merge as well, as the various game providers continue to seek ways to make their product more realistic. Such seamless transitions between the manufactured game and the enacted game will be of growing interest to communication scholars as they continue to seek out what makes each game format so appealing.

Suggested Additional Reading

Bowman, N.D., Spinda, J.S.W., & Sanderson, J. (2016). *Fantasy sports and the changing sports media industry: Media, players, and society.* Lanham, MD: Lexington.

Conway, S. C., & Leonard, D. J. (2009). Starting at "start": An exploration of the nondiegetic in soccer video games. *Sociology of Sport Journal, 26*(1), 67–88.

Lee, W. Y., Kwak, D., Lim, C., Pederson, P., & Miloch, K. (2010). Effects of personality and gender on fantasy sports game participation: The moderating role of perceived knowledge. *Journal of Gambling Studies, 27*(3), 427–441.

Ordine, B. (2016). *Fantasy sports: Real money: The unlikely rise of daily fantasy, how to play—how to win.* Las Vegas, NV: Huntington Press.

Plymire, D. C. (2009). Remediating football for the posthuman future: Embodiment and subjectivity in sport video games. *Sociology of Sport Journal, 26,* 17–30.

Spinda, J. S. W., & Haridakis, P. M. (2008). Exploring the motives of fantasy sports: A uses and gratifications approach. In L. W. Hugenberg, P. M. Haridakis, & A. C. Earnheardt (Eds.), *Sports mania: Essays on fandom and the media in the 21st century* (pp. 187–202). Jefferson, NC: McFarland.

16

COMMUNICATION AND SPORT IN THE FUTURE

At this point of the book, you probably have an understanding of sport that is a very fixed part of modern culture and yet is rapidly changing in a variety of manners. In an era in which there appears to be a sports crisis emerging every single day in the form of injury threats, corruption, gambling, deviant behavior, and economic pressures, the headline always seems to be akin to "Is the death of [insert sport element] near?" However, what this book highlights from a communicative perspective is that the constructs may shift, yet the core elements are still viable and important. For instance, one major facet of our discussions has been sports media, yet many highly regarded experts are arguing against even the use of the word *media*, claiming that the concept itself is too ambiguous and outdated. Consider *Wired* editor Chris Anderson's beliefs about the traditional terminology no longer applying:

> I don't use the word "journalism." I don't use the word "media." I don't use the word "news." I don't think that those words mean anything anymore. They defined publishing in the 20th century. Today, they are a barrier. They are standing in our way, like a horseless carriage. . . . We're in one of those strange eras where the words of the last century don't have meaning. What does news mean to you, when the vast majority of news is created by amateurs? Is news coming from a newspaper, or a news group or a friend? . . . You don't need this access to a commercial channel to distribute (news), anyone can do it. (Hornig, 2009, paras. 1, 3, 4, 12)

It is not just media that is undergoing dramatic change. Technology, economic models, and the advent of social networking ultimately have already been changing and will continue to change the way we interact within and about sport in the future, emphasizing the role of communication even more. Within the more traditional subdisciplines of the communication field, much evidence exists that the influence of sport is escalating. Church sports leagues are *growing,* meaning that the study of this pairing from organizational and interpersonal viewpoints must *grow* as well. The use of sport-laden language in other public arenas, such as politics and public relations, is *growing,* meaning the study of sports rhetoric must *grow* as well. The number of fantasy sports participants is *growing*; therefore, the study of the media outlets partnering with these new media players must *grow* as well. The number of ways athletes and fans can interact is *growing*, meaning that the channels of communication may shift away from one social media platform and toward another, yet the core interactions are still very worthy of study. The wider the field of communication and sport becomes, the more direct the ties between the two flagpole terms become.

The future (and relative present of sport communication), however, is not relegated to growth-based matrices. Instead, the future of sport may be best described in the desire for convergence or integration. There are increased ways to enjoy mediated sports while making the event very interpersonal (via smartphones and other second-screen advents). There is a desire to consume mediated sport products while being live at the game itself (and stadiums are attempting redesigns to accommodate such tastes, along with bolstering the bandwidth necessary for full enjoyment from a 21st-century fan).

This chapter outlines the potential ramifications of these types of changes in the communication and sport combination by reexamining the key players within the community of sport that were outlined in Chapter 2. Specifically, we delve into what the future looks like for sports participants, organizations, media entities, and fans and then finish by combining them into the eclectic mix of communication phenomena that will inherently get messier and more blurry in the years to come.

THE FUTURE SPORT PARTICIPANT

The role of the sport participant continues to change based on a number of outside influences ranging from economic to political to cultural to mediated. A person who participates in sport is now more likely to do so in a structured manner or not do it at all, opting for indoor-based video games (now often dubbed "e-sports"; see Rai & Yan, 2009; Stein, Mitgutsh, & Consalvo, 2012) and other forms of entertainment that supersede free-form play. Those who do participate in organized sports will continue to be pushed to specialize as the concept of the well-rounded athlete is trumped by the notion of keeping up with the others if you wish to succeed or even participate. Most athletic trainers would counter that children should not specialize in sports, mostly because year-round play of any sport such as soccer, basketball, or baseball results in the overuse of some muscles and bones to the exclusion of others. Yet, for almost every trainer that you find that holds this belief, parents can find others who are willing to take advantage of the desire for parents (at the right price) to ensure their child has a competitive advantage. Children now participate in leagues that travel much greater distances than ever before and push the limits of the human body in ways not expected for previous generations. Children participate in multiple games in a single day and often try to gain competitive advantages through potentially dangerous physical maneuvers, such as Little League baseball players throwing curveballs at early ages, when such practices are not recommended (Pennington, 2012). This constant pressure to get ahead of other children so they can excel athletically has even led to the concept of "redshirting" kindergarten, whereby parents opt to have their children start school one year later specifically because they will be bigger, faster, and stronger by being the oldest in their grade (Safer, 2012). This has become such a prevalent trend that states like New Jersey are considering bills to safeguard against students repeating middle school grades for athletic advantages even though they are academically on track for promotion (Stanmyre, 2015).

Athletes at all levels will also increasingly find themselves debating appropriate uses of performance-enhancing drugs (PEDs), even debating what constitutes performance enhancement. Currently, each sport faces different challenges based on the PED that aids athletes the most, whether that involves human growth hormone (HGH) in football or erythropoietin (EPO) in cycling. Moreover, medicinal advantages that are currently considered fair and ethical could counter the advantages from illegal sources. For instance, when athletes such as Rafael Nadal recover from injuries more quickly using German-based "bloodspinning" techniques, there is presumably less need to even consider other options. Similarly, other athletes such as football's Adrian Peterson find that injuries that were career-ending decades ago now involve procedures that can have people in healthy, exemplary form in a matter of months.

Medical advances continue to make steroids that are more effective and safer to use than ever before, and an increasing number of people use steroids for nonathletic purposes, including treating allergies and chronic ailments. Thus, the controversy surrounding the use of steroids in sports will likely continue to percolate, if not escalate, over time. If and when steroids become commonplace remedies for mainstream America (and international societies), is it fair to exclude athletes from being able to use them if they hold the potential to make their lives better outside the sporting arena? Is it reasonable to think steroids (and other PEDs) can be regulated in any meaningful way when they continue to evolve in substance and usage?

At higher levels, athletes are finding an increased expectation for a pseudo relationship with those who consume sport, a concept known in communication circles as parasocial interaction (see Rubin, Perse, & Powell, 1985). Rubin and McHugh (1987) find that physical attraction is not as important as social interaction within parasocial relationships; this is undoubtedly true in 21st-century sport. Athletes are offering dramatically increased access to their personal and everyday lives. As of the summer of 2013, soccer's Cristiano Ronaldo had 18.8 million followers on the social networking website Twitter. Athletes such as basketball's James Harden find their celebrity image is bigger because of appearing on reality television shows than because he is a professional athlete, while other athletes are given their own reality shows or find themselves more popular because of reality shows based on sport, such as HBO's *Hard Knocks*. Athletes also find themselves participating in other shows with other skill formats, such as boxer Mike Tyson on *Lip Synch Battle* or NASCAR driver Michael Waltrip on *Dancing With the Stars,* offering people an opportunity to see what they are like beyond the arena in which they perform. Athlete blogs and websites are now commonplace, sometimes revealing ignorance (such as retired baseball player Jose Canseco's tweet

"Titanic. 100 years. Wow. Global warming could have saved titanic. Sad to say."). Other outlets, such as the 2014 rise of The Players Tribune, purportedly reveal athletes' voices in unvarnished lights (away from cameras and immediate interviews), yet have a considerably larger public relations tint to entries.

This relates well to another way in which the role of the athlete changes at its highest levels—an enhanced perception of the cult of celebrity. The athletes regarded as the common everyman such as Joe DiMaggio have morphed into figures that, almost out of necessity in popular culture, become larger than life. A hybrid form of commercialism now exists in which sports become a vehicle for attaining a certain lifestyle. Sports are not always played because people even like sports, let alone just because an athlete regards it as a job. Instead, sport becomes a vehicle for selling records, attaining modeling contracts, and celebrating "bling" and other lifestyles. Famous underperforming athletes, such as Anna Kournikova and Johnny Manziel, have increased their celebrity status by being ubiquitous within other media formats.

Finally, one must note the dramatic degree to which sport is becoming increasingly internationalized. Sometimes, the effects are positive (cultures become exposed to soccer or American football in ways that previously were ignored), yet other issues prove problematic (such as the Ladies Professional Golf Association [LPGA] attempt to market Asian players with similar-sounding names who lack proficiency in English to a resistant public). Regardless of these largely commercialized effects, the bottom line is that athletes from different nations have ample opportunities to compete together, and this will become even more common in the future (former National Basketball Association [NBA] commissioner David Stern foresees a European division in the somewhat near future, while other sports continually expand the brand with popular international players, such as Chinese golfer Guan Tianlang, who made the cut at the 2013 Masters at age 14). Integration is good, yet the result may be sports in which the preponderance of winners may not be from one's home country. The very international sport of tennis, for instance, nonetheless has a hard time garnering U.S. public interest in the sport when an American is not in contention. As of the summer of 2016, the top-ranked American men's tennis player was Jon Isner (#17). As much as tennis aficionados exalt the golden age of tennis with a big four of Novak Djokovic, Roger Federer, Rafael Nadal, and Andy Murray, Americans still view tennis in much smaller numbers compared to when Andre Agassi and Pete Sampras competed in a plethora of Grand Slam finals.

Thus, from the ways in which kids are accustomed to playing sports to the expectations professional athletes bring to athletic competition, it is fair to surmise a major sea change that results from a hyperconnected sports culture.

THE FUTURE SPORTS ORGANIZATION

Turning to the player in the sports communication process, that is, the sports organization, perhaps one of the biggest influences that currently resides in sport and may only be exacerbated in the future regards access not just to sports but also to

CASE STUDY

THE RIGHT SPORT PEDIGREE

A sport program's success has always been intertwined with the coach's ability to recruit talented athletes. While this has been a basic feature of college sports for quite some time, an increasing number of high school athletes are making decisions about their high school careers as open-enrollment policies throughout the country have made it possible to relocate. The intent behind open enrollment is to allow families the right to ensure their children receive an appropriate educational experience. It is not uncommon, though, to find sport participation as a major factor in such decisions. Football is one such sport where parental positioning is likely to occur, as key player matchups, supporting personnel, or coaching strategies can be deciding factors for landing college scholarships. Having a son who is interested in being a quarterback at a Division I program, then playing for a coach who prefers an offensive ground game, is unlikely to help your chances.

At the start of the 2008 high school season in California, Joe Montana (a Hall of Fame quarterback in the National Football League [NFL]) made a decision to transfer his son to Oaks Christian School, which had won five championships since it was established in 2000. The tuition is more than $20,000 each year, and the school employs both academics and athletics to attract families of some of the state's most gifted athletes. For instance, despite his father's athletic pedigree, at the time, Nick Montana was considered to be just one of three high-profile athletes competing on the school's football team. Wayne Gretsky's son Trevor and Will Smith's son Trey also attended and played at Oaks Christian during this same time period.

As a result, the school was often referred to as "Celebrity High." The Montanas' decision to move rested not only on the possibility of working with the coaching staff for the program (when they made their decision to enroll, the current starting quarterback for Notre Dame had recently attended the school) but also on the ability to be in closer proximity to Steve Clarkson (one of the most prominent private quarterback trainers in the country). At the start of fall camp his first year, Montana's arrival brought about the departure of three other quarterback hopefuls whose families made decisions to transfer their sons to another school. It's easy to see that with Joe Montana's experience in the NFL, it was likely that Nick would be assuming the starting position. Regardless of the starter's talent, it is unlikely that a college coach would recruit the team's backup quarterback.

1. In what way can state open enrollment policies be detrimental to the future of high school athletics? Do private schools present an unfair advantage when compared to public high schools in a state?
2. What message is communicated to children when a family is motivated to change schools based largely on the athletic program's prowess?
3. What do you think the future holds regarding the merged communication of high school, collegiate, and professional sport practices (redshirting, pay for play, etc.)?

sport instruction and facilities that are necessary for an athlete to become successful (or sometimes even just healthy). There are fundamental issues, such as the lack of innercity swimming pools or recreational club funding. High schools are developing funding models for athletic teams based on "pay for play" policies, which involve a student paying a fee in order to participate in a varsity sport. These fees vary widely; in Connecticut, for instance, some students play sports for free, whereas others have fees assessed that are as high as $1,450 per sport (Thomas, 2013). This significantly affects lower income levels; placing a $200 fee lowers participation rates among those with household incomes of $60,000 or greater by 45% but lowers participation rates among household incomes lower than $60,000 by *328%* (C.S. Mott Children's Hospital National Poll on Children's Health, 2015).

However, there are even larger issues that make access to sports cavernous between the "haves" and "have nots." Multitudes of people may play the same sport but experience it in starkly different ways. As an example, for decades, foreign athletes have moved to the United States to be offered better facilities and a higher level of personal instruction. Now this is happening within the United States, with families uprooted to move to where the opportunities reside, usually accompanied by a great deal of financial hardship. For example, gold medal winning gymnast Gabby Douglas left her home town of Virginia Beach, Virginia, when she was 14, moving to Des Moines, Iowa, so she could train with Olympian Shawn Johnson's former coach, Liang Chow.

This relates to sports organizations because they are becoming tiered in the process. Those who can afford to be in Class A programs have opportunities as never before seen; those who cannot experience a drop-off from people who seek better options. Even in college athletics, this is increasingly the case. The University of Texas generates $131 million from its football program alone, a figure higher than what all but two other universities generate for their entire athletic program. A great deal of that amount gets funneled back into the program, making it even more likely to produce a consistent winner.

These disparities happen with professional organizations as well. Certainly, salary caps and luxury taxes are enacted as a necessary counterbalance for a healthy overall league, but money continually yields disparate results. For instance, the New York Yankees have always been a financial behemoth in the world of baseball; however, the advent of the Yankee Entertainment and Sports (YES) Network in 2002 made the team even wealthier in a way that very few other teams could ever conceive. For all of the discussion of parity in baseball, the 2012 season featured four final teams in the American League and the National League Championship series that each were in the top nine in total payroll, and even moderate payroll success stories such as the 2015 World Series champion Kansas City Royals cannot blunt the overall advantage enjoyed by larger market teams with lucrative local television contracts.

Thus, many sports organizations (from professional down to secondary schools and local public entities) must find their market and work within it. For professional teams, this can involve finding ways to market a team that will very likely be a consistent loser. Because of expansion, leagues such as the NFL now offer an extensive 32-team lineup. Even if a different team won a championship from the year 2017 on, it would take

OFF THE BEATEN PATH

KITEBOARDING

While some sports organizations are looking to secure their place in the sports marketplace, American kiteboarders are on a mission to find their voice. Kiteboarding, a wind-powered surface watersport, is growing in popularity around the world. The International Kiteboarding Association (IKA) manages the global administration of kiteboarding, and three American kiteboarders, Johnny Heineken, Andrew Koch, and Adam Koch, partnered to found the American Kiteboarding Association (AKA) in 2012 with intentions of representing the United States in IKA. The organization was founded 4 months after kiteboarding was selected to debut at the Rio 2016 Olympics. However, kiteboarders were granted only a short period of time to celebrate. The International Sailing Federation (ISAF), the world governing body for sailing, overturned its May 2012 decision to replace windsurfing with kiteboarding after only 6 months. Thus, organizations such as IKA and AKA are charged with continuing to draw attention to and support for kiteboarding in order to compete for a spot in the 2020 Games.

until 2048 before each team had a taste of winning the Super Bowl. Even assuming random odds (claiming each team was of the same relative skill level), the chances of that happening are well into billions to one.

The odds of producing a successful (as defined by winning championships) program at local levels are no less daunting. School systems continue to receive a major portion of their funding through property taxes, essentially ensuring a tiered system of hegemonically entrenched power for public school attendees. To make matters even more challenging, towns change demographically to the point that teams that experienced "glory days" in the 1960s or 1970s may have little chance of ever revisiting them today. Thus, the game for organizations becomes finding a niche and redefining what success would mean for their organizations. The future will inevitably involve financial realities in the face of increasing hypercompetitive mind-sets from young athletes and the people who influence them.

THE FUTURE SPORTS MEDIA ENTITY

When *TIME* magazine named its 2006 Person of the Year, one had to wonder if the editors realized how prescient their choice would become. Past honorees had included Nikita Khrushchev, Martin Luther King, Jr., and Queen Elizabeth II, yet the magazine opted to think outside the box in 2006, naming "You" the recipient of the award. Their reasoning was simple and possessed no small amount of foreshadowing of the world in which we currently reside: The massive amount of contributed content from millions of people on the Internet was influencing daily lives in virtually all realms of society. This is certainly the case with the current state of sports media.

In 1964, communication theorist Marshall McLuhan proclaimed that the "medium is the message." The argument was that the media used to convey a message influenced how it was received. Lou Gehrig's "Luckiest Man on the Face of the Earth" speech is different when hearing it as opposed to reading it. However, we currently live in a world where one must query "what medium"? When *TIME* named You as its choice, the examples were largely based on aggregate Internet sites, venues such as Wikipedia and YouTube, in which collective contributions provide a wide swath of information. In his 2004 book *The Wisdom of Crowds,* James Surowiecki (2004) articulated the thesis that "when our imperfect judgments are aggregated in the right way, our collective intelligence is often excellent" (p. xiv). These sites still thrive, but the media convergence (sports highlights on smart phones, news updates on Twitter, websites that beget their own TV shows) merges sport in a way in which the delivery of it is no longer about the medium as much as it is immediacy combined with access. ESPN once was almost exclusively a television company. Now, it has secured measurable markets in traditional media, such as radio and magazines, as well as in new media, such as interactive websites and personal digital assistants, embodying what we now refer to as Web 2.0. ESPN started as a television station; now, it's a brand.

Given the understandings of social media that we have explored in Chapter 3, sports media entities know they need to cross-promote in a multitude of formats, offering a diverse set of information and entertainment options for people to consume. Instead, the question is where to focus one's energies. For instance, at the time of this writing, Pew Research Center indicates that Facebook remains the dominant player in social media (71% of all Americans report having a Facebook account), followed by Pinterest (28%), LinkedIn (28%), Instagram (26%), and Twitter (23%). The second most popular social media site was Pinterest, which moved slightly ahead of Twitter in terms of web traffic and number of people with accounts. However, sports media entities have opted to focus more on Twitter than other secondary outlets, partly because of the breaking news and parasocial interaction aspects in which it thrives but also presumably because women currently outnumber men on Pinterest by a five to one ratio. Accordingly, sports media entities must continue to assess not just where people are migrating but also the degree to which different platforms are built to facilitate sports media interests. For example, Billings, Qiao, Conlin, and Nie (2016, in press) report significant advancements in the use of Snapchat and the enactment of sports fandom.

The result could be increased fragmentation of sports media offerings, even megasporting events that are currently shared experiences. ESPN has already experimented with offerings such as "360" coverage of certain major games. For instance, the January 2016 college football National Championship Game between Alabama and Clemson featured 14 different ways to consume the game (dubbed the "MegaCast"), ranging from a traditional (main) feed to a view from the camera inside the goal-line pylon to another focusing exclusively on student section reactions. DirecTV satellite coverage fragments sports event coverage as well, offering, for instance, one channel just devoted to the 12th tee at Augusta's Amen Corner during Masters coverage or mosaic screens to offer more than one tennis match simultaneously. Fragmentation may take on new perspectives for fans seeking different things. Already, websites such as nfl.com offer different simultaneous tabs of coverage, ranging from chatting with like-minded fans to focuses on fantasy football implications to reading expert analysis, and, yes, the unfolding of the actual game itself.

Media entities continue to struggle with these distinctions when deciding who should be allowed in media rooms and press conferences. Who should be let in—the blogger with half a million Twitter followers or the local newspaper journalist with a readership one tenth of that size? A modicum of journalism is to be first, be best, or be different; increasingly, quality measures are difficult to discern, with quantity measures (page views, likes, followers, bounce rates) becoming paramount to determining credibility. Without question, these types of nebulous definitions are a major issue for the future of sports media, as they literally affect who has access to covering major sporting events.

Moreover, the economic models for sports media offerings are becoming blurred as well. Broadcast networks (e.g., ABC, CBS, FOX, NBC) are finding that rights fees no longer justify purchasing major sports contracts, leaving cable networks (e.g., ESPN, TNT, TBS) to become increasingly prevalent players, as their funding model can include increases in subscription rates that make sports programming more viable. Events that were mainstays of certain broadcast networks are migrating to other outlets because of the economics. For instance, TBS aired the National Collegiate Athletic Association (NCAA) men's basketball semifinals in 2014 and 2015 and added the entire Final Four to its coverage in 2016.

Additionally, channels have now been created by sports leagues themselves, ranging from the professional leagues (MLB Network, Tennis Channel, NBA TV) to collegiate conferences (Big Ten Network, SEC Network). All of these changes force new economic

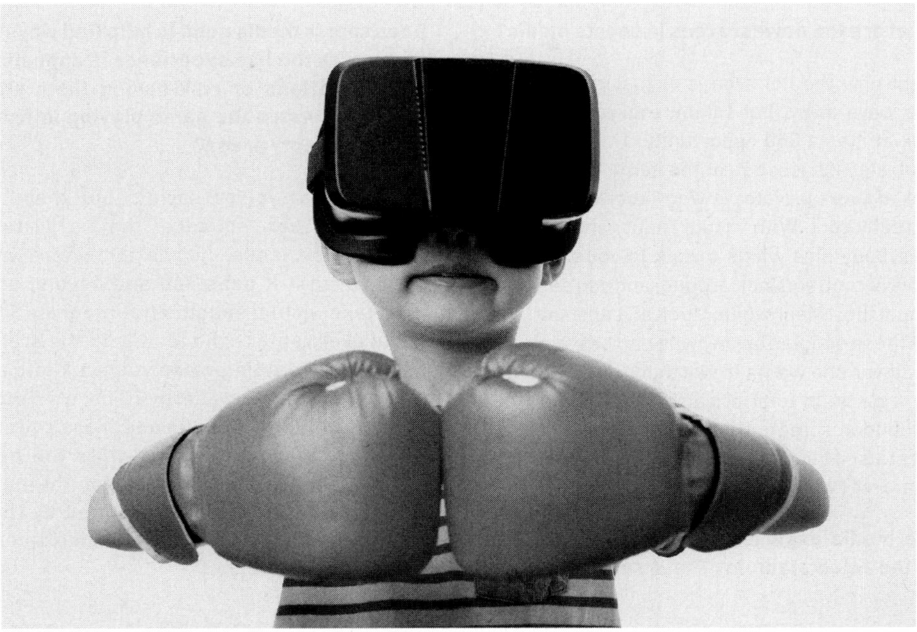

Source: © iStockphoto.com/real44

Child embracing VR technology

models to the fore, particularly as some sports rise because of a young fan base (such as BMX cycling, snowboarding, and Ultimate Fighting Championship), while others may diminish as older fan bases continue to age (such as in baseball, boxing, and tennis).

At this point, one could conclude that the future for sports media is economically bleak and operationally problematic. However, there are other sides to the media equation that could be viewed in a more positive light. One could easily argue that the Internet is the most democratic form of media ever introduced. Hegemony involves power and influence over others, which were implemented in forms of dominance of traditional media. However, when anyone can create a blog or aggregate sports website, the people who drive a story can literally be the fans. Media outlets can let fans help with the work, with websites now offering breaking news and holding the potential to highlight stories that were previously stifled when media sources were limited (by page limitations in print and by time limitations in television). What percolates to the top of the media conversation may not be the most important stories of the day, and it may not be driven by the most credible journalists of our time, yet it has the opportunity to enter the sports media zeitgeist, providing insight into our society simply by underscoring what is of greatest import to sports fans today.

INTERVIEW

MARK CUBAN, OWNER, DALLAS MAVERICKS

Q: What are the newest areas in sports media?

A: Right now the hot area is virtual reality. 360 is a ways away, but I think everyone should look at it as a 360 opportunity. There are net neutrality issues, but, at the same time, if you look at it as a private viewing experience it can be really cool. With virtual reality and sports, everybody else wants to talk to you and say, "This is cool, you look around, and you see this virtual life." Meanwhile, I look at it and say, "If I put these goggles on, my wife can be watching whatever she wants to watch, I can be watching a game in total privacy, and it looks like a 200 inch screen. If I look to my right, I can get stats; if I look to the left, I can get a feed of whatever I want." It's an amazing experience.

Q: The media experience is partly enhanced by the filled stadium. The screaming fans. Does sports media need to help find ways to make sure the live experience is appealing enough to fans or risk having them stay home and watch the game playing in front of a half-empty arena?

A: I know what you're saying, but there is absolutely zero chance that a virtual reality experience, no matter where you do it—even if it goes 360 and beyond and they take virtual magic and integrate it—could ever replace the feeling in the arena because the feeling when you walk into an arena and feel the energy? There's nothing better. When 20,000 people are collectively holding their breath while the ball is in the air, and their mood for the next 24 hours or longer is determined by that ball and what happens 2 seconds later? You can't replace that.

Q: You argue that in a few years all sports gambling will be legal. If that happens, how does the sports media landscape change?

A: It changes it because more people care. They'll gamble more on sports, and they'll care more about sports. I guess I'm selling my own book when I say I'm for sports gambling and gambling in general. If we allow gambling now, sports get bigger. There's a reason why all those people stood in line for Powerball. It wasn't just because the line looked interesting.

Q: You were also one of the first professional team owners who expanded the definition of what someone needed to get credentialed for a game. It used to be it was legacy media only, and you said there should be a place for bloggers and other popular websites without legacy media connections. How did you make the decision without opening the floodgates for everyone? Is it really just the audience size?

A: Yes. You can go by the size of the audience because nobody has really any more or less credibility anymore. It's not like there's a 20-year learning curve to be able to write about a game or do interviews. We had a kid, Ben Collins, who now writes for some major magazines, that we brought in when he was 13. He just had a different perspective. A 13-year-old's mind is much different from a 30-year-old's, and that perspective is welcome. So, if you have an audience and a redeeming quality, you're in. I know it when I see it.

Q: The interaction that we have between different parts of sports media—athletes, owners, fans—are all very different because of social media platforms. Have the relationships changed between these constituencies, and will it continue to grow as these platforms expand?

A: It shouldn't change; it should get closer. They pay the bills! I've never been in a business where the customer didn't matter. When I got the Mavs in 2000, I put my e-mail—a lot of people didn't have e-mail back then—on the Jumbotron and let people e-mail me. Now I'm available on an app called Cyberdust just because it's private, and it's troll-free. The challenge with anything isn't that communication has increased; the challenge is dealing with trolls; however, you want to define that. When you're on a social platform, it becomes far less social if everyone's trolling. Trolls don't try to communicate with Mark Cuban; trolls try to communicate with everybody who's paying attention to Mark Cuban or the Mavs. They're the scorpions riding your back trying to get to your audience and that's the problem that I think the future holds.

For a full transcript of the interview with Mark Cuban, consult Billings, A.C. (2016). An interview with Mark Cuban. *International Journal of Sports Communication*, *9*(2), 163-166.

THE FUTURE SPORTS FAN

As we have already learned, issues of social class used to divide athletes into stratified groups, with higher classes being amateur athletes and lower classes being professional or, if not talented enough, marginalized. Now, the economics of modern sport separate fans in even larger dimensions. Tickets to Super Bowl I were seen as extravagant at $12 each, causing 30,000 no-shows; tickets to Super Bowl 50 were resold for an

Source: © Ryan McVay/Lifesize/Thinkstock

Skyboarding

average of $4,639—and there was not an empty seat to be found. Some football teams have difficulty filling stadiums, while others are thriving. The continual influx of money creates an even more stark notion of the haves and have-nots. Jerry Jones's $1.2 billion stadium for the Cowboys offers extreme luxury for some fans, while others purchase "party passes" ($199 per season) that do not even include actual admission to see the game but rather just the opportunity to be present at the stadium during the game, enjoying the festivities from a bar-like atmosphere while watching on television. Cities are increasingly told that their constituents must pay additional taxes to fund modern sports "cathedrals" (see Trumpbour, 2007); St. Louis recently lost their NFL team to Los Angeles in part because their contract required that the team play in a "state-of-the-art" facility, inherently bolstering the arms race. Meanwhile, baseball teams in Atlanta and Texas secured new stadium deals to replace stadiums that were perceived to be obsolete—even though they were just two decades old. Examples of the economic divide could be offered *ad nauseam,* but the bottom line is that the current (and likely future) sports fan will often display a great deal of resentment—toward players with contracts north of $100 million and toward teams that continue to find new and innovative ways to make money off of their "product." Fans who do spend significant amounts of dollars to attend games can feel entitled to display their fandom in any manner they feel necessary. As a consequence, some find athletic events are becoming coarser in their decorum, with some families opting to skip attending live games because of deviant behaviors and obscene language.

Beyond the influence of dollars, the integration of new media influences fandom, most notably in how they receive and interpret their news. While media entities struggle in their attempts to differentiate between investigative journalism and blog entries, many fans take these forms of information as one and the same, with few distinctions being made. Rumors become fact; opinions become talking points in press conferences; and social media perceptions result in changed fan behavior, usually in a negative direction.

In light of the economic realities combined with more uncertain elements of fandom, it is not that surprising that an increasing number of fans are opting to avoid the entire live enactment of fandom altogether, opting to become the home-dwelling devotees outlined in Chapter 2. When tickets to the game cost thousands of dollars, the decision to invest in high-definition televisions and comfortable seating becomes the lesser (and more practical) of two economic evils. The same trend happened earlier in the film industry; the more movies and movie food cost, the more people opted to rent movies instead. The more people talked and had cell phones ring during movies at the theater, the more

Video screen at AT&T Stadium in Arlington, Texas

people felt staying in their own media rooms was more of an escape than actually leaving the house. Sport fans experience a fair amount of cognitive dissonance with the cost and hassles of fandom, making simpler at-home options more appealing.

COMMUNICATION AND SPORT: ENTERING HYPERDRIVE

It is difficult not to notice that whenever we talk about the current state of sport within a communicative context, words such as *extreme* or *ultimate* come to mind. All "players" within the community of sport tend to regard it like surfers looking for the next wave, always hoping for a better ride than before. When attempting to extrapolate on the future of sports, the extreme really does seem to be where the sporting action is. Consider the X Games, hardly a new event given their introduction to the sports world in 1995. Still, the X Games continue to expand, setting new ratings and Internet streaming records (Hargrove, 2012) and influencing more mainstream sporting events, such as the Olympics, which now offers several events featured in the X Games, such as snowboarding. It is no accident that the X Games are experiencing growth, particularly with younger people, because they offer a sense of adrenaline-packed hypersport.

Take another case of old versus new sport. Earlier generations were enamored of boxing. Fights of the Week were commonplace, everyone knew who held the heavyweight title, and the sport was heavily featured on *Wide World of Sports* and the Summer Olympics telecasts. Now, boxing has been superseded by Mixed Martial Arts (MMA)/Ultimate Fighting Championship (UFC), a sport originating in the 1990s and once referred to by Senator John McCain as "human cockfighting" before it had formalized rules. UFC regularly draws higher pay-per-view numbers than boxing, and, in a stunning indication of the future of sports viewership, has considerably more male viewers in the 18–to–34 age demographic than baseball's World Series (Meltzer, 2009). When factoring in that UFC costs money via pay-per-view while the World Series is offered for free on a mainstream broadcast network (FOX), the trend toward more violent sports and away from slow-paced traditional sports like baseball is underscored. Indeed, FOX has added UFC to its growing list of sports properties, highlighting it on its main broadcast channel while considering it a cornerstone of its new efforts in its all-sports network, which launched in 2013, FOX Sports 1.

Hypersport appears to be the future, if not at least part of the present. For instance, as this shift toward singular sports events of a more violent nature has increased, so has the payout to athletes to compete in these events. Brock Lesner's payout for UFC 200 was $2.5 million, increasing the likelihood that his "on loan" status from WWE will not be a one-time occurrence, encouraging more athletes from different sport backgrounds to enter the cage because of the potential payout that it produces. This is not to say that the major sports that we loved as children will disappear in the near future; it simply is an argument that the expanding world of sport tends to be gravitating toward Ronda Rousey and 1080-degree flips and away from prolonged games and tennis passing shots.

What are the key phrases to remember regarding different levels of the sporting populace? For participants in the enactment of sport at the amateur levels, the key word is likely *specialization.* This book has outlined the new attempts to start honing athletic skills earlier and in more precise (sometimes overwhelming) ways. For those who play sport at the highest levels, the word is likely *globalization.* Leagues are constantly

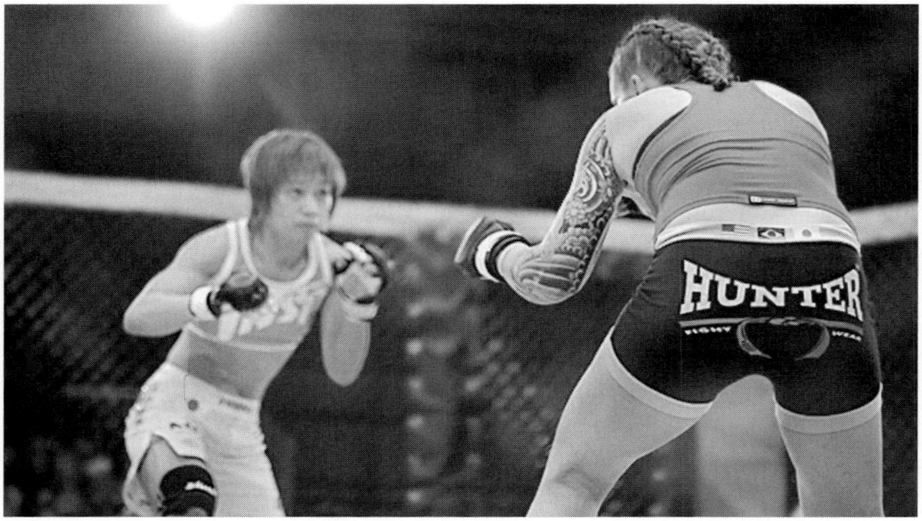

A Mixed Martial Arts bout

looking for new fans (and, hence, revenue streams). Thus, the National Football League features regular season games in London and Mexico City, with other avenues on the horizon. Baseball focuses efforts on the World Baseball Classic; basketball continues to make in-roads to Asian and European markets. For those who consume sport, the word is likely *integration*. No matter the media format, one will undoubtedly be gaining new information and finding new ways to consume sports in ways that offer an immense amount of information with an emphasis placed on minutiae; many avid sports fans still cannot decipher all of the new statistical analyses and their related degree of meaningfulness. For all of these various entities together, that word is likely *cross-pollination*. No single form of sport, no "player" in the community of sport, can be discussed without the other elements. Convergence will often result in confusion but also in a sense of cultures and tastes colliding that could benefit sport in the long term.

In essence, people involved in the community of sport are continually looking for a value-added proposition. Maybe it is the professional athlete seeking additional forms of celebrity. Maybe it is the third grader playing sports because he or she seeks the added value of a better relationship with parents or classmates. Maybe it is the fan playing fantasy sports or placing a monetary bet on the game he or she is watching. Maybe it is the sports organization seeking to commodify its product in ways both inventive and previously unimaginable. Sport in the future will very likely be about offering a new edge, an ancillary component to the act of participating or consuming itself.

Nonetheless, the basics of sport remain relatively the same. Think back to Chapter 1. The basic tenets remain in place for the foreseeable future. Sports will still be fun. They will continue to be educational. They will foster unity—and sometimes division. They will continue to be among the most vital and diverse industries in the United States. The other variables may change, but the basics will not. A first introduction to sport will likely still consist of a small child playing catch with a parent or, perhaps, batting around a balloon with a sibling. The love of that activity is innate, before any notion of sport takes hold. Those tendencies will not change; however, the communication-laden enactments, protocols, dialogues, and conceptions will be in constant flux. Winners will survive, losers will fade away. As it is with sport, so it is with trends that will shape it in the years to come.

Suggested Additional Reading

Eitzen, S. (2009). *Sport in contemporary society: An anthology* (8th ed.). Boulder, CO: Paradigm.

Fort, R. D. (2006). *Sports economics*. Upper Saddle River, NJ: Prentice Hall.

Leonard, D. (2006). An untapped field: Exploring the world of virtual sports gaming. In A. Raney & J. Bryant (Eds.), *Handbook of sports and media* (pp. 393–407). Mahwah, NJ: LEA.

Paolantonio, S. (2008). *How football explains America*. Chicago, IL: Triumph.

Rowe, D. (2011). *Global media sport: Flows, forms and futures*. London, UK: Bloomsbury Academic Press.

Wenner, L. A. (2015). Communication and sport, where art thou?: Epistemological reflections on the moment and fields of play. *Communication & Sport, 3*(3), 247–260.

REFERENCES

Chapter 1

Abeza, G., O'Reilly, N., & Nadeau, J. (2014). Sport communication: A multidimensional assessment of the field's development. *International Journal of Sport Communication, 7,* 289–316.

Alberts, J. K., Nakayama, T. K., & Martin, J. N. (2012). *Human communication in society (3rd ed.).* Upper Saddle River, NJ: Pearson.

At the gate: Outlook for the sports market in North America through 2019. (October 2015). *Price Waterhouse Coopers.* Retrieved from http://www.pwc.com/us/en/industry/entertainment-media/publications/assets/pwc-sports-outlook-north-america-2015.pdf

Baxter, K. (2015, July 4). Early criticism of Jill Ellis turns to awe as U.S. reaches World Cup final. *Los Angeles Times.* Retrieved from http://www.latimes.com/sports/soccer/la-sp-usa-world-cup-20150704-story.html

Bell, J. B. (1987). *To play the game: An analysis of sports.* New Brunswick, NJ: Transaction Press.

Billings, A. C. (2007). From diving boards to pole vaults: Gendered athlete portrayals in the 'big four' sports at the 2004 Athens Summer Olympics. *Southern Communication Journal, 72,* 329–344.

Blaney, J. R., Lippert, L. R., & Smith, J. S. (Eds.). (2013). *Repairing the athlete's image: Studies in sports image restoration.* Lanham, MD: Lexington Books.

Brown, R. S. (2004). Sport and healing in America. *Society, 42,* 37–41.

Chan, W. (2015, July 7). Abby Wambach, wife Sarah Huffman share kiss after U.S. World Cup win. *CNN.com.* Retrieved from http://edition.cnn.com/2015/07/06/football/womens-world-cup-abby-wambach-wife-kiss

Dean, J. (2014, March 31). How a risky ad campaign turned the Portland Timbers into one of pro sports' hottest startups. *Fast Company.* Retrieved from http://www.fastcompany.com/3026949/marketing-with-a-kick-portland-timbers

Deitsch, R. (2015, July 6). USA-Japan Women's World Cup final shatters American TV ratings record. *Sports Illustrated.* Retrieved from http://www.si.com/planet-futbol/2015/07/06/usa-japan-womens-world-cup-tv-ratings-record

Dubois, L. (2015, June 24). Artificial turf controversy a constant in backdrop of Women's World Cup. *Sports Illustrated.* Retrieved from http://www.si.com/planet-futbol/2015/06/23/womens-world-cup-artificial-turf-canada

Farrell, T. B. (1989). Media rhetoric as social drama: The Winter Olympics of 1984. *Critical Studies in Mass Communication, 6,* 158–182.

Goldberg, J. (2016, January 5). Portland Timbers still exploring feasibility of expanding seating capacity at Providence Park. *The Oregonian.* Retrieved from http://www.oregonlive.com/timbers/index.ssf/2016/01/

portland_timbers_still_decidin.html

Grano, D. A., & Zagacki, K. S. (2011). Cleansing the Superdome: The paradox of purity and post-Katrina guilt. *Quarterly Journal of Speech, 97*, 201–223.

Grez, M. (2015, July 21). Alex Morgan: U.S. star shares FIFA 16 cover with Lionel Messi. *CNN.com*. Retrieved July 14, 2016, from http://edition.cnn.com/2015/07/21/football/alex-morgan-fifa-16

Guttmann, A. (1978). *From ritual to record: The nature of modern sports*. New York, NY: Columbia University Press.

Hawkins, K., & Tolzin, A. (2002). Examining the team/leader interface: Baseball teams as exemplars of postmodern organizations. *Group and Organization Management, 27*, 97–112.

Isidore, C. (2015, July 7). Women World Cup champs win waaaaay less money than men. *CNN.com*. Retrieved July 14, 2016, from http://money.cnn.com/2015/07/07/news/companies/womens-world-cup-prize-money

Kassing, J. W., Billings, A. C., Brown, R. S., Halone, K. K., Harrison, K., Krizek, B., Meân, L. J., & Turman, P. D. (2004). Communication in the community of sport: The process of enacting, (re)producing, consuming, and organizing sport. *Communication Yearbook, 28*, 373–409.

Kassing, J. W., & Infante, D. A. (1999). Aggressive communication in the coach-athlete relationship. *Communication Research Reports, 16*, 110–120.

Kremer-Sadlik, L., & Kim, J. L. (2007). Lessons from sports: Children's socialization to values through family interaction during sports activities. *Discourse & Society, 18*, 35–52.

Krizek, B. (2008). Introduction: Communication and the community of sport. *Western Journal of Communication, 72*, 103–106.

Leibowitz, B. (2010, July 12). It's just a game, dad? Pa. youth baseball coach accused of hitting Son. *CBS News*. Retrieved from http://www.cbsnews.com/8301–504083_162–20010177–504083.html

Lipsyte, R. (1975). *SportsWorld: An American dreamland*. New York, NY: Quadrangle.

McCarthy, M. (2011, June 7). NBC wins rights to Olympics through 2020. *USA Today*. Retrieved from http://content.usatoday.com/communities/gameon/post/2011/06/olympic-tv-decision-between-nbc-espn-and-fox-could-come-down-today/1#.UgPB55K1H6M

Mandell, N. (2015, July 5). Celebrities, athletes, politicians celebrate U.S. World Cup victory on Twitter. *USA Today*. Retrieved from http://ftw.usatoday.com/2015/07/uswnt-twitter

Moss, R. (2015, July 1). Women's World Cup 2015: "Sexist" profile on FIFA's website focuses on Alex Morgan's "good looks" before mentioning her football skills. *Huffington Post*. Retrieved from http://www.huffingtonpost.co.uk/2015/07/01/alex-morgan-sexist-fifa-profile_n_7705760.html

Norlander, M. (2016, April 12). NCAA, CBS, Turner extend NCAA Tournament deal through 2032. *CBSSports.com*. Retrieved from http://www.cbssports.com/college-basketball/news/ncaa-cbs-turner-extend-ncaa-tournament-deal-through-2032

O'Toole, T. (2010, April 22). NCAA reaches 14-year deal with CBS/Turner for men's basketball tournament, which expands to 68 teams for now.

USA Today. Retrieved from http://content.usatoday.com/communities/campusrivalry/post/2010/04/ncaa-reaches-14-year-deal-with-cbsturner/1#.UgPA4ZK1H6M

Pfahl, M. E., & Bates, B. R. (2008). This is not a race, this is a farce: Formula One and the Indianapolis Motor Speedway tire crisis. *Public Relations Review, 34*, 135–144.

Pheifer, P. (2012, October 16). St. Paul dad gets 6 months for attack on coach. *Minneapolis Star-Tribune*. Retrieved from http://www.startribune.com/local/south/174407021.html

Price, J. (1992). The Super Bowl as religious festival. In S. J. Hoffman (Ed.), *Sport and religion* (pp. 13–15). Champaign, IL: Human Kinetics.

Real, M. (1975). Super Bowl: Mythic spectacle. *Journal of Communication, 25*, 31–43.

Rowe, D. (2007). Sports journalism: Still the 'toy department' of the news media? *Journalism, 8*, 385–405.

Sabo, D., & Veliz, P. (2008). *Go out and play: Youth sports in America*. East Meadow, NY: Women's Sports Foundation. Retrieved from http://www.womenssportsfoundation.org/sitecore/content/home/research/articles-and-reports/mental-and-physical-health/go-out-and-play.aspx

Sanderson, J. (2011). *It's a whole new ballgame: How social media is changing sports*. New York, NY: Hampton.

Segrave, J. O. (2000). The sports metaphor in American cultural discourse. *Culture, Sport, and Society, 3*, 48–60.

Shannon, C., & Weaver, W. (1948). *The mathematical theory of communication*. Urbana, IL: University of Illinois Press.

Shear, M. D., & Leibovich, M. (2013, May 28). No partisan fire at the shore: An Obama-Christie reunion. *New York Times*. Retrieved from http://www.nytimes.com/2013/05/29/us/obama-and-christie-to-view-recovery-on-jersey-shore.html?pagewanted=all&_r=0

Shugart, H. A. (2003). She shoots, she scores: Mediated constructions of contemporary female athletes in coverage of the 1999 US women's soccer team. *Western Journal of Communication, 67*, 1–31.

Smith, A. (2015, July 6). U.S. soccer fans' "Pearl Harbor" barbs cause Twitter storm. *NBC News*. Retrieved from http://www.nbcnews.com/news/us-news/u-s-soccer-fans-pearl-harbor-jokes-cause-twitter-storm-n387176

Sperber, M. (2000). *Beer and circus: How big-time college sports is crippling undergraduate education*. New York, NY: Owl Books.

Tomlinson, A. (2005). *Sport and leisure cultures*. Minneapolis: University of Minnesota Press.

Trujillo, N. (1991). Hegemonic masculinity on the mound: Media representations of Nolan Ryan and American sports culture. *Critical Studies in Mass Communication, 8*, 290–308.

Trujillo, N. (2003). Introduction. In R.S. Brown & D. J. O'Rourke (Eds.), *Case studies in sport communication* (pp. xi-xv). Westport, CT: Praeger.

Trujillo, N., & Ekdom, L. R. (1985). Sportswriting and American cultural values: The 1984 Chicago Cubs. *Critical Studies in Mass Communication, 2*, 262–281.

Turman, P. D. (2003). Coaches and cohesion: The impact of coaching techniques on team cohesion in the small group sport setting. *Journal of Sport Behavior, 26*, 86–104.

Walker, R. (2016, September 15). High school football players following Kaepernick's lead. *The Undefeated.* Retrieved from http://theundefeated.com/features/high-school-football-players-following-kaepernicks-lead

Wanta, W., & Leggert, D. (1988). "Hitting paydirt": Capacity theory and sports announcers' use of clichés. *Journal of Communication, 38*, 82–89.

Wenner, L. A. (Ed.). (1989). *Media, sports, & society.* Newbury Park, CA: Sage.

Chapter 2

Billings, A. C. (2008). *Olympic media: Inside the biggest show on television.* London, UK: Routledge.

Billings, A. C. (2010). *Communicating about sports media: Cultures collide.* Barcelona, ESP: Aresta.

Bryant, J., Comisky, P., & Zillmann, D. (1977). Drama in sports commentary. *Journal of Communication, 27*, 140–149.

Burke, K. (1969). *A rhetoric of motives.* Berkeley: University of California Press. (Original work published 1950)

Gill, M. (2012). Communicating organizational history to sports fans. In A. C. Earnheardt, P. M. Haridakis, & B. S. Hugenberg (Eds.), *Sports fans, identity, and socialization: Exploring the fandemonium* (pp. 151–164). Lanham, MD: Lexington Books.

Guttmann, A. (1978). *From ritual to record.* New York, NY: Columbia.

Hartmann, D., & Depro, B. (2006). Rethinking sports-based community crime prevention: A preliminary analysis of the relationship between midnight basketball and urban crime rates. *Journal of Sport and Social Issues, 30*(2), 180–196.

Hugenberg, L. W., Haridakis, P. M., & Earnheardt, A. C. (Eds.). (2008). *Sports mania: Essays on fandom and the media in the 21st Century.* Jefferson, NC: McFarland.

Lipscomb, S. (2006). Secondary school extracurricular involvement and academic achievement: A fixed effects approach. *Economics of Education Review, 26*(5), 463–472.

Nylund, D. (2007). *Beer, babes, and balls: Masculinity and sports talk radio.* Albany, NY: SUNY.

Raney, A. A. (2006). Why we watch and enjoy mediated sports. In A. Raney & J. Bryant (Eds.), *Handbook of sport and media* (pp. 313–329). Mahwah, NJ: LEA.

Solomon, J. (2015, Sept. 30). Court shuts down plan to pay athletes, says NCAA violates anti-trust law. Retrieved at: http://www.cbssports.com/college-football/news/court-shuts-down-plan-to-pay-athletes-says-ncaa-violates-antitrust-law

Trujillo, N. (2003). Introduction. In R. S. Brown & D. J. O'Rourke (Eds.), *Case studies in sport communication.* Westport, CT: Praeger.

Trulson, M. E. (1986). Martial arts training: A novel "cure" for juvenile delinquency. *Human Relations, 39*, 1131–1140.

Wann, D. L. (2006). The causes and consequences of sports team identification. In A. Raney & J. Bryant (Eds.), *Handbook of sport and media* (pp. 331–352). Mahwah, NJ: LEA.

Wann, D. L., & Branscombe, N. R. (1990). Die-hard and fair-weather fans: Effects of identification on BIRGing and

CORFing tendencies. *Journal of Sport & Social Issues, 14*(2), 103–117.

Weinreb, M. (2011, November 8). Growing up Penn State. *Grantland.com.*

Zillmann, D. (1988). Mood management through communication choices. *American Behavioral Scientist, 31*(3), 327–341.

Chapter 3

Bi, F. (2015, Jan. 8). ESPN leads all cable networks in affiliate fees. *Forbes.* Retrieved from http://www.forbes.com/sites/frankbi/2015/01/08/espn-leads-all-cable-networks-in-affiliate-fees/#2f24aa17e60c

Billings, A. C., & Eastman, S. T. (2003). Framing identities: Gender, ethnic, and national parity in network announcing of the 2002 Winter Olympics. *Journal of Communication, 53,* 569–586.

Billings, A.C., Qiao, F., Conlin, L.T., & Nie, T. (2016, in press). Permanently desiring the temporary?: Snapchat, social media, and the shifting motivations of sports fans. *Communication & Sport.*

Browning, B., & Sanderson, J. (2012). The positives and negatives of Twitter: Exploring how student-athletes use Twitter and respond to critical tweets. *International Journal of Sport Communication, 5,* 503–521.

Conlin, L., McLemore, D. M., & Rush, R. (2014). Pinterest and the female sports fan: Gaining a foothold in the male-dominated sports world. *International Journal of Sport Communication, 7*(3), 357–376.

Dickerson, N. (2015). Constructing the digitized sporting body: Black and White masculinity in NBA/NHL Internet memes. *Communication & Sport*, available via Online First.

Duggan, M. (2013). *The demographics of social media users—2015.* Washington, DC: Pew Internet & American Life Project. Retrieved from http://www.pewinternet.org/2015/08/19/the-demographics-of-social-media-users

Entman, R. M. (1993). Framing: Toward clarification of a fractured paradigm. *Journal of Communication, 43,* 51–58.

Frederick, E., Lim, C. H., Clavio, G., Pederson, P. M., & Burch, L. M. (2014). Choosing between the one-way or two-way street: An exploration of relationship promotion by professional athletes on Twitter. *Communication & Sport, 2,* 80–99.

Frederick, E., Lim, C. H., Clavio, G., & Walsh, P. (2012). Why we follow: An examination of parasocial interaction and fan motivations for following athlete archetypes on Twitter. *International Journal of Sport Communication, 5*(4), 481–502.

Friedman, T. (2007). *The world is flat: A brief history of the twenty-first century.* New York, NY: Picador.

Goffman, E. (1974). *Frame analysis: An essay on the organization of experience.* New York, NY: Harper & Row.

Goggin, G. (2013). Sport and the rise of mobile media. In B. Hutchins & D. Rowe (Eds.), *Digital media sport: Technology and power in the network society.* New York, NY: Routledge.

Hambrick, M. E., Simmons, J. M., Greenhalgh, G. P., & Greenwell, T. C. (2010). Understanding professional athletes' use of Twitter: A content analysis of athlete tweets. *International Journal of Sport Communication, 3,* 454–471.

Holton, A. (2012). Baseball's digital disconnect: Trust,

media credentialing, and the independent blogger. *Journal of Sports Media, 7*(1), 39–58.

Hutchins, B., & Mikosza, J. (2010). The Web 2.0 Olympics: Athlete blogging, social networking and policy contradictions at the 2008 Beijing Games. *Convergence, 16*(3), 279–297.

Hutchins, B., & Rowe, D. (2009). From broadcast scarcity to digital plenitude: The changing dynamics of the media sport content economy. *Television & New Media, 10*(4), 354–370.

Kaiser, T. (2012, Mar. 7). Government job applicants, college students asked to surrender Facebook information. *DailyTech.* Retrieved from http://www.dailytech.com/Government+Job+Applicants+College+Students+Asked+to+Surrender+Facebook+Information/article24186.htm

Laird, S. (2012, February 24). Pinsanity: How sports teams are winning on Pinterest. *Mashable.* Retrieved from http://mashable.com/2012/02/24/pinterest-sports

Pilkington, E. (2012, July 30). Twitter suspends British journalist critical of NBC's Olympics coverage. *The Guardian.* Retrieved from http://www.guardian.co.uk/technology/2012/jul/30/twitter-suspends-guy-adams-account-nbc

Sanderson, J. (2008). Spreading the word: Emphatic interaction displays on BlogMaverick.com. *Journal of Media Psychology: Theories, Methods, and Applications, 20,* 157–168.

Sanderson, J. (2011). *It's a whole new ballgame: How social media is changing sports.* Creskill, NJ: Hampton Press.

Smith, L. R., & Sanderson, J. (2015). I'm going to Instagram it!: An analysis of athlete self-presentation on Twitter. *Journal of Broadcasting & Electronic Media, 59*(2), 342–358.

Sporting News Media Group. (2013). Social media use: 2013. Retrieved from http://www.knowthefan.com/US

Weber, J. D., & Carini, R. M. (2013). Where are the female athletes in *Sports Illustrated?* A content analysis of covers (2000–2011). *International Review for the Sociology of Sport, 48*(2), 196–203.

Whiteside, E., Yu, N., & Hardin, M. (2012). The new "toy department": A case study on differences in sports coverage between traditional and new media. *Journal of Sports Media, 7*(1), 23–38.

Wolverton, B. (2012, August 12). *Two universities bar athletes from using hundreds of words on Twitter.* Retrieved from http://chronicle.com/blogs/players/u-of-kentucky-louisville-ban-athletes-from-using-hundreds-of-words-on-twitter/31096

Chapter 4

American Institute of Food Distribution. (2004). *The Food Institute report.* Retrieved from http://www.foodinstitute.com/firsample216.pdf

Branscombe, N. R., & Wann, D. L. (1991). The positive social and self-concept consequences of sports team identification. *Journal of Sport & Social Issues, 15,* 115–127.

Bryant, J., & Cummins, R. G. (2010). The effects of outcome of mediated and live sporting events on sports fans' self- and social identities. H. L. Hundley & A. C. Billings (Eds.), *Examining identity in sports media* (pp. 217–238). Thousand Oaks, CA: Sage.

Byers, D. (2013). Old media vs. new media, sports edition. *Politico*. Retrieved from http://www.politico.com/blogs/media/2013/02/old-media-vs-new-media-sports-edition-156932.html

Brown, N. A., & Billings, A. C. (2013). Sports fans as crisis communicators on social media websites. *Public Relations Review, 39*(1), 74–81.

Burns, E. B. (2014). When the Saints went marching in. Social Identity in the world champion New Orleans Saints football team and its impact on their host city. *Journal of Sport and Social Issues, 38*, 148–163.

Carbaugh, D. (1996). The playful self: Being a fan at college basketball games. In D. Carbaugh, *Situating selves: The communication of social identities in American scenes* (pp. 39–61). Albany: State University of New York Press.

Cottingham, M. B. (2012). Interaction ritual theory and sport fans: Emotion, symbols, and solidarity. *Sociology of Sport Journal, 29*, 168–185.

Courneya, K. S., & Carron, A. V. (1992). The home-field advantage in sports competitions: A literature review. *Journal of Sport & Exercise Psychology, 14*, 28–39.

Courtney, J. J., & Wann, D. L. (2010). The relationship between sport fan dysfunction and bullying behaviors. *North American Journal of Psychology, 12*, 191–198.

Eichelberger, C. (2013). Sports revenue to reach $67.7 billion by 2017, PwC report says. *Bloomberg*. Retrieved from http://www.bloomberg.com/news/articles/2013–11–13/sports-revenue-to-reach-67–7-billion-by-2017-pwc-report-says

Elliot, S. (2007). The know list 6: Work that net. *Sporting News, 231*(9), 5.

Epting, L. K., Riggs, K. N., Knowles, J. D., & Hanky, J. J. (2011). Cheers vs. jeers: Effects of audience feedback on individual athletic performance. *North American Journal of Psychology, 13*, 299–312.

Ferriter, M. M. (2009). "Arguably the greatest": Sport fans and communities at work on Wikipedia. *Sociology of Sport Journal, 26*, 127–154.

Gantz, W. (2012). Reflections on communication and sports: On fanship and social relationships. *Communication and Sport, 1*, 176–187.

Giles, H., & Stohl, M. (2016). Sport and intergroup communication: Fans, rivalries, communities and nations. In A. C. Billings (Ed.), *Defining sport communication* (pp. 150–164). New York, NY: Routledge.

Golden, J. (2016). Billions of dollars lost due to March Madness. *CNBC*. Retrieved from http://www.cnbc.com/2016/03/14/billions-of-dollars-lost-due-to-march-madness.html

Griggs, G., Leflay, K., & Groves, M. (2012). "Just watching it again now still gives me goose bumps!": Examining the mental postcards of sport spectators. *Sociology of Sport Journal, 29*, 89–101.

Haridakis, P. M. (2010). Rival sports fans and intergroup communication. In H. Giles, S. A. Reid, & J. Harwood, J. (Eds.), *The dynamics of intergroup communication* (pp. 249–262). New York, NY: Peter Lang.

Hyatt, C. G. (2007). Who do I root for now? The impact of franchise relocation on the loyal fans left behind: A case study of Hartford Whalers fans. *Journal of Sport Behavior, 30*, 36–56.

Jamieson, J. P. (2010). The home field advantage in athletics: A meta-analysis.

Journal of Applied Social Psychology, 40, 1819–1848.

Krizek, B. (1992). Remembrances and expectations: The investment of identity in the changing of Comiskey. *Elysian Fields Quarterly, 20*, 30–50.

Love, J., & Walker, A. (2012). Football versus football: Effect of topic on /r/ realization in American and English sports fans. *Language and Speech, 56*, 443–460.

Martin, C. R., & Reeves, J. L. (2001). The whole world isn't watching (but we thought they were): The Super Bowl and U.S. solipsism. *Culture, Sport Society, 4*, 213–236.

Miller, J. B. (1999). Indians, Braves, and Redskins: A performative struggle for control of an image. *Quarterly Journal of Speech, 85*, 188–202.

Moskowitz, B. J., & Wertheim, L. J. (2011). Scorecasting: The hidden influences behind how sports are played and games are won. New York, NY: Crown Archetype.

Oates, T. P. (2009). New media and repackaging of NFL fandom. *Sociology of Sport Journal, 26*, 31–49.

Ruihley, B. J., & Hardin, R. (2011). Beyond touchdowns, homeruns, and 3-pointers: An examination of fantasy sport participation motivation. *International Journal of Sport Management and Marketing, 10*, 232–256.

Rushin, S. (2004). Take me out to the . . . whatever. *Sports Illustrated, 100*(24), 15.

Schechner, R. (2002). *Performance studies: An introduction*. New York, NY: Routledge.

Serazio, M. (2012). The elementary forms of sports fandom: A Durkheimian exploration of team myths, kinship, and totemic rituals. *Communication and Sport, 1*, 303–325.

Solberg, H. A., Hanstad, D. V., & Thoring, T. A. (2010). Doping in elite sports—Do the fans care? Public opinion on the consequences of doping scandals. *International Journal of Sports Marketing & Sponsorship, 12*, 185–199.

Sutton, W. A., McDonald, M. A., Miline, G., & Cimperman, J. (1997). Getting and fostering fan identification in professional sports. *Sport Marketing Quarterly, 6*, 15–22.

Trail, G. T., Robinson, J., Dick, R. L., & Gillentine, A. L. (2003). Motives and points of attachment: Fans versus spectators in intercollegiate athletics. *Sport Marketing Quarterly, 12*, 217–227.

Wann, D. L., Allen, B., & Rochelle, A. R. (2004). Using sport fandom as an escape: Searching for relief from under-stimulation and over-stimulation. *International Sports Journal, 8*, 104–113.

Wann, D. L., Peterson, R. R., Cothran, C., & Dykes, M. (1999). Sport fan aggression and anonymity: The importance of team identification. *Social Behavior and Personality, 27*, 597–602.

Wann, D. L., & Robinson, T. N. (2002). The relationship between sport team identification and integration into and perceptions of a university. *International Sports Journal, 24*, 36–44.

Wann, D. L., Royalty, J. L., & Rochelle, A. L. (2002). Using motivation and team identification to predict sport fans' emotional responses to team performance. *Journal of Sport Behavior, 25*, 207–216.

Weed, M. (2007). The pub as a virtual football fandom venue: An alternative to "being there"? *Soccer & Society, 8,* 399–414.

Chapter 5

Aden, R. C. (1999). *Popular stories and promised lands: Fan cultures and symbolic pilgrimages*. Tuscaloosa: University of Alabama Press.

Aden, R. C. (2008). *Huskerville: A story of Nebraska football, fans, and the power of place*. Jefferson, NC: McFarland.

Andrews, M., & Chapman, B. (Directors), & Sarafian, K. (Producer). (2012). *Brave* [Motion picture]. United States: Walt Disney Studios.

Beal, B. (1997). The Promise Keepers' use of sport in defining 'Christlike' masculinity. *Journal of Sport & Social Issues, 21*, 274–284.

Billings, A. C. (2013). Tiger Woods lands in the rough: Gold, apologia, and the heroic limits of privacy. In L. A. Wenner (Ed.), *Fallen sports heroes, media, & celebrity culture* (pp. 51–63). New York, NY: Peter Lang.

Boaz, Y. (Director), & Bruckheimer, J. (Producer). (2000). *Remember the Titans*. United States: Walt Disney Pictures.

Butterworth, M. L. (2005). Ritual in the 'church of baseball': Suppressing the discourse of democracy after 9/11. *Communication and Critical/Cultural Studies, 2*, 107–129.

Butterworth, M. L. (2007). Race in 'the race': Mark McGwire, Sammy Sosa, and heroic constructions of whiteness. *Critical Studies in Media Communication, 24*, 228–244.

Butterworth, M. L. (2011). Saved at home: Christian branding and faith nights in the "church of baseball." *Quarterly Journal of Speech, 97*, 309–333.

Butterworth, M. L. (2013). The passion of the Tebow: Sports media and heroic language in the tragic frame. *Critical Studies in Media Communication, 30*, 17–33.

Cameron, J. (Director & Producer). (2009). *Avatar*. Untied States: Twentieth Century Fox.

Campbell, J., & Moyers, B. (1988). *The power of myth*. (Ed. Betty Sue Flowers). New York, NY: Doubleday.

Cole, C. L., & King, S. (2003). The new politics of urban consumption: *Hoop Dreams*, *Clockers*, and "America." In R. C. Wilcox, D. L. Andrews, R. Pitter, & R. L. Irwin (Eds.), *Sporting dystopias: The making and meanings of urban sport cultures* (pp. 221–246). Albany, NY: State University of New York Press.

Deegan, M. J., & Stein, M. (1989). The big red dream machine: Nebraska football. In M. J. Deegan (Ed.), *American ritual dramas: Social rules and cultural meanings* (pp. 77–88). New York, NY: Greenwood Press.

Doty, W. G. (1986). *Mythography: The study of myths and rituals*. Tuscaloosa: University of Alabama Press.

Drucker, S. J. (1994). The mediated sports hero. In S. J. Drucker & R. S. Cathcart (Eds.), *American heroes in a media age* (pp. 82–93). Cresskill, NJ: Hampton.

Drucker, S. J., & Cathcart, R. S. (1994). The hero as a communication phenomenon. In S. J. Drucker & R. S. Cathcart (Eds.), *American heroes in a media age* (pp. 1–11). Cresskill, NJ: Hampton.

Eastwood, C (Director and Producer). (2009). *Invictus*. United States: Warner Bros.

Fainaru-Wada, M., & Fainaru, S. (2013). *League of denial: The NFL, concussions, and the battle for truth*. New York, NY: Crown.

Fisher, W. (1984). Narration as a human communication paradigm: The case of moral public argument. *Communication Monographs, 51,* 1–22.

Gartner, J. (Director), & Bruckheimer, J. (Producer). (2006). *Glory road.* United States: Walt Disney Pictures.

Giardina, M. D., & Magnusen, M. (2013). Dog bites man? The criminalization and rehabilitation of Michael Vick. In L. A. Wenner (Ed.), *Fallen sports heroes, media, & celebrity culture* (pp. 165–178). New York, NY: Peter Lang.

Grano, D. A. (2009). Muhammad Ali versus the 'modern athlete': On voice in mediated sports culture. *Critical Studies in Media Communication, 26,* 191–211.

Grano, D. A. (2014). The greatest game ever played: An NFL origin story. In T. P. Oates & Z. Furness (Eds.), *The NFL: Critical and cultural perspectives* (pp. 13–39). Philadelphia, PA: Temple University Press.

Grano, D. A., & Zagacki, K. S. (2011). Cleansing the Superdome: The paradox of purity and post-Katrina guilt. *Quarterly Journal of Speech, 97,* 201–223.

Grant, C. (1998). *Myths we live by.* Ottawa: University of Ottawa Press.

Hart, R. (1990). *Modern rhetorical criticism.* Glenview, IL: Scott Foresman.

Hoffman, S. J. (1992). Sport as religion. In S. J. Hoffman (Ed.), *Sport and religion* (pp. 1–12). Champaign, IL: Human Kinetics.

James, S. (Director). (1994). *Hoop dreams* [Motion picture]. United States: Fine Line Features.

Kurtz, J. B. (2016). Elegy for the McPheean moment: False idols and the tyrannical faith of celebrity-sports culture. In B. Schultz & M. L. Sheffer (Eds.), *Sport and religion in the twenty-first century* (pp. 31–46). Lanham, MD: Lexington.

Landesman, P. (Director). (2015). *Concussion* [Motion picture]. United States: Columbia Pictures.

Lewis, T. V. (2013). Religious rhetoric in southern college football: New uses for religious metaphors. *Southern Communication Journal, 78,* 202–214.

MacCambridge, M. (2004). *America's game: The epic story of how pro football captured a nation.* New York, NY: Random House.

Newman, R. (2001). The American church of baseball and the National Baseball Hall of Fame. *Nine: A Journal of Baseball History and Culture, 10,* 46–63.

Okrent, D. (1998, December 28). A mac for all seasons: Mark McGwire's 70 home runs shattered the most magical record in sports and gave America a much-needed hero. *Time,* pp. 138–144.

Olsen, R. (2003). Fifty-eight American dreams: The NBA draft as mediated ritual. In R. S. Brown & D. J. O'Rourke (Eds.), *Case studies in sport communication* (pp. 171–200). Westport, CT: Praeger.

O'Rourke, D. J. (2003). The talk of the town: A rhetorical analysis of the Browns' departure from and return to Cleveland. In R. S. Brown & D. J. O'Rourke (Eds.), *Case studies in sport communication* (pp. 63–80). Westport, CT: Praeger.

Paolantonio, S. (2008). *How football explains America.* Chicago, IL: Triumph Books.

Perez, A. J. (2016, July 12). Joe Paterno knew of alleged sexual abuse by Jerry Sandusky in 1976, court documents say. *USA Today.* Retrieved from http://www.usatoday.com/story/sports/ncaaf/2016/07/12/

joe-paterno-jerry-sandusky-penn-state-sexual-assault-complaint/86982048

Rader, B. (2002). *Baseball: A history of America's game* (2nd ed.). Urbana: University of Illinois Press.

Real, M. (1975). Super bowl: Mythic spectacle. *Journal of Communication*, *25*, 31–43.

Real, M. (1989). *Super media: A cultural studies approach.* Newbury Park, CA: Sage.

Rinehart, R. E. (2012). All things in moderation: "Saint" Joe Paterno. *Cultural Studies ó Critical Methodologies, 12,* 365–368.

Roessner, L. A. (2014). Sixteen days of glory: A critical-cultural analysis of Bud Greenspan's official Olympic documentaries. *Communication, Culture & Critique, 7,* 338–355.

Ross, G. (Director), & Jacobson, N. (Producer). (2012). *The hunger games* [Motion picture]. United States: Lionsgate Films.

Rothenbuhler, E. W. (1989). Values and symbols in orientations to the Olympics. *Critical Studies in Mass Communication*, *6*, 138–157.

Rothenbuhler, E. W. (1998). *Ritual communication: From everyday conversation to mediated ceremony.* Thousand Oaks, CA: Sage.

Serazio, M. (2013). The elementary forms of fandom: A Durkheimian exploration of team myths, kinship, and totemic rituals. *Communication & Sport, 1,* 303–325.

Vande Berg, L. R. (1998). The sports hero meets mediated celebrityhood. In L. A. Wenner (Ed.), *Mediasport* (pp. 134–153). London, UK: Routledge.

Wenner, L. A. (2013). The fallen sports hero in the age of mediated celebrityhood. In L. A. Wenner (Ed.), *Fallen sports heroes, media, & celebrity culture* (pp. 3–16). New York, NY: Peter Lang.

Whedon, J. (Director), & Feige, K. (Producer). (2012). *The avengers* [Motion picture]. United States: Walt Disney Studios.

Chapter 6

Anderson, E. (2005). *In the game: Gay athletes and the cult of masculinity.* Albany, NY: SUNY.

Angelini, J. R., MacArthur, P. J., & Billings, A. C. (2012). What's the gendered story? Vancouver's primetime Olympic glory on NBC. *Journal of Broadcasting & Electronic Media, 56*(2), 261–279.

Billings, A. C. (2008). Clocking gender differences: Televised Olympic clock-time in the 1996–2006 Summer and Winter Olympics. *Television & New Media, 9*(5), 429–441.

Billings, A. C. (2009). *Communicating about sports media: Cultures collide*. Barcelona, ESP: Aresta.

Billings, A. C., Angelini, J. R., & Duke, A. H. (2010). Gendered profiles of Olympic history: Sportscaster dialogue in the 2008 Beijing Olympics. *Journal of Broadcasting & Electronic Media, 54*(1), 9–23.

Billings, A. C., & Young, B. D. (2015). Comparing flagship news programs: Women's sport coverage in ESPN's *SportsCenter* and FOX Sports 1's *FOX Sports Live*. *Electronic News*, *9*(1), 3–16.

Blinde, M. E., Greendorfer, S. L., & Sankner, R. J. (1991). Differential media coverage of men's and women's intercollegiate basketball: Reflection of gender ideology. *Journal of Sport & Social Issues, 15,* 98–114.

Cooky, C., Messner, M. A., & Musto, M. (2015). "It's dude time!": A quarter century of excluding women's sports in televised news and highlight shows. *Communication & Sport, 3*, 261–287.

Connell, R. W. (1987). *Gender and power: Society, the person and sexual politics.* Palo Alto, CA: Stanford University Press.

Daddario, G. (1998). *Women's sport and spectacle.* Westport, CT: Praeger.

Eastman, S. T., & Billings, A. C. (2000). Sportscasting and sports reporting: The power of gender bias. *Journal of Sport & Social Issues, 24*(1), 192–212.

Genovese, J. (2015). Sports television reporters and the negotiation of fragmented professional identities. *Communication, Culture, & Critique, 8*(1), 55–72.

Godoy-Pressland, A. (2014). 'Nothing to report': A semi-longitudinal investigation of the print media coverage of sportswomen in British Sunday newspapers. *Media, Culture & Society, 36*, 595–609.

Gramsci, A. (1971). *Selections from the prison notebooks.* New York, NY: International.

Griffin, P. (2007). Changing the game: Homophobia, sexism, and lesbians in sport. In J. O'Reilly & S. K. Cahn (Eds.), *Women and sports in the United States* (pp. 217–234). Lebanon, NH: Northeastern Univ. Press.

Halbert, C., & Latimer, M. (1994). "Battling" gendered language: An analysis of the language used by sports commentators in a televised coed tennis competition. *Sociology of Sport Journal, 11*, 298–308.

Hardin, M. (2009). The Rene Portland case: New homophobia and heterosexism in women's sport coverage. In H. Hundley & A. C. Billings (Eds.), *Examining identity in sports media* (pp. 17–36). Thousand Oaks, CA: Sage.

Hardin, M., & Greer, J. D. (2009). The influence of gender-role socialization, media use, and sports participation on perceptions of gender-appropriate sports. *Journal of Sport Behavior, 32*(2), 207–226.

Hardin, M., & Shain, S. (2005). Strength in numbers? The experiences and attitudes of women in sports media careers. *Journalism & Mass Communication Quarterly, 84*(4), 804–819.

Hardin, M., Whiteside, E., & Ash, E. (2014). Ambivalence on the front lines? Attitudes toward Title IX and women's sports among Division I sports information directors. *International Review for the Sociology of Sport, 49*(1), 42–64.

Hargreaves, J. A. (1994). *Sporting females: Critical issues in the history and sociology of women's sports.* London, UK: Routledge.

Hartsock, N. (1983). *Money, sex, and power: Toward a feminist historical materialism.* New York, NY: Longman.

Hauser, M. (1999). Selling their game. In L. Danziger (Ed.), *Nike is a goddess: The history of women in sports* (pp. 81–101). New York, NY: Atlantic Monthly Press.

Helm, B. (2009, April 29). The race for Kentucky Derby viewers. Retrieved from http://www.businessweek.com/bwdaily/dnflash/content/apr2009/db20090428_323412.htm?chan=top+news_top+news+index+-+temp_news+%2B+ analysis

Hundley, H. L., & Billings, A. C. (2010). *Views from the fairway: Media explorations of identity in golf.* Cresskill, NJ: Hampton Press.

International Olympic Committee. (2012). *Fact sheet: Women in the Olympic movement*. Retrieved from http://www.olympic.org

Kane, M. J. (2013). The better sportswomen get, the more the media ignore them. *Communication & Sport, 1*(3), 231–236.

Kane, M. J., Lavoi, N. M., & Fink, J. S. (2013). Exploring elite female athletes' interpretations of sport media images: A window into the construction of social identity and "selling sex" in women's sports. *Communication & Sport, 1*(3), 269–298.

Marshall, P. (Director), & Abbott, E. (Producer). (1992). *A league of their own* [Motion picture]. United States: Columbia Pictures.

Meân, L. J., & Kassing, J. (2008). "I would just like to be known as an athlete": Managing hegemony, femininity, and heterosexuality in female sport. *Western Journal of Communication, 72*, 126–144.

Messner, M. (2002). *Taking the field: Women, men and sports.* Minneapolis: University of Minnesota Press.

Miller, J. A., & Shales, T. (2011). *Those guys have all the fun: Inside the world of ESPN.* New York, NY: Little, Brown, & Company.

National Bureau of Economic Research. (2016, Feb. 11). *Why do women outnumber men in college?* Retrieved at: http://www.nber.org/digest/jan07/w12139.html

Oates, T. P. (2012). Representing the audience: The gendered politics of sport media. *Feminist Media Studies*, 603–607.

Sandoz, J., & Winans, J. (Eds.). (1999). *Whatever it takes: Women on women's sport.* New York, NY: Farrar, Straus, and Giroux.

Schmidt, H. C. (2013). Women, sports, and journalism: Examining the limited role of women in student newspaper sports reporting. *Communication & Sport 1*(3), 246–268.

Shugart, H.A. (2003). She shoots, she scores: Mediated constructions of contemporary female athletes in coverage of the 1999 US women's soccer team. *Western Journal of Communication, 67*(1), 1–31.

Spice girls of centre court. (1999, June 20). *The London Times*, p.1.

Suggs, W. (2006). *A place on the team: The triumph and tragedy of Title IX.* Princeton, NJ: Princeton University Press.

Thomas, K. (2010, April 20). *NCAA praises change of rule for Title IX compliance*. Retrieved from http://www.nytimes.com/2010/04/21/sports/21titleix.html

Trujillo, N. (1991). Hegemonic masculinity on the mound: Media representations of Nolan Ryan and American sports culture. *Critical Studies in Mass Communication, 9*, 290–308.

Walker, N. A., & Melton, E. N. (2015). The tipping point: The intersection of race, gender, and sexual orientation in intercollegiate sports. *Journal of Sport Management, 29*(3), 257–271.

Weber, J. D., & Carini, R. M. (2013). Where are the female athletes in *Sports Illustrated?* A content analysis of covers (2000—2011). *International Review for the Sociology of Sport, 48*(2), 196–203.

Whiteside, E., & Hardin, M. (2011). Women (not) watching women: Leisure time, television, and implications for televised coverage of women's sports. *Communication, Culture & Critique, 4*(2), 122–143.

Women's Sports Foundation. (2009). *Sport careers for women*. Retrieved from http://www.womenssportsfoundation.org/Content/

Articles/Careers/S/Sport-Careers-for-Women.aspx

Wulf, S. (2009, March 23). Page 2. *ESPN: The Magazine*, p. 16.

Chapter 7

Anderson, T. (2009, September 1). *CC Sabathia works to bring more Blacks to baseball*. Retrieved from http://www.thegrio.com/entertainment/yankee-pitcher-unhappy-with-number-of-blacks-in-mlb-1.php

Andrews, D. L., & Silk, M. L. (2010). Basketball's ghettocentric logic. *American Behavioral Scientist, 53,* 1626–1644.

Baker, A., & Boyd, T. (1997). *Sports, media, and the politics of identity.* Bloomington: Indiana University Press.

Bass, A. (2002). *Not the triumph but the struggle: The 1968 Olympics and the making of the Black athlete.* Minneapolis: University of Minnesota Press.

Billings, A. C. (2003). Portraying Tiger Woods: Characterizations of a "Black" athlete in a "White" sport. *The Howard Journal of Communications, 14*(1), 29–38.

Blackistone, K. B. (2012). The Whitening of sports media and the coloring of Black athletes' images. *Wake Forest Journal of Law & Policy, 2*(1), 215–225.

Buffington, D. (2005). Contesting race on Sundays: Making meaning out of the rise in the number of Black quarterbacks. *Sociology of Sport Journal, 21,* 19–37.

Butterworth, M. L. (2007). Race in "the race": Mark McGwire, Sammy Sosa, and heroic constructions of Whiteness. *Critical Studies in Media Communication, 24*(3), 228–244.

Byrd, J., & Utsler, M. (2007). Is stereotypical coverage of African-American athletes as "dead as disco"? An analysis of NFL quarterbacks in the pages of *Sports Illustrated. Journal of Sports Media, 2*(1), 1–28.

Carrington, B. (2010). *Race, sport, and politics: The sporting Black diaspora.* Thousand Oaks, CA: Sage.

Carver, R. (1834). *The book of sports.* Boston, MA: Lily, Wait, Colman, & Holden.

Chen, M. (2010, July 21). Black women don't swim? *Color Lines.* Retrieved from http://colorlines.com/archives/2010/07/black_women_dont_swim.html

Coakley, J. (2009). *Sports in society: Issues and controversies.* New York, NY: McGraw-Hill.

Cox, J. W., Clement, S., & Vargas, T. (2016, May 19). New poll finds 9 in 10 Native Americans aren't offended by Redskins name. *Washington Post.* Retrieved from https://www.washingtonpost.com/local/new-poll-finds-9-in-10-native-americans-arent-offended-by-redskins-name/2016/05/18/3ea11cfa-161a-11e6-924d-838753295f9a_story.html

Edwards, H. (1970). *Revolt of the Black athlete.* New York, NY: Free Press.

Entine, J. (2000). *Taboo: Why Black athletes dominate sports and why we're afraid to talk about it.* New York, NY: Public Affairs.

Fitzgerald, T. (2005, December 16). Philadelphia NAACP head rebuked for McNabb remarks. *The Philadelphia Inquirer,* p. 1A.

Ford, B. (2004, December 27). Complex legacy left by White: One of NFL's greatest lineman died yesterday. *The Philadelphia Inquirer,* p. S6.

Gartner, J. (Director), & Bruckheimer, J. (Producer). (2006). *Glory road* [Motion picture]. United States: Walt Disney Pictures.

Gerbner, G., Gross, L., Morgan, M., & Signorielli, N. (1986). Living with television: The dynamics of the cultivation process. In J. Bryant & D. Zillmann (Eds.), *Perspectives on media effects* (pp. 17–40). Hillsdale, NJ: LEA.

Gerbner, G., Gross, L., Morgan, M., Signorielli, N., & Shanahan, J. (2002). Growing up with television: The cultivation perspective. In J. Bryant & D. Zillmann (Eds.), *Media effects: Advances in theory and research* (pp. 43–67). Hillsdale, NJ: LEA.

Goss, B. D., Tyler, A. L., & Billings, A. C. (2009). A content analysis of racial representations of NBA athletes on *Sports Illustrated* magazine covers, 1970–2003. In H. Hundley & A. C. Billings (Eds.), *Examining identity in sports media* (pp. 173–194).

Grano, D. A. (2010). Risky dispositions: Thick moral description and character-talk in sports culture. *Southern Communication Journal, 75,* 255–276.

Griffin, R. A., & Calafell, B. M. (2011). Control, discipline, and punish: Black masculinity and (in)visible Whiteness. In M. G. Lacy & K. A. Ono (Eds.), *Critical rhetorics of race* (pp. 117–136). New York: New York University Press.

Hoberman, J. (2007). Race and athletics in the twenty-first century. In J. A. Hargreaves & P. Vertinsky (Eds.), *Physical culture, power, and the body* (pp. 208–231). London, UK: Routledge.

Hutchison P. (2016). The legend of Texas Western: Journalism and the epic sports spectacle that wasn't. *Critical Studies in Media Communication, 33,* 154–167.

Khan, A. I. (2012). *Curt Flood in the media: Baseball, race, and the demise of the activist athlete.* Oxford: University of Mississippi Press.

King, C. R. (2016). *Redskins: Insult and brand.* Lincoln: University of Nebraska Press.

King, C. R., Leonard, D. J., & Kusz, K. K. (2007). White power and sport: An introduction. *Journal of Sport & Social Issues, 31,* 3–10.

Lavelle, K. (2017, in press). No room for racism: Restoration of order in the NBA. *Communication & Sport* (Online First).

Lumpkin, A., & Williams, L. D. (1991). An analysis of *Sports Illustrated* feature articles, 1954–1987. *Sociology of Sport Journal, 8,* 16–32.

Margolis, B., & Piliavin, J. A. (1999). "Stacking" in Major League Baseball: A multivariate analysis. *Sociology of Sport Journal, 16,* 16–34.

McDonald, M. G. (2005). Mapping Whiteness in sport: An introduction. *Sociology of Sport Journal, 22,* 245–255.

Mocarski, R. A., & Billings, A. C. (2014). Manufacturing a messiah: How Nike and LeBron James co-constructed the legend of King James. *Communication & Sport, 2*(1), 3–23.

Page, C. (2009, July 30). The audacity of hops. On Keith Olbermann's *Countdown* (television).

Pearson, M., & Sutton, J. (2015). Black football players at Missouri: We'll sit out until system president resigns. *CNN.* Retrieved on July 7, 2016 from: http://www.cnn.com/2015/11/08/us/missouri-football-players-protest/index.html

Rada, J., & Wulfemeyer, K. T. (2005). Color coded: Racial

descriptors in television coverage of intercollegiate sports. *Journal of Broadcasting & Electronic Media, 49,* 65–85.

Rhoden, W. C. (2006). *Forty million dollar slaves: The rise, fall, and redemption of the black athlete.* New York, NY: Crown.

Ross, C. K. (Ed.). (2006). *Race and sport: The struggle for equality on and off the field.* Oxford: University Press of Mississippi.

Sailes, G. (1998). *African-Americans in sport: Contemporary themes.* New Brunswick, NJ: Transaction.

Stone, J. (2012). A hidden toxicity in the term "student-athlete": Stereotype threat for athletes in the college classroom. *Wake Forest Journal of Law & Policy, 2*(1), 179–197.

Sweet, F. W. (2005). *Legal history of the color line: The rise and triumph of the one-drop rule.* Palm Coast, FL: Bakintyme.

Wonsek, P. L. (1992). College basketball on television: A study of racism in the media. *Media, Culture and Society, 14,* 449–461.

Zenovich, M. (Director). (2016). *Fantastic lies* [Motion picture]. United States: ESPN.

Chapter 8

About First Pitch. (n.d.). *ESPN.com.* Retrieved July 10, 2016, from http://espn.go.com/30for30/film?page=firstpitch

Allison, L. (2000). Sport and nationalism. In J. Coakley & E. Dunning (Eds.), *Handbook of sports studies* (pp. 344–355). London, UK: Sage.

Anderson, B. (1991). *Imagined communities: Reflections on the origin and spread of nationalism* (Rev. ed.). London, UK: Verso.

Barber, B. (1995). *Jihad vs. McWorld: How the planet is both falling apart and coming together and what this means for democracy.* New York, NY: Crown.

Bass, A. (2002). *Not the triumph but the struggle: The 1968 Olympics and the making of the black athlete.* Minneapolis: University of Minnesota Press.

Beer, F. A., & de Landtsheer, C. (2004). Introduction: Metaphors, politics, and world politics. In F. A. Beer & C. de Landtsheer (Eds.), *Metaphorical world politics* (pp. 5–52). East Lansing: Michigan State University Press.

Benjamin, J. (2015, August 12). Milwaukee Bucks' new arena is a multimillion dollar mistake. *Forbes.* Retrieved, from http://www.forbes.com/sites/joshbenjamin/2015/08/12/milwaukee-bucks-new-arena-is-a-multimillion-dollar-mistake/#58080ca63055

Benoit, W. L., Stein, K. A., & Hansen, G. J. (2005). *New York Times* coverage of presidential campaigns. *Journalism & Mass Communication Quarterly, 82,* 356–376.

Billings, A. C. (2008). *Olympic media: Inside the biggest show on television.* London: Routledge.

Billings, A. C., Brown, K. A., & Brown, N. A. (2013). 5, 355 hours of impact: Effects of Olympic media on nationalism attitudes. *Journal of Broadcasting & Electronic Media, 57,* 579–595.

Billings, A. C., Brown, N. A., Brown, K. A., Guoqing, Leeman, M. A., Li en, S., Novak, D. R., & Rowe, D. (2013). From pride to smugness and the nationalism between: Olympic media consumption effects on nationalism across the globe. Mass *Communication and Society, 16*, 910–932.

Billings, A. C., & Eastman, S. T. (2003). Framing identities: Gender, ethnic, and national parity in network announcing of the 2002 Winter Olympics. *Journal of Communication, 53*, 569–586.

Bineham, J. L. (1991). Some ethical implications of team sports metaphors in politics. *Communication Reports, 4*, 35–42.

Brown, R. S. (2004). Sport and healing America. *Society, 42*, 37–41.

Brown, K. A., Billings, A. C., Schallhorn, C., Schramm, H., & Brown-Devlin, N. (2016, in press). Power within the Olympic rings? Nationalism, Olympic media consumption, and comparative cases in Germany and the USA. *Journal of International Communication, 22*, 143–149.

Butterworth, M. L. (2005). Ritual in the 'church of baseball': Suppressing the discourse of democracy after 9/11. *Communication and Critical/Cultural Studies, 2*, 107–129.

Butterworth, M. L. (2007). The politics of the pitch: Claiming and contesting democracy through the Iraqi national soccer team. *Communication and Critical/Cultural Studies, 4*, 184–203.

Butterworth, M. L. (2012). Militarism and memorializing at the Pro Football Hall of Fame. *Communication and Critical/Cultural Studies, 9*, 241–258.

Dave Zirin on the whitewashing of Muhammad Ali: He wasn't against just war, but empire. (2016, June 10). *Democracy Now!* Retrieved from http://www.democracynow.org/2016/6/10/dave_zirin_on_the_whitewashing_of

Delgado, F. (2003). The fusing of sport and politics: Media constructions of U.S. versus Iran at France '98. *Journal of Sport & Social Issues, 27*, 293–307.

Devlin, M. B., & Billings, A. C. (2016). Examining the world's game in the United States: Impact of nationalized qualities on fan identification and consumption of the 2014 FIFA World Cup. *Journal of Broadcasting & Electronic Media, 60*, 40–60.

Eagleton, T. (1991). *Ideology: An introduction*. London, UK: Verso.

Fleder, G. (Director), & Davis, J. (Producer). (2008). *The express* [Motion picture]. United States: Universal Pictures.

Florio, M. (2016, July 9). Carmelo Anthony calls on all athletes to demand change. *NBC Sports.com*. Retrieved from http://profootballtalk.nbcsports.com/2016/07/09/carmelo-anthony-calls-on-all-athletes-to-demand-change

Hartmann, D. (2003). *Race, culture, and the revolt of the black athlete: 1968 Olympic protests and their aftermath*. Chicago, IL: University of Chicago Press.

Helgeland, B. (Director), & Tull, T. (Producer). (2013). *42* [Motion Picture]. United States: Warner Brothers.

Herbeck, D. A. (2004). Sports metaphors and public policy: The football theme in Desert Storm discourse. In F. A. Beer & C. de Landtsheer (Eds.), *Metaphorical world politics* (pp. 121–139). East Lansing: Michigan State University Press.

Hester, M. (2005). *America's #1 fan: A rhetorical analysis of presidential sports encomia and the symbolic power of sports in the articulation of civil religion in the United States*. Unpublished doctoral dissertation. Georgia State University.

Hopkins, S. (Director), & Brünig, K., Dayan, L., Garwood, K., Hopkins, S., Levy, J-C., Manuel, N., Rochon, L-P., & Séguin, D. (Producers). (2016). *Race* [Motion picture]. United States: Focus Features.

Howard, R. (Director & Producer), & Marshall, P., & Grazer, B. (Producers). (2005). *Cinderella man* [Motion picture]. United States: Universal Pictures.

Jarvie, G. (2003). Internationalism and sport in the making of nations. *Identities: Global Studies in Culture and Power, 10*, 537–551.

Jhally, S. (1989). Cultural studies and the sports/media complex. In L. A. Wenner (Ed.), *Media, sports, & society* (pp. 70–93). Newbury Park, CA: Sage.

Keown, T. (2016, October 7). Colin Kaepernick is a real American. *The Undefeated.* Retrieved from http://theundefeated.com/features/colin-kaepernick-is-a-real-american

Khan, A. I. (2012). *Curt Flood in the media: Baseball, race, and the demise of the activist-athlete.* Jackson: University Press of Mississippi.

King, C. R. (2008). Toward a radical sport journalism: An interview with Dave Zirin. *Journal of Sport & Social Issues, 32*, 333–344.

Lipsyte, R. (2002). Prophets. In J. Lovinger (Ed.), *The Gospel according to ESPN: Saints, saviors & sinners* (pp. 9–58). New York, NY: Hyperion.

Maguire, J. (2006). Sport and globalization: Key issues, phases, and trends. In A. A. Raney & J. Bryant (Eds.), *Handbook of sports and media* (pp. 435–446). Mahwah, NJ: Lawrence Erlbaum.

Miller, T. (2004). Manchester, USA? In D. L. Andrews (Ed.), *Manchester United: A thematic study* (pp. 241–248). London, UK: Routledge.

Moretti, A. (2013). The interference of politics in the Olympic Games, and how the U.S. media contribute to it. *Global Media Journal, 6*, 5–18.

Mouffe, C. (2000). *The democratic paradox*. London, UK: Verso.

Nauright, J. (2014). Sport and the neo-liberal world order. *Catalan Journal of Communication & Cultural Studies, 6*, 281–288.

Olson, R. (2016, July 10). As stadium opens, Vikings and city sail into new era. *Minneapolis Star-Tribune.* Retrieved from http://www.startribune.com/as-stadium-opens-vikings-and-city-sail-into-a-new-era/386100791

Ono, K. A. (1997). 'America's' apple pie: Baseball, Japan-bashing, and the sexual threat of miscegenation. In A. Baker & T. Boyd (Eds.), *Out of bounds: Sports, media and the politics of identity* (pp. 81–101). Bloomington: Indiana University Press.

Ross, G. (Director), & Kennedy, K., Marshall, F., Ross, G., & Sindell, J. (Producers). (2003). *Seabiscuit* [Motion picture]. United States: Universal Pictures.

Rowe, D. (1999). *Sport, culture, and the media: The unruly trinity.* Buckingham, UK: Open University Press.

Rowe, D. (2013). Reflections on communication and sport: On nation and globalization. *Communication & Sport, 1*, 18–29.

Ryan, B. (2002, October). Memory serves us better. *Boston Globe*, E5. Retrieved from http://web.lexis-nexis.com/universe

Scherer, J., & Koch, J. (2010). Living with war: Sport, citizenship, and the cultural politics of post-9/11 Canadian identity. *Sociology of Sport Journal, 27*, 1–29.

Segrave. J. O. (2000). The sports metaphor in American cultural discourse. *Culture, Sport, Society, 3*, 48–60.

Tomlinson, A. (1998). Power: Domination, negotiation, and resistance in sports cultures. *Journal of Sport & Social Issues, 22*, 235–240.

Chapter 9

Amaechi, J. (2007). *Man in the middle*. New York, NY: ESPN.

Bean, B., & Bull, C. (2003). *Going the other way: Lessons from a life in and out of Major League Baseball*. New York, NY: Marlowe.

Billings, A. C., Moscowitz, L. M., Rae, C., & Brown, N. (2015). The art of coming out: Traditional and social media frames surrounding the NBA's Jason Collins. *Journalism & Mass Communication Quarterly, 92*(1), 142–160.

Birrell, S., & Cole, C. L. (1990). Double fault: Renee Richards and the construction and naturalization of difference. *Sociology of Sport Journal, 7*, 1–21.

Butterworth, M. L. (2008). "Katie was not only a girl, she was terrible": Katie Hnida, body rhetoric, and football at the University of Colorado. *Communication Studies, 59*, 259–273.

Butler, J. (1999). *Gender trouble: Feminism and the subversion of identity*. New York, NY: Routledge.

Carmack, H. J. (2011). Everythang's gonna be all white: The fightin whities' use of parody and incongruity for social change. *Florida Communication Journal, 39*, 35–44.

Carrington, B. (2008). "What's the footballer doing here?" Racialized performativity, reflexivity, and identity. *Cultural Studies ó Critical Methodologies, 8*, 423–452.

Chadha, G. (Director & Producer), & Nayare, D. (Producer). (2002). *Bend it like Beckham* [Motion picture]. UK: Redbus Film Distribution.

Cherney, J. L. (2003). Sport, (dis)ability, and public controversy: Ableist rhetoric and Casey Martin v. PGA Tour, Inc. In R. S. Brown & D. J. O'Rourke III (Eds.), *Case studies in sport communication* (pp. 81–104). Westport, CT: Praeger.

Cherney, J. L., & Lindemann, K. (2010). Sporting images of disability: Murderball and the rehabilitation of masculine identity. In H. Hundley & A. C. Billings (Eds.), *Examining identity in sports media* (pp. 195–215). Thousand Oaks, CA: Sage.

Cherney, J. L., & Lindemann, K. (2014). Queering Street: Homosociality, masculinity, and disability in *Friday Night Lights*. *Western Journal of Communication, 78*, 1–21.

Cherney, J. L., Lindemann, K., & Hardin, M. (2015). Research in communication, disability, and sport. *Communication & Sport, 3*, 8–26.

Chidester, P. (2012). Farewell to the Chief: Fan identification and the sports mascot as postmodern image. In A. C. Earnheardt, P. M. Haridakis, & B. S. Hugenberg (Eds.), *Sports fans, identity, and socialization: Exploring the fandemonium* (pp. 49–62). Lanham, MD: Lexington Books.

Collins, J. (2013, April 29). Why NBA center Jason Collins is coming out now. *Sports Illustrated*. Retrieved from http://sportsillustrated.cnn.com/magazine/news/20130429/jason-collins-gay-nba-player

Cunningham, P. L. (2009). "Please don't fine me again!!!!!" Black athletic defiance in the NBA and NFL. *Journal of Sport & Social Issues, 33*, 39–58.

de Haan, D., Osborne, A., & Sherry, E. (2015). Satire or send-up? Paddy power and blind football: A case for managing public relations for disability sport. *Communication & Sport, 3*, 411–433.

Disch, L. J., & Kane, M. J. (2000). When a looker is really a bitch: Lisa Olson, sport, and the heterosexual matrix. In S. Birrell & M. G. McDonald (Eds.), *Reading sport: Critical essays on power and representation* (pp. 108–143). Boston, MA: Northeastern University Press.

Duncan, M. C. (2001). The sociology of ability and disability in physical activity. *Sociology of Sport Journal*, 18, 1–4.

Fagan, K. (2013, May 27). Griner: No talking sexuality at Baylor. *ESPN.com*. Retrieved from http://espn.go.com/wnba/story/_/id/9289080/brittney-griner-says-baylor-coach-kim-mulkey-told-players-keep-quiet-sexuality

Fenske, M. (2007). *Tattoos in American visual culture*. New York, NY: Palgrave Macmillan.

Giardina, M. D. (2003). "Bending it like Beckham" in the global popular. *Journal of Sport & Social Issues, 27*, 65–82.

Grano, D. A. (2007). Ritual disorder and the contractual morality of sport: A case study in race, class, and agreement. *Rhetoric & Public Affairs, 10*, 445–474.

Griffin, R. A., & Calafell, B. M. (2011). Control, discipline, and punish: Black masculinity and (in)visible whiteness in the NBA. In M. G. Lacy & K. A. Ono (Eds.), *Critical rhetorics of race* (pp. 117–136). New York: New York University Press.

Houck, D. W. (2006a). Sporting bodies. In A. A. Raney & J. Bryant (Eds.), *Handbook of sports and media* (pp. 543–558). Mahwah, NJ: Lawrence Erlbaum.

Houck, D. W. (2006b). Crouching Tiger, hidden blackness: Tiger Woods and the disappearance of race. In A. A. Raney & J. Bryant (Eds.), *Handbook of sports and media* (pp. 469–484). Mahwah, NJ: Lawrence Erlbaum.

Iannotta, J. G., & Kane, M. J. (2002). Sexual stories as resistance narratives in women's sports: Reconceptualizing identity performance. *Sociology of Sport Journal, 19*, 347–369.

Kahrl, C. (2016, May 9). Christina Kahrl on clearing the way for the next Chris Mosier. *ESPN.com*. Retrieved from http://espn.go.com/sports/endurance/story/_/id/16560259/chris-mosier-first-trans-athlete-compete-ioc-back-championship-leading-way-other-trans-athletes

Khan, A. I. (2016). Michael Sam, Jackie Robinson, and the politics of respectability. *Communication & Sport*, online first. doi: 10.1177/2167479515616407

Lindemann, K., & Cherney, J. L. (2008). Communicating in and through 'murderball': Masculinity and disability in wheelchair rugby. *Western Journal of Communication, 72*, 107–125.

Lord, M. A., & Lord, Jr., W. J. (2000). Effects of the Special Olympics of Texas *Athletes for Outreach* program on communication competence among individuals with mental retardation. *Communication Education, 49*, 267–283.

Markazi, A. (2015, July 30). July has been a significant, memorable month for women in sports. *ESPN.com*. Retrieved from http://espn.go.com/espnw/news-commentary/article/13333138/uswnt-becky-hammon-jen-welter-help-make-july-historic-women-sports

Martin, J., & Tatum, S. (2015, July 9). Court rules against Redskins trademark registration. *CNN.com*. Retrieved from http://www.cnn.com/2015/07/08/politics/redskins-lose-trademark-battle-in-federal-court

Miller, J. B. (1999). "Indians," "Braves," and "Redskins." A performative struggle for control of an image. *Quarterly Journal of Speech, 85*, 188–202.

Miller, S. (2010). Making the boys cry: The performative dimensions of fluid gender. *Text and Performance Quarterly, 30*, 163–182.

Mozisek, K. D. (2013). *Throwing like a girl! Constituting citizenship for women and girls through the American pastime*. (Doctoral dissertation).

Palmer, T. (2014, September 30). NFL says Chiefs' Husain Abdullah shouldn't have been penalized for slide, prayer in end zone. *Kansas City Star*. Retrieved from http://www.kansascity.com/sports/nfl/kansas-city-chiefs/article2324330.html

Patterson, R., & Corning, G. (1997). Researching the body: An annotated bibliography for rhetoric. *Rhetoric Society Quarterly, 27*, 5–29.

Postema, P. (1992). *You've gotta have balls to make it in this league*. New York, NY: Simon & Schuster.

Rubin, H. A., & Shapiro, D. A. (Directors), & Mandel, J. V., Shapiro, D. A. (Producers). (2005). *Murderball* [Motion picture]. United States: ThinkFilm.

Schultz, J. (2005). Reading the catsuit: Serena Williams and the production of blackness at the 2002 U.S. Open. *Journal of Sport & Social Issues, 29*, 338–357.

Sloop, J. M. (2005). Riding in cars between men. *Communication and Critical/Cultural Studies, 2*, 191–213.

Sloop, J. M. (2012). "This is not natural": Caster Semenya's gender threats. *Critical Studies in Media Communication, 29*, 81–96.

Smith, L. R. (2015). The blade runner: The discourses surrounding Oscar Pistorius in the 2012 Olympics and Paralympics. *Communication & Sport, 3*, 390–410.

Wood, J. T. (2009). *Gendered lives: Communication, gender, and culture* (8th ed.). Boston, MA: Wadsworth.

Young, S. L. (2015). Running like a man, sitting like a girl: Visual enthymeme and the case of Caster Semenya. *Women's Studies in Communication, 38*, 331–350.

Chapter 10

Armour, N. (2015). In 6th grade and being primed for the pros. *Detroit Free Press*. Retrieved from http://www.freep.com/story/sports/2015/02/27/this-boy-is-in-6th-grade-and-being-primed-for-the-pros/24106481

Arthur-Banning, S., Wells, M. S., Baker, B. L., & Hegreness, R. (2008). Parents behaving badly? The relationship between the sportsmanship behaviors of adults and athletes in youth basketball games. *Journal of Sport Behavior, 32*, 3–18.

Baxter-Jones, A. D., & Maffulli, N. (2003). Parental influence on sport participation in elite young athletes. *Journal of Sports Medicine and Physical Fitness, 43*(2), 250–255.

Bigelow, B. (2005). *Youth sports survey results*. Retrieved from http://www.bobbigelow.com/documents

Blom, L. C., & Drane, D. (2009). Parents' sideline comments: Exploring the reality of a growing issue.

Online Journal of Sport Psychology, 10(3), 12.

Brown, L. (April 28, 2016). Canadian high school basketball star claims he did not know his real age. *Larry Brown Sports*. Retrieved from http://www.msn.com/en-ae/news/offbeat/canadian-high-school-basketball-star-claims-he-did-not-know-his-real-age/ar-BBsmhNz

Brustad, R. J. (1988). Affective outcomes in competitive youth sport: The influence of intrapersonal and socialization factors. *Journal of Sport & Exercise Psychology, 10*, 307–321.

Butterfield, F. (2000, July 11). A fatality, parental violence and youth sports. *The New York Times*, A14.

Cho, M., (2014). The influence of family's participation in recreational sports on its resilience and communication facilitation. *Journal of Exercise Rehabilitation, 10*(5), 313–318.

Dorsch, T. E., Smith, A. L., & McDonough, M. H. (2009). Parents' perceptions of child-to-parent socialization in organized youth sports. *Journal of Sport and Exercise Psychology, 31*, 444–468.

Feller, B. (2014, August 15). There's no off in this season: Team sports are taking over kids' lives. *The New York Times*. Retrieved from http://www.nytimes.com/2014/08/17/fashion/team-sports-are-taking-over-kids-lives.html

Glanville, D. (2012). The high cost of youth sports: Nothing opens parent's checkbook like guilt and fear, as a new book on the big business of kids' sports shows. *Time*. Retrieved from http://ideas.time.com/2012/03/21/the-high-cost-of-youth-sports

Gregory, S. (2013). A national basketball championship—For second graders. *Time*. Retrieved from http://keepingscores.blogs.time.com/2013/07/11 /a-national-basketball-championship-for-second-graders

Hardy, L. L., Kelly, B., Chapman, K., King, L., & Farrell, L. (2010). Parental perceptions of barriers to children's participation in organized sport in Australia. *Journal of Pediatrics and Child Health, 46*, 197–203.

Heinzmann, G. S. (2002, March). Parental violence in youth sports: Facts, myths and videotapes. *Park & Recreation, 37*, 66–73.

Henson, S. (2012). What makes a nightmare sports parent—And what makes a great one. *The Ticket*. Retrieved from http://www.thepostgame.com/blog/more-family-fun/201202/what-makes-nightmare-sports

Kane, R. (2014). Play dates: Scripps' Youthletic site aims to connect kids with sports organizations. *Editor & Publisher, 147*, 12–13.

Kassing, J., Billings, A. C., Brown, R., Halone, K. K., Harrison, K., Krizek, B., . . . Turman, P. D. (2004). Enacting, (re)producing, consuming, and organizing sport: Communication in the community of sport. *Communication Yearbook, 28*, 373–409.

Lavoi, N. M., & Stellino, M. B. (2008). The relation between perceived parent-created sport climate and competitive male youth hockey players' good and poor sport behavior. *Journal of Psychology, 142*, 471–496.

Leff, S. S., & Hoyle, R. H. (1995). Young athletes' perceptions of parental support and pressure. *Journal of Youth & Adolescence, 24*, 187–203.

Lord, M. (2000, May 15). When cheers turn into jeers. *U.S. News & World Report, 128*, 52.

Mach, F. (1994). Defusing parent–coach dissidence. *Scholastic Coach, 63*(10), 5–6.

McCullagh, P., Matzkanin, K. T., Shaw, S. D., & Maldonado, M. (1993). Motivation for participation in physical activity: A comparison of parent–child perceived competencies and participation motives. *Pediatric Exercise Science, 5,* 224–233.

McMillian, R., McIsaac, M., & Janssen, I. (2016). Family structure as a correlate of organized sport participation among youth. *PLoS One, 11,* 1–12.

Mead, G. H. (1934). *Mind, self, & society, from the standpoint of a social behaviorist.* Chicago, IL: University of Chicago Press.

Meân, L. J., & Kassing, J. W. (2007). Identities at youth sporting events: A critical discourse analysis. *International Journal of Sport Communication, 1,* 42–66.

Minnesota Amateur Sports Commission. (2015). *Youth sports statistics.* Retrieved from http://www.statisticbrain.com/youth-sports-statistics

Na, J. (2015). Parents' perceptions of their children's experiences in physical education and youth sport. *The Physical Educator, 72,* 139–167.

Roberts, G. C., Treasure, D. C., & Hall, H. K. (1994). Parental goal orientations and beliefs about the competitive sports experience of their child. *Journal of Social Psychology, 24,* 631–645.

Segura, M. (2013). The beautiful game, turned ugly. *Sport Illustrated, 118*(2), 58–62.

Starcher, S. C. (2015). Memorable messages from fathers to children through sports: Perspectives from sons and daughters. *Communication Quarterly, 63,* 204–220.

Trussell, D. E., & Shaw, S. M. (2012). Organized youth sport and parenting in public and private spaces. *Leisure Studies, 34,* 377–394.

Turman, P. (2007). Parental sport involvement: Parental influence to encourage young athlete continued sport participation. *Journal of Family Communication, 7,* 151–175.

Vandenabeele, R. (2004, August). Save our sportsmanship. *Coach & Athletic Director,* p. 72.

Wagner, M., Jones, T., & Riepenhoff, J. (2010). Children may be vulnerable in $5 billion youth-sports industry. *The Columbus Dispatch.* Retrieved from http://www.dispatch.com/content/stories/local/2010/08/29/"children-may-be-vulnerable-in-5-billion-youth-sports-industry.html

Wojciechowski, G. (February 8, 2008). College 'recruit' lie, a tale gone horribly wrong. *ESPN.Com.* Retrieved from http://sports.espn.go.com/ncaa/recruiting/football/news/story?id=3234302

Wood, J. T. (1996). She says/he says: Communication, caring, and conflict in heterosexual relationships. In Julia T. Wood (Ed.), *Gendered relationships* (pp. 149–162). Mountain View, CA: Mayfield.

Chapter 11

Andersen, J. F. (1979). Teacher immediacy: A predictor of teaching effectiveness. In D. Nimmo (Ed.), *Communication Yearbook 3* (pp. 543–559). New Brunswick, NJ: Transaction.

Austin, M. (2011). Just don't call him coach. *Sports Illustrated, 115*(20), 15–16.

Blidner, R. (2014, November 17). Calif. high school basketball coach sues parent for $1 million in libel lawsuit. *New York Daily News.*

Retrieved from http://www.nydailynews.com/sports/high-school/calif-high-school-coach-sues-parent-1-million-article-1.2014094

Butterworth, M. (2013). Coaches gone wild: Media, masculinity, and morality in big-time college football. In L. A. Werner (Ed.), *Fallen sports heroes, media and celebrity culture* (pp. 284–297). New York, NY: Peter Lang.

Chelladurai, P., & Saleh, S. D. (1978). Preferred leadership in sports. *Canadian Journal of Applied Sport Science, 3,* 85–92.

Cote, J. (1999). The influence of family in sports: A review. *International Journal of Sport Psychology, 21,* 328–354.

Craig, S., & Lynn, O. (2011). Behavioral characteristics of "favorite" coaches: Implications for coach education. *Physical Educator, 68*(2), 90–98.

Cranmer, G. A., Anzur, C. K., & Sollitto, M. (2016). Memorable messages of social support that former high school athletes received from their head coaches. *Communication & Sport, 4*(1), 1–18

Cranmer G., A., & Goodboy, A. K. (2015). Power play: Coach power use and athletes' communicative evaluations and responses. *Western Journal of Communication, 79,* 614–633.

Cranmer, G. A., & Sollitto, M. (2015). Sport support: Received social support as a predictor of athlete satisfaction. *Communication Research Reports, 32,* 253–264.

Dimec, T., & Kajtna, T. (2009). Psychological characteristics of younger and older coaches. *Kinesiology, 41,* 172–180.

Felton, L., & Jowett, S. (2013). "What do coaches do" and "how do they relate?": Their effects on athletes' psychological needs and functioning. *Scandinavian Journal of Medicine & Science in Sports, 23,* 130–139.

Gallmeier, C. P. (1987). Putting on the game face: The staging of emotions in professional hockey. *Sociology of Sport Journal, 4,* 347–362.

Hamilton, A. (2011, August). Dan Gable: Hall of famer is retired now, but he's left a lasting legacy as one of the best wrestlers and coaches in history. *USA Wrestling, 39*(5), 6–9.

Hastie, P. A. (1999). An instrument for recording coaches' comments and instructions during time-outs. *Journal of Sport Behavior, 22,* 467–478.

Jowett, S. (2007). Interdependence analysis and the 3 + 1C's in the coach–athlete relationship. In S. Jowett & D. Larallce (Eds.), *Social psychology in sport* (pp. 15–27). Champaign, IL: Human Kinetics.

Jowett, S. (2009). Validating coach–athlete relationship measures with the nomological network. *Measurement in Physical Education and Exercise Science, 13,* 34–51.

Kassing, J. W., & Anderson, R. L. (2014). Contradicting coach or grumbling to teammates: Exploring dissent expression in the coach-athlete relationship. *Communication & Sport, 2*(2), 172–185.

Katzowitz, J. (2014. September 17). Adrian Peterson's high school coach says he used corporal punishment. *CBS Sports.* Retrieved from http://www.cbssports.com/nfl/eye-on-football/24713131/adrian-petersons-high-school-coach-says-he-used-corporal-punishment

Kirk, D., & MacPhail, A. (2003). Social positioning and the construction of a youth sports club. *International*

Review for the Sociology of Sport, 38, 23–45.

Kruse, N. W. (1981). Apologia in team sport. *Quarterly Journal of Speech, 67,* 270–283.

Mach, F. (1994). Defusing parent–coach dissidence. *Scholastic Coach, 63*(10), 5–6.

Martin, M. M., Rocca, K. A., Cayanus, J. L., & Weber, K. (2009). Relationship between coaches use of behavior alteration techniques and verbal aggression on athletes' motivation and affect. *Journal of Sport Behavior, 32,* 227–241.

Mazer, J. P., Barnes, K., Grevious, A., & Boger, C. (2013). Coach verbal aggression: A case study examining effects of athlete motivation and perceptions of coach credibility. *International Journal of Sport Communication, 6*(2), 2013, 203–213.

Masin, H. L. (2007, September). Remember the "only thing"? *Coach & Athletic Director,* p. 5.

Mehrabian, A. (1967). Attitudes inferred from non-immediacy of verbal communications. *Journal of Verbal Learning and Verbal Behavior, 6,* 294–295.

Naylor, A. H. (2007). The coach's dilemma: Balancing playing to win and player development. *Journal of Education, 187,* 31–48.

Roberts, G. C. (1984). Achievement motivation in children's sport. In J. G. Nicholls (Ed.), *Advances in motivation and achievement: Vol. 3* (pp. 251–281). Greenwich, CT: JAI Press.

Sagar, S. S., & Jowett, S. (2012). Communicative acts in coach-athlete interactions: When losing competitions and when making mistakes in training. *Western Journal of Communication, 76,* 148–174.

Solomon, G. B., DiMarco, A. M., Ohlson, C. J., & Reece, S. D. (1998). Expectations and coaching experience: Is more better? *Journal of Sport Behavior, 21,* 444–455.

Turman, P. D. (2005). Coaches' use of anticipatory and counterfactual regret messages during competition. *Journal of Applied Communication Research, 33,* 116–138.

Turman, P. (2007). Coach regret messages: The influence of athlete sex, context, and performance on high school basketball coaches' use of regret messages during competition. *Communication Education, 56,* 333–353.

Turman, P. (2008). Coaches' immediacy behaviors as predictors of athletes' perceptions of satisfaction and team cohesion. *Western Journal of Communication, 72,* 162–179.

Turman, P., & Schrodt, P. (2004). Coaching as an instructional communication context: Relationships among coaches' leadership behaviors and athletes' affective learning. *Communication Research Reports, 21,* 130–143.

Turman, P., Zimmerman, A., & Dobesh, B. (2009). Parent-talk and sport participation: Interaction between parents, children, and coaches regarding level of play in sports. In T. Socha & G. Stamp (Eds.), *Parents and children communicating with society: Managing relationships outside of home* (pp. 171–188). New York, NY: Lawrence Erlbaum.

Vella, S., Oades, L., & Crowe, T. (2011). The role of coach in facilitating positive youth development: Moving from theory to practice. *Journal of Applied Sport Psychology, 22,* 33–48.

Chapter 12

Aden, R. (2007). *Huskerville: A story of Nebraska football, fans, and the power of place.* Minneapolis, MN: McFarland.

Anderson, E., McCormack, M., & Lee, H. (2012). Male team sport hazing initiations in a culture of decreasing homohysteria. *Journal of Adolescent Research, 27,* 427–448.

Backer, M. D., Boen, F., Cuyper, B. D., & Brock, G. V. (2015). A team fares well with a fair coach. Predictors of social loafing in interactive female sport teams. *Scandinavian Journal of Medicine and Science in Sports, 25,* 897–908.

Bormann, E. (1996). *Small group communication: Theory and practice.* Edina, MN: Burgess.

Brennan, C. (November 8, 2013). NFL bullying saga not so cut-and-dried. *USA Today Sports.* Retrieved from http://www.usatoday.com/story/sports/nfl/2013/11/07/christine-brennan-nfl-bullying-miami-dolphins/3470541

Bruner, M. W., Eys, M., Blair Evans, M., & Wilson, K. (2015). Interdependence and social identity in youth sport teams. *Journal of Applied Sport Psychology, 27,* 351–358.

Burtis, J. O., & Turman, P. D. (2009). *Leadership communication as citizenship.* Thousand Oaks, CA: Sage.

Cronin, L. D., Arthur, C. A., Hardy, J., & Callow, N. (2015). Transformational leadership and task cohesion in sport: The mediating role of inside sacrifice. *Journal of Sport & Exercise Psychology, 37,* 23–36.

Crozier, A. J., Loughead, T. M., & Munroe-Chandler, K. J. (2013). Examining the benefits of athlete leaders in sport. *Journal of Sport Behavior, 26,* 346–363.

Dupuis, M., Bloom, G. A., & Loughead, T. M. (2006). Team captains' perceptions of athlete leadership. *Journal of Sport Behavior, 29,* 60–78.

French, J. R., & Raven, B. (1959). The bases of social power. In D. Cartwright (Ed.), *Studies in social power* (pp. 150–167). Ann Arbor: University of Michigan Press.

Grandzol, C. Perlis, S., & Draina, L. (2010). Leadership development of team captains in collegiate varsity athletics. *Journal of College Student Development, 51,* 403–418.

Hoigaard, R., Tofteland, I., & Ommundsen, Y. (2006). The effect of team cohesion on social loafing in relay teams. *International Journal of Applied Sports Sciences, 19,* 59–73.

Hoover, N. C. (1999). *National survey of sports teams.* Alfred, NY: Alfred University. Retrieved from http://www.alfred.edu/sports_hazing

Jones, I. (2000). A model of serious leisure identification: The case of football fandom. *Leisure Studies, 19,* 283–298.

Karmel, J. (2009). The top 10 sports rivalries of all time. *Bleacher Buzz.* Retrieved from http://bleacherreport.com/articles/119042-top-10-sports-rivalries/page/11

Krzysztof, T., & Craig, S. (2010). Defining high school hazing: Control through clarity. *Physical Educators, 67,* 204–209.

Latané, B., Williams, K., & Harkins, S. (1979). Many hands make light the work: The causes and consequences of social loafing. *Journal of Personality and Social Psychology, 37,* 822–832.

Maltz, D. N., & Borker, R. (1982). A cultural approach to male–female miscommunication. In J. J. Gumpertz (Ed.), *Language and social identity* (pp. 196–216). New York, NY: Cambridge University Press.

Martin, K. A. (2002). Development and validation of the coaching staff cohesion scale. *Measurement in Physical Education and Exercise Science, 6,* 23–42.

Merrill, E. (2013, September 17). What is Pelini's place among fans? *ESPN*. Retrieved from http://espn.go.com/college-football/story/_/id/9685394/how-do-nebraska-fans-feel-bo-pelini-recent-behavior

Messner, M. (1990). Boyhood, organized sports, and the construction of masculinities. *Journal of Contemporary Ethnography, 18,* 416–444.

Messner, M. (2011). Gender ideologies, youth sports, and the production of sport essentialism. *Sociology of Sport Journal, 28,* 151–170.

Munroe, K., Estabrooks, P., Dennis, P., & Carron, A. (1999). A phenomenological analysis of group norms in sport teams. *Sport Psychologist, 13,* 171–182.

Rains, P. (1984). The production of fairness: Officiating in the National Hockey League. *Sociology of Sport Journal, 1,* 150–162.

Ringelmann, M. (1913). Research on animate sources of power: The work of man. *Annales de l'Institut National Agronomique, 12,* 1–40.

Schelling-Kamphoff, C., & Huddleston, S. (1999). *Jealousy in collegiate track and field athletes.* Proceedings of the Association for the Advancement of Applied Sport Psychology annual convention, Banff, Alberta, Canada.

Seyed-Mahmoud, A., & Kwasi, K. (2009). A quantitative assessment of factors affecting college sport team unity. *College Student Journal, 43,* 294–303.

Tannen, D. (1990). *You just don't understand: Women and men in conversation.* New York, NY: Ballantine.

Tauber, S., & Sassenberg, K. (2012). The impact of identification on adherence to group norms in team sports. Who is going the extra mile? *Group Dynamics: Theory, Research & Practice, 16,* 231–240.

Turman, P. (2003). Coaches and cohesion: The impact of coaching techniques on team cohesion in the small group sport setting. *Journal of Sport Behavior, 26*(1), 86–104.

Van Raalte, J. L., Cornelius, A. E., Linder, D., E., & Brewer, B. W. (2007). The relationship between hazing and team cohesion. *Journal of Sport Behavior, 30,* 491–507.

Wann, D. L. (2006). Examining the potential causal relationship between sport team identification and psychological well-being. *Journal of Sport Behavior, 29,* 79–95.

Wann, D. L., Keenan, B., & Page, L. (2009). Testing the team identification–social psychology health model: Examining non-marquee sports, seasonal differences, and multiple teams. *Journal of Sport Behavior, 32,* 112–124.

Widmeyer, W. N., Carron, A. V., & Brawley, L. R. (1993). Group cohesion in sport and exercise. In R. N. Singer, M. Murphey, & L. K. Tennant (Eds.), *Handbook of research on sport psychology* (pp. 672–692). New York, NY: Macmillan.

Wood, J. T. (1996). She says/he says: Communication, caring, and conflict in heterosexual relationships. In Julia T. Wood (Ed.), *Gendered relationships* (pp. 149–162). Mountain View, CA: Mayfield.

Chapter 13

Benoit, W. L. (1995). *Accounts, excuses, and apologies: A theory of image restoration strategies*. Albany: State University of New York Press.

Benoit, W. L. (2013). Tiger Woods's image repair: Could he hit one out of the rough? In J. Blaney, L. R. Lippert, &

J. C. Smith (Eds.), *Repairing the athlete's image: Studies in sport image restoration* (pp. 89–96). Boulder, CO: Lexington Books.

Benoit, W. L., & Hanczor, R. S. (1994). The Tonya Harding controversy: An analysis of image restoration strategies. *Communication Quarterly, 42,* 416–433.

Benoit, W. L., & McHale, J. (1999). "Just the facts, ma'am": Starr's image repair discourse viewed in 20/20. *Communication Quarterly, 47,* 265–280.

Billings, A. C. (2008). *Olympic media: Inside the biggest show on television.* London, UK: Routledge.

Brazeal, L. (2008). The image repair strategies of Terrell Owens. *Public Relations Review, 34,* 145–150.

Brazeal, L. (2013). Belated remorse: Serena Williams's image repair rhetoric at the 2009 U. S. Open. In J. R. Blaney, L. R. Lippert, & J. S. Smith (Eds.), *Repairing the athlete's image: Studies in sports image restoration* (pp. 239–252). Lanham, MD: Lexington.

Brown, K. A., Billings, A. C., Mastro, D., & Brown-Devlin, N. (2015). Changing the image repair equation impact of race and gender on sport-related transgressions. *Journalism & Mass Communication Quarterly, 92*(2), 487–506.

Brown, K., Dickhaus, J., & Long, M. (2012). "The Decision" and LeBron James: An empirical examination of image repair in sports. *Journal of Sports Media, 7,* 149–167.

Grano, D. A. (2014). Michael Vick's "Genuine Remorse" and problems of public forgiveness. *Quarterly Journal of Speech, 100,* 81–104.

Harris, C. (1990). Caught in a crisis. *College Athletic Management, 2*(6), 30–34.

Jerome, A., M. (2013). A death, a family feud, and a merger: The image repair of Teresa Earnhardt and Dale Earnhardt, Inc. In J. R. Blaney, L. R. Lippert, & J. S. Smith (Eds.), *Repairing the athlete's image: Studies in sports image restoration* (pp. 239–252). Lanham, MD: Lexington.

Kihl, L., & Richardson, T. (2009). "Fixing the mess": A grounded theory of a men's basketball coaching staff's suffering as a result of academic corruption. *Journal of Sport Management, 23,* 278–304.

Kinkhabwala, A. (2007, April 23). The righteous Scarlet Knights. *Sports Illustrated, 106*(17), 16–18.

Kruse, N. W. (1981). *Apologia* in team sport. *Quarterly Journal of Speech, 67,* 270–283.

McDorman, T. (2003). The rhetorical resurgence of Pete Rose: A second chance apologia. In R. S. Brown & D. O'Rourke (Eds.), *Case studies in sport communication* (pp. 1–26). Westport, CT: Praeger.

Meng, J., & Pan, P. L. (2013). Revisiting image-restoration strategies: An integrated case study of three athlete sex scandals in sports news. *International Journal of Sport Communication, 6,* 87–100.

Mullen, L. J., & Mazzocco, D. W. (2000). Coaches, drama, and technology: Mediation of Super Bowl broadcasts from 1969 to 1997. *Critical Studies in Media Communication, 17,* 347–363.

Nelson, J. (1984). The defense of Billie Jean King. *Western Journal of Communication, 48,* 92–102.

Rogers, R. P. (2003). *Adultery, sexual assault, and the management of sports imagery: Kobe Bryant and image repair.* Paper presented at the annual meeting of the National Communication Association, Miami Beach, FL.

Ryan, H. R. (1982). *Kategoria* and *apologia*: On their rhetorical criticism as a speech set. *Quarterly Journal of Speech, 68,* 256–261.

Smith, J. (2007). *Steroids in Major League Baseball: Image restoration strategies of the players accused of steroid use.* Conference Paper—National Communication Association, 1–26.

Smith, J. S. (2013). Bad newz kennels: Michael Vick and dogfighting. In J. R. Blaney, L. R. Lippert & J. S. Smith (Eds.), *Repairing the athlete's image: Studies in sports image restoration* (pp. 239–252). Lanham, MD: Lexington.

Stein, K. A. (2006). *Apologia, antapologia* and the 1960 Soviet U-2 spy plane incident. *Communication Studies, 59,* 19–34.

Stein, K., Turman, P., & Barton, M. (2013). In the dark at Texas Tech: News coverage involving the image repair discourse of Mike Leach and Adam James. In J. Blaney, L. R. Lippert, & J. C. Smith (Eds.), *Repairing the athlete's image: Studies in sport image restoration* (pp. 203–222). Boulder, CO: Lexington Books.

Torres, C. R., & McLaughlin, D. W. (2003). "Indigestion?" An apology for ties. *Journal of the Philosophy of Sport, 30,* 144–158.

Turman, P., Stein, K., & Barton, M. (2008). Understanding the voice of the fan: *Apologia, antapologia,* and the 2006 World Cup controversy. In L. W. Hugenberg, P. Haridakis, & A. Earnheart (Eds.), *Sports mania: Essays on fandom and the media in the 21st century* (pp. 86–102). Jefferson, NC: McFarland.

Utsler, M., & Epp, S. (2013). Image repair through TV: The Strategies of McGwire, Rodriguez and She. *Journal of Sports Media, 8,* 139–161.

Ware, B. L., & Linkugel, W. A. (1973). They spoke in defense of themselves: On the generic criticism of apologia. *Quarterly Journal of Speech, 50,* 273–283.

Zagacki, K. S., & Grano, D. (2005). Radio sports talk and the fantasies of sport. *Critical Studies in Media Communication, 22,* 45–63.

Chapter 14

Aden, R. C. (1995). Nostalgic communication as temporal escape: *When It Was a Game*'s re-construction of a baseball/ work community. *Western Journal of Communication, 59,* 20–38.

Andrews, D. L. (2006). Disneyization, Debord, and the integrated NBA spectacle. *Social Semiotics, 16,* 89–102.

Armfield, G. G., & McGuire, J. (2015). You've come a long way, baby. In J. McGuire, G. G. Armfield, & A. Earnheardt (Eds.), *The ESPN effect: Exploring the worldwide leader in sports* (pp. xiii-xvii). New York. NY: Peter Lang.

Boyd, J. (2000). Selling home: Corporate stadium names and the destruction of commemoration. *Journal of Applied Communication Research, 28,* 330–346.

Bryant, H. (2005). *Juicing the game: Drugs, power, and the fight for the soul of Major League Baseball.* New York, NY: Viking.

Burke, T., & Dickey, J. (2013, January 16). Manti Te'o's dead girlfriend, the most heartbreaking and inspirational story of the college football season, is a hoax. *Deadspin.com*. Retrieved from http://deadspin.com/manti-teos-dead-girlfriend-the-most-heartbreaking-an-5976517

Caplan, J. (2016, May 23). National reaction to Texas Rangers' proposed stadium: Huh? *Fort Worth Star-Telegram*. Retrieved from http://www.star-telegram.com/sports/mlb/texas-rangers/article79379487.html

Cowboys Stadium to be renamed AT&T Stadium. (2013, July 25). *USA Today*. Retrieved from http://www.usatoday.com/story/sports/nfl/cowboys/2013/07/25/cowboys-stadium-at-t-stadium/2586977

Dart, J. J. (2009). Blogging the 2006 FIFA World Cup finals. *Sociology of Sport Journal, 26*, 107–126.

Dear, W. (Director), & Smith, I., Roth, J., & Birnbaum, R. (Producers). (1994). *Angels in the outfield* [Motion picture]. United States: Buena Vista Pictures.

Duvall, S., & Guschwan, M. (2013). Commodifying global activism and racial unity during the 2010 FIFA World Cup. *Communication, Culture & Critique, 6*, 298–317.

Evans, D. M. (Director), & Burg, M., & Zarpas, C. (Producers). (1993). *The Sandlot* [Motion picture]. United States:20th Century Fox.

Goldberg, D. T. (1998). Call and response: Sports, talk radio, and the death of democracy. *Journal of Sport & Social Issues, 22*, 212–223.

Halone, K. K., & Billings, A. C. (2010). The temporal nature of racialized sport consumption. *American Behavioral Scientist, 53*, 1645–1668.

Isidore, C. (2013, July 26). New $444 million hockey arena is still a go in Detroit. *CNNMoney.com*. Retrieved from http://money.cnn.com/2013/07/26/news/economy/detroit-bankruptcy-arena/index.html

Jackson, S. (2013). Reflections on sport communication, advertising and promotional culture, commodification, and globalization. *Communication & Sport, 1*, 100–112.

Jhally, S. (1984). The spectacle of accumulation: Material and cultural factors in the evolution of the sports/media complex. *The Insurgent Sociologist, 12*, 41–57.

Kellner, D. (1996). Sport, media culture, and race—some reflections on Michael Jordan. *Sociology of Sport Journal, 13*, 458–467.

Kercheval, N., & Novy-Williams, E. (2011, August 23). MetLife sets 25-year naming rights deal for Jets-Giants New Jersey stadium. *Bloomberg*. Retrieved August 12, 2013, from http://www.bloomberg.com/news/2011-08-23/metlife-sets-25-year-naming-rights-deal-for-jets-giants-new-jersey-stadium.html

Kidd, B. (2013). The Olympic movement and the sports-media complex. *Sport in Society, 16*, 439–448.

King, S. (2006). *Pink ribbons, inc.: Breast cancer and the politics of philanthropy*. Minneapolis: University of Minnesota Press.

Lane, J. (2007). *Under the boards: The cultural revolution in basketball*. Lincoln: University of Nebraska Press.

McAllister, M. P. (1998). College bowl sponsorship and the increased commercialization of amateur sports. *Critical Studies in Mass Communication, 15*, 357–381.

McAllister, M. P. (2010). Hypercommercialism, televisuality, and the changing nature of college sports sponsorship. *American Behavioral Scientist, 53*, 1476–1491.

McCarthy, M. (2012, May 22). First look: Inside Brooklyn Nets new $1 billion arena. *USA Today*. Retrieved from http://content.usatoday.com/communities/gameon/post/2012/05/first-look-inside-the-brooklyn-nets-new-arena-barclays-center-nba-bruce-ratner-jay-z/1#.UglRJpK1H6M

McChesney, R. W. (1989). Media made sport: A history of sports coverage in the United States. In L. A. Wenner (Ed.), *Media, sport, and society* (pp. 49–67). Newbury Park, CA: Sage.

Meân, L., Kassing, J. W., & Sanderson, J. (2010). The making of an epic (American) hero fighting for justice: Commodification, consumption, and intertextuality in the Floyd Landis defense campaign. *American Behavioral Scientist, 53*, 1590–1609.

Meltzer, M. (2015, March 2). Braves complex to cost $1.1 billion. *Atlanta Business Chronicle*. Retrieved from http://www.bizjournals.com/atlanta/news/2015/03/02/braves-complex-to-cost-1-1-billion.html

Moor, L. (2007). Sport and commodification: A reflection on key concepts. *Journal of Sport & Social Issues, 31*, 128–142.

Pegoraro, A., Ayer, S. M., & O'Reilly, N. J. (2010). Consumer consumption and advertising through sport. *American Behavioral Scientist, 53*, 1454–1475.

Real, M. (2013). Reflections on communication and sport: On spectacle and mega-events. *Communication & Sport, 1*, 30–42.

Rhoden, W. C. (2006). *Forty million dollar slaves: The rise, fall, and redemption of the black athlete*. New York, NY: Crown.

Ritzer, G., & Stillman, T. (2001). The postmodern ballpark as a leisure setting: Enchantment and simulated de-McDonaldization. *Leisure Sciences, 23*, 99–113.

Robinson, P. A. (Director), & Gordon, L., Gordon, C. (Producers). (1989). *Field of dreams* [Motion picture]. United States: Universal Pictures.

Roche, M. (2000). *Mega-events and modernity*. London, UK: Routledge.

Rosensweig, D. (2005). *Retro ball parks: Instant history, baseball, and the new American city*. Knoxville: University of Tennessee Press.

Sandomir, R., & Miller, J. A. (2013, January 22). As ESPN debated, Manti Te'o story slipped away. *New York Times*. Retrieved from http://www.nytimes.com/2013/01/23/sports/ncaafootball/as-debate-raged-at-espn-manti-teo-story-slipped-from-its-hands.html?_r=0

Scheinman, A. (Director), & Nicolaides, S., Bergman, N., & Lobell, M. (Producers). (1993). *Little big league* [Motion picture]. United States: Columbia Pictures.

Smith, R. (1988). *Sports and freedom: The rise of big-time college athletics*. New York, NY: Oxford University Press.

Sobchack, V. (1997). Baseball in the post-American cinema, or life in the minor leagues. In A. Baker & T. Boyd (Eds.), *Out of bounds: Sports, media, and the politics of identity* (pp. 175–197). Bloomington: Indiana University Press.

Sperber, M. (2001). *Beer and circus: How big-time college sports is crippling undergraduate education*. New York, NY: Holt.

Springwood, C. F. (1996). *Cooperstown to Dyersville: A geography of baseball nostalgia*. Boulder, CO: Westview Press.

Staton, D. (2015). Lipsyte, the league, and the "leader." In J. McGuire, G. G. Armfield, & A. Earnheardt (Eds.), *The ESPN effect: Exploring the worldwide leader in sports* (pp. 183–196). New York, NY: Peter Lang.

Stern, D. (Director), & Harper, R. (Producer). (1993). *Rookie of the year* [Motion picture]. United States: 20th Century Fox.

Team marketing report: 2016. (2016). *Team Marketing Research*. Retrieved from https://www.teammarketing.com/public/uploadedPDFs/MLB-FCI-2016.pdf

Thibodeau, I. (2016, March 18). Crews start work on roof at new Red Wings arena in Detroit. *MLive.com*. Retrieved from http://www.mlive.com/business/detroit/index.ssf/2016/03/crews_start_on_roof_at_new_red.html

Thompson, W. (2009). Yankee Stadium's legends suite was sparsely populated at times this season—a sign of what greed does to loyalty. *Outside the Lines*. Retrieved from http://sports.espn.go.com/espn/eticket/story?page=091005yankeestickets

Trumpbour, R. C. (2007). *The new cathedrals: Politics and media in the history of stadium construction*. Syracuse, NY: Syracuse University Press.

Wenner, L. A. (2004). Recovering (from) Janet Jackson's breast: Ethics and the nexus of media, sports, and management. *Journal of Sport Management, 18*, 315–334.

Wenner, L. A. (2010). Sport, communication, and the culture of consumption: On language and Identity. *American Behavioral Scientist, 53*, 1571–1573.

Wenner, L. A. (2013). The mediasport interpellation: Gender, fanship, and consumer culture. *Sociology of Sport Journal, 30*, 83–103.

Wojnarowski, A. (2011, December 24). Jordan's shadow hangs over new NBA season. *Yahoo!Sports*. Retrieved from http://sports.yahoo.com/nba/news?slug=aw-wojnarowski_michael_jordan_nba_2011-12_season_122411

Zirin, D. (2011, March 16). Slaves to the game? Adrian Peterson and the "s" word. *The Nation*. Retrieved from https://www.thenation.com/article/slaves-game-adrian-peterson-and-s-word

Chapter 15

American Gaming Association.(2012). *Fact sheet*. Retrieved from http://www.americangaming.org/industryresources/research/fact-sheets/sports wagering

Anderson, C. A., & Carnagey, N. L. (2009). Causal effects of violent sports video games on aggression: Is it competitiveness or violent content? *Journal of Experimental Social Psychology, 45*, 731–739.

Bernhard, B. J., & Earle, V. H. (2005). Gambling in a fantasy world: An exploratory study of rotisserie baseball games. *UNLV Gaming Research & Review Journal, 9*(1), 29–42.

Berkowitz, S. (2016, Mar. 31). Federal judge: NCAA must pay $42.3 million in O'Bannon anti-trust case. *USA Today*. Retrieved fromhttp://www.usatoday.com/story/sports/college/2016/03/31/federal-judge-ncaa-must-pay-423-million-obannon-anti-trust-case/82493298

Billings, A.C., & Ruihley, B.J. (2013).Why we watch, why we play: The relationship between fantasy sport and fandom motivations. *Mass Communication & Society, 16*(1), 5–25.

Billings, A. C., & Ruihley, B. J. (2014). *The fantasy sport industry: Games within games*. London, UK: Routledge.

Billings, A. C., Ruihley, B. J., & Yang, Y. (2018, in press). Fantasy gaming on steroids?: Contrastingperce ptions of traditional and daily fantasy sport participants. *Communication & Sport*.

Bolitho, Z. C. (2006). When fantasy meets the courtroom: An examination of the intellectual property issues surrounding the burgeoning fantasy sports industry. *The Ohio State Law Journal, 67*(4), 911–960.

Brookey, R.A., & Oates, T.P. (2015). *Playing to win: Sports, video games, and the culture of play*. Bloomington: Indiana University Press.

Cianfrone, B. A., Zhang, J. J., Trail, G. T., & Lutz, R. J. (2008). Effectiveness of in-game advertisements in sport video games: An experimental inquiry on current gamers. *International Journal of Sport Communication, 1*(2), 195–218.

Crawford, G., & Gosling, V. (2009). More than a game: Sports-themed video games & player narratives. *Sociology of Sport Journal, 26*(1), 50–66.

Davis, N. W., & Duncan, M. C. (2006). Sports knowledge is power: Reinforcing masculine privilege through fantasy sport league participation. *Journal of Sport & Social Issues, 30*, 244–264.

Drayer, J., Shapiro, S., Dwyer, B., Morse, A., & White, J. (2010). The effects of fantasy football participation on NFL consumption: A qualitative analysis. *Sport Management Review, 13*, 129–141.

Fantasy Sports Trade Association. (2013). *Media kit*. Retrieved from fsta.org/mk/MediaKit.org

Fantasy Sports Trade Association. (2016). *Industry demographics*. Retrieved from http://fsta.org/research/industry-demographics

Farquhar, L. K., & Meeds, R. (2007). Types of fantasy sports users and their motivations. *Journal of Computer-Mediated Communication, 12*(4), article 4. Retrieved from http://jcmc.indiana.edu/v0112/issue4/farquhar.html

Felps, P. (2000, September 20). Fantasy sports players getting a big assist from the Internet. *The Dallas Morning News*. Retrieved from http://www.amarillo.com/stories/092300/tec_fantasysports.shtml

Fisher, E. (2015, Mar. 16). Daily pushes to continue growth streak. *Sport Business Journal*, p. 1.

Gaudiosi, J. (2015, Oct. 29). League of Legends video game championship is like the World Series and Super Bowl, combined. *Fortune*. Retrieved from http://fortune.com/2015/10/29/league-of-legends-video-game-championship

Gillentine, A., & Schulz, J. (2001). Marketing the fantasy football league: Utilization of simulation to enhance sport marketing concepts. *Journal of Marketing Education, 23*(3), 178–186.

Jones, J. M. (2008). One in six Americans gamble on sports. *Gallup poll*. Retrieved from www.gallup.com/poll/104086/one-six-americans-gamble-sports.aspx

Katz, D. (2012, October 3). New fantasy football law legalizes fantasy league prizes. Retrieved from http://blogs.findlaw.com/tarnished_twenty/2012/10/new-fantasy-football-law-legalizes-fantasy-league-prizes.html

Keating, P. (2012, July 10). Betting nation: How much sports gambling is going on out there?*ESPN: The Magazine,* p. 23.

Kim, Y. J., & Ross, S. D. (2006). An exploration of motives in sport video gaming. *International Journal of Sports Marketing and Sponsorship,8*(1), 34–46.

Kim, Y. J., Walsh, P., & Ross, S. D. (2008). An examination of the psychological and consumptive behaviors of sport video gamers. *Sport Marketing Quarterly, 17*(1), 44–53.

Kwak, D. H., Clavio, G. E., Eagleman, A. N., & Kim, K. T. (2010). Exploring the antecedents and consequences of personalizing sport video game experiences. *Sport Marketing Quarterly, 19*(4), 217–225.

Lefton, T., & Ourand, J. (2015, Apr. 3). ESPN agrees to buy stake in DraftKings. *Sports Business Daily.* Retrieved at: http://www.sportsbusinessdaily.com/SB-Blogs/On-The-Ground/2015/04/0403-ESPN-DraftKings.aspx

Lomax, R. G. (2006). Fantasy sports: History, game types, and research. In A. Raney & J. Bryant (Eds.), *Handbook of sports and media* (pp. 383–392). Mahwah, NJ: LEA.

Mahan, J. E., Drayer, J., & Sparvero, E. (2012). Gambling and fantasy: An examination of the influence of money on fan attitudes and behaviors. *Sport Marketing Quarterly, 21*(3), 159–169.

McGonigal, J. (2011). *TED conversations*. Retrieved from http://www.ted.com/conversations/44/we_spend_3_billion_hours_a_wee.html

Millman, C. (2010). The odds of a college athlete betting on March Madness are enough to scare the NCAA. *ESPN: The Magazine.* Retrieved from http://insider.espn.go.com/insider/insider/news/story?id=4987360

Plunkett, L. (2012, Dec. 13). *The most popular video games of 2012, according to Google search results.* Retrieved from http://kotaku.com/5968318/the-most-popular-video-games-of-2012-according-to-googlessearch-results

Raney, A. A., & Bryant, J. (Eds.). (2006). *Handbook of sport and media.* Mahwah, NJ: LEA.

Rovell, D. (2014, Nov. 12). NBA partners with FanDuel. *ESPN.com*. Retrieved from http://espn.go.com/nba/story/_/id/11864920/nba-fanduel-reach-4-year-exclusive-daily-fantasy-deal

Ruihley, B. J., & Billings, A. C. (2013). Infiltrating the boys club: Motivations for women's fantasy sport participation. *International Review for the Sociology of Sport, 48*(4), 435–452.

Rubin, A., & Perse, E. (1987). Audience activity and soap opera involvement: A uses and effects investigation. *Human Communication Research, 14*(2), 246–268.

Rushin, S. (2013, April 8). It's time to build a bettor world. *Sports Illustrated,* p. 68.

Sacco, J. (2015, July 14). FanDuel announces Series E financing of $275M from KKR, Google Capitol, and Time-Warner. *Business Wire.* Retrieved from http://www.businesswire.com/news/home/20150714005506/en/FanDuel-Announces-Series-Financing-275-Million-KKR#.VdSynXiqy0s

Sandomir, R. (2002, September 13). Reality of fantasy football: Root, root, root for no team. *The New York Times.* Retrieved from http://query.nytimes.com/gst/fullpage.html?res=

9F05E4DE1131F930A25
75AC0A9649C8B63

Schwartz, A. (2005). *The numbers game: Baseball's lifelong fascination with statistics.* New York, NY: St. Martin's.

Serazio, M. (2008). Virtual sports consumption, authentic brotherhood: The reality of fantasy football. In L. W. Hugenberg, P. M. Haridakis, & A. C. Earnheardt (Eds.), *Sports mania: Essays on fandom and the media in the 21st century* (pp. 229–242). Jefferson, NC: McFarland.

Smith, B., Sharman, P., & Hooper, P. (2006). Decision making in online fantasy sports communities. *Interactive Technology and Smart Education, 3*(4), 347–360.

Snyder, B. (2014, Aug. 17). Fantasy football could cost businesses $13.4 billion a season. *Fortune.* Retrieved at: http://fortune.com/2014/08/17/fantasy-football-13-4-billion

Spangler, T. (2015, Sept. 23). Turner, WME/IMG form esports league, with TBS to air live events. *Variety.* Retrieved from http://variety.com/2015/tv/news/turner-wme-img-esports-league-tbs-1201600921

Van Voris, B., & St. Onge, J. (2007, October 16). *Fantasy sports win right to player names, statistics.* Retrieved from http://www.bloomberg.com/apps/news?pid=newsarchive&sid=a7JHYb1118mY

Waelchli, P. (2008). Librarians' sport of choice: Teaching information literacy through fantasy football. *College Research Library News, 69,* 10–15.

Chapter 16

Billings, A.C., Qiao, F., Conlin, L.T., & Nie, T. (2016, in press). Permanently desiring the temporary?: Snapchat, social media, and the shifting motivations of sports fans. *Communication & Sport.*

C.S. Mott Children's Hospital National Poll on Children's Health. (2015). *Pay-to-play sports keeping some kids on the sidelines.* Retrieved from http://mottnpch.org/reports-surveys/pay-play-sports-keeping-some-kids-sidelines

Hargrove, K. (2012, February 9). *X Games 2012 ratings soar.* Retrieved from http://business.transworld.net/86566/news/x-games-2012-ratings-soar

Hornig, F. (2009, July 28). *Who needs newspapers when you have Twitter?* Retrieved from http://www.salon.com/news/feature/2009/07/28/wired

Meltzer, D. (2009, September 18). *Kimbo still ratings gold.* Retrieved from http://sports.yahoo.com/mma/news?slug=dm-tufratings091809&prov=yhoo&type=lgns

Pennington, B. (2012, Mar. 11). Young arms and curveballs: A scientific twist. *New York Times.* Retrieved from http://www.nytimes.com/2012/03/12/sports/baseball/debate-grows-over-how-to-protect-young-pitching-arms.html?_r=0

Rai, L., & Yan, G. (2009). Future perspectives on next generation e-sports infrastructure and exploring their benefits. *International Journal of Sports Science and Engineering, 3*(1), 27–33.

Rubin, A. M., Perse, E. M., & Powell, R. A. (1985). Loneliness, parasocial interaction and local television viewing. *Human Communication Research, 12,* 155–180.

Rubin, R. B., & McHugh, M. P. (1987). Development of parasocial interaction relationships. *Journal of Broadcasting & Electronic Media, 31*(3), 279–292.

Safer, M. (2012, Mar. 4). *Redshirting: Holding kids back from kindergarten*. Retrieved from http://www.cbsnews.com/8301–18560_162–57390128/redshirting-holding-kids-back-from-kindergarten

Stanmyre, M. (2015, Oct. 6). *Senator Codey to push bill penalizing athletes who repeat grades for athletic edge*. Retrieved from http://highschoolsports.nj.com/news/article/3878963304204887534/sen-richard-codey-to-introduce-bill-penalizing-athletes-who-repeat-a-grade-for-athletic-advantage

Stein, A., Mitgutsch, K., & Conslavo, M. (2012). Who are sports gamers? A large scale study of sports video game players. *Convergence: The International Journal of Research Into New Media Technologies*, *1*, 1–19.

Surowiecki, J. (2004). *The wisdom of crowds*. New York, NY: Random House.

Thomas, J. R. (2013, May 8). *Legislators take aim at controversial "pay-to-play" sports fees*. Retrieved from http://www.ctmirror.org/story/legislators-take-aim-controversial-pay-play-sports-fees

Trumpbour, R. C. (2007). *The new cathedrals: Politics and media in the history of stadium construction*. Syracuse, NY: Syracuse University Press.

INDEX

ABOUT THE AUTHORS

Andrew C. Billings is the director of the Alabama Program in Sports Communication and Ronald Reagan Chair of Broadcasting in the Department of Journalism & Creative Media at the University of Alabama. His research interests lie in the intersection of sport, mass media, consumption habits, and identity-laden content. With 12 books and over 130 journal articles and book chapters, he is one of the most published sports media scholars in the world. His books include *Olympic Media: Inside the Biggest Show on Television* (Routledge, 2008) and *Defining Sport Communication* (Routledge, 2017), and his journal outlets include the *Journal of Communication, Journalism & Mass Communication Quarterly, Mass Communication & Society*, and the *Journal of Broadcasting & Electronic Media*. His writings have been translated into five languages. He also serves on many editorial boards, including as an associate editor of the journals *Communication & Sport* and *Journal of Global Sport Management*. Billings's work has won numerous awards from organizations such as the International Communication Association, National Communication Association, Broadcast Education Association, and the Association for Education in Mass Communication and Journalism. He is the current chair of the Communication & Sport Division of the National Communication Association and a former chair of the Sport Communication Interest Group of the International Communication Association. He has lectured in nations around the world, from Spain to China to Austria. His work in the classroom has also earned him many teaching awards. He has been interviewed over 500 times by media outlets ranging from *The New York Times* to *The Los Angeles Times* to ESPN. Billings has also consulted with many sports media agencies and is a past holder of the Invited Chair of Olympism at the Autonomous University of Barcelona.

Michael L. Butterworth (PhD, Indiana University) is director and associate professor of Communication Studies at Ohio University. His research focuses on the rhetorical relationships between democracy and sports, and he has taught undergraduate and graduate courses in communication and sport, with particular emphasis on metaphor, myth, and politics. He is the author of *Baseball and Rhetorics of Purity: The National Pastime and American Identity during the War on Terror* (University of Alabama Press, 2010), editor of *Sport and Militarism: Contemporary Global Perspectives* (Routledge, 2017), and author of scholarly articles in journals such as *Communication and Critical/Cultural Studies, Communication & Sport, Critical Studies in Media Communication*, the *Journal of Communication*, and the *Quarterly Journal of*

Speech. He also serves on several editorial boards and was the founding executive director for the International Association for Communication and Sport.

Paul D. Turman (PhD, University of Nebraska) is the vice president for Academic Affairs for the South Dakota Board of Regents. His scholarly research focuses on the role of communication in the coach-athlete and parent–child relationship within a sport context. Prior to his time with the Board of Regents, he taught courses in communication and sport at the University of Northern Iowa. His scholarly work has been published in journals such as *Communication Education*, the *Journal of Applied Communication Research*, the *Journal of Family Communication*, and *Communication Studies*.